DATE DUE

SIXTH
EZRA

SIXTH EZRA

The Text and Origin

THEODORE A. BERGREN

New York · Oxford

Oxford University Press

1998

Oxford University Press

Oxford   New York

Athens   Auckland   Bangkok   Bogota   Bombay   Buenos Aires
Calcutta   Cape Town   Dar es Salaam   Delhi   Florence   Hong Kong
Istanbul   Karachi   Kuala Lumpur   Madras   Madrid   Melbourne
Mexico City   Nairobi   Paris   Singapore   Taipei   Tokyo   Toronto   Warsaw

and associated companies in
Berlin   Ibadan

Published by Oxford University Press, Inc.
198 Madison Avenue, New York, New York 10016

Oxford is a registered trademark of Oxford University Press

Library of Congress Cataloging-in-Publication Data
Bergren, Theodore A.
Sixth Ezra : the text and origin / Theodore A. Bergren.
p.   cm.
Appendix includes text of 2 Esdras 15–16 in English and Latin
Includes bibliographical references and index.
ISBN 0-19-511201-6
1. Bible.   O.T.   Apocrypha.   Esdras, 2nd, XV–XVI—Criticism,
Textual.   2. Bible.   O.T.   Apocrypha.   Esdras, 2nd, XV–XVI—
Criticism, interpretation, etc.   I. Bible.   O. T. Opocrypha.
Esdras, 2nd, XV–XVI.   Polyglot.   1997. II. Title.
BS1715.2.B48   1997
229'.1—dc20   96-34718

1 3 5 7 9 8 6 4 2

Printed in the United States of America
on acid-free paper

In loving memory of my mother,

Joan M. Bergren

Preface

This book is an introduction to the early Christian writing known as 6 Ezra (2 Esdras 15–16). Since 6 Ezra has never been critically edited or studied in depth, my first concern has been to establish the book's text and then to proceed inductively from there. My main objectives are to determine as closely as possible the book's most accurate text, religious affiliation, date, original language, provenance, and *Sitz im Leben*. Although comments on various parts of the text appear where they are relevant, I have not attempted to provide a systematic commentary.

Although 6 Ezra has never been edited or surveyed in detail, scholars have, of course, been aware of its existence and have commented on it. Since it is important to take into consideration past scholarship before making a new effort, I have included in chapter 1 a chronological survey of all published scholarship to date that has contributed to the book's study. Also, like any text from antiquity, 6 Ezra has its own history of transmission through the ages, in this case a relatively complicated one; chapter 1 reviews this history.

As stated, the starting point for this study is the text of 6 Ezra. Proper consideration of this topic involves several stages: first, collecting all of the relevant textual evidence; second, evaluating this evidence; and third, attempting to construct a text that most closely approximates the original. Chapter 2 surveys all of the primary and secondary witnesses to the text of 6 Ezra. The "primary" witnesses are eight complete Latin manuscripts and one fragmentary Greek one. The "secondary" evidence comprises three apparent quotations of 6 Ezra in later literature and one epitome of the book.

The next step is to construct a *stemma*—a chart tracing the genealogical relationships and avenues of descent—of all the main textual witnesses. Although this task is often impossibly convoluted, in the case of 6 Ezra it proves to be manageable. In turn, such a stemma allows one to evaluate more intelligently the readings of the witnesses. As it happens, the textual witnesses for 6 Ezra fall into two main groups, or *recensions*; chapter 3 traces the stemma from the individual manuscripts up to the level of these two recensions.

The two recensions of 6 Ezra are distinct enough that a careful analysis is necessary to determine their relationship and relative merit. This final phase of textual study is the subject of chapter 4, which concludes that one recension (the "French") is the more original, while the other (the "Spanish") is a secondary adaptation of it.

The present volume is constructed deliberately so that summaries of all of the major issues and points of concern—text, authorship, date, and so on—are provided in the first chapter, under the heading "goals and conclusions of the present study." Thus, a summary of our deliberations on the text of 6 Ezra in chapters 2–4 is included under the heading "text and recensional relationship" in chapter 1. Furthermore, the concrete "realium" underlying the sometimes abstract discussion in chapters 2–4—the text of 6 Ezra itself—is presented in complete form in Appendix 1, in a critical edition. A "running," sequential version of this text, without variants, is given in Appendix 2, while Appendix 3 provides an English translation.

An area of scholarly concern closely related to the text of 6 Ezra is the Latin vocabulary of the book—its character, its affinities, and especially its more unusual elements. This topic is treated in chapter 5.

A further avenue of investigation which, in this case, logically precedes consideration of date, provenance, and so on, is the question of the religious affiliation of the author of 6 Ezra. This issue is pursued in chapter 6. The conclusions reached there are also summarized in the "goals and conclusions" section of chapter 1. The book's date of composition, perhaps the most vexed issue in the study of 6 Ezra, is dealt with in chapter 7; again, the conclusions arrived at there are reprised in chapter 1.

Finally, there are a number of important elements of our study that, although highly significant, do not warrant a full chapter of discussion. These topics—6 Ezra's original language, provenance, *Sitz im Leben*, and eschatology—are all treated under separate headings in the "goals and conclusions" section of chapter 1.

To summarize the conclusions of this study, we argue that 6 Ezra is a Christian composition, written in Greek, deriving from Asia Minor (probably) or Egypt. It seems to date from the second or third century, probably between 262 and 313 C.E. These conclusions are influenced largely by evidence within the text for a persecution of the Christian community within which the book was composed, a persecution which had occurred in the past, was being experienced in the present, or was expected in the near future. This persecution is reflected in virtually every aspect of the text, including its eschatology, which interprets the present sufferings as a time of testing by God and a precursor of the end. The book envisages a future in which those in the community who remain faithful will be rewarded, while backsliders will be like a field which is devoured by fire (16:78). In sum, 6 Ezra claims to record the words of God speaking through an unnamed prophet, predicting worldwide eschatological catastrophes as a result of human wrongdoing, warning unrepentant "sinners" of their imminent destruction, and promising deliverance from the tribulations to those of God's "elect" who remain steadfast and keep God's commandments in the time of trial.

Richmond, Virginia   T.A.B.
February 1997

Acknowledgments

My major debt of gratitude in the writing of this volume is owed to Robert A. Kraft, my *Doktorvater* and former graduate adviser at the University of Pennsylvania. Dr. Kraft not only introduced me to 6 Ezra, in a graduate seminar many years ago, but also provided me with the intellectual, scholarly, and computer tools with which to carry out this study. Those familiar with his scholarly dedication and one-pointedness, sense of humor, and joie de vivre will appreciate what a pleasure it was to have worked with him.

I have also enjoyed an ongoing working relationship with Michael E. Stone of the Hebrew University of Jerusalem, at various times both in Jerusalem and here in Virginia. Dr. Stone, besides having a deserved reputation as a master of Ezra lore, is generally a boundless source of creative ideas and has provided input on many aspects of this project.

As the book developed, I sought the advice of many experts in the history and literature of the period from which 6 Ezra stems. Among these have been Professors William Adler of the North Carolina State University, Glen Bowersock of the Institute for Advanced Study in Princeton, David Frankfurter of the University of New Hampshire, John Gager and Martha Himmelfarb of Princeton University, Frederick Knobloch of the University of Maryland, Ross Kraemer of the University of Pennsylvania, David Levenson of the Florida State University, George Nickelsburg of the University of Iowa, David Potter of the University of Michigan, Walter Stevenson of the University of Richmond, and Benjamin Wright of Lehigh University.

Much of the early work on this book was done in connection with my previous study of 5 Ezra (*Fifth Ezra: The Text, Origin and Early History* [Atlanta: Scholars Press, 1990]). In this connection I am indebted to two distinguished European scholars of the Latin Bible, Dr. Hermann Josef Frede, Director of the Vetus Latina Institut in Beuron, and Dr. André Thibaut of the Abbazia San Girolamo in Rome. Each of these scholars not only provided me with copies of manuscripts but also graciously responded to numerous inquiries.

The following individuals and institutions have provided copies of manuscripts of 6 Ezra: Drs. A. F. J. Klijn and H. E. Gaylord Jr. of the Rijksuniversiteit Groningen; Dr. Manuel Sánchez Mariano of the Biblioteca Nacional in Madrid; Mr. Emile Defrene of the Bibliothèque Royale Albert 1er in Brussels; the Bibliothèque Nationale in Paris; the Bibliothèque Municipale in Amiens, France; and the Hill Monastic Manuscript Library of St. John's University in Collegeville, Minnesota.

As noted earlier, this study of 6 Ezra, in its early, textual stages, had close affinities with my earlier work on 5 Ezra, in that the two documents share a similar manuscript tradition and history of transmission. For this reason, it was most efficient in a few parts of this volume, mostly in the initial sections of chapter 2, simply to reproduce material from the book on 5 Ezra. I am grateful to Scholars Press for their permission in this regard.

The Faculty Research Committee of the University of Richmond provided a generous grant that enabled me to devote my full attention to this project during the summer of 1993. The same committee gave another grant that enabled proofreading of the penultimate version of the manuscript, which was done by Ms. Dorrie Turner of the University of Richmond.

Contents

Abbreviations

AB	Anchor Bible
ABD	*Anchor Bible Dictionary*
AGLB	Aus der geschichte der lateinische Bibel
ANRW	Aufstieg und Niedergang der römischen Welt
CAH	*Cambridge Ancient History*
CATSS	Computer Assisted Tools for Septuagint Studies
CCL	Corpus Christianorum—Series Latin
CP	*Classical Philology*
CRINT	Compendia rerum iudicarum ad novum testamentum
Fr	"French" version of 6 Ezra
GCS	Griechischen christlichen Schriftsteller
HTR	*Harvard Theological Review*
Int	*Interpretation*
JRS	*Journal of Roman Studies*
JSPSup	*Journal for the Study of the Pseudepigrapha*, Supplements
LCL	Loeb Classical Library
MT	Masoretic Text
NCBC	New Century Biblical Commentaries
NICNT	New International Commentary on the New Testament
NTTS	New Testament Tools and Studies
OCD	*Oxford Classical Dictionary*
OG	Old Greek
OL	Old Latin
OLD	*Oxford Latin Dictionary*
PVTG	Pseudepigrapha Veteris Testamenti graece
PW	Pauly-Wissowa, *Real-Encyclopädie der classischen Altertumswissenschaft*
RBén	*Revue bénédictine*
RTP	*Revue de théologie et de philosophie*
SBLDS	SBL Dissertation Series
SBLRBS	SBL Resources for Biblical Study
SBLSCS	SBL Septuagint and Cognate Studies
SJLA	Studies in Judaism in Late Antiquity
SNTSMS	Society for New Testament Studies Monograph Series
Sp	"Spanish" version of 6 Ezra
TextsS	Texts and Studies
TLL	*Thesaurus Linguae Latinae*
TU	Texte und Untersuchungen
VC	*Vigiliae christianae*
Vg	Vulgate
VTSup	*Vetus Testamentum*, Supplements
ZWT	*Zeitschrift für wissenschaftliche Theologie*

SIXTH
EZRA

ONE

Introduction and Summary of Results

Sixth Ezra is a short, oracular Christian writing that is cast as the words of God mediated through an unnamed prophet.[1] The main part of the work sets forth predictions of impending doom for the world at large and for certain specific sections of it, conveying this message with eschatological language and imagery. In this regard 6 Ezra is reminiscent of, and stands in the tradition of, Jewish and Christian prophetic writings of the Hebrew Bible and elsewhere[2] that enunciate God's threats and "woes" against humankind for their sinfulness and envisage imminent destruction on the earth as a result.[3] Sixth Ezra is furthermore concerned to exhort a group of God's "chosen" people to remain faithful and resist sin in order to escape the imminent calamities.[4]

In the first part of the work (15:1–4), God instructs the prophet to speak and write down the words of the prophecy, and reassures the prophet of the validity of the message. The discourse then moves directly to a prophetic declamation of God's threats of impending doom against the world, and certain parts of it, for the iniquity that prevails on the earth (15:5–16:34). This "threat discourse" comprises a series of vignettes that depict God's anger and judgment being exercised in certain specific situations. For example, 15:28–33 portrays a terrifying vision of war being waged between two mighty powers in the east. Other, similar vignettes appear in 15:5–11, 20–27, 34–45, 46–63; 16:1–17, 18–34, 35–39, 40–50, and 63–67.

The first part of the threat discourse (15:5–16:1) is organized around a successive focus on four separate locales: Egypt (15:10–13); Assyria (15:28–33); "Babylon" (almost certainly a coded designation for Rome) (15:43–45); and Asia Minor (15:46–63). This focus is replicated, in brief, in reverse order, in 16:1: "Woe to you, Babylon and Asia! Woe to you, Egypt and Syria!" The latter section of the threat discourse (16:2–34) is directed against the sinful world in general.

As a whole, the threat discourse envisages "evils" (Lat. *mala*)—warfare, famine, civil strife, poverty, bloodshed, and pestilence—being inflicted by God on the earth as punishment for human sinfulness and the persecution of the just. The destruction will be wholesale and universal, including fire from God burning "the foundations of the earth" (15:23; 16:15). All parts of the world will suffer the tragic consequences of human iniquity. Especially destructive will be widespread warfare and famine, which will decimate the earth's population. It is noteworthy that 6 Ezra focuses its attention almost exclusively on the eschatological calamities themselves; little attention is given to their aftermath.

The final section of 6 Ezra (16:35–78) constitutes an exhortation to the "servants of the Lord," "my [God's] people," or "my [God's] elect" (presumably the actual audience of the book) to abstain rigorously from sin and remain ethically inviolate if they wish to escape the coming calamities. People are advised to be "like strangers on the earth" (16:40) during the eschatological period of testing, since any worldly activity will be useless. God's elect should also expect to experience dire persecution and tribulation before the end times come (16:68–75).

Several leitmotifs recur in the various sections of 6 Ezra. One is a strong polemic against sin and sinners (15:22–27; 16:20, 48–54, 63–67, 76–78). The iniquity and oppression of the just perpetrated by these people are largely responsible for the coming worldwide catastrophes, and the sinners will face certain destruction.

Also scattered throughout the book are allusions to a group or groups of people who are specially chosen, innocent, or righteous (15:8–11, 20–22, 52–56; 16:35–44, 68–78). The persecution and unjust suffering endured by these individuals have prompted God to introduce the eschaton and destroy evil in the world, and, as a result, they will enjoy a new, coming era of righteousness (16:52–53). In order to receive this reward, however, they must resist sin and adhere strictly to the moral and ethical evocations of the book. Indeed, moral and ethical exhortation is one of the dominant concerns of 6 Ezra, especially in its latter section (16:35–78). This latter part of the book also predicts that God's chosen will undergo specific types of persecution at the time of the end (16:68–73). We can probably assume that these descriptions reflect events in the real world of the author and the author's community.

The theme of persecution of the just is linked closely to the motif mentioned earlier of the "sinners" who, among other activities, carry out this persecution. These individuals are sometimes represented in 6 Ezra as "kings" or "rulers" of the earth (15:20–21). Especially excoriated are the ruling classes of "Babylon" (Rome) and Asia (15:43–63).

Other leitmotifs that characterize the eschatological sections of 6 Ezra are the pronouncement of "woes" against various individuals and locales (15:12–15, 24–25, 46–47; 16:1, 63, 77), and the idea of a coming desolation of the earth and a radical reduction in its population (16:22–34). Also, certain sections of 6 Ezra manifest markedly misogynistic language and imagery, displayed specifically in polemic against "whores" (15:55; 16:49), "consort[ing] in the beauty of Babylon" (15:46), "adorn[ing] one's] daughters in fornication" (15:47), and "mak[ing] up the beauty of [one's] face" (15:54) (for the motif of misogyny in general see 15:46–55, 63; 16:47–51). The theme of God's omniscience and omnipotence is prominent in 16:54–67. Finally, it is worth noting that several of the narrative vignettes in 6 Ezra are composed in a highly elaborate style, utilizing such literary and rhetorical devices as parallelism of discourse, rhetorical questions, and elaborate metaphor. Noteworthy examples appear in 16:3–17, 18–20, 25–34, 40–45, and 54–63.

As noted previously, 6 Ezra's language, style, imagery, literary form, ideology, and modes of expression display striking parallels to the prophetic traditions of the Hebrew Bible and related literature. The fact that 6 Ezra seems to have been written at a relatively late date (second to third century c.e.)[5] suggests that it stands self-consciously within these traditions and was influenced by them.[6] The book's date, authorship, provenance, religious affiliation, eschatology, and *Sitz im Leben* are addressed in the following discussion.

TRANSMISSION HISTORY

Sixth Ezra was transmitted through the Middle Ages and into the modern period as part of a larger literary complex often called "2 Esdras."[7] Second Esdras is in fact an artificial literary creation, composed of three originally independent units: 4, 5, and 6 Ezra. (In the present study, the designation "2 Esdras" is used for the corpus 4, 5, and 6 Ezra taken as a group.) The account of how, why, and when these three works came into association is a complex one, about which much remains unclear.

Fourth Ezra (2 Esdras 3–14), the longest and central work of the complex, is a sophisticated Jewish apocalypse that was probably written in Hebrew, in the land of Israel, during the last decade of the first century c.e.[8] It was translated into Greek at some time before 190, when Clement of Alexandria quotes it; the Greek text is now lost except for a few citations.[9] Fourth Ezra was then translated from Greek into a panoply of tertiary language versions, of which no fewer than eight survive.[10] A Latin translation, one of the eight, was made at some time before 374, when Ambrose begins to quote the work in his writings.[11]

Sixth Ezra (2 Esdras 15–16), as noted earlier, was written during the second to third century c.e. It was probably composed in Greek, in the eastern Mediterranean region. A *terminus ante quem* in the fourth century is provided by a small vellum Greek fragment of the work, containing 15:57–59, that was found at Oxyrhynchus.[12] Sixth Ezra was translated into Latin, the only language in which it survives in toto,[13] at some time before the mid–sixth century, when it is quoted by Gildas, a historian of Britain.[14] There are also two known liturgical citations of 6 Ezra, a response in the ancient Mozarabic (Hispanic) liturgy that quotes 15:8–9[15] and an antiphon in the Roman liturgy that seems to reflect 16:52.[16] Although the liturgical sources cannot be dated precisely, both the Roman and Hispanic types are thought to go back in their earliest forms to at least the fifth to sixth centuries.[17] A phrase in Ambrose's Epistle 11(29) .22 is sometimes claimed to cite 6 Ezra 16:59,[18] but this is by no means certain.[19]

At some point 6 Ezra, which in its present form is anonymous, came to be associated with 4 Ezra. Although it is sometimes surmised that this association occurred in the Greek tradition, or even that 6 Ezra was composed as an appendix to the Greek version of 4 Ezra, these possibilities are discounted by two considerations. First, no other daughter version of the Greek text of 4 Ezra besides the Latin includes 6 Ezra. Second, a study of the Oxyrhynchus Greek fragment of 6 Ezra 15:57–59 by A. S. Hunt indicates that, given the pagination of the fragment, it is improbable that the copy of 6 Ezra to which the fragment belonged was preceded by a work as long as 4 Ezra.[20]

Thus, it seems likely that the textual connection between 4 and 6 Ezra was made in the Latin tradition.

The manuscript tradition suggests that the Latin text of 6 Ezra was first simply placed after 4 Ezra, retaining its separate identity.[21] Later, in some manuscript streams, the two works actually became textually conjoined, as they are in modern editions of 2 Esdras.[22]

The rationale and the date for the association of 4 and 6 Ezra are both difficult to ascertain. As noted previously, 6 Ezra in its present form is anonymous and nowhere mentions the name Ezra. This would imply that the connection was not made on the basis of a common attribution. There are, however, reasons to believe that both the end of 4 Ezra and the beginning of 6 Ezra might have been textually modified when or after the two works became connected. First, virtually every language version of 4 Ezra *besides* the Latin features an ending to the book which describes Ezra's assumption to heaven, his transcription of 4 Ezra, and his continuing function as a heavenly scribe.[23] The Latin version lacks all of this, ending with Ezra still on the earth. Presuming that the original Latin translation of the Greek text had the longer ending, it seems reasonable to postulate that it was excised when 6 Ezra became connected to the end of 4 Ezra, in order to allow the seer to continue to prophesy in an earthbound setting.

Also, it is often observed that the present text of 6 Ezra begins rather abruptly, without the name of a prophet or a context for prophecy ever being given. It seems possible that part of the original beginning of 6 Ezra, which might have included these elements, was removed when it was connected to 4 Ezra, perhaps to afford a smoother transition between the two works.[24] Indeed, when the two are read together, 4 Ezra provides both the name of the seer and a prophetic context.

It is possible in theory, then, that 6 Ezra was in its original form attributed to an Ezra, and that the textual connection with 4 Ezra occurred on the basis of a common attribution. This is, however, purely speculative. In their content, the two works do not show enough parallels or common material to make the factor of thematic similarity a possible cause for connection, nor does either work show an indication of knowing the other. In theory, the connection might also have occurred by chance: 6 Ezra might have followed 4 Ezra in some collection or manuscript, and the association between the two might have become traditional.

With regard to date, the earliest definite evidence for the textual connection between 4 and 6 Ezra occurs in a two-volume Bible manuscript (S) from St. Germain des Prés that is dated to 821/22.[25] There are, however, reasons to believe that the connection was made long before that time. First, Gildas's quotations of 6 Ezra, made between 516 and 547 C.E., are prefaced by the words "Hear, besides, what the blessed prophet Ezra, library (*bibliotheca*) of the law, has threatened. . . ."[26] This reference may reflect a knowledge of the episode related in 4 Ezra 14 and may indicate, therefore, that 4 and 6 Ezra were associated by the time of Gildas. Furthermore, Gildas quotes 6 Ezra in the context of other "canonical" prophets of the Hebrew Bible and clearly considers it to be of equal authority to them; it could reasonably be argued that this status accrued to 6 Ezra only in its connection with 4 Ezra, which had a long history of high prestige in Christian circles.[27]

The latest possible date for a connection between 4 and 6 Ezra can be pushed back even further by appeal to the third textual component of 2 Esdras, 5 Ezra.

Fifth Ezra (2 Esdras 1–2) is a short work that indicts God's people for their sinfulness and ingratitude and predicts the advent of a "coming people" who will inherit their patrimony. It seems to be a Christian writing of the second or third century; its provenance and original language remain uncertain.[28] The work survives only in a Latin text, the earliest datable witnesses to which come from the fifth century.[29]

At some point 5 Ezra became associated with, and in some cases connected to the end of, a Latin corpus that by that time apparently already consisted of 4/6 Ezra. At a later stage of revision, 5 Ezra was moved to the beginning of the corpus, resulting in the sequence 5/4/6 Ezra; this sequence occurs in many Latin manuscripts, in editions of the Vulgate, and in modern translations of 2 Esdras. The earliest witness to the full Latin text of 5 Ezra, and the earliest definite attestation of its textual connection with 4 and 6 Ezra, occurs in the ninth-century St. Germain manuscript mentioned earlier.[30]

As with the 4–6 Ezra connection, there are other indications that may help to push back the probable date of the textual association between 5 Ezra and 4/6 Ezra. The *Inventiones Nominum*, a Latin composition of the seventh century or earlier, cites in close connection material that derives from 4 and 5 Ezra, suggesting that the two works were linked by that time.[31] Furthermore, the citations of 5 Ezra in three of the fifth-century witnesses alluded to above—namely, the *De altercatione ecclesiae et synagogae* and the Roman and Mozarabic liturgies—clearly imply that 5 Ezra is considered to be as authoritative as the other "canonical" writings in whose context it is quoted.[32] As is the case with 6 Ezra as quoted in the history of Gildas, 5 Ezra probably gained this authoritative status only in its association with the prestigious 4 Ezra.

We may, therefore, conclude that 5 Ezra probably became connected with the unit 4/6 Ezra as early as 450, and perhaps even before. This makes it likely that the earlier textual connection between 4 and 6 Ezra had occurred at least by 400.

One other datum pertinent to the early textual history of 6 Ezra is the issue of the book's recensions. The Latin text of 6 Ezra—like those of 4 and 5 Ezra—survives in two distinct recensions. One, normally labeled the "French," is attested in two manuscripts (S and A); the other, the "Spanish," is present in six (CMNEVL).[33] This recensional situation is discussed in detail in chapter 4, where it is argued that the French recension represents the earliest recoverable text of 6 Ezra and that the Spanish recension is a revision of this text made on stylistic and grammatical grounds.[34]

The main issue in this context is the date at which the Spanish recension was made. Although the earliest manuscript attesting this recension in full, manuscript C, can only be dated approximately to the ninth to tenth centuries, it happens that the earliest Latin manuscript of 6 Ezra, S (see earlier discussion), contains one section (15:59–16:31) in which the usual "French" text of this manuscript gives way to a "Spanish" form. Apparently, at some stage in the transmissional background of this manuscript, a leaf of a manuscript was lost and later recopied from a Spanish exemplar. Thus, the Spanish recension of 6 Ezra must have been made prior to 821/22. Regrettably, there is at present no other evidence that sheds light on the recensional history of 6 Ezra prior to this date.[35]

Thus, in summary, the only firm data available concerning the textual history of 6 Ezra before its first appearance in full, in Latin, in the St. Germain manuscript of 821/22, are those listed in the preceding discussion. To recapitulate, the book was composed in Greek during the second to third centuries c.e. The Greek text was known in

Egypt in the fourth century, as evidenced by the Oxyrhynchus fragment. Sixth Ezra was translated into Latin before 400 C.E., and also probably became connected with 4 Ezra, in Latin, before that time. The Latin text of 4/6 Ezra was known in Britain in the mid–sixth century, and that of 4/6/5 Ezra is attested in Italy around the same period.[36] At some point before 821, a secondary recension (the Spanish recension) of 6 Ezra was made on stylistic and grammatical grounds.

This brings us to the stage at which 6 Ezra begins to be attested in Latin manuscripts.

Significant versions of the complete Latin text of 6 Ezra appear in eight manuscripts, ranging in date from the ninth to the thirteenth century.[37] All of these are Bibles (manuscripts SCMNEVL) or collections of biblical materials (manuscript A). Furthermore, these same eight manuscripts also contain the only significant complete Latin texts of 4 and 5 Ezra. Thus, in the tradition of significant Latin manuscripts, 6 Ezra occurs only in its complete form, and only in conjunction with complete forms of 4 and 5 Ezra.[38]

In each of these eight manuscripts, 6 Ezra follows immediately upon 4 Ezra. In those manuscripts with Spanish texts of 2 Esdras (manuscripts CMNEVL), 5 Ezra follows 4/6 Ezra; this is the literary sequence whose development is traced in the preceding discussion, and it almost certainly represents the more original placement of 5 and 6 Ezra within the 2 Esdras corpus. The order in the French manuscripts (S and A), 5/ 4/6 Ezra, probably reflects a secondary repositioning of 5 Ezra (see earlier discussion).

The earliest Latin manuscripts of 6 Ezra, and of the 2 Esdras corpus as a whole, are, however, the French manuscripts S and A, both of which were written in the ninth century around Paris. The first extant manuscript with a Spanish text, C, was copied in Spain in the ninth to tenth century. Two other Spanish manuscripts which are textually related to C—V and L—were written in Spain in the twelfth to thirteenth century. The remaining three manuscripts with Spanish texts—M, N, and E—are closely related textually, and were all copied in north-central Europe in the eleventh to twelfth century. Further details about each of these eight manuscripts are provided in chapter 2, while the textual relationships between them are discussed in chapter 3.

There are, in fact, numerous additional Latin manuscripts of 6 Ezra, and of the 2 Esdras corpus as a whole, that were copied in Europe in the thirteenth to sixteenth century.[39] To my knowledge, all of these are in Bibles. None of these manuscripts, however, is considered text-critically significant for 2 Esdras; this situation is explained in chapter 2.

A final pertinent piece of information regarding the transmission history of 6 Ezra, and of the 2 Esdras corpus, concerns decisions made regarding 2 Esdras at the Council of Trent. At the fourth session of this council, in 1546, 2 Esdras, together with 1 Esdras and the Prayer of Manasseh, were pronounced of secondary scriptural authority and relegated to an "appendix" at the end of the Vulgate. These works continue to occupy that position in modern editions of the Vulgate.

Furthermore, this session mandated a revision of the Vulgate text that was not completed until 1592 under Pope Clement VIII. This revised edition, the "Clementine" Vulgate, remained the standard printed text of the Vulgate until modern times. Although it is not known precisely which manuscripts were used for this revision, the Clementine text of 2 Esdras seems to be based mainly on manuscripts that can be shown to derive from the St. Germain manuscript. An authoritative new edition of the Vulgate, using for 2 Esdras only certain of the "significant" manuscripts listed earlier, was published by the Deutsche Bibelgesellschaft in Stuttgart, in 1969.[40] The new multivolume Vulgate edition issuing from the Abbey of San Girolamo in Rome does not include 2 Esdras. Another significant new Latin text edition of the Bible, the Vetus Latina project at Beuron, Germany, will, to my understanding, eventually include 2 Esdras.

HISTORY OF SCHOLARSHIP

Sixth Ezra, like its "companion piece" 5 Ezra, has received relatively little modern scholarly attention.[41] The reasons for this are difficult to discern, although the work's placement in modern editions and translations at the end of, and thus in the shadow of, the more important and influential 4 Ezra has probably contributed to the relative lack of attention.

The first significant modern edition of 6 Ezra after the Clementine Vulgate is P. Sabatier's *Bibliorum sacrorum latinae versiones antiquae seu vetus Italica* (1743).[42] Although Sabatier simply reprints the Clementine version in his main text, he provides the variants of the important St. Germain manuscript (S) in notes.

Perhaps the earliest attention given to 6 Ezra in modern critical scholarship is a brief notice in F. Lücke's 1852 *Versuch einer vollständingen Einleitung in die Offenbarung des Johannes*.[43] Lücke holds that 6 Ezra is clearly Christian, citing a number of apparent New Testament references and allusions. It was written in Greek, in Egypt, at a time when Christianity was persecuted there, during either the persecution of Decius (249–251) or that of Diocletian (303–313). The narrative details of 6 Ezra are, according to Lücke, too obscure to allow for any definite historical identification; one can only say that the book was written during, or between, these two periods of persecution.

The first, and most influential, sustained critical investigation of the date and provenance of 6 Ezra is A. von Gutschmid's article "Die Apokalypse des Esra und ihre spätern Bearbeitungen," published in 1860.[44] Von Gutschmid maintains, on the basis of 15:10–13, that 6 Ezra was written by an Egyptian Christian. He argues that the book's date can be established precisely in 263 by the confluence of three indicators. First, 15:28–33 must refer to the battles waged between the Palmyrenes ("Arabs") under Odaenathus and the Persians ("Carmonians") under Sapor 1 on the eastern borders of the Roman Empire in 261–266; moreover, 15:31–32 specifically reflects knowledge of events between 263 and 266. Second, 15:34–45 envisages a situation where Rome ("Babylon") is under a threat of invasion and destruction; given the period indicated earlier, this must refer to the Gothic incursions of 260–263. Third, various parts of 6 Ezra—namely, 15:8–10, 20–22, 52–56; and 16:68–74—reflect persecution of a "chosen" group; Egyptian Christians were liable to persecution not only under Valerian in 257–260 but also under Macrianus in 261–262 and Aemilianus in 262–264. Von Gutschmid concludes that 6 Ezra must have been written in 263, when the second campaign of Odaenathus against the Persians had already begun, but before the Goths had withdrawn from Rome and Asia.

Von Gutschmid's arguments, which have been extremely influential in subsequent scholarship, are evaluated in extenso in chapter 7 of this study.

In 1863, G. Volkmar published a Latin text, commentary, German translation, and detailed study of 4 Ezra.[45] Although Volkmar's text edition does not include 6 Ezra, he does comment on the work. Sixth Ezra, he claims, is an early Christian apocalyptic piece reflecting the periods of persecution and martyrdom under Decius and Aurelian, written around 260.[46]

A. Hilgenfeld's *Messias Judaeorum* (1869) offers a comprehensive treatment of the entire 2 Esdras corpus, including an edition of the Latin texts based on three manuscripts.[47] Hilgenfeld views 5 and 6 Ezra (in that order) as two continuous parts of the same literary work, which he labels "the second book of Ezra the prophet" (as opposed to 4 Ezra, "the first book . . .").[48] This piece was composed in Greek by a Western Christian author, perhaps at Rome, around 268;[49] it was translated into Latin by a different person than was 4 Ezra (p. xlix). Hilgenfeld relies on von Gutschmid for the basic framework of his dating of 5/6 Ezra but differs on the interpretation of several details in the text, thus coming to a slightly later date.

Another major critical investigation of the date and provenance of 6 Ezra was published in 1869 by A.-M. Le Hir, in his *Etudes bibliques*.[50] Le Hir characterizes 6 Ezra as an early Christian apocalyptic treatise that imitates Revelation and the *Sibylline Oracles*, and that was written between 260 and 268, during the reign of Gallienus. Although again following von Gutschmid's basic framework for dating, Le Hir believes that *unum ex illis* in 15:33 refers to Valerian rather than to Odaenathus (Hilgenfeld) or an unknown Persian general (von Gutschmid), and thus sets the *terminus post quem* in 260. He places the book's composition in Syria or Palestine and, adopting a rather unusual position, argues that it was written in Hebrew.[51]

In 1871, another edition of the Latin text of 2 Esdras was published, by O. F. Fritzsche.[52] Fritzsche's edition is based on the same manuscripts used by Hilgenfeld. Fritzsche follows Hilgenfeld's opinions regarding the tradition history and original language of 5/6 Ezra but maintains that its date cannot be fixed with certainty.

A study with important implications for the textual history of 6 Ezra is R. L. Bensly's *Missing Fragment of the Fourth Book of Ezra*, published in 1875.[53] Bensly located the so-called missing fragment of 4 Ezra 7:36–105 in a ninth-century Latin manuscript from Amiens (A) and noted that the missing fragment could also be shown to have been excised physically from the St. Germain manuscript.[54] He correctly deduced from this that all Latin manuscripts of 4 Ezra known up to his time derived, directly or indirectly, from the St. Germain manuscript. His conclusions probably extend to 5 and 6 Ezra as well (see the discussion in chapter 2). For the purposes of this study, this means that only manuscripts of 2 Esdras *including* the "missing fragment" of 4 Ezra may be taken as independent, and thus text-critically "significant," witnesses to the texts of 4, 5, or 6 Ezra. Bensly includes 5 and 6 Ezra in his discussions in *The Missing Fragment* and makes a number of important observations on 6 Ezra that will figure in what follows. His chief point is that manuscripts S and A diverge significantly in certain sections of 6 Ezra, and that the quotations of Gildas consistently follow manuscript A.[55]

In 1877, J. S. Wood published an article revealing that J. Palmer, a British clergyman and scholar, had in fact preceded Bensly in discovering a Latin manuscript of

4 Ezra that included the missing fragment.[56] Palmer, in 1826, had found in the university library in Alcalá de Heñares (Complutum), Spain, a tenth-century manuscript (C)[57] containing the missing section. He recorded the text of the fragment in personal papers, which are printed by Wood.

Another manuscript, manuscript M (eleventh to twelfth century), of 2 Esdras containing the missing fragment of 4 Ezra was discovered in 1885 by S. Berger in the Bibliothèque Mazarine in Paris.[58] The same scholar, in his 1893 *Histoire de la Vulgate pendant les premiers siècles du Moyen Age*,[59] identifies two additional complete manuscripts of 2 Esdras: one in the well-known "Bible of Ávila" (Spain) (V; twelfth to thirteenth century)[60] and the other in a twelfth-century Bible from León, Spain (L).[61] Berger thus brings to six the number of known complete Latin manuscripts of the 2 Esdras corpus.

A seminal piece of scholarship on 6 Ezra, and on the 2 Esdras corpus as a whole, is R. L. Bensly and M. R. James's *Fourth Book of Ezra*, appearing in 1895.[62] The main text edition of 2 Esdras, done by Bensly, is based on the French manuscripts S and A; in addition the Spanish texts of 5 and 6 Ezra, based on manuscripts C and M, are supplied in an appendix.[63] James, who wrote an extensive introduction to the edition after Bensly's death, provides exemplary discussions of several topics; most important for our purposes are detailed studies of the "quotations from," "text of," and "character of" 6 Ezra.

James concurs with von Gutschmid's dating of 6 Ezra around 263, proposing that it was written as an appendix to 4 Ezra. He assumes the original language to be Greek and remarks that, except for a few Christian touches, the book "might almost be a Jewish composition" (p. lxiv). With regard to the recensional differences, James argues that the French text represents more accurately the book's original form; the Spanish text, although often preserving correct readings, is "on the whole an emended text" (p. lxxvii). James points out a number of parallels to 6 Ezra in the text of the *Sibylline Oracles* and notes that the book imitates both this collection and, more especially, the "prophetical invective" of the Old Testament (p. lxiii).

Another influential treatment of 6 Ezra is that of H. Weinel in E. Hennecke's collections *Neutestamentliche Apokryphen*[64] and *Handbuch zu den neutestamentlichen Apokryphen*,[65] both first published in 1904. The former volume contains a general introduction to and translation of the text; the latter provides a slightly more technical introduction and a commentary. Weinel views 6 Ezra as a Christian composition written in Greek, perhaps as an appendix to 4 Ezra. He argues that the attempts of von Gutschmid and others to date 6 Ezra precisely in the 260s are overambitious and unfounded; there are no certain indicators that allow us to place the book more specifically than in the period between 120 and 300 C.E. Furthermore, 6 Ezra is more likely to have been written in Asia Minor than in Egypt.

Regarding the text and the issue of the two recensions, Weinel takes an eclectic approach, choosing whichever reading seems preferable in each individual case. He normally favors the French recension.

In 1907, D. de Bruyne announced the discovery of another complete Latin text of 2 Esdras in a twelfth-century manuscript in Brussels (N).[66] De Bruyne collated this manuscript against the Mazarine manuscript for several parts of 2 Esdras, including all of 5 and 6 Ezra.

In the same year C. Marbach, in his *Carmina scripturarum*, was the first to point out a striking similarity between 6 Ezra 16:52 and an antiphon *Ad laudes* in the *In Vigilia Nativitatis Domini* of the Roman liturgy.[67]

A publication of indirect significance for the study of 6 Ezra is B. Violet's 1910 text edition of 4 Ezra.[68] Violet, in his introduction (pp. xv–xxiv), gives the fullest account of the (then known) seven full manuscripts of 2 Esdras that is available even today.

Also in 1910 appeared the announcement of what is probably the single most important event for the textual history of 6 Ezra: the discovery of a small, fourth-century vellum Greek fragment of 6 Ezra 15:57–59, at Oxyrhynchus, Egypt.[69] Besides establishing that the extant Latin text of 6 Ezra was based on a Greek original,[70] which had already been widely surmised, and providing a paleographically based *terminus ante quem* for the book, this fragment also has important implications for the issue of the relative value of the two recensions. Although the Greek text of 15:57–59 does not side unambiguously with either Latin recension, it does favor the French over the Spanish by a margin of four variant readings to two. This confirms James's earlier, independent assessment of the relative superiority of the French text. Further remarks on the Oxyrhynchus fragment and its text-critical significance are provided in chapters 2 and 3. A. S. Hunt's 1910 edition of the fragment also contains photographic plates.

Discoveries of further manuscript witnesses to the text of 2 Esdras were announced by de Bruyne in 1920.[71] Relevant for 6 Ezra is yet another copy of the complete Spanish text of 2 Esdras, in an eleventh-century manuscript from Echternach (E).[72]

In 1924, B. Violet, with H. Gressmann, published a comparison of the text of 4 Ezra with that of 2 Baruch.[73] In the introduction, he provides extensive discussion of the Echternach manuscript, which had not figured in his previous edition, and proposes a manuscript stemma of the Latin 4 Ezra (p. xxii) that is still widely accepted today.

P. Riessler included 6 Ezra in his wide-ranging 1928 collection *Altjüdisches Schrifttum ausserhalb der Bibel*.[74] Characteristically, Riessler maintains that the book is Jewish and that the Greek *Vorlage* of the Latin is in turn "clearly" based on a Hebrew original. Riessler divides 6 Ezra into seven sections which, he claims, stem from different periods.

A major critical commentary on the 2 Esdras corpus was published in 1933 by W. O. E. Oesterley.[75] Oesterley's treatment of 6 Ezra is on the whole heavily dependent on that of James; he follows the lead of von Gutschmid and James in dating the book in the 260s and maintains that—apart from 16:68–78 and a few New Testament allusions, which could be Christian interpolations—6 Ezra could be a Jewish composition. Nevertheless, he disputes (perhaps on the basis of A. S. Hunt's observations)[76] James's claim that 6 Ezra was composed as an appendix to 4 Ezra, proposing instead that 6 Ezra was originally part of some other work, now lost.

In 1959, L. Brou and J. Vives published an edition of an important tenth-century Mozarabic antiphonary from León, Spain.[77] Although the editors did not recognize it, this antiphonary contains a quotation of 6 Ezra 15:8–9, indicating that 6 Ezra was known and recognized as authoritative scriptural material by the compilers of the antiphonary.[78] Brou maintains that the antiphonary, although itself rather late, accurately reflects liturgical practice in Spain in the fifth to sixth centuries. Fourth and Fifth Ezra are also quoted extensively in the Mozarabic liturgy.

A third edition of Hennecke's *Neutestamentliche Apokryphen* by W. Schneemelcher appeared in 1959–64, with a new treatment of 6 Ezra by H. Duensing.[79] Duensing in large measure follows the lead of the original articles by Weinel, arguing that 6 Ezra was written by a Christian author somewhere in the eastern Mediterranean area, at an unspecifiable date between 120 and 300 c.e. The work was composed in Greek as an appendix to 4 Ezra; in the Latin translation, the French recension is, on the whole, superior to the Spanish.

In 1969 appeared the first edition of the "Stuttgart" Vulgate, edited by R. Weber with several collaborators.[80] This Vulgate contains a fresh edition of the 2 Esdras corpus, with many of the manuscripts being collated anew. The editors follow established tradition in deciding for the superiority of the French text in 6 Ezra; additionally, the readings of three Spanish manuscripts—C, M, and E—are cited in the apparatus.[81] The edition of 6 Ezra is superb.

A commentary on the 2 Esdras corpus by J. M. Myers appeared in 1974.[82] Myers follows von Gutschmid in viewing 15:28–33 as a description of events of the early 260s but also interprets parts of 6 Ezra as referring to an even later period, extending up to around 270 (the revolt of Palmyra against Rome following Zenobia's conquest of Egypt and Aurelian's departure; see *Cambridge Ancient History* 12.301–7). He maintains that, in theory, the book could be Jewish or Christian. Myers's commentary is especially noteworthy first for the attention paid to the Spanish manuscripts C and M in the notes to the translation, and second for the remarkable number of outside literary parallels that he has gathered to 6 Ezra.

Another commentary on the 2 Esdras corpus, by M. Knibb, was published in 1979.[83] According to Knibb, 6 Ezra was composed in Greek as an appendix to the Greek version of 4 Ezra. Its author was a Christian who utilized Jewish traditions. Knibb follows established tradition in referring 15:28–33 to events of the 260s and concludes that 6 Ezra was written in the latter part of the third century, in the eastern section of the Roman Empire. Because 4 Ezra was held in such high esteem in the Christian churches, a Christian author added this piece as an appendix in a time of persecution, in order to adapt 4 Ezra to the new situation.

A new, fifth edition of (Hennecke-) Schneemelcher's *Neutestamentliche Apokryphen*, published in 1987–89, contains an article on 6 Ezra by H. Duensing and A. de Santos Otero that is slightly revised in its details, notes, and bibliography from earlier editions of the collection.[84]

Two new treatments of 5 and 6 Ezra have been announced but have not yet appeared in print. A text edition of the two books by P. Geoltrain will be included in the "Series Apocryphorum" of *Corpus Christianorum*. A treatment of both works by H. Stegemann is projected in the series Jüdische Schriften aus hellenistisch-römischer Zeit.

GOALS AND CONCLUSIONS OF THE PRESENT STUDY

It is clear from the summary of research given in the preceding discussion that there are numerous aspects of the textual situation and origin of 6 Ezra on which definite or satisfactory conclusions have not been reached. Critical study of the book's text, and particularly of the relationship between the two recensions, is certainly the most pressing need, since it forms the basis on which other aspects of the book's origin can be assessed. It is these issues of text and recensional relationship that will form the first subjects of the present study.

Closely related to the textual questions in 6 Ezra are such issues as the original language of the book, its date and place of composition, and the religious affiliation of its author. In the subsequent part of this chapter, separate sections are devoted to each of these issues. In several cases (viz., the religious affiliation of the author of 6 Ezra and the date of the book), these issues also receive extended discussion in a separate chapter of this volume. The following part of this chapter also contains considerations of the *Sitz im Leben* and eschatology of 6 Ezra.

Text and Recensional Relationship

As noted earlier, the text of 6 Ezra survives in two distinct recensions, usually labeled the "French" (manuscripts S and A) and "Spanish" (manuscripts CMNEVL). It is important at the outset to establish the origins of and relationship between these recensions.

Chapter 4 of the present work treats this issue in detail; the following is a summary of that analysis. The first topic addressed in chapter 4 is the state of correlation between the two texts. From a purely statistical point of view, the recensions agree in 72 percent of their readings. Thus the texts proceed from the same base but also offer substantial variation. Analysis of the lexical variants between the recensions reveals that a high proportion, more than one-third, are differences in synonyms: the texts say the same thing using different words.

This situation indicates that the differences between the recensions are a product of conscious intention rather than of textual corruption. Two main possibilities suggest themselves: either the two recensions represent independent translations of a Greek original or originals, or the variations arose within a Latin context, with one recension perhaps being a revision of the other.

Examination of the places where the recensions differ in content reveals only a few cases in which the variations could be accounted for on the basis of a Greek original or originals; none of these is decisive. There are, on the other hand, numerous instances in which variation between the recensions is explicable within a Latin context.

Two other factors suggest that the two recensions arose within a Latin medium. First, in several passages the two recensions are identical for stretches of twenty-five to thirty-five words; one would not expect independent translations to be so close. Second, the figure of 72 percent of overall verbal agreement between the recensions again seems rather high for independent translations. Thus, I argue that the two texts arose on the basis of intra-Latin recension rather than being independent translations of a Greek *Vorlage*.

In determining exactly in what context the two recensions originated, one main consideration is to find how often and in what situations one or the other recension offers a superior text, that is, one that seems to be temporally prior to the other.

The differences between the two recensions can be analyzed under four main categories: (1) grammatical and stylistic features; (2) synonymous lexical variants; (3) differences in meaning (including theological factors and apparent corruptions); and (4) quantitative differences (additions and deletions). In each case, examination of the recensional variations strongly suggests the superiority, or temporal priority, of the French text. In the category of grammar and style, this text consistently manifests readings that are stylistically primitive or grammatically incorrect; these readings are inevitably ameliorated in the Spanish version. The French recension features a plethora of exotic lexical elements and Greek loanwords, which regularly appear in the Spanish as more common, native Latin equivalents. Differences in meaning between the two texts, including textual corruptions, can usually be explained most easily by assuming the priority of the French text. Finally, quantitative differences between the recensions can also normally be accounted for by assuming that a Spanish reviser wished to improve the style or content of the French text.

These data suggest that, on the whole, the French recension of 6 Ezra represents the more original Latin form of the work, and that the Spanish is a revision of it based mainly on criteria of style and grammar. The priority of the French recension is also supported by the Oxyrhynchus fragment and by the extant citations of 6 Ezra in other writings.

In practical text-critical terms, this means that the French text is adopted whenever there is no obvious reason for choosing the Spanish. The results of these text-critical investigations are presented in Appendix 1, which gives a critical edition of 6 Ezra based on the two recensions; the main text is also printed in running form in Appendix 2.

The Religious Affiliation of the Author

The contents and style of 6 Ezra make it almost certain that the book was written by a Jew or a Christian. Deciding between these two, however, is more difficult. As indicated in the survey of scholarship presented earlier, several commentators have noted that the book could be either Jewish or Christian. This issue is addressed in chapter 6 of the present work; the following discussion summarizes that analysis.

Two factors suggest strongly that 6 Ezra was written by a Christian. The first is the striking linguistic and thematic parallels between 6 Ezra and the book of Revelation, specifically between 6 Ezra 15:43–16:1 and Revelation 14:8; 16:19–19:3. Both documents discuss in some detail a city called "Babylon," and both describe the city's characteristics and fate in a remarkably similar way. Both label Babylon with certain negative features associated with femininity. In 6 Ezra many of the negative points connected with Babylon are extended also to "Asia." Both books attribute to Babylon (or Asia) the persecution and murder of God's elect, and both describe Babylon's cataclysmic overthrow and the subsequent mourning of those around her.

The parallels between these documents in this regard are, in fact, so close that dependence of one upon the other, or of both upon a common source, seems almost certain. Of these three options, by far the most historically plausible is that the author of 6 Ezra knew and used Revelation. Such dependence would suggest that the author of 6 Ezra was a Christian.

A second factor indicating Christian authorship of 6 Ezra lies in the book's descriptions of an impending persecution of God's "elect" in 16:68–74. These descriptions are so vivid and concrete that they seem to reflect an actual setting in life in the community of 6 Ezra. Sixth Ezra was probably written in the second or third centuries C.E. (chapter 7), in either Asia Minor or Egypt (see "Provenance," this chapter). A survey of Jewish history in these places during this period reveals little, if any, incidence of violent pagan persecution of Judaism of the type that seems to be envisioned in 6 Ezra.

An examination of Christian history in the same locales and period, however, reveals numerous situations that are remarkably close to that apparently reflected in 6 Ezra 16:68–74. These situations arose in the context of Roman persecution of Christianity as an illegal and dangerous cult. Indeed, each aspect of the persecution envisioned in 6 Ezra 16:68–74—the outbreaks of mob violence against "God's elect," the destruction of their property, their forced eating of sacrificial meat, and the mockery of those who acceded to this demand—is graphically documented in historical accounts of Roman persecution of Christians in the second and third centuries. The striking parallels between documented historical evidence of Christian persecution in the Roman empire and the literary record of 6 Ezra 16:68–74, in conjunction with the almost total lack of evidence for persecution of Jews in the same period, strongly suggest that 6 Ezra is a Christian document. The combination of this factor and the parallels between 6 Ezra and Revelation noted earlier effectively clinches the case for Christian authorship.

Date of Composition

To start with the broadest possible limits, it is fairly certain that 6 Ezra was composed between 95 and 313 C.E. The *terminus post quem* is set by the apparent date of the book of Revelation, which 6 Ezra almost certainly knows (see especially chapter 6). The *terminus ante quem* is suggested by the fact that 6 Ezra seems to be a Christian work and to reflect a situation in which persecution of Christians is a live issue; such persecution had effectively ceased by the year 313.

Although these are the closest firm boundaries that can be set, it is possible to narrow the limits somewhat based on other internal indications in the text. These possibilities are pursued in detail in chapter 7 of the present work and are outlined here.

A. von Gutschmid's determination in 1860 that 6 Ezra was written precisely in the year 263, a theory that in its broad outlines has decisively influenced virtually all subsequent commentary on the book—despite its erudition and the many cogent points that it advances—is overly optimistic, depends on outmoded views regarding the nature and methods of apocalyptic eschatology, and furthermore is based on several faulty historical assumptions. Consequently, it seems advisable to adopt a more flexible position on the book's dating.

One of von Gutschmid's most compelling arguments is that 6 Ezra 15:28–33 refers historically to conflicts between the Palmyrene ruler Odaenathus, fighting in cooperation with the Romans, and the Perian king Shapur I that took place in 262–267 C.E. on the frontiers between the Roman and Persian empires. If this pericope does in fact refer in principle to concrete events locatable in history, von Gutschmid's identification of it would seem by far the most plausible choice. This would place the composition of 6 Ezra between ca. 262 and 313. Furthermore, several additional factors suggest a date toward the beginning of this period.

There are, however, various considerations indicating that 15:28–33 may not in fact refer to locatable historical events. First, certain details within the pericope suggest that it possesses a more "mythological" or paradigmatic eschatological than a "historical" frame of reference; and second, the details of the pericope do not fit particularly well with what little is known from independent historical sources about the Persian-Palmyrene wars and their sociohistorical context. If, then, 15:28–33 is not intended to refer to the specific historical events of the Persian-Palmyrene wars, then 6 Ezra could indeed have been written at almost any time between 95 and 313 C.E.

Although it is impossible to resolve this issue with certainty, it seems somewhat more likely that 15:28–33 does in fact refer to the Persian-Palmyrene wars, and that 6 Ezra is therefore to be dated between 262 and 313 C.E., probably in the earlier part of this period. Nevertheless, as historians we are well advised to tread a path of methodological caution and to acknowledge that, in principle, 6 Ezra could have been written at almost any time during the second or third century C.E.

Original Language

The fragment of a Greek text of 6 Ezra 15:57–59 found at Oxyrhynchus strongly suggests that the surviving Latin version was based on a Greek *Vorlage*. That is, there is no evidence, nor any reason to speculate, that the Greek version preserved at Oxyrhynchus was translated from the Latin. This is indicated both by the early date of the Oxyrhynchus fragment (fourth century C.E.) and by the fact that, in the first centuries of the common era, translation of Jewish and Christian literature from Greek to Latin was far more common than that in the opposite direction.

Another, equally compelling factor indicating that the Latin text of 6 Ezra was translated from Greek lies in the vocabulary and character of the Latin text itself. As pointed out in chapter 5, the Latin 6 Ezra abounds both in Greek calques and in highly distinctive Latin lexical elements that are best explained as translations from Greek. The nature and quantity of these elements make it almost certain that the Latin text was based on a Greek *Vorlage*.

There are also various grammatical and syntactic features in the Latin text of 6 Ezra that indicate a Greek original. For example, *deficiet semina* in 15:13 makes best sense on the supposition of an original like ἐπιλείψει σπέρματα, in which the Greek neuter plural subject takes a singular verb. In 16:13, the unexpected *gloriae* in *quoniam fortis gloriae qui tendit sagittam* could represent a misreading or corruption in Greek between δεξιά and δόξα. In 16:20, the two occurrences of *super* in *et super his omnibus non se avertent ab iniquitatibus suis nec super has plagas memorantur sempiterna* make more sense as translations of Greek ἐπί or ὑπέρ than as native Latin elements. The same observation could be made for *super* in *erit enim . . . exsurrectio multa super timentes Dominum* (16:70).

The phrase *in adpropinquante hora partus eius* ("when the hour of her delivery draws near"; 16:38) appears to be a Latin rendering of a Greek temporal construction with ἐν (ἐν τῷ ἐγγίζειν ὥραν τῆς ὠδῖνος αὐτῆς) rather than a native Latin construction. Likewise, *ad emittendum flumina ab eminenti* ("to send forth streams from the height";

16:60) would seem to be a crude translation of a Greek purpose clause with πρός or εἰς (πρὸς τὸ ἀφιέναι ποταμοὺς ἀπὸ τοῦ ὑψώματος) (in Greek, the phrase actually makes grammatical sense!). Finally, *iram illam* (15:37), *in diebus illis* (16:17, 31), and *in die illo* (16:65) all reflect the normal Greek postposition of ἐκεῖνος rather than the usual Latin pre-position of *ille*.

If the extant Latin text of 6 Ezra was in fact translated from a Greek *Vorlage*, we must inquire in turn whether this alleged Greek text depended on a version in some other language. Based on our knowledge of Jewish and Christian Greek and Latin translation literature in antiquity, by far the leading candidates would be Hebrew and Aramaic. And there are, in fact, a few elements in the Latin text that could suggest a Semitic original.

In *aut sicut in vinea vindemiata et subremanet racemus*...(16:30), the unexpected *et* could be seen as resembling the occasional Hebrew use of ן between the introductory and main clauses of a sentence (e.g., "And it will be when . . . , and . . .). A similar situation occurs in 15:30: *Carmonii insanientes in ira et exient de silva.* . . . In neither case, however, does the wording in 6 Ezra exactly replicate a syntactic situation that might be expected in a Semitic text. Moreover, in 16:30, the *et* could be taken as simply meaning "also." Likewise, in 15:30, it is possible that the shift from participle to finite verb is accidental or a product of mistranslation, and that the *et* is not as intrusive as it first appears.

Vindicans vindicabo (15:9) and *Dominus scrutinando scrutinavit* (16:64) are examples, respectively, of a cognate present nominative participle with finite verb and a cognate gerund ablative (of means) with finite verb, both of which derive ultimately from the Hebrew infinitive absolute with finite verb, which marks emphasis.[85] This construction is a common and distinctive feature of Hebrew biblical idiom, which feature Greek or Latin authors writing in a self-consciously "biblicistic" tone could easily have attempted to imitate. Therefore, these elements also do not provide conclusive evidence for a Hebrew stage of 6 Ezra.

In considering the possibility of a Semitic original, it should be kept in mind that Hebrew or Aramaic literature deriving from our period would most likely have come from a Jewish pen. On other grounds, however, it seems most likely that 6 Ezra is, in its present form, a Christian rather than a Jewish composition (see chapter 6).

Given the ambiguous character of the "Semitisms" discussed previously, the fact that 6 Ezra contains no Semitic loanwords (see chapter 5), the a priori unlikelihood of 6 Ezra's being a Jewish composition (at least in its present form), and a lack of any other compelling evidence, it seems most reasonable to postulate that the Greek text of 6 Ezra did not have a Hebrew or Aramaic *Vorlage*.[86] It is most probable, then, that the book was composed in Greek, and then translated into the Latin text(s) that survive today.

Provenance

There are no direct, certain internal or external indicators as to the provenance of 6 Ezra. There are, however, several factors both within and outside the text that allow reasonable conjectures as to its place of origin.

The most obvious indicators in this regard are (1) the probable original language of the book (Greek) and (2) geographical references within the text. The first factor indicates that 6 Ezra originated in a Greek-speaking milieu; this, however, could be virtually anywhere in the Mediterranean world.

More useful are the extensive geographical notices within the text of 6 Ezra. As noted in the introductory section of this chapter, the first part of 6 Ezra (15:5–63) focuses successively on four distinct locales: Egypt (15:10–13); Assyria (15:28–33); Rome (figuratively called "Babylon")[87] (15:43–45); and Asia (15:46–63). The verse immediately following this section, 16:1, recapitulates these geographical loci in reverse order: "Woe to you, Babylon and Asia! Woe to you, Egypt and Syria!" These four locales, of course, constitute a ring around the northern and eastern Mediterranean from Italy to Egypt (excluding Greece).

The contents and character of the geographical references in chapter 15 (mostly "threat-" or "woe-discourses") suggest that 6 Ezra was written in one of the locales mentioned there. Of the four places alluded to, "Asia" seems, on internal grounds, to be the most likely possibility. Not only is the section devoted to Asia in 6 Ezra the most extensive of the four locales (eighteen verses, as opposed to three to six verses for the other places), but the contents of that section are highly direct, vivid, and personal, in contrast to the more stylized treatments given the other places.[88] The following excerpt is indicative of the lively interest that the author shows in this region:

> And you, Asia, consort in the beauty of Babylon and the glory of her person: woe to you, miserable one, because you have made yourself like her. You have adorned your daughters in fornication in order to please and glory in your lovers, who have always wanted you to fornicate. You have imitated that hateful one in all her deeds and designs.
>
> Therefore, says God, I will unleash evils upon you—want, poverty, and famine, and the sword, and pestilence—in order to destroy your houses for injury and death. And the glory of your strength will be dried up like a flower, when the heat that has been sent upon you rises up. And you will be weakened and (made) poor by a blow and beaten from (the) wounds [sic], so that it is impossible for you to receive powerful ones and lovers.
>
> Would I have acted so zealously against you, says the Lord, if you had not killed my elect [pl.], always exulting with clapping of hands and talking about their death when you were drunk? Make up the beauty of your face! The wages of a whore (are) in your bosom; therefore, you'll get your recompense! (15:46–55)

This passage, which extends in the same tone for eight additional verses, imparts the distinct impression that Asia, and its transgressions, represent immediate and pressing concerns for the author.

As for the other places mentioned in chapter 15, the allusions to Babylon/Rome (15:43–45) are extremely brief and serve mainly to provide a backdrop for the more extensive plaint against Asia in 15:46–63. The description of the battle that takes place in Syria/Assyria (15:28–33) is highly stylized and is almost certainly intended to provide an exotic, "mythological" element within the larger eschatological framework of 6 Ezra (on this point see chapter 7 of the present volume); there is no reason to suppose that it indicates the book's place of composition. Finally, the brief references to Egypt in 15:10–13 explicitly utilize the biblical trope of the Exodus; there is no indication that the author has any direct interest in that region beyond the exploitation of that trope.

It is true, of course, when we argue for a place of composition in Asia, that the mere direction of extensive polemical attention against a particular region does not necessarily indicate the provenance of the polemicist. Were this the case, the biblical prophets would be as readily locatable in Babylon, Egypt, Edom, or Moab as in the land of Israel. But given the absence of any other likely provenance for the book, and especially given the highly personal and immediate tone of the treatment of Asia in 15:46–63, this seems, on purely internal grounds, to be by far the most likely possibility for the provenance of 6 Ezra. Even further indication of such a provenance is provided by the compelling and imaginative way in which the language and imagery used in the Book of Revelation for "Babylon" are apparently taken over in 6 Ezra and reapplied to "Asia" (see chapter 6 for an extended discussion of this phenomenon).

The conclusion of an Asian provenance for 6 Ezra is confirmed by the fact that the apparent references to persecution of the book's audience (God's "elect") in 16:68–78 accord well with what is known about persecution of Christians in Asia Minor in the second and third centuries C.E. This evidence is discussed in detail in chapter 6 (especially relevant in that discussion is the consideration of the implications of the book's historical background for its provenance).

One other piece of potential internal evidence for provenance should be mentioned here. The earliest recoverable text of 6 Ezra 16:70 apparently runs as follows: *Erit enim lociis et in vicinas civitates exsurrectio multa super timentes Dominum.* It is most common to read *lociis* as a corruption of *locis*, and to translate, as we have, "For there will be in (various) places and in neighboring cities a great insurrection against those who fear the Lord" (NRSV has "For in many places and in neighboring cities there shall be a great uprising against those who fear the Lord"). This interpretation, however, is forced in two respects: first, because the text apparently reads *lociis*, not *locis*; and second, because the context of the verse clearly seems to call for a place-*name*. That is, the wording "in place X and in neighboring cities . . ." would make far more sense than "in (various) places and in neighboring cities. . . ."

If *lociis* is understood as a place-name, several options present themselves. To my knowledge, Lociis itself is not attested as a locale either in Latin or in a Greek form, so we must consider the possibility of textual corruption. One option is to read *lociis* as a corruption of Locris, of which there are several in the Greco-Roman world.[89] On the eastern coast of Achaia, directly south of the northwestern end of the island of Euboea and of the Euboean Straits, lies a large region known as "Locris"; it is subdivided into "Epiknemidian Locris" (on Mount Knemis, south of the Maliac Gulf) to the northwest[90] and "Hypoknemidian" or "Opuntian Locris" (directly on the Euboean Straits) to the southeast. There is also, on the western end of the northern shore of the Gulf of Corinth, below Mount Parnassus, a region known as "Ozolian Locris" (sometimes called Locris Hesperia);[91] it is usually supposed that this western Locris and the more easterly one were originally one territory, which was split by invasion or immigration. Finally there is, several miles northeast of the extreme southern tip of the Italian peninsula, on the eastern (Ionian) coast, a town called Locri Epizephyrii (or Lokroi Epizephyrioi; also known as Narycium or Gerace), founded in the seventh century B.C.E. by colonists from one or both of the Greek Locris.[92] It is, then, conceivable that the strange term *lociis* in 6 Ezra 16:70 is a corruption of Locris, and originally designated one of the regions described previously.

Two other possibilities are worth noting. Lochias (Greek λοχιάς) is the name of a promontory of land situated on the northern coast of Alexandria, on the eastern perimeter of the large, eastern harbor, which "in the Ptolemaic layout of the city bore the royal palace and the temple of Artemis, and to which the royal harbor was also connected."[93] This area, however, according to Pauly-Wissowa, was deserted after the third century C.E., that is, at or shortly before the presumed time of composition of 6 Ezra.

Finally, Locheia (Greek λοχέεα, λοχείᾱ), while not explicitly attested as a place-name, is an epithet of Artemis found (1) in the cult at Halos in Phthiotis (Thessaly) and (2) in the cult at Pergamum.[94] It is theoretically possible that locales near one of these sites, or near other places where Artemis was worshiped with this epithet, bore this name of Artemis.

While each of the previously mentioned sites is a viable possibility for a place-name of which lociis in 16:70 may be a corruption, none seems certain enough to adopt with confidence. Based on other considerations, discussed both earlier in this chapter and in chapters 6 and 7, the potential locations in Asia Minor ("Locheia") and Egypt ("Lochias") seem prima facie preferable; but the sites in Greece ("Locris") and Italy ("Locri") cannot be excluded. In the final analysis, however, given the uncertainty of the situation, it seems preferable to translate lociis provisionally as a corruption of locis, even while acknowledging the problems with this interpretation and the viable possibilities for corruption of geographical place-names, as discussed.

Thus far we have discussed only indicators of provenance that are internal to the text of 6 Ezra. Still, there is one important external factor that should be kept in mind. This is the fact that a fragment of the Greek text of 6 Ezra which bears an extremely early date was found at Oxyrhynchus, Egypt. The fragment's editor places it in the fourth century,[95] which would, of course, be very shortly after we have dated the composition of 6 Ezra. The early date of the fragment could therefore be taken as support for an Egyptian provenance of the book.

In final consideration, however, the internal textual indicators discussed here regarding 6 Ezra's provenance seem to me to outweigh the factor of the early date of the Oxyrhynchus fragment. The arguments presented for situating 6 Ezra in Asia Minor, based mainly on the quantity of material in the text focusing on this locale and the intimate tone of this material, seem strong enough to justify placing 6 Ezra here, at least provisionally. Egypt would be a strong second choice. It should be recognized, however, that neither of these sites is by any means certain. In theory, 6 Ezra could have been written almost anywhere in the Roman Empire where Greek was in currency.

Sitz im Leben

It is notoriously difficult to place ancient, anonymous eschatological documents, especially ones that employ vaticinatio ex eventu, as 6 Ezra seems to do, in a concrete social setting. Nevertheless, 6 Ezra does contain indications that may help to establish its social context.

We begin with the issue of religious affiliation. I argue in chapter 6 that 6 Ezra was written by a Christian. Presumably this person lived and worked in a community which to some degree shared the author's ideas and worldview, and which was envisaged by the author as one potential audience for the book's urgent message. We also keep in mind the fact that the author of 6 Ezra perceives and presents himself as a prophet. Even if 6 Ezra is a purely literary creation rather than a message that was delivered orally, its creator considers himself the authentic and inspired medium of a message issuing from God. We will return to this point in the following discussion.

The author of 6 Ezra, then, "prophesied" in a Christian community in the second or third century c.e. It seems most probable to me that the references to various types of persecution in the closing section of the book (especially 16:68–72) are not topoi, imaginative constructions, or socioliterary "ideal types" but rather reflect actual events in the real world of the author—events that had happened, were presently happening, or were expected in the near future. This is indicated by the highly charged, vivid, and concrete character of the descriptions:

> For behold, the burning (wrath) of a great crowd will be kindled over you, and they will seize certain of you, and will feed (them) what was killed for [or: to] idols. And those who consent to them will be held by them in derision and disgrace and will be trampled under foot.
>
> For there will be in (various) places [or: in Lociis/Locii/Lociae] and in neighboring cities a great [or: many an] insurrection against those who fear the Lord. For people pressed by their own evils will be like madmen, sparing no one, in order to pillage and destroy those who still fear the Lord. For they will destroy and pillage their property, and will drive them out of their house(s). (16:68–72).

These descriptions are, in my opinion, too direct, detailed, graphic, and emotionally charged to derive abstractly from the mind of an author. The community within which 6 Ezra was written either had experienced such persecution firsthand or had had contact with other communities that had.

Assuming that 6 Ezra was in fact written by a Christian, the details of 16:68–72 suggest that the persecution was a religious one, directed by pagans against a Christian community or communities with religious motivations. The persecution appears to have been a pogrom, or mob action, of an ad hoc nature (16:68), probably local in extent (16:70), not necessarily officially sanctioned, involving the forced eating of animals sacrificed in pagan rites (16:68). These were probably sacrifices to a Roman deity that were viewed as establishing an individual's allegiance to the Roman state. Such forced eating is known to have occurred during the persecutions of Christians by Decius in 249–251 and Maximin Daia in 308–311;[96] presumably it also occurred with some frequency in other persecutory contexts. Normally, the forced eating followed the offering of sacrifice to the deity and the pouring of a libation. It can thus be viewed as a concrete reinforcement or reification of the act of sacrifice, an indication that the individual involved in the sacrifice fully acknowledged its efficacy. It was also doubtless connected with the traditional Christian prohibition against eating food offered to idols (see the discussion in chapter 6).

The persecution envisaged in 6 Ezra also seems to have involved mob action of indiscriminate violence against its victims: pillaging, destruction of property, and forcible eviction from domiciles. Such acts of mob violence are frequently documented in the sources describing the persecution of Christians in the Roman Empire in the second and third centuries c.e. (see the more detailed discussions in chapters 6 and 7).

Besides the specificity and highly charged character of the persecutions described in 6 Ezra, the book's heartfelt ethical and moral exhortations suggest a social setting in which such evocations were not simply abstract points of advice designed to edify an audience living in a relative state of security. Rather, these exhortations (cf. 16:20, 35–36, 40–45, 51–54, 63–67, and 74–78) strike one as impassioned pleas to individuals whose very salvation, in the mind of the author, depends on a correct response to an immediate and pressing life situation. The author adopts a strong position against whatever sorts of religious compromise are being practiced in his community and pleads with his audience to do the same. Furthermore, the book evinces a strong sense of self-righteousness, a strong impression that the author believes himself to know absolutely which course of action is correct for himself and his coreligionists, and will spare no effort to impress this understanding on others.

Another, related issue is whether the polemic against "sin" and "sinners" in 6 Ezra is directed against the "opposition," in the form of pagan persecutors of Christianity, or whether some of it may in fact be applicable to parties within the author's own community who are responding to the challenges of persecution in ways that he feels are inadequate. Although certainty on this question is difficult, it is my sense that the author of 6 Ezra is indeed speaking to some extent against groups within his own community, indeed, perhaps primarily against them. That is, several of the pointed references to "sinners" mentioned in the review at the beginning of this chapter leave the distinct impression that they are directed against persons or groups within the author's own, Christian community.

Especially telling is the polemic in 16:51–53, 63–67 against sinners who claim not to have sinned, and against "those who wish to hide their sins" (16:63). The latter are counseled in 16:67 to "fear [God], and give up your sins and forget your iniquities . . . and God will deliver you and free you from every tribulation." It seems highly doubtful that such a message is directed toward the "great crowd" of persecutors mentioned in the following verse! Rather, the intended objects of this advice seem to be individuals within the author's own community, persons he, for some reason, feels are acting irresponsibly in the situation at hand. The same impression is created by 15:25, which warns God's "faithless children" against "defil[ing his] holiness," and by the impassioned plea in 16:35–36 for the reader to accept the author's prophecy as the authentic "word of the Lord."

Again, the exhortation to God's "elect" in 16:76 not to "let your sins weigh you down or your iniquities mount up" and the following two verses, which explain that those who are "choked by their sins" are "relegated to a devouring by fire," are clearly best understood not as polemic against pagan persecutors but as warnings to slackers within the author's own community to adopt a stricter moral stance. Although the private ethical positions of these people were doubtless important to the author, he was probably mainly concerned with the public ramifications of their actions, the ways in which their responses to persecution would affect the community as a whole.

The author of 6 Ezra, then, both in his exhortations to moral purity and in his polemics against sinners who pervert the word of the Lord, is concerned largely, perhaps mainly, with elements within his own community. The attitudes and actions of certain of these persons, he feels, are detrimental to the social cohesion and integrity of the group, and also to these people's own individual salvation. This overriding concern of the author, that the community as a whole and its individual members conform to the point of view and modes of behavior promulgated by him, is highly significant. The author of 6 Ezra, according to this view, perceives himself as the arbiter and enforcer of a specific, strict set of community ethical and social norms, attempting through his work to impose this set of norms on the group as a whole. In order for the integrity of the group to be maintained in the face of radical social and theological challenges, and for the validity of the author's own sociotheological position to be upheld, it is important that the attitudes and behavior of potentially deviant subgroups within the community be brought into conformity with the norms advanced by the author.

It is widely recognized sociologically that times of crisis within religious communities often involve narrowing of the bounds of what is considered theologically permissible within the community. This is a way of strengthening the group's cohesion and, therefore, its ability to withstand challenge. This seems to represent one dimension of the theological claims and challenges laid down within the text of 6 Ezra.

There is one further aspect of the polemic of 6 Ezra that deserves special note. This is the diatribe, expressed mainly in 15:46–63, against "whores" and evil women who "make up the beauty of [their] face" (15:54), are consorts in beauty and glory (15:46), "adorn [their] daughters in fornication" (15:47), and "receive powerful ones and lovers" (15:51). This imagery, which I haved argued is drawn from Revelation (see chapter 6), and which is directed in 6 Ezra mainly against the ruling classes of Asia Minor, reflects a clear misogyny. Even if the images and leading ideas are taken from another text, their use here in such a dramatic and forceful way, and the fact that they occupy such a significant position in the text, speak worlds about the attitudes of the author, and perhaps of his community.

It is furthermore significant that precisely these same images are then applied in a later context (16:47–52), in a more general way, to the sinners who form the object of the polemic in 16:47–67. 16:47–52 states:

> For as long as they adorn their cities and houses and possessions and their own persons, so much more will I strive zealously against them, because of (their) sins, says the Lord. Just as a whore strives very zealously against a dignified and good woman, so righteousness will strive zealously against iniquity, when she adorns herself, and accuses her to her face, when the one comes who will defend the one seeking out every sin on the earth.
>
> Therefore, do not imitate her or her actions! Because behold, a little while longer and iniquity will be taken away from the earth, and righteousness will rule over [or: among] us.

I have just argued that these sections of text refer specifically to individuals *within* the community of the author, individuals he feels are thinking and acting in ways that do not conform to his own ethic, and who therefore threaten the integrity of the group. The same misogynistic imagery and attitudes, then, that were taken over from Revelation and previously directed against the Christian-persecuting rulers of Asia Minor are now extended by the author to elements within his own Christian community! Again, this polemical strategy tells us a great deal about both the author of 6 Ezra and the social milieu in which he wrote.

Finally, some attention should be given to *Sitz im Leben* in the sense of the origin of what now appears as the literary text of 6 Ezra. As noted earlier, the discourse of 6 Ezra is prophecy, which may be broadly defined as the expression of an individual who has a message of a "higher" origin to communicate that he feels is relevant, indeed urgent, to those around him. Classically, prophecy is an oral phenomenon; when it is written down, it is done by those around the prophet who feel that the message is important enough to be preserved. It seems, especially in the Jewish-Christian tradition, that the prophecies that came to be written down in this way, many of which acquired a religiously authoritative, or "canonical," status, were often then imitated by later "prophets," in either oral or literary contexts. The authoritative status attained by the earlier prophets was an important factor in the later continuation of the prophetic tradition in literary form, for example, in the apocalypses.

It is possible in theory that the prophecy in 6 Ezra is a written record of an originally oral utterance or series of utterances. It is also conceivable that the various sections, or vignettes, in 6 Ezra represent oral prophecies that were delivered at different times and were then collected into a literary unit. It is important not to underestimate the significance of the living, oral prophetic tradition in the social world of early Christianity.

In the case of 6 Ezra, however, it seems to me more likely that we are dealing with prophecy that was written from the beginning. This is indicated perhaps most clearly by the text itself, in its opening lines: "Speak out the words of this prophecy, and cause them to be written down on paper, for the words are trustworthy and true" (16:1). One would not expect an originally oral prophecy to contain this type of injunction for writing. The first clause of the verse, wherein the prophet is enjoined to speak out the prophecy, would, according to this interpretation, be a literary device intended to establish the validity of the prophecy (speaking being the traditional form of delivering a prophecy). It is also possible that this prophet actually combined oral utterance with written recording.

Aside from this observation, it is difficult to make sure statements about the context in which the prophecy was delivered. The many scriptural allusions in the text could as easily have come as part of the inspired speech of someone imbued with the Jewish Scriptures as in a more deliberately constructed written composition. Likewise, the highly crafted rhetorical structure of certain parts of 6 Ezra could as plausibly have been the oral product of a living, inspired poet as the constructions of a writing author. The explicit reference to writing in 16:1, however, leads us to theorize that 6 Ezra originated as a literary composition.[97]

Eschatology

The eschatology of 6 Ezra, which is the predominant theme in the book, is rather simple and primitive in form. There is no complex eschatological timetable or elaborate apocalyptic scenario. Simply put, God will, in the near future, bring a variety of "evils" on the world and its inhabitants—warfare, famine, civic unrest, bloodshed, death, destruction, pestilence, and poverty. These evils are intended as punishment for the iniquity that has generally overtaken humankind and as recompense for the persecution of the just, both of which elements have reached a breaking point. It is due to an accumulation of human sinfulness and unrighteous deeds that God will strike the earth in anger: "I will no longer be silent about their impieties . . . innocent and just blood cries out to me, and the souls of the just cry out continuously" (15:8).

Sixth Ezra does not specify any one particular agency or event through which God's eschatological wrath will be unleashed. Rather, the book's form, a series of smaller vignettes, leads to the expression of a number of eschatological devices and scenarios. The eschatological "evils" will manifest variously as civic disorder (15:16–19); as divine fire devouring the earth's foundations and sinners (15:23); as conflict in remote areas of the world (15:28–33); as terrible storm clouds that will rain down fire, hail, floods, and general destruction (15:34–45, 60–63); as earthquakes, thunder, and cosmic turmoil (16:3–20); and as conquest by foreign peoples (16:40–48). Warfare and famine are the two main avenues through which God wreaks consternation, terror, havoc, and destruction among the earth's inhabitants.

Although much of the threat discourse of 6 Ezra is directed against the "world" and humankind in general, in several instances specific areas or individuals are singled out. In 15:10–13, the focus is on Egypt, utilizing the biblical trope of the Exodus: God's people will be delivered from oppression, and God will once again strike Egypt with destruction and blight. In 15:20–22, the "kings of the earth" are excoriated for their persecution of God's elect, and their punishment is promised. In 15:28–33, an eschatological conflict between two powers in the remote east is depicted: the "Arabians" and "Carmonians" wreak desolation in the "land of the Assyrians." In 15:43–45, 60 the destruction of Babylon/Rome by malefic, rampaging storm clouds is described, while 15:46–63 envisages the devastation of Babylon/Rome's protégé, Asia, by these same storm clouds.

Sixth Ezra pays little attention to the *aftermath* of the eschatological catastrophes that will plague the earth. One section, 16:22–34, describes the severe desolation and reduction of population that will result from widespread warfare and famine, but even this can be considered part of the eschatological woes. The only hints at a state following the eschatological calamities occur in the parenetic section at the end of the book, 16:35–78. Here, two statements allude to the possibility of a state of salvation or redemption for God's servants who remain faithful during the tribulations. These are: "Behold, a little longer and iniquity will be taken away from the earth, and righteousness will rule over us" (16:52); and "Behold, the days of tribulation are here, and I will deliver you from them" (16:74). While the second statement could simply mean that the elect are removed from the evil world, the first clearly envisages a state of eschatological redemption that will one day obtain on the earth.

It may also be worthwhile to consider a few of the noteworthy eschatological scenarios and themes in 6 Ezra that have not been touched on so far. Chapter 15, verse 23 states that "fire has gone out from [God's] wrath, and it has devoured the foundations of the earth and the sinners, like straw that is burned up." This clearly anticipates world destruction on a cosmic level; strangely, however, 6 Ezra never describes the details or envisions the consequences of such a world destruction.

In 15:34–45, 60–63, the movements and clashes of terrible storm clouds that pour out destruction on the earth are depicted. At various times they let loose fire, hail, flying swords, and, more predictably, floodwaters. These clouds cause widescale bloodshed (15:35–36), and, when they reach "Babylon," they completely destroy the city, so that "the dust and smoke will rise to the sky, and everyone around will mourn her" (15:44). To my knowledge, this imagery of storm clouds that cause widespread devastation on the earth is virtually unique here in Jewish and Christian eschatological literature.

A beautifully crafted narrative unit, 16:3–20, contains striking eschatological imagery. Here the events of the end times are compared to "a hungry lion in the woods," a bed of straw on fire, and an "arrow shot by a strong archer": that is, they are inexorable. The destruction of the world will take place on a cosmic order: "[God] will quake, and who will not be afraid? He will thunder, and who will not tremble? . . . The earth and its foundations will quake; the sea is shaken from the depth, and its waves and fish will be thrown into turmoil" (16:10–12). God is depicted as a mighty bowman: "Just as an arrow shot by a strong archer does not return, so the evils that will be sent out over the earth will not return" (16:16). In this section also the idea is found that fire will consume "the foundations of the earth" (16:15).

A number of the images in 16:3–20 are intended to emphasize the inevitability of the eschatological calamities, once they are set in motion. This idea is also stressed in the metaphor in 16:38–39, in which the eschaton is compared to the birth of a child: "Just as a woman pregnant with her child in the ninth month, when the hour of her delivery draws near, groans for two or three hours beforehand . . . , and when the baby comes out of the womb, it will not delay for one moment, so the evils will not delay in coming forth over the earth, and the world will groan." The application of imagery from childbirth in eschatological contexts is familiar from 4 Ezra 4:40–42 and 1 Thess 5:3.

The eschatology of 6 Ezra, then, encompasses a variety of scenarios and images. The eschatological descriptions focus almost entirely on the threat of imminent catastrophes of a worldly and concrete nature—warfare, famine, poverty, bloodshed, and destruction—that will take place within the physical, earthly sphere. There is no historical review, no heavenly journey, no questioning of angels, no afterlife or resurrection, no eschatological timetable, no Messiah or other heavenly agent, no eschatological state of salvation, and very little of what could be called direct heavenly intervention in earthly affairs. There is, it is true, some hint of a state of deliverance or salvation for the righteous, but this occurs only in the parenetic section at the end of the book, which abandons the arena of eschatology and focuses instead on ethical issues and individual salvation. In one sense, however, it could be argued that the last sentence of 6 Ezra actually links the earlier eschatological sections of the book, with their threats of destruction and desolation, with the later ethical/parenetic section: "Woe to those who are choked by their sins and covered over by their iniquities, as a field is choked by the forest and its path covered over by thorn bushes . . . it is shut off and relegated to a devouring by fire" (16:77–78).

TWO

Evidence for the Text of 6 Ezra

PRIMARY EVIDENCE: THE MANUSCRIPTS

As noted in chapter 1, the primary textual base for 6 Ezra consists of eight Latin manuscripts that are known not to depend exclusively on any other extant manuscript of the work. They are as follows:

S Sangermanensis: Paris, Bibliothèque Nationale latin (11504–)11505; 821/22 c.e., from St. Riquier, later at St. Germain des Prés

A Ambianensis: Amiens, Bibliothèque Communale 10; 9th c., from Corbie

C Complutensis 1: Madrid, Biblioteca de la Universidad Central 31; 9–10th c., from Toledo or southern Spain, then at Alcalá de Heñares

M Mazarinaeus: Paris, Bibliothèque Mazarine (3–)4; 11–12th c., from les Cordeliers (Paris)

N Bruxellensis: Brussels, Bibliothèque Royale 1er Série (9107–)9109(–9110); 12th c., origin unknown

E Epternacensis: Luxembourg, Bibliothèque Nationale 264; 1051–1081 c.e., from Echternach

V Abulensis: Madrid, Biblioteca Nacional vitr. 15–1; 12–13th c., from Ávila

L Legionensis 2: León, Real Colegiata de San Isidoro I,3; 1162 c.e., from León

To these witnesses, which also form the main textual base for 5 Ezra and for the Latin version of 4 Ezra, must be added the fourth-century Greek fragment of 15:57–59 found at Oxyrhynchus (X).

In the case of the Latin version of 4 Ezra, the reason for limiting the number of complete significant manuscripts to these eight is well known. They are the only Latin manuscripts that contain (or contained, in the case of S) the celebrated "missing fragment" of 4 Ezra 7:36–105. Accounts of the unpublished discovery of this lost section in manuscript C by J. Palmer, the independent deduction of its existence by J. Gildemeister, and finally its discovery in manuscript A and publication by R. L. Bensly are readily available[1] and need not be repeated here. It suffices to state that the "missing fragment" can be shown to have been excised physically from manuscript S, and that all manuscripts lacking this section (i.e., the vast majority of Latin manuscripts of 4 Ezra) must therefore derive genealogically from this manuscript.[2]

The principle that textual criticism of the Latin 4 Ezra must depend on manuscripts containing the lost fragment, although it has not gone unchallenged,[3] was cogently defended by B. Violet[4] and has been accepted by almost every editor of the text since Bensly.[5] The extension of this principle to include 5 and 6 Ezra is, however, somewhat less certain.[6] This is because, in manuscript S, the units of 5 and 6 Ezra are set off from 4 Ezra and given separate titles. The relevant contents of this manuscript, set out in detail below, may be summarized as follows:

. . .

Chronicles
Canonical Ezra-Nehemiah ("The first book of Ezra")
1 Esdras 3:1–5:3 (apparently in a second hand; not titled)
5 Ezra (return to the first hand)("The second book of Ezra")
1 Esdras 1:1–2:15 ("The third book of Ezra")
4 Ezra ("The fourth book of Ezra")
6 Ezra ("The fifth book of Ezra")
Esther

. . .

Although 5 and 6 Ezra are closely connected with 4 Ezra in virtually every aspect of the Latin textual tradition, the attribution of separate titles to them in this crucial manuscript indicates that the principle of exclusion of manuscripts on the basis of the "missing fragment" need not also apply to 5 and 6 Ezra. After all, to my knowledge, manuscripts lacking the "missing fragment" are not on that basis excluded from the textual criticism of canonical Ezra and Nehemiah, Chronicles, or Esther.[7]

At this point, elements of probability and practicality enter into consideration. First, other factors being equal, the manuscripts that contain the "missing fragment" in 4 Ezra are those most likely to be text-critically valuable for 5 and 6 Ezra, which are almost always connected with 4 Ezra in the Latin tradition. That is, an investigation of the texts of 5 and 6 Ezra most logically *begins* with the eight manuscripts that contain the missing fragment. In this connection we may refer to Violet's comments on 4 Ezra that were already mentioned.[8] Violet notes that, although it is possible that manuscripts containing the gap in 4 Ezra 7 may occasionally, through "horizontal contamination," offer superior readings, practical considerations demand that the text of 4 Ezra initially be established on the basis of the complete manuscripts. The same principle of practicality applies to 5 and 6 Ezra, especially in the early stages of their textual study.

Second, it is in fact possible to check the texts of 5 and 6 Ezra in the eight complete manuscripts against manuscripts that lack the fragment in question. Several Latin editions of the 2 Esdras corpus appeared before Bensly's publication of the missing fragment;[9] these presumably were based on what were thought to be the best manuscripts available at the time.

Examination of the manuscripts used in these editions in the case of 5 Ezra revealed that they almost exclusively feature readings that are characteristic of the French family (manuscripts S and A).[10] Although the other manuscripts did contain a few alternate readings of apparently equal merit to those in manuscripts S and A, they did not offer any readings that could not be accounted for as copies, corruptions, or attempted emendations of manuscript S.[11] In fact, R. L. Bensly, who collated a large number of manuscripts of 2 Esdras (including 5 and 6 Ezra) that contained the gap, was unable to find any readings in those manuscripts that could not be explained as deriving from S.[12]

On the basis of these considerations, there is no compelling reason to believe that superior readings in 6 Ezra may be found in manuscripts that lack the missing fragment in 4 Ezra 7. Thus, our text-critical investigation is based on the eight "significant" manuscripts described previously.

Description of the Significant Manuscripts

Each of the eight significant Latin manuscripts of 6 Ezra is described in detail in text editions of 4 Ezra, library manuscript catalogues, and other sources. In addition, they are discussed together in convenient form by both Violet[13] and Klijn.[14] The Oxyrhynchus Greek fragment is best consulted in Hunt's *editio princeps*.[15] All the sources of information known to me for each manuscript are listed in the note that heads the description of that manuscript.

In this survey, special attention is given to (1) the date and place of origin of the manuscripts, (2) the location, titling, and disposition of the 2 Esdras material within them, and (3) the other writings that they contain. This section is largely identical to the analogous portion of this author's edition of 5 Ezra, except for the Oxyrhynchus fragment and manuscripts S, M, V, and L, where new information is available.

Oxyrhynchus Fragment 1010 (X)

This is a miniature vellum leaf dating from the fourth century that contains a Greek text of 6 Ezra 15:57–59.[16] The leaf measures eight by six centimeters and is inscribed on both sides. The recto is numbered at the top μ with an overstroke (i.e., 40); the verso does not show a page number, but this may be due to its damaged condition.

A. S. Hunt, the editor of the fragment, devotes much attention to the issue of pagination: does μ denote the fortieth leaf or the fortieth page? It is usual in manuscripts such as this for each page to be numbered. It is, however, problematic that the Greek on both sides of the leaf, taken together, corresponds to four lines of Bensly's text, in which 6 Ezra 15:1–56, the section of text coming before the fragment, occupies ninety-six lines. This means that 6 Ezra 15:1–56 in Greek could be expected to have occupied about 24 leaves (48 pages) of the lost portion of the Oxyrhynchus manuscript. The numeration of the extant fragment, however, suggests that either 39 leaves (78 pages)(if μ is the number of the leaf) or 19.5 leaves (39 pages)(if μ is the number of the page) are missing. Hunt concludes that μ probably denotes the fortieth page, and that the writing was somewhat smaller at the beginning of the manuscript, accounting for the discrepancy.[17] This would mean that the verso of the Oxyrhynchus fragment was once numbered ($\mu\alpha$) but that the number has been lost because of damage.

Of greater moment is the implication of this pagination for the form in which 6 Ezra circulated in this manuscript. It is impossible, given the pagination of the fragment, that the far longer 4 Ezra preceded 6 Ezra in this manuscript. Furthermore, Hunt observes that had this manuscript been intended as part of a multivolume work, it probably would not have been rendered on such small pages and in such a large script. Thus it is almost certain that, in the form of the Greek text of 6 Ezra preserved at Oxyrhynchus, 4 Ezra did not precede 6 Ezra. This contravenes the theory, generally accepted in Hunt's time and promoted even by many modern scholars, that 6 Ezra was written as an appendix to the Greek version of 4 Ezra.

Sangermanensis (S)
Paris, Bibliothèque Nationale latin (11504–)11505

This is probably the oldest known Latin manuscript of 6 Ezra.[18] It is a full Bible in two volumes that, through a scribal note, can be dated to 821/22 C.E.[19] The manuscript, in a Carolingian minuscule, was written "perhaps at St. Riquier, in any case in the north of France."[20] It was later housed at the Benedictine abbey of St. Germain des Prés in Paris.[21] The text of 2 Esdras has undergone modification by several correcting hands. According to Violet, various characteristic errors in the manuscript point toward a *Vorlage* in a Visigothic minuscule.[22]

The 2 Esdras corpus stands in the second volume of the Bible. It is preceded by the canonical books of Ezra and Nehemiah, is intermixed with material from 1 Esdras (see below), and is followed by Esther.

Canonical Ezra, beginning with Jerome's prologue, appears on ff. 51r–55r; Nehemiah, titled separately, stands on ff. 55r–60r. These two are labeled in the explicit as one book: *Liber primus in Ezra secundum Hieronimum*. Following this, on f. 60v, appears 1 Esdr 3:1–5:3, apparently in a different hand.[23] This section has no incipit; its explicit is illegible to me. Fifth Ezra, clearly in the original hand, follows immediately after this on ff. 61r–62r. The book begins *Incipit liber Ezrae secundus*; the explicit repeats this title.

Next, on f. 62rv, stands 1 Esdr 1:1–2:15.[24] Both an incipit and an explicit designate this as *Liber Ezrae tertius*. Fourth Ezra proper appears on ff. 62v–70v. It begins with *Incipit liber Ezrae quartus cum versus* [*sic*] *iidc*; the explicit reads *Liber quartus Ezre homini Dei*. Fourth Ezra is followed by 6 Ezra, on ff. 70v–73r[25]: *Incipit liber quintus Ezrae cum versis ii ccxxx . . . Explicit liber Ezrae quintus*. A colophon appears after 6 Ezra. The 2 Esdras material is followed, on ff. 73vff., by Esther, with Jerome's preface.

The text of the St. Germain manuscript is that of the Vulgate, with the exception of the "Prayer of Solomon" in 1 Chronicles 6, Tobit, and Judith, which are Old Latin texts.[26] The order of books in the manuscript is: Oct, Reg, Proph, Job, Ps, L. sap, Chr, 1–4 Esdr, Esth, Tob, Jud, Macc, Ev, Act, Cath, Pa, Ap.[27] The first published collation of the 2 Esdras corpus in manuscript S is that of Sabatier, mentioned in chapter 1; other collations are listed by Klijn.[28] The text of the 2 Esdras corpus is that of the "French" recension.[29]

Ambianensis (*A*)
Amiens, Bibliothèque Communale 10

This manuscript of one volume contains five writings attributed to Ezra: the canonical Ezra/Nehemiah (written as one book), 1 Esdras, 5 Ezra, 4 Ezra, and 6 Ezra.[30] It dates from the ninth century and is written in a Carolingian minuscule. The manuscript comes from the Benedictine abbey at Corbie, in Picardy, Diocese of Amiens.[31] It has received correction by several hands.

The five works in the manuscript are written virtually consecutively—they have only short incipits and explicits, and often follow one another in midline.

Ezra/Nehemiah, entitled "The first book of Ezra," stands on ff. 1r–27v. First Esdras, designated "The second book of Ezra," is on ff. 28r–49r; it ends with *Explicit saecundus liber Aezrae.*

Fifth Ezra begins in the middle of the same line on f. 49r and extends to f. 53r. It begins with *Incipit tertius* and ends with *Explicit liber tertius* (*liber* written above the line). Fourth Ezra appears on ff. 53r–78r: *Incipit quartus liber . . . Explicit liber quartus.* Sixth Ezra occupies ff. 78r–82r and begins with *Incipit quintus.* The book ends with *Finiunt quinque libri Ezrae profaete,* followed by a short colophon.

The text of the canonical Ezra/Nehemiah in this manuscript is that of the Vulgate. The 2 Esdras corpus, which appears in the "French" recension, was first collated by Bensly (see chapter 1); other published collations are listed by Klijn.[32]

Complutensis 1 (*C*)
Madrid, Biblioteca de la Universidad Central 31

This renowned, one-volume Bible manuscript dates from the ninth to tenth century.[33] Written in Toledo, or some other location in the Arabic sphere of southern Spain,[34] it formerly belonged to the University Library at Alcalá de Heñares (Complutum) and is often designated "the first Bible of Alcalá." The script is Visigothic.

The 2 Esdras material is situated between the canonical books of Ezra and Nehemiah, and the book of Esther. Nehemiah ends on f. 231r with *Explicit liber Esdre secundus.* The 2 Esdras corpus begins on the next line of f. 231r with *Secuntur libri hisdem Esdre tertius et quartus.* This is followed by six lines of writing which, in the microfilm available to me, are difficult to read. Fourth Ezra proper begins with the incipit *Liber tertius* and extends to f. 236v. Although 4 Ezra has no explicit, the extremely large letters with which the following incipit of 6 Ezra begins clearly signal a break in the text.

Sixth Ezra stands on ff. 236v–237v. It has the incipit *Liber Esdre prophete quartus* but no explicit. Fifth Ezra begins on the next line of f. 237v. Although there is no incipit, the enlarged initial letter (V) of the first word marks a break in the text. This letter is larger than that with which paragraphs normally begin, but not as large as the letters that signal the beginnings of 4 Ezra, 6 Ezra, and Esther. Fifth Ezra extends to f. 238v, ending with *Expliciunt libri Esdre prophete.* Thus, 6 and 5 Ezra are apparently intended to be read as one "book" (labeled "4 Ezra") with two parts. The book of Esther begins on the next line of f. 238v.

While the Bible text of Complutensis 1 is mostly that of the Vulgate, it has several exceptional features. Ruth, Tobit, Judith, Esther, 2 Chronicles, the "Prayer of Solomon," the Psalter (Mozarabic), and Maccabees are Old Latin texts. Old Latin versions of Exodus 15 and 1 Samuel 2 are also found in the otherwise Vulgate texts of these books. Also, the Wisdom of Solomon and Sirach appear in distinctive recensions.[35]

The order of books is: Oct, Reg, Proph, Job, Ps, Sal, Chr, 1–4 Esdr, Esth, Sap, Sir, Tob, Jud, Macc, Ev, Pa, Cath, Act, Ap.[36] The manuscript was first fully collated in 2 Esdras by Bensly (see chapter 1); other collations are listed by Klijn.[37] Complutensis 1 preserves the "Spanish" text of 2 Esdras.

Mazarinaeus (M)
Paris, Bibliothèque Mazarine (3–)4 (formerly [6–]7 [so in Berger])

This Bible in two volumes dates from the eleventh to twelfth century and came from the monastery of les Cordeliers in Paris.[38] The 2 Esdras material stands in the second volume of the manuscript between the canonical Ezra/Nehemiah with a fragment of 1 Esdras (all written as one book) and 1 Maccabees.

Ezra/Nehemiah, preceded by Jerome's preface and introduced by *Incipit liber Esdre*, is found on ff. 187v–201r. This is followed without interruption, on ff. 201r–202v, by the fragment 1 Esdr 3:1–5:3 (i.e., the same section of 1 Esdras that appeared immediately before 5 Ezra in the St. Germain manuscript).[39] This section concludes with *Explicit liber I Esdre*. Thus, Ezra/Nehemiah and 1 Esdr 3:1–5:3 are grouped together as one book, entitled "1 Ezra."

Fourth, Sixth, and Fifth Ezra, in that order, are also read as one book, entitled "2 Ezra," which occupies ff. 202v–219r. Fourth Ezra begins with *Incipit liber II*. The text continues, without any break (other than enlarged letters indicating chapter markers) being indicated between 4 (ff. 202v–215r), 6 (215r–217v), and 5 Ezra (217v–219r). Fifth Ezra concludes with *Explicit liber secundus Esdrae scribae*. First Maccabees, with Jerome's preface, follows on ff. 219r ff.

The Mazarine manuscript exhibits a Vulgate text type throughout. The order of books is: (1) Oct, Reg, Chr, Proph (through Jer); (2) Proph (from Baruch), Job, Ps, L. sap, Tob, Jud, Esth, 1–4 Esdr, Macc, Act, Cath, Ap, Pa.[40] The text of 2 Esdras was first collated by Bensly (see chapter 1); later collations are listed by Klijn.[41] The manuscript contains the "Spanish" text of 2 Esdras.

Bruxellensis (N)
Brussels, Bibliothèque Royale 1er Série (9107–)9109(–9110)

This Bible in four volumes dates from the twelfth century.[42] Its place of origin is unknown, but it belonged to an archbishop of Malines (Belgium) in the eighteenth century.

The 2 Esdras corpus, again written as one book in the order 4, 6, 5 Ezra, stands in the third volume between 2 Maccabees and the Psalms.

Second Maccabees concludes on f. 64r. Fourth Ezra begins on f. 64r with *Incipit liber secundus Esdrae* and extends through f. 76r. Sixth Ezra occupies ff. 76r–78r. Fifth

Ezra is on ff. 78r–79v, ending with *Explicit liber Esdrae secundus* (the explicit is written in a second hand). There are no breaks of any kind between the three texts. The
Psalter commences on f. 80r with Jerome's preface.

The Bible text of manuscript N is that of the Vulgate throughout. The order of books
is: (vol. 1) Oct; (vol. 2) Reg, Chr, 1 Esdr, L. sap, Tob; (vol. 3) Jud, Esth, 1–2 Macc, 2
Esdr, Ps, Proph (a); (vol. 4) Proph (b), Act, Cath, Ap, Ev, Pa.[43] The text of 4 Ezra was
first collated by Violet (see chapter 1); de Bruyne, who had discovered the full text of
2 Esdras in this manuscript, collated 5 and 6 Ezra against the Mazarine manuscript
(see chapter 1). The text of 2 Esdras is of the "Spanish" recension and agrees closely
with manuscript M.

Epternacensis (E)
Luxembourg, Bibliothèque Nationale 264

This is a Bible in one volume ("pandect") that can be dated through a scribal note to
1051–1081 C.E.[44] It was written at the Benedictine abbey in Echternach (Luxembourg)
and later belonged to the Herzoglich Bibliothek in Gotha.

The 2 Esdras corpus, again written as one book in the order 4, 6, 5 Ezra, stands
between Nehemiah and the Solomonic books.

Nehemiah ends on f. 126r with *Explicit liber I.* Fourth Ezra begins on the next line
of f. 126r with *Incipit liber II Ezre* and extends to f. 132r. Sixth Ezra stands on
ff. 132r–133r. There is no indication of any textual break between 4 and 6 Ezra. Fifth
Ezra begins on f. 133r; the initial *V* of the first word is somewhat enlarged, indicating
a minor textual division. Fifth Ezra ends on f. 133v with *Explicit liber secundus Ezre.*
Jerome's preface to the Solomonic books follows on f. 133v.

The Bible text of this manuscript is of the Vulgate type. The order of books is: Oct,
Reg, Chr, Esdr, L. sap, Job, Tob, Jud, Esth, Macc, Proph, Ps, Ev, Act, Cath, Pa, Ap.[45]
The first full collation of 4 Ezra was undertaken by B. Fischer for the Stuttgart Vulgate;
5 Ezra was collated by the present author in *Fifth Ezra.* The present edition includes
the first full collation of 6 Ezra. The text of the 2 Esdras corpus is of the "Spanish"
recension and is closely allied to manuscripts M and N.

Abulensis (V)
Madrid, Biblioteca Nacional vitr. 15–1

This huge pandect of the twelfth to thirteenth century formerly belonged to the
Cathedral of Ávila in Spain and is known as the Bible of Ávila.[46] It is written in a
Carolingian minuscule. Although several hands are represented in the manuscript,
the 2 Esdras material seems to have been copied by one scribe.

An account of the location of the 2 Esdras corpus in this manuscript is complicated by the fact that the manuscript's contents were rearranged, and its pages renum-
bered, at some point in its history.

In the original form of the codex (with page numbers in black ink), 2 Esdras stood
as the last textual unit, after the New Testament and 1 Esdras. The order of contents
was: . . . Esther; Ezra; Nehemiah; 1 Maccabees; New Testament (to f. 417); 1 Esdras
(ff. 417–420v); 4 Ezra (written in two separate units, as described below: 4 Ezra

3:1–13:56 on ff. 420v–426r; 4 Ezra 13:56–14:47 on f. 426rv); 6 Ezra (ff. 426v–427v); and 5 Ezra (ff. 427v–428r).[47]

When the contents of the manuscript were rearranged and it was repaginated (with page numbers in red ink), 1 and 2 Esdras were moved together to a position before the New Testament, following the canonical Ezra and Nehemiah, and followed by the Prayer of Manasseh. The new order is: . . . 1–2 Chronicles; Ezra; Nehemiah; 1 Esdras; 4 Ezra; 6 Ezra; 5 Ezra; Prayer of Manasseh; and New Testament. The apparent rationale for this reordering was to place 1 and 2 Esdras together with the Ezra-Nehemiah material in the Jewish Scriptures, where 1 and 2 Esdras also stand in most of the other manuscripts we have surveyed. In the original order, 1 and 2 Esdras could be seen as occupying secondary positions.

In the new order, Ezra and Nehemiah, labeled "Ezra I" and "Ezra II," stand on ff. 152–160. First Esdras, entitled *Hesdre III*, occupies ff. 161–164v; it ends with *Explicit liber tercius feliciter amen.*

Fourth Ezra 3:1–13:56 stands as a separate unit, with the designation (*Liber*) *quartus*, on ff. 164v–170r. Fourth Ezra 13:56–14:47 occupies f. 170rv and begins with *Liber Hesdre quintus.* There is absolutely no textual break between this section and 6 Ezra, which is on ff. 170v–171v. Sixth Ezra has no explicit, but its text ends without filling the line, the remainder of which is left blank. This indicates a textual break between it and 5 Ezra, which begins on the next line.

Fifth Ezra stands on ff. 171v–172r. Although there is no incipit, the initial *V* is quite large and distinctive, signaling a major textual break. Fifth Ezra has no explicit but ends in the middle of a page (originally the last page of the Bible), the rest of which is left blank.

Manuscript V exhibits a Vulgate text type throughout. The order of books, in the rearranged form of the codex, is: Oct, Reg, [Proph], Job, Tob, Jud, Esth, Ps, L. sap, Chr, 1–4 Esdr, Macc, Ev, Act, Cath, Ap, Pa.[48] The text of 4 Ezra in this manuscript was first collated by Violet (see chapter 1); 5 Ezra was collated by the present author in *Fifth Ezra.* This edition is the first published collation of 6 Ezra. The text of 2 Esdras is of the "Spanish" recension.

Legionensis 2 (L)
León, Real Colegiata de San Isidoro I,3

This Bible in three volumes is traditionally dated to 1162.[49] Although Violet argued that it was actually written around 1300,[50] recent commentators tend to favor the traditional date.[51] The manuscript probably originated at San Isidoro, León, Spain.[52]

Until recently, it was thought that the whole of this manuscript except the 2 Esdras corpus was copied from the renowned Codex Gothicus Legionensis of San Isidoro ("Legionensis 1"), which was written at Valeranica, Castile, in 960.[53] (Codex Gothicus Legionensis does not contain 2 Esdras.) This theory, however, has been challenged by John Williams.[54] Williams attempts to demonstrate, through careful comparison of both the miniature illustrations and the marginal Old Latin glosses in the two Bibles, that the scribe/illuminator of the 1162 Bible "had before him as a pictorial and textual model an illustrated manuscript very similar to, but not identical with, the Bible of 960."[55] Williams actually claims to be able to identify this manuscript: it is

Florentius's great illustrated master Bible of 943, written at Valeranica, and once housed in the Castilian monastery of Oña. Today this manuscript survives only in fragments, but there is every indication that it was virtually identical to the later Legionensis 1 of 960 and thus was presumably its model.[56] Williams argues that it was the model of Legionensis 2 as well.[57] Unfortunately, if Williams's theory is accepted, there is no sure way to ascertain whether Florentius's Bible contained 2 Esdras—which would then have been omitted by Legionensis 1 but retained by Legionensis 2—or lacked the corpus, in which case Legionensis 2 would have had to copy it from another source.[58]

The 2 Esdras material in Legionensis 2 is situated near the end of the third volume, after the New Testament. It is of particular interest not only because it is the only biblical part of the manuscript not present in Legionensis 1 but also because it features epitomes of 4/6 and 5 Ezra and a preface to 4 Ezra, none of which is paralleled in any other known manuscript. The 2 Esdras corpus is followed by a nonbiblical tractate entitled *Vita vel obitum santorum.*

Between the end of the NT and the beginning of 2 Esdras, the manuscript has about ten folios of miscellaneous material that is catalogued by Violet.[59] This material concludes on f. 217r.

Fourth Ezra, with its supplementary material, stands on ff. 217r–231v. It begins with an extremely interesting preface that is reprinted by both Violet and Klijn.[60] This preface is closely related to the sections on Ezra in the *Inventiones Nominum*, a medieval Latin Christian composition that discusses various biblical names.[61] The preface begins with *Incipit premium prefatio in libro Esdre filius Cusi prophete*; it has no explicit.

The preface is followed by an epitome of 4 and 6 Ezra, which are treated as one book.[62] The epitome has twenty-five numbered "capitula," of which twenty-one are devoted to 4 Ezra and four to 6 Ezra. The epitome begins on f. 217v with *Incipiunt brebis capitulacio in libro Esdre prophete* and concludes with *Finit.*

The text of 4 Ezra stands on ff. 218v–231v. It is introduced with *Incipit liber Esdre filius Cusi prophete.* There is absolutely no textual break between it and 6 Ezra, which extends from f. 231v to f. 233v. Sixth Ezra has no explicit.

The text of 5 Ezra is preceded by a separate epitome, in four "capitula," on f. 234r. The text of this epitome is printed in the present author's *Fifth Ezra*, appendix 6.[63] Fifth Ezra occupies ff. 234r–235v. It is introduced with *Incipit liber Esdre filius Cusi prophete sacerdos* but has no explicit. The next work in the manuscript begins on f. 235v with *Incipit vita vel obitum santorum.*

Legionensis 2, like Legionensis 1, is a Vulgate manuscript with Old Latin glosses in the margins of many books.[64] The order of books is: Oct, Reg, Chr, Job, Ps, L. sap, Proph, Tob, Jud, Esth, Esdr, Macc, Ev, Pa, Cath, Act, Ap, 2 Esdr.[65]

The text of 4 Ezra in Legionensis 2 was first collated by Violet (see chapter 1); 5 Ezra was collated by the present author in *Fifth Ezra*. The present edition is the first published collation of 6 Ezra. On the whole, the 2 Esdras corpus in this manuscript follows the Spanish recension.[66]

Conclusion to the Discussion of the Manuscripts

Several points of interest arise from the preceding review. First, both manuscripts of the French recension, S and A, have the order 5/4/6 Ezra. In both of these manuscripts, the three books are clearly differentiated by title. In both, a total of five books of Ezra is explicitly denoted—however, the specifics of the numeration differ. Both manuscripts seem to come from the area around Paris, and both were written in the ninth century.

All of the complete manuscripts of 2 Esdras that follow the Spanish recension (viz., CMNEVL) feature the order 4/6/5 Ezra. However, these manuscripts have little else in common in terms of their organization. A subgroup of the Spanish family, manuscripts MNE, cohere in that they present the 2 Esdras corpus as one book, entitled "the second book of Esdras." Furthermore, these three manuscripts are relatively close in time (eleventh to twelfth century), appear to come from the same geographical area of north, western-central Europe, and are extremely similar in their texts of 2 Esdras.

The three remaining complete Spanish manuscripts — C, V, and L—are the only significant manuscripts of 2 Esdras that come from Spain. However, the disposition and titling of the 2 Esdras material differ dramatically among them. In C, 4 Ezra is "3 Esdras" and 6/5 Ezra are "4 Esdras." In V, the first part of 4 Ezra (to 13:56) is "4 Esdras" and the remaining material is "5 Esdras." In L, 4/6 Ezra is clearly distinguished from 5 Ezra, but neither of them bears numeration. Even in C and V, however, there is some indication of a textual division between 6 and 5 Ezra.

Concerning geographical provenance, it is of interest that all the known significant manuscripts of 2 Esdras come from Spain or north-central continental Europe; there is none, for example, from Italy or Britain.

It is also noteworthy that the two latest manuscripts—V and L—which are closely related textually and geographically, both originally placed the 2 Esdras material at the very end of the Bible, after the NT. In the earlier manuscripts, on the other hand, 2 Esdras is found among the Jewish Scriptures, usually in connection with the books of Ezra, Nehemiah, and 1 Esdras. This may reflect a tendency, in the time and area where V and L were copied, to view 2 Esdras as suspect, or at least secondary, from a "scriptural" point of view.[67] Note, however, that when the contents of manuscript V were later rearranged (the date of this is uncertain), 1 and 2 Esdras were moved from the end of the codex to their customary position among the Jewish Scriptures. Note also that the tenth-century León antiphonary, written in the same city as Legionensis 2 but about two centuries earlier, freely includes material from 4, 5, and 6 Ezra among the scriptural materials of the Hebrew Bible and the New Testament (for details, see this chapter, "The Mozarabic Liturgy," and chapter 3, "The Mozarabic Liturgy").

SECONDARY EVIDENCE: QUOTATIONS AND AN EPITOME

Quotations of 6 Ezra are rare. To my knowledge, the book is cited in only three sources, all Latin: Gildas's *De excidio Britanniae* and the Mozarabic and Roman liturgies. It is sometimes claimed that Ambrose quotes 6 Ezra 16:59 (*qui extendit caelum quasi cameram*) in Epistle 11(29):22 (*extendit caelum sicut cameram*).[68] This phrase, however, is too short for the attribution to be certain; moreover, Isa 40:22 is another possible candidate.[69]

As noted previously, the León manuscript contains an epitome of 6 Ezra which could also potentially be of text-critical significance.

The citations and epitome are discussed below; their implications for the textual criticism of 6 Ezra are treated in chapter 3.

Gildas's "De excidio Britanniae" (ca. 540)

Gildas was a British monk and writer of the sixth century about whose life little certain is known. Known as Gildas Sapiens, he apparently was born in Scotland around the turn of the sixth century. He is said to have studied in South Wales, to have traveled in Wales and Ireland, and later to have settled in Rhuys (Morbihan, southern Brittany), where he founded a monastery, now called St. Gildas de Rhuys. He apparently died in Rhuys around 570.

Probably around 540, apparently in South Wales,[70] Gildas wrote his best-known work, entitled in full *De excidio et conquestu Britanniae ac flebili castigatione in reges, principes et sacerdotes*.[71] This is a scathing historical and ethical attack on the moral laxity that, according to the author, prevailed in sixth-century Britain, especially among the royalty and clergy.

The *De excidio* is divided into three main sections. The first (chapters 1–26) is a summary of British history to around 500 C.E. In the second (chapters 27–65), Gildas launches a "complaint" against contemporary political powers, focusing on the moral shortcomings of five British kings ("tyrants") of Cornwall and Wales. This critique is buttressed by an extensive chain of biblical citations from the "prophets," in which Gildas literally works his way through the entire biblical prophetic corpus, citing passages that seem to him to support his claims (chapters 37–65). The third and final section of the book (chapters 66–110) constitutes another "complaint," this one directed against contemporary British clergy.

The *De excidio* is generally important for several reasons. First, it represents one of the few extant sources for fifth- and sixth-century British history.[72] Second, Gildas's biblical citations are of value because they exhibit an Old Latin text type.

In the long string of prophetic citations against amoral rulers appear two extended quotations from 6 Ezra. As mentioned, Gildas in this section basically works his way through the biblical prophetic corpus. He begins, in chapter 38, with 1 and 2 Samuel, and then proceeds through the books of Kings and Chronicles, Isaiah, Jeremiah, and the twelve minor prophets. Chapter 59 treats Job. Chapter 60 begins with the words "Hear, besides, what the blessed prophet Ezra, library (*bibliotheca*) of the law, has threatened."[73] Gildas then quotes in succession 6 Ezra 15:21–27 (*Haec dicit . . . mala multa*) and 16:3–12 (*Inmissus est . . . fluctuantur de profundo*). There is no break indicated between the two citations. The section from the prophets concludes with quotations from Ezekiel, the Wisdom of Solomon, and Sirach (chapters 61–64).

One major concern of our study lies with the Latin text of Gildas's quotations of 6 Ezra: this is addressed in chapter 3. Another equally important issue, however, is that of the context in which 6 Ezra is quoted. Given the data presented previously, it hardly needs to be emphasized that 6 Ezra was an integral part of the prophetic corpus of Gildas's biblical text. Sixth Ezra was clearly considered of equal authority to the other writings in whose context it is quoted. This section of the *De excidio*, in fact, contains no nonbiblical references: it is an unbroken catena of quotations from biblical prophets.

Another significant issue is the sequence in which the prophetic books are cited. Sixth Ezra seems to have stood in Gildas's Bible text after the former prophets, Isaiah, Jeremiah, the Twelve, and Job, but before Ezekiel, the Wisdom of Solomon, and Sirach. The survey of significant manuscripts of 6 Ezra presented earlier in this chapter evidences no manuscript that shows anything approximating this order of texts.

Finally, one must ask how a book like 6 Ezra managed to find its way into the biblical canon of a sixth-century British/Brittanish monk. A survey of the transmission history of 6 Ezra is given in chapter 1. It can, I believe, be inferred from this survey that 6 Ezra would have gained the type of authoritative, indeed "canonical," status indicated in Gildas's work only in its connection with 4 Ezra. Sixth Ezra is virtually unattested in the history or literature of the church before the sixth century, and therefore cannot be assumed to have been a widely circulated work. Fourth Ezra, on the other hand, is widely known, is frequently quoted as being authoritative and inspired,[74] and appears in numerous translated language versions.[75] It is my opinion that, although Gildas happens not to quote from 4 Ezra 3–14, 6 Ezra was already connected textually to 4 Ezra by the time of Gildas, and that it was in this form that 4/6 Ezra entered into the biblical corpus from which Gildas quotes. Another consideration supporting this position is the fact that Gildas introduces his quotations of 6 Ezra as statements of "the blessed prophet Ezra, library of the law." Not only does the extant Latin text of 6 Ezra lack any reference to Ezra, but 4 Ezra calls Ezra a "prophet,"[76] and the phrase "library of the law (*bibliotheca legis*)" may well allude to the episode related in 4 Ezra 14.

Of course, all of this still leaves uncertain the status of 5 Ezra in relation to the 4/6 Ezra corpus at the time of Gildas.

The Mozarabic Liturgy (Date Uncertain)

An early citation of 6 Ezra which, to my knowledge, has not been noticed before occurs in the Spanish (Mozarabic) liturgy. A tenth-century Visigothic antiphonary from León, Spain contains the following response:

> Sanguis innocens et iustus clamat ad me et anime innocentum suspirant vehementer. Iam non feram dicit Dominus sed faciam vindictam illorum cito. Effuderunt sanguinem eorum.[77]

This may be compared to 6 Ezra 15:8–9:

> Ecce sanguis innoxius et iustus clamat ad me et animae iustorum clamant perseveranter. Vindicans vindicabo illos dicit Dominus et accipiam omnem sanguinem innocuum ex illis ad me.[78]

Clearly, these pericopae are closely related. The first sentences are virtually identical, and the second and third share the same structure, rhythm, and concepts. In theory, either pericope could derive from the other, or they could depend on a common source. The key to understanding their relationship lies in the structural framework of the Mozarabic liturgy. The section of the liturgy in which this passage occurs, which carries the theme *In diem allisionis infantum*, constitutes a florilegium of biblical texts centering on the theme of persecution and suffering of the innocent, especially inno-

cent children. The passage quoted above is directly preceded in the liturgy by citations from Jeremiah, Revelation, Isaiah, and the Psalms, and is followed by ones from
the Psalms, Matthew, the Wisdom of Solomon, Revelation, and Isaiah. Thus, this
liturgical passage stands in the context of a series of disjointed citations of biblical Scriptures centering on a common theme. Its parallel in 6 Ezra, on the other hand, forms
part of a smooth and continuous narrative.

These considerations make it unlikely that 6 Ezra is quoting the liturgy. There is
no evidence of a common source for the two passages. Furthermore, the intent of this
section of the liturgy is to quote Scripture, and we know that 2 Esdras was considered
scriptural in many places, including Spain, at an early date.[79] In fact, the León
antiphonary quotes both 4 and 5 Ezra in the midst of other biblical books, indicating
that these works were also considered of "canonical" status by the compilers of the
Mozarabic liturgy. It seems virtually certain, then, that the liturgy is quoting 6 Ezra.
Furthermore, like Gildas, it quotes 6 Ezra as an authoritative scriptural document, in
the same context as other sources whose "canonical" status is beyond dispute.

As noted here, it is not surprising that 6 Ezra should be quoted in the Mozarabic
liturgy, since both 4 and 5 Ezra are cited there liberally,[80] and since 6 Ezra seems to
have been connected with 4 Ezra at an early date, almost certainly earlier than 5 Ezra.[81]
This is, however, the first citation of 6 Ezra that has been identified in this liturgical
corpus. As argued, it is most probable that 6 Ezra achieved "scriptural" or "canonical" status only in its association with 4 Ezra. Thus, this liturgical citation provides
further evidence that the 2 Esdras corpus, including 4, 5, and 6 Ezra, was considered
scripturally authoritative in Spain at a relatively early date.[82]

As noted, the antiphonary in which this quotation stands dates from the tenth
century. However, the antiphonary's editor and commentator, L. Brou, maintains that
it represents a liturgical situation current in Spain in the fifth to sixth century.[83] Furthermore, Brou holds that the León antiphonary contains "almost all the elements of
the chant" of the ancient Hispanic liturgy.[84] Thus it seems that 6 Ezra, as a part of
2 Esdras, was considered ecclesiastically authoritative in Spain at least by the sixth century. Evidence of liturgical usage of 5 Ezra, again as part of the 2 Esdras corpus, may
push this date back to the fifth century, and in a wider variety of contexts—namely,
Spain, France, Italy, and North Africa.[85]

Finally, we should comment on the rather free form of the quotation, especially in
its second part. Citations in the Mozarabic liturgy tend to be free, and this one therefore fits the general pattern. In the present case, for example, with the liturgical substitutions of *innocentum* for *iustorum,* *suspirant* for *clamant,* and *vehementer* for *perseveranter,* it seems likely that the liturgist, or a written or oral source, was quoting
from memory, due to which synonymous equivalents entered the text.

It is also possible in theory, however, that there was at one time a longer, continuous written text of 6 Ezra, no longer preserved, that approximated the text in
the liturgy. This possibility, while hypothetical, is supported by the fact that one
unique reading of 6 Ezra in manuscript L, the twelfth-century manuscript that also
happens to come from León, agrees with the liturgical citation. This situation is
discussed in chapter 3, "The Mozarabic Liturgy." For comments on the text-critical
significance of the unique elements of manuscript L in 5 Ezra, see Bergren, *Fifth
Ezra,* pp. 112–16 and 140–42.

The Roman Liturgy (Date Uncertain)

Carl Marbach, in his 1907 work *Carmina scripturarum*,[86] lists an antiphon (no. 3) from the *Ad laudes* in the *In Vigilia nativitatis Domini* (24 December) that, although somewhat different in wording, expresses a thought that is almost identical to 6 Ezra 16:52.[87] The antiphon reads as follows:

> Crastina die delebitur iniquitas terrae, et regnabit super nos salvator mundi.[88]

> On the next day the iniquity of the earth will be wiped out, and the savior of the world will rule over us.

Sixth Ezra 16:52, in the French recension, reads:

> Quoniam ecce adhuc pusillum et tolletur iniquitas a terra et iustitia regnabit in nos.[89]

> Because behold, a little longer and iniquity will be taken away from the earth, and righteousness will rule over us.
>   (The Spanish recension differs only in omitting *ecce* and substituting *nobis* for *nos.*)

Although these pericopae are short and the verbal parallels are not as striking as in the passage considered previously, there is little question that the pericopae are related. It seems reasonable to hypothesize that one is dependent on the other. As in the case of the Mozarabic liturgical passage discussed, the question is in which direction the influence has occurred.

There are several reasons to believe that the liturgical reading depends on 6 Ezra. First, it is commonplace for the Roman liturgy, like the Mozarabic, to cite scriptural works. It has been shown elsewhere that the Roman liturgy quotes both 4 and 5 Ezra.[90] Thus, given the transmissional history of 2 Esdras traced in chapter 1, it would not be surprising if 6 Ezra were also cited here. Second, whereas 6 Ezra is known to have been composed by about 300 C.E., the early history of the liturgy is vague and is not generally extended back much before the fifth century. Third, the liturgical phrase "the savior of the world will rule over us" is more specific and theologically developed than 6 Ezra's "righteousness will rule over us." In cases like this, the theologically developed reading is usually secondary. Similar cases are found in the liturgical use of 4 and 5 Ezra.[91] Finally, the verse as it appears in 6 Ezra forms part of an extended and coherent narrative, whereas the liturgical sentence is an isolated pericope. Again, the isolated fragment is more likely to be a secondary citation.

Assuming, then, with Marbach, that the liturgy here quotes or alludes to 6 Ezra, the next issue to consider is the relationship between the two texts. They have several verbal elements in common: namely, *iniquitas, terra/terrae, regnabit,* and *nos*. There are, on the other hand, some differences in word choice: the liturgy has *crastina die* for 6 Ezra's *adhuc pusillum, delebitur* for *tolletur,* and *super* for *in.* There is also one major difference in content: the liturgy's *salvator mundi* for 6 Ezra's *iustitia.*

The latter element can be accounted for easily enough: as noted previously, it is relatively common in liturgical contexts for specific theological terms to replace more general ones. (The possibility that there was a text of 6 Ezra 16:52 that read *salvator mundi* cannot, however, be ruled out.)

The differences in word usage are more problematic. As with the Mozarabic citation treated above, there are two basic alternatives. One is that the Latin text of 6 Ezra existed in antiquity in multiple forms. (In fact, the Spanish recension of 6 Ezra is itself an example of this.) It is possible in theory that the liturgist quoted a Latin text of 6 Ezra 16:52 that no longer survives. Another is that the liturgist has freely adapted 6 Ezra or quoted from memory. The Roman liturgists, like the Hispanic, are known to have quoted freely or paraphrastically.[92]

The apparent use of 6 Ezra in the Roman liturgy indicates that here, as in Spain, the book was considered authoritative by individuals responsible for liturgical formulation. Unfortunately, as noted, the early tradition history of the Roman liturgy is not well known. Nevertheless, as with the quotations in Gildas and in the Mozarabic liturgy, this citation from Rome suggests not only that 6 Ezra was considered scripturally authoritative there at an early period (fifth to seventh centuries) but also that it was probably attached to 4 Ezra by that time. The scriptural or "canonical" status of 6 Ezra, as part of the 2 Esdras corpus, is, therefore, now attested in the fifth to seventh centuries for Britanny and/or England (Gildas's provenances), Spain, and Rome. Again, it is not a coincidence that both 4 and 5 Ezra are amply cited in the Hispanic and Roman rites.

The Epitome of 6 Ezra in the León Manuscript (Twelfth Century)

The setting of this epitome in the León manuscript (L) was discussed previously (see "Description of the Significant Manuscripts, Legionensis 2"). The text of the epitome, the only extant epitome of 6 Ezra, is printed by Klijn in *Der lateinische Text der Apokalypse des Esra*, page 100. The epitome's text-critical significance is discussed in the following chapter.

THREE

Reconstructing the
Two Recensions

Examination of the Latin manuscripts of 6 Ezra indicates that they constitute a "closed recension": that is, it is possible to construct a genealogical stemma of the manuscripts that reasonably accounts for all the variant readings, without having to take recourse to hypothetical outside sources, cross-influence between manuscript families, and so on. Analysis of the manuscripts suggests the following stemma:

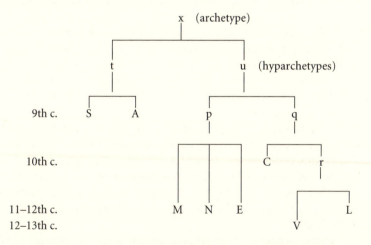

In what follows, an attempt is made to establish each link in this stemma, up to the level of the hyparchetypes t and u, through established principles of textual criticism.[1] Since it is widely recognized that these hyparchetypes represent two distinct textual recensions, and since the relationship between these recensions will require special attention, discussion of this relationship and reconstruction of the archetype x are reserved for chapter 4.

In the present analysis, the manuscripts are first examined individually to determine their orthographic peculiarities and characteristic types of scribal errors.[2] In the process the manuscripts' "separative errors," that is, errors that indicate that no other of the eight significant Latin manuscripts is dependent on them, are pointed out. The same methods are then applied to the hypothetical common ancestors of families of manuscripts. For the latter, it is also necessary to demonstrate "conjunctive errors," that is, shared errors that prove that two or more manuscripts had a common and distinctive ancestor.

As noted in the survey of the transmission history of 6 Ezra in chapter 1 and in the discussion of the significant manuscripts in chapter 2, the Latin text tradition of 6 Ezra is closely related to those of 4 and 5 Ezra. It is therefore worthy of note that the stemma proposed here for 6 Ezra is virtually identical both to that commonly accepted for the Latin 4 Ezra[3] and to that suggested by the present writer for 5 Ezra.[4]

A few methodological comments about manuscripts and the stemmatic method are in order here. First, the stemma proposed above comprises entirely manuscripts from the ninth century and later. This leaves a considerable amount of time between the earliest full witnesses to the text of 6 Ezra and its probable date of composition in the second or third century. It should therefore be emphasized that the text of the archetype x that this study aims to reconstruct is only an "earliest recoverable text" and not necessarily the "original" form of 6 Ezra.

Similarly, the eight significant Latin manuscripts available to us represent only a small proportion of the hundreds of manuscripts (most now lost) that must have made up the full textual history of the Latin 6 Ezra. It is not inconceivable that all the extant manuscripts represent, for example, only one stream of a more complex Latin textual tradition.

Moreover, consideration of the prior stage of the (mostly lost) Greek text introduces a further level of uncertainty. Although we possess a small fragment of the Greek text, it is difficult to judge on this basis the overall accuracy of the extant Latin translation, how close the Greek fragment may be to the original Greek form of 6 Ezra, and indeed how closely the Greek *Vorlage* of the extant Latin version of 6 Ezra approximated the original Greek text.

Finally, it is in the nature of the stemmatic method to seek out the simplest possible situation that reasonably accounts for all of the available textual evidence. Real historical situations, however, are usually far from being the simplest possible situations. Given the vagaries of history and the factors indicated above, it is quite possible that the "simplest solution" will be inaccurate and misleading to some extent. It is important to recognize and make allowance for the inherent limitations of the stemmatic method.

I also call attention here to the chart of quantitative textual relationships among the eight Latin manuscripts of 6 Ezra presented in Appendix 4. Although these data do not allow us to determine the *direction* of influence among the manuscripts, they do show the extent of textual agreement between any given pair of manuscripts, and thus are helpful in forming an initial impression of the textual situation. Furthermore, the analogous data given there for 4 and 5 Ezra permit a comparison of 6 Ezra with these other, related books.

THE READINGS OF THE LATIN MANUSCRIPTS

Sangermanensis (S)

Manuscript S has traditionally been regarded as the *codex optimus* of 6 Ezra, and in fact of the entire 2 Esdras corpus. The pervasive influence of this manuscript on the medieval Latin manuscript tradition of 2 Esdras is graphically illustrated by the situation of the "lost fragment" of 4 Ezra, described in chapters 1 and 2. The present treatment concerns the first hand of the manuscript; the correcting hands are discussed later.

One important feature of the text of S that should be mentioned at the outset is that in 15:59–16:30 (inclusive) plus two words of 16:31 (i.e., the text section *infelix primaria venies . . . scrutantur sic relinquentur*), this manuscript, which normally manifests the French recension in 2 Esdras, suddenly switches to a Spanish text. This phenomenon is most easily explained by the theory that, at some point in the chain of transmission between the French hyparchetype t and manuscript S, a manuscript leaf (or leaves) dropped out of a (now lost) exemplar. The missing text was noticed and recopied, but from a "Spanish" manuscript.

We may speculate whether anything more can be deduced about the exemplar from which the leaf or leaves were lost. In manuscript S itself, the section of text in which the affiliation shifts occupies about three-quarters of one side of a page. In manuscript C, the earliest extant Spanish manuscript (and the closest in date to S and A), this section of text occupies less than one-half of one side of a page. In manuscript A, however, the other French manuscript, the section in which S switches affiliation occupies, almost to the line, two sides of a page, or one full folio. In fact, were the text of A to be shifted forward by seven lines, this section of text would literally fill folio 80 (recto and verso) exactly. Given the fact that manuscript A has relatively short pages (as indicated here), this shows almost certainly that it was only one leaf that dropped out of the unknown exemplar of S. This exemplar seems to have had pages whose capacity almost exactly matched those of A.

The shift of affiliation in S between 15:59 and 16:31 shows that the Spanish recension, which we will argue to be secondary, circulated in northern France[5] before the ninth century. It furthermore establishes that in at least one location and at one point in time, the French and Spanish recensions existed side by side. The text type of the unknown Spanish manuscript from which 15:59–16:31 of S was copied is discussed in this chapter, "The Lost Exemplar."

The text of 6 Ezra in manuscript S is on the whole quite good, but it has undergone some corruption and also some attempts at emendation and stylistic improvement. The manuscript's text contains forty-eight unique readings,[6] some of which are orthographic variants.

Manuscript S shows the following orthographic traits:[7]

ae → e	*procelle* 15:34; *magne* 15:40; *aque* 15:58; *terre* 15:60; *et passim*	
e → ae	*aequi* 15:35; *caeteros* 16:22	
t → c	*iusticia* 16:50, 52	
t → th	*cartha* 15:2	
v → b	*superelebent* 16:76	
loss of h	*ora* 16:38	

The manuscript contains a number of simple copying errors, often unusual words that were misread by a scribe. These include: *me vendum* for *movendum* 15:20; *a potestate* for *apostatae* 15:25; *sic flatus* for *sibilatus* 15:29; *vinxit* for *finxit* 16:61; *exresurrectio* for *exsurrectio* 16:70; and *semina* for *semita* 16:77. There are many errors in case and gender endings of nouns and adjectives and in verbal tense endings. S has relatively few omissions or additions; those that occur may be deliberate (see below). There are also few places in which one error has prompted a chain of attempted emendations.

The manuscript does show some attempts at emendation and stylistic improvement, usually minor in scope. These include: addition of *in* 15:6; *inhabitant* for *habitant* 15:14; omission of *et* 15:20; 16:67; *peccatores* for *peccantes* 15:22; *tradidit* for *tradet* 15:26; *aut* for *vel* 16:29, 31; and *fornicariam mulierem idonea et bona* for *fornicaria mulierem idoneam et bonam* 16:49. Perhaps the most striking change is the substitution of *coram Deo et angelis eius* for *coram Domino et gloria eius* in 16:66.

The latter two passages serve as separative errors for the text of 6 Ezra in S, as does *sic flatus* 15:29, mentioned previously. That is, since these corrupt or emended readings are unlikely to have been independently restored by a scribe, they indicate that no other of the eight manuscripts of 6 Ezra is dependent exclusively on S.

We should mention one other unusual feature of S. There are twelve passages in 6 Ezra (15:2, 3, 6, 12, 16, 20, 26, 33 [bis], 55; 16:43, 62) in which, in a phrase or sentence, S agrees with the Spanish manuscripts, whereas A presents a variant text. Normally, on the basis of our stemma, an agreement of S and Sp against A would indicate that A is in error. However, it is in precisely these passages that A exhibits some of the most primitive and unusual vocabulary in the book: *mastigati* 15:12 (a Latin *hapax legomenon*); *supervalesco* 15:16 (very rare); *subsessor* 15:33 (rare); and *inconstabilitio* 15:33 (a Latin *hapax legomenon*). This factor, in combination with the fact that these twelve readings of A can often be judged stylistically more primitive than the readings of S/Sp on other grounds, has led us to conclude that, in these passages, A is superior, and that S has been altered to conform to the (secondary) Spanish text. This is a rather unusual text-critical decision, but it seems to be mandated by the evidence. It is, of course, difficult to tell when this assimilation of S to Sp occurred, or how many other readings besides those indicated here might have been affected. It is possible in theory that this phenomenon was connected with the copying of 6 Ezra 15:59–16:31 into an exemplar of S from an unknown Spanish manuscript, as described previously.

The text of 6 Ezra in manuscript S shows significant activity of correcting hands.[8] Berger believes that the oldest of these corrections were made by a hand contemporary with the original scribe, if not by that scribe himself.[9] Bensly affirms this observation, noting also that the correctors tended to assimilate abnormal spelling, inflection, and syntax to the classical standards of biblical Latin, that many archaic forms characteristic of the original have therefore been removed, and that the alterations are ubiquitous.[10] It is difficult to judge how many correcting hands are represented in the text and which alterations, if any, come from the original scribe.

The text of 6 Ezra in this manuscript has been altered some ninety-three times. As noted, many of these changes attempt to bring the text into accord with the norms of classical biblical Latin. Thus, there are numerous changes in spelling and orthography, and many grammatical improvements. In addition, the correctors frequently, and often successfully, emend tense and number of verbs, and case and gender endings of nouns and adjectives. In several cases, words are added or deleted for reasons of style or sense. Two examples of successful emendation are the substitution of *vindemiabit* for *vindiamit* 16:25 and *esitemini* for *sitemini* 16:75. On the other hand, in 15:53 the correct *mortem* is altered to *montem*.

In evaluating the corrections in S, it should be asked whether any of them evidence clear signs of influence from other manuscripts. In 6 Ezra there are two possible cases of such influence: the restoration of the missing *qui sunt* in 15:20 and the correct substitution of *subsessor* for *obsessor* in 15:33. Neither of these emendations conclusively indicates an influence from other manuscripts, however, since both could conceivably be successful "guesses" by a scribe. There is no evidence of influence from the Spanish recension on the correcting hands of S.

Ambianensis (A)

The text of 6 Ezra in Ambianensis is more idiosyncratic than that in S.[11] The original hand of A contains, for example, 110 unique readings, more than twice the number of its congenitor.[12]

The following orthographic traits characterize the manuscript:

b	→ v	*odivilem* 15:48
e	→ ae	*speciae* 15:46; *famae* 15:58; passim
e	→ i	*vindimiam* 16:26, 30; *vinia* 16:30
e	→ oe	*foena* 15:42; *concoeptum* 16:57
l	→ ll	*camelli* 15:36
o	→ u	*curuscabit* 16:10; *nun* 16:10; passim
s	→ ss	*Assia* 15:46; 16:1; *possuit* 16:61
ss	→ s	*inmisus* 16:3; *abysum* 16:57; passim
t	→ c	*recuciet* 16:6, 8
t	→ th	*notho* 15:20; *natho* 15:39
tt	→ t	*sagitam* 16:7; *sagitario* 16:7, 16

Many of the corruptions in A are simply careless copying errors: missing letters, misread words, and so on (e.g., *repetentur* for *trepidentur* 15:29; *averterit orio* for *a territorio* 15:33). As with S, there are numerous errors in verbal tense endings,[13] and in case and gender endings of nouns and adjectives. Manuscript A also shows a tendency toward omission: the longest are of ten (15:8), four (15:16), five (16:33), thirteen (16:42), and three words (16:54). (At least one of these, in 15:16, however, may be a deliberate attempt to circumvent a difficult text.)

Manuscript A does essay a few emendations and stylistic improvements: for example, transposition of *ire* 15:17; omission of *et* 15:30, 38; 16:11; omission of *et erit* and substitution of *sanguinem* for *sanguis* 15:35; and *possitis* for *possit* 15:51. There is one example of substitution of *Dominus* for *Deus* (15:20), and one of the reverse (16:64).

Any of the longer omissions serve as separative errors for this manuscript.

The text of 6 Ezra in manuscript A has been altered by correcting hands even more frequently than in S: A has 185 corrections, almost twice as many as S.[14] The comments of Bensly, cited earlier in the discussion of the correctors of S, were also made with reference to A: its correctors tend to modify the text toward conformity with the grammatical and orthographic norms of classical biblical Latin. As with S, it is difficult to judge how many correcting hands were active and how many corrections might have been made by the original scribe.

The correcting hands of A (in our notation, A2) show more than forty orthographic changes and numerous adjustments of minor grammatical points. The correctors often attempted to emend the tense and number of verbs and the case and gender of nouns and adjectives. There are numerous efforts to improve the text by adding words or by emending corrupt or difficult readings. Many of these emendations are successful. A2 successfully restores omissions of five words in 16:33 (*sponsos lugebunt mulieres non habentes*) and three words in 16:54 (*et corda illorum*), as well as correctly emending many individual errors.

Again, we must ask whether correctors of A can be shown to have had recourse to other manuscripts of 6 Ezra. Here the answer is clearly positive, since neither of the restorations indicated previously could have been accomplished through the simple ingenuity of a scribe. (In both cases, however, it is possible that the restoration was made by, or at the time of, the original copyist.) On the other hand, the numerous incorrect attempts at emendation in A suggest that at least one corrector worked without reference to other manuscripts. There is no indication of influence of the Spanish recension on the correcting hands of A.

Complutensis 1 (C)

The text of 6 Ezra in manuscript C is relatively faithful to the manuscript's hyparchetype q.[15] Although C contains some 124 unique readings, a relatively high number, almost half of these (59) are orthographic variants.

Especially characteristic of this manuscript is substitution of *b* for *v*: this is a well-known feature of late Latin stemming from an approximation in sound of the two letters.[16] Additionally, the following orthographic traits appear:

ae	→ e	*profetie* 15:1; *que* 15:8; passim
b	→ v	*supervia* 15:18
ch	→ c	*bracio* 15:11
d	→ t	*illut* 16:59[17]
e	→ ae	*aeducam* 15:11; *aenim* 15:16; passim
h	→ c	*mici* 16:17 (bis)
i	→ y	*ydoneam* 16:49
oo	→ o	*coperitur* 16:77
th	→ t	*tesauros* 16:57
t	→ tt	*tritticum* 15:42
v	→ f	*deforabit* 15:23 (cf. 15:62; 16:78)

alliteration	*quemammodum* 16:29, 73, 77
adds initial h	*hedificat* 16:42
removes h	*odie* 15:21; *adpreendet* 15:37

Most of the corruptions in the manuscript are minor copying errors or mistakes in case, gender, or verbal ending. There are a few omissions of one or two words.

Manuscript C does make some stylistic changes and faulty attempts at emendation. These include replacement of *his* with *eis* 15:24 and of *eorum* with *ipsorum* 15:29,[18] and the addition of *minus* 16:30. In 16:39, *tardabitur* is written for *morabitur*.

Because the manuscript contains so few omissions and major copying mishaps, there are relatively few candidates for separative errors. However, *tuum* for *fructiferum* 15:62 and *tardabitur* for *morabitur* 16:39 can count as such.

Mazarinaeus (M)

Except for one long omission, this manuscript is an extremely faithful representation of its hyparchetype p.[19] Most of its twenty-five unique readings either stem from this omission or are orthographic in character.

The following orthographic traits appear:

ae	→ e	*misere* 15:47; *seculum* 16:58
e	→ ae	*praecepta, praeponderent* 16:76
h	→ ch	*michi* 16:17 (bis)
i	→ y	*Babyloniam* 15:43
n	→ m	*septemtrione* 15:34
t	→ c	*contricio* 15:15; 16:2

M has only a few copying errors. *et ce* appears for *ecce* 15:27, *convenerint* for *cum venerint* 16:18, and *portaret* for *potaret* 16:60. The omission mentioned above is of eighteen words in 16:6–7 and was prompted by homoioteleuton.

Likewise, the manuscript manifests only a few attempts at emendation. *sic* is substituted for *sicut* in 15:29, *est qui* is added in 16:10, and *omnia* is transposed in 16:62.

The long omission in 16:6–7 serves as a separative error.

Bruxellensis (N)

Manuscript N,[20] like its congenitor M, is faithful to the hyparchetype p.[21] It contains only thirteen unique readings in 6 Ezra, equally divided between errors, attempted emendations, and orthographic peculiarities. The following are orthographic traits:

ae	→ e	*cecabunt* 16:68
d	→ c	*ociosam* 15:60
e	→ ae	*aebria* 15:53
t	→ c	*inconstabilicio* 15:16; *porcio* 15:38; passim
xsu	→ xu	*exurget* 15:15, 50

The manuscript has only a few minor errors: for example, *multis* for *multos* 15:29 and *sui* for *tui* 15:54. A scribe has deliberately emended the style in several places: for example, additions of *in* 15:48 and *et* 16:43, and transposition of *populi* 16:68. The most interesting attempt at emendation is the transformation of *defendat* (". . . when the one comes who will *defend*, seeking out every sin . . .") to *descendat* (". . . *descend* . . .") 16:50.

Although N contains no dramatic separative errors, the four emendations mentioned previously, when considered in combination, are unlikely to have been independently restored.[22]

Epternacensis (E)

Manuscript E is more idiosyncratic than its congenitors M and N, with fifty-eight unique readings.[23] As in the case of 4 and 5 Ezra,[24] however, many of these are not corruptions but rather deliberate attempts to improve the grammar, style, or readability of the text. In Violet's words, "the scribe was a good Latinist . . . who thought independently and therefore often made wrong emendations (exactly like present-day editors)."[25]

The following orthographic traits occur:

l → ll	*tollerantia* 16:73
m → n	*nunquid* 15:52; 16:6, 7
y → i	*Babilonis* 15:46

alliteration   *assunt* 16:74

The text of 6 Ezra in E shows several errors. The most substantial is a ten-word omission in 16:4, caused by homoioteleuton. Most of the others are relatively minor: for example, *multitudo* for *multus* 15:36; *examinent* for *exterminent* 15:40; and *terram* for *iram* 15:44.

The vast majority of unique readings in E are, as indicated here, attempted emendations. Many of these are made for reasons of grammar or style: for example, the substitution of *tuas* for *tuos* and *concupierunt* for *cupierunt*[26] 15:47; addition of *es* 15:53; and omission of *omnes* 15:62. The substitution of *et occidente* for *ab euro* 15:20, addition of *aquam et* 15:41, and omission of *qui defendat* 16:50 all attempt to improve the sense or flow of the text. A scribe has several times interchanged pronouns (e.g., *eorum* for *illorum* 15:19; cf. 15:23, 40, 45)[27] and nomina sacra (e.g., *Dominus* for *Deus* 15:12; cf. 15:24; 16:62, 70). An apparently innocent change in verbal ending in 16:14 may actually be of Christological intent: *veniant*, "evils are sent out, and they will not return until *they come* over the earth," becomes *veniat*, ". . . until *he comes* upon the earth."

The ten-word omission in 16:4 is a separative error.

Abulensis (V)

Manuscript V, with 209 unique readings, presents a highly idiosyncratic text of 6 Ezra.[28] Most of the unique readings are careless copying errors and omissions; there are also numerous attempts at emendation and orthographic peculiarities.

The following are orthographic traits:

ae → e	*que* 15:3; *ve* 16:1; *celum* 16:59
ii → i	*fili* 15:25
l → ll	*camilli* 15:36; *demollient* 15:42
m → n	*famen* 15:19, 49
rr → r	*oribilis* 15:28
t → c	*porcio* 15:38; *inicium* 16:18; passim
y → i	*Assiriorum* 15:33; *Siria* 16:1

alliteration   *appropinquavit* 15:15
addition of initial h   *hodibilem* 15:48

Most of the corruptions in the manuscript are simple reading errors or short, one-word omissions. Examples of the former are *omnibus* for *hominibus* 15:16; *a vevtro* for *ab euro* 15:20; and *molabitur* for *violabitur* 15:39. The manuscript also has several longer omissions, the most substantial being of fifteen (15:44), ten (15:62), and eight (16:12) words. There are numerous errors in verbal and nominal endings.

On the other hand, V evidences many attempts at grammatical and stylistic improvement. Most of these involve changes in verbal ending, transpositions, and short additions or deletions. Examples are *convocabo* for *convoco* 15:20; transposition of *multa* 15:27, *eum* 16:9, and *illam* 16:26; addition of *ad* 15:39; and *habitant* for *inhabitant* 15:40. There are also several cases of deliberate substitution of words: *eum* for *illum* 15:27; *illa* for *ea* 16:8; *de* for *ex* 16:28;[29] and *peccatis* for *iniquitatibus* 16:77.

Any of the longer omissions noted previously can serve as separative errors.

Legionensis 2 (L)

The text of the 2 Esdras corpus in manuscript L[30] is notorious for several reasons.[31] First, the scribe either of this manuscript or of an exemplar has added numerous words and phrases to the text. In 6 Ezra alone, there are some fifty additions, ranging from one to five words.[32] Furthermore, this manuscript presents the most idiosyncratic and corrupt text of 2 Esdras of all the significant manuscripts in other ways as well. Manuscript L contains 270 unique readings in 6 Ezra, making up more than 10 percent of the words in the text.

L has the following orthographic traits:

a → e	*Esaye* 15:46; 16:1	
ae → e	*celum* 16:55	
cc → c	*sicabitur* 15:50	
e → ae	*grandinae* 15:13; *irae* 15:17; passim	
h → ch	*michi* 16:17	
m → mm	*consummet* 15:33	
m → n	*ronfea* 15:22	
n → m	*septemtrionae* 15:34	
r → rr	*derridens* 15:53	
ss → s	*obsesor* 15:33	
t → c	*dicencium* 15:3; *paciar* 15:10; passim	
t → th	*cathaginis* 15:39	
u → i	*Assirioru* 15:30	

loss of initial h   *oras* 16:38

The majority of unique readings in L are textual corruptions due to copying error. These are ubiquitous, occurring at the rate of two to three per verse. The most common types of errors are misread words, corruption of endings, and short omissions. There are also cases of dittography and careless transposition.

Equally striking, however, are a scribe's intentional alterations of the text, mostly in the form of short additions. The text of 6 Ezra features fifty-two additions, spanning from one to five words. Most of these are intended either to clarify the text, to supplement it by adding extra elements, or to enhance its dramatic effect. In 15:2, for example, when God instructs the prophet to be sure that the words of the prophecy are "written on paper," L adds "and placed in a book" (*et in libro ponantur*). L supplements God's promise that "everyone who believes will be saved by their faith" (15:4) with the assurance *in eternum*. In 15:23, where the Spanish text states that "sinners will be burned like straw," L has ". . . like fresh straw of trees" (*quasi stramen lignorum viridis*). To 6 Ezra's charge that sinners have killed the elect, "ridiculing their death when you were drunk," L adds "with their blood" (*de sanguine eorum*; 15:53).

In the present author's study of 5 Ezra, it was noted first that certain of the additions of L in that book show clear signs of correlation with the secondary French recension, and second that some of the additions of L in 4 Ezra seem to be related to unique readings of the Armenian version.[33] In the present context, it is noteworthy first that none of the additions of L in 6 Ezra shows a correlation with the French recension. This may be related to the fact that the French recension in 6 Ezra seems to be primary and the Spanish secondary, the reverse of the situation in 5 Ezra. Second, further investigation of the relationship between L and the Armenian version of 4 Ezra has caused me to doubt that there are, in fact, significant links between those two texts.

Although the correlations of manuscript L with the Armenian version of 4 Ezra have not proven significant, there is one other factor that may bear on the highly idiosyncratic and expansionistic tendencies of manuscript L in the texts of 4, 5, and 6 Ezra. N. Fernández Marcos's recent study of the Old Latin glosses in the margins of the books of Samuel-Kings in five medieval Spanish Vulgate Bibles, *including manuscript L*, has shown that these Old Latin texts have several distinct characteristics.[34] Primary among these are their textual expansions, which typically account for more than 30 percent of the text, and most of which have no parallels in other known Bible texts in any language (pp. 45–46, 49). According to Fernández Marcos, such textual expansions are highly unusual in any textual tradition of the Bible,[35] were virtually unknown until now, and are especially surprising because the Old Latin translations are generally known for their literalness (pp. 45–46). In general he finds that these expansions show no evidence of having been copied from the Greek *Vorlagen* of the Old Latin; rather, most seem to be the work either of the translator or of later copyists.

The main features of these expansions are as follows. First there are numerous double readings ("doublets"). Second, "when a passage is obscure or the translator is faced by a perplexing translation, VL [Vetus Latina = Old Latin] adopts a text twice as long in order to clarify the original" (pp. 62–63). Third, there are numerous "midrashic expansions, exegetical interpretations and editorial notes that bear witness to an intense redactional activity by the translators or early copyists" (p. 63).

It is especially this final type of scribal activity that reminds us of the textual expansions in manuscript L in 4, 5, and 6 Ezra. Since manuscript L is one of the manuscripts under investigation by Fernández Marcos, and since the other four manuscripts that he discusses are all cognate to it in date, locale, and text type, it is difficult to believe that these phenomena are coincidental. One is almost forced to conclude that the textual expansions in 4, 5, and 6 Ezra in manuscript L are the work of the same scribe, or at least the same scribal tradition, that is responsible for the textual expansions in the Old Latin marginal glosses in Samuel-Kings in that manuscript. The primary difference is, of course, that in 2 Esdras these readings have been integrated into the main text. This may have something to do with the fact that 2 Esdras was widely regarded, and in fact is explicitly indicated through its placement in manuscript L, as being of "secondary" scriptural status.

We may draw several conclusions. First, the majority of the textual expansions in 2 Esdras in manuscript L would seem, as Violet claimed long ago, to derive from late editorial activity and to be the work of an "independently-thinking person,"[36] not, if the Old Latin marginal glosses are indicative, to reflect a different Greek *Vorlage* of the book. Second, these textual expansions are not a unique phenomenon but reflect wider Latin scribal practices in copying biblical materials in central Spain in the tenth through the sixteenth century. Third, presumably something may be gained by comparing the expansions in 2 Esdras with those in the marginal Old Latin readings in the five biblical manuscripts studied by Fernández Marcos. This, however, is beyond the scope of this study.

The text of L in 6 Ezra shows other signs of intentional scribal intervention besides the additions. There are several cases of substitution of words: for example, *conturbent* for *turbent* 15:3;[37] *eorum* for *ipsorum* 15:21; and *innocentem* for *innocuum* 15:22. A scribe also tended to favor the *-que* suffix over *et*: for example, *domusque* 15:18; *exientque* 15:29; *erbasque* 15:42.

The numerous additions and the five-word omission in 15:48 are separative errors, proving that no other significant manuscript depends exclusively on L.

The Lost Exemplar of 15:59–16:31 in Manuscript S

As noted in the discussion of manuscript S, in the first part of this chapter, S in 15:59–16:31 switches affiliation from the French to the Spanish text type. It may be presumed that a leaf dropped out of a lost ancestor of S, and that the missing text was recopied from an (unknown) Spanish manuscript. This manuscript, of course, represents yet another variable in the text-critical situation of 6 Ezra, and it should be situated in the stemma of the Spanish family. We will label it "T."

It will be recalled that the Spanish recension has two main manuscript groups, MNE (hyparchetype p) and CVL (hyparchetype q), and that V and L share a hyparchetype r. Since T does not share any conjunctive errors, or even any unique or significant readings, with any of the individual Spanish manuscripts, or with r, we assume that it does not fall under the hyparchtypes p or q. Since T, p, and q all exhibit separative errors (for T, see *ad* in 15:60 and *ut* in 15:61; for p, see *potest* in 16:21; for q, see the three-word omission in 15:60), none of these witnesses is directly dependent on any other. Thus, T must have a position in the stemma independent of and equal to p and q.

T agrees with q (CVL) against p (MNE) as follows:

In readings that are almost surely correct: 9 times
In readings that are apparently correct: 6 times
In uncertain readings: 5 times
In probable errors: once (*succenditur* 16:15)
In certain errors: never

T agrees with p (MNE) against q (CVL) as follows:

In readings that are almost surely correct: 7 times
In readings that are apparently correct: 6 times

In uncertain readings: 7 times

In probable errors: 6 times (*otiosam* 15:60; *surgebit* 16:10; *disturbabuntur* 16:12; ~ *se* 16:20; *perdet* 16:22; omission of *in* 16:28)

In an almost certain error: once (omission of *agricola* 16:24)

The agreements in readings that are surely or apparently correct are not significant, first because the figures are so close, and second because these readings could simply indicate errors in p or q. It is the shared (conjunctive) errors that are telling. Unfortunately, the one instance where T sides with p in an almost certain error (16:24) is not conclusive, since two scribes theoretically could have omitted the same word independently. Nevertheless, the situation indicated previously strongly suggests that T and p share a common archetype, which we call d:

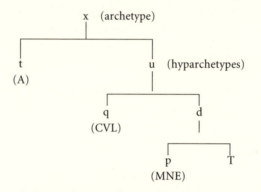

Since T and p have no certain conjunctive errors, d cannot be proven, but it seems the most logical way to account for the textual evidence. Our text-critical evaluation of T thus proceeds on the basis of the stemma shown.

THE LATIN MANUSCRIPT GROUPS AND HYPARCHETYPES

The following section analyzes the various manuscript groups and hyparchetypes proposed earlier. According to the stemmatic method as elucidated by P. Maas,[38] each junction point in the stemma, representing a (usually hypothetical) common ancestor of two or more manuscripts or hypothetical texts, must be proven by both conjunctive and separative errors. Conjunctive errors, characterized by their improbability of independent commission by different scribes, demonstrate that all the manuscripts or texts in a group derive from a common ancestor. Separative errors, that is, errors incapable of emendation, show that no *other* extant manuscripts than those within the proposed group derive from the hypothetical common ancestor.

Text r (Common Ancestor of V and L)

The following conjunctive errors indicate that manuscripts V and L had a common ancestor (r): addition of *et dixit ad me* 15:1; *caronii* for *carmonii* 15:30; *habitantis* for *navitatis* 15:31; and *fortissimam* for *forti missam* 16:7. Numerous separative errors show that no other known manuscript derived from this ancestor: for example, *orbem terrae* for *omnem terram* 15:6; omission of *in unum* 15:44; and *suscitabunt* for *cibabunt* 16:68.

Although its descendants V and L are both highly idiosyncratic, r can usually be reconstructed from their convergence or at least hypothesized from their corruptions. Like its two witnesses, r features a very corrupt text.

The following orthographic traits appear:

ae → e   *hec* 15:21; *celum* 15:44
t   → c   *percuciam* 15:11; *contricio* 15:15
tt → t   *quatuor* 16:29

Most of the corruptions in r are simple copying errors: for example, *orbem terrae* 15:6; *habitantis* 15:31; *fortissimam* 16:7; and the omission of *in unum* 15:44.

Several unique readings appear to be intentional changes. The addition of *et dixit ad me* in 15:1 attempts to smooth the transition between 4 and 6 Ezra. *Concupierunt* for *cupierunt* 15:47 illustrates the late Latin tendency to prefer compound to simplex verbs.[39]

There is no indication that V or L, the descendants of r, underwent contamination or cross-fertilization from any other known manuscript or manuscript group of 6 Ezra.

Text q (Common Ancestor of C and r)

Conjunctive errors demonstrating the existence of q are *ibi planctus* for *sibilatus* 15:29; the addition of *ideo sciant* 16:46; and *facte* for *fundatae* 16:56. The most important separative error is the four-word omission in 15:60.

The text of q can be reconstructed by comparing C and r. Where it is impossible to decide between or reconcile these readings, the reading of C is usually preferable, since r is quite corrupt (see above). Text q contains a number of errors, equally divided between corruptions and attempted emendations.

The most common orthographic trait of q is the writing of *e* for *ae* (passim). Also present are:

oe → e   *ceperit* 16:6, 13, 38
p   → b   *poblites* 15:36; *abtate* 16:40
ph → f   *romfea* 15:15

loss of initial h   *orribilis* 15:28

The most characteristic errors of q are to miscopy words (*ibi planctus* 15:29; *exterrent* 15:60) and to corrupt endings (*manebit* 15:27; *morabitur* 16:39). There are also numerous attempts at emendation. The two substitutions of *vobis* for *tibi* in 16:1 intend to improve the text grammatically. The additional of *ideo sciant . . . quoniam* in 16:46 renders the sentence more elegant. The omission of *scrutans* in 16:64 eliminates a primitive-sounding Hebraism. The substitutions of *illos* for *eos* 15:26 and *illas* for *eas* 16:32 are probably stylistically motivated.[40]

Comparison of the reconstructed text of q with the readings of C and r shows no compelling evidence that either C or r was contaminated by other known manuscripts or text groups of 6 Ezra.

Text p (Common Ancestor of M, N, and E)

Before discussing a common source for manuscripts M, N, and E, it is necessary to consider whether any pair of these manuscripts shared an ancestor. Proof of this would require the demonstration of an error in two of the three manuscripts that is both conjunctive and separative. Examination of the manuscripts reveals no such reading. Thus, we tentatively conclude that no two of these manuscripts had a common ancestor. This conclusion is supported by the fact that this situation also obtains in 4 and 5 Ezra.

Conjunctive errors for p include *egentes tenorum* for *egestanorum* 15:16; *et arabunt* for *Arabum* 15:29; and *exorta sit* for *exornant se* 16:50. The omissions of four words in 15:13, six words in 15:19, and five words in 15:32 and 16:77 are separative errors.

Although p cannot be characterized as "corrupt," it does contain a number of erroneous readings. The majority of these are attempted emendations. The scribe of p, like that of its descendant E, was alert to try to improve the grammar, style, wording, and sense of the text at every opportunity. The result is a version of 6 Ezra that is more elegant, but less accurate, than that of p's ancestor u, the hyparchetype of the Spanish family. Setting aside the tendency of E toward independent emendation, the three manuscript witnesses to p are of approximately equal value.

The most noteworthy orthographic trait of p is a tendency toward alliteration: for example, *collident* for *conlident* 15:35. The following also appear:

c → ch   *choruscabit* 16:10
e → ae   *caeteri* 15:45
e → oe   *foemur* 15:36
tt → t   *quatuor* 16:29

As noted previously, most of the errors in p are attempted emendations. These are too numerous to catalogue; examples include *inmittam* for *in* 15:19; addition of *moventur* 15:3 and *montem* 15:40; and *gement* for *gemitus* 16:18. The six-word omission in 15:19 is almost certainly deliberate. Alterations of pronouns include *eorum* for *illorum* 15:15; 16:46; *eorum* for *ipsorum* 15:21; and *ipsorum* for *eorum* 16:31.[41] The omission of *gladios volantes* in 15:41 may be a deliberate excision of an overly sensationalistic turn of phrase. An especially interesting alteration is the substitution of *octo* for *novem* in 16:38 as the length in months of a human pregnancy.

The most substantial inadvertent corruptions are the omissions in 15:13, 15:32, and 16:77 noted here. In a number of places, the scribe has miscopied individual words. Especially amusing are two corruptions of unusual proper nouns: *et arabunt* for *Arabum* 15:29 and *carmine* for *Carmonii* 15:30.

A comparison of the reconstructed text of p with its descendants M, N, and E gives no reason to suspect that any of these three were subject to contamination from any other known manuscript or manuscript family of 6 Ezra.

Text t (Common Ancestor of S and A;
Hyparchetype of the French Family)

The clearest conjunctive errors demonstrating the existence of t are *uredine* for *aurugine* 15:13; *frumenta* for *fundamenta* 16:15; and *diis (dies) credatis* for *discredatis* 16:36. The six-word omission in 16:71 is a separative error. The analysis of the Spanish and French families in chapter 4 of this study bears on the question of indicative errors for both t and u.

Since t has only two independent witnesses that are closely allied, its readings are normally easy to deduce. In almost all cases where S and A disagree, one or the other is either validated by agreement with the Spanish or obviously corrupt. Where S and A disagree and text-critical methods cannot solve the problem, S is to be preferred, since A exhibits slightly more errors in places where disagreements can be arbitrated with certainty.

The text of t exhibits several orthographic traits:

ae → e   *magne* 15:40; *fena* 15:42
e → ae   *Aegyptae* 16:1
e → i   *vindimiaturus* 16:43

Text t contains only a few obvious errors. Besides those listed here, we note *alios/ aliis* 15:16; *exterruerunt* 15:45; and *portaret* (for *potaret*) 16:60. There are also several corruptions in verbal tense endings.

A comparison of the reconstructed text of t with S and A gives no indication that either manuscript suffered contamination from any other known manuscript or manuscript family of 6 Ezra.

Text u (Common Ancestor of p and q; Hyparchetype of the Spanish Family)

Conjunctive errors demonstrating the existence of u are *egestanorum* 15:16 and the addition of *ne discedatis a Domino et nolite increduli esse his* 16:36. The latter and *ab oriente* 15:20 constitute separative errors.

The text of u is established through comparison of p and q. Where these texts are at odds and standard text-critical methods do not avail, q is to be preferred, since p contains almost three times as many demonstrable errors.

The overall worth of u can be established only through comparison with t, the progenitor of the French family. This comparison forms the basis of the next chapter.

Orthographic traits of the text include:

ae → e   *precingite* 16:2; *querens* 16:50
i → y   *sydus* 15:39, 40, 44
t → c   *iusticia* 16:50, 52
tt → t   *quatuor* 16:31

loss of initial h   *orrida* 15:34; *orrebit* 16:10

Text u contains only a few obvious errors, all of which are mentioned here. *Egestanorum* for *megestanorum* 15:16 and *ab oriente* for *a borea* 15:20 are both corruptions of unusual Greek loanwords. The long addition in 16:36 appears to be a miscopying of and gloss on the unusual word *discredatis* (see the discussion in chapter 4, "Methodological Considerations").

A comparison of the reconstructed text of u with p and q yields no indication that either of the latter suffered contamination from any other known manuscript or manuscript family of 6 Ezra.

THE RELATIONSHIP BETWEEN THE OXYRHYNCHUS GREEK
FRAGMENT AND THE LATIN RECENSIONS

The Greek text of 6 Ezra 15:57–59 in Oxyrhynchus papyrus 1010 is clearly of immense text-critical import, since it offers a fragment of the language version from which the extant Latin text was translated. It is of value both in indicating the accuracy, or degree of literalness, of the Latin translation(s) and in showing which recension is closer to the Greek.

The Greek fragment contains about fifty words, as follows:

μω διαφθαρησεται και συ εν ρομφαια πεση και αι πολεις σου συντριβησονται και
παντες σου οι εν τοις πεδιοις πεσουνται εν μαχαιρη και οι εν τοις ορεσι και
μετεωροις εν λειμω διαφθαρησονται και εδονται τας σαρκας αυτων και το αιμα
αυτων πιονται απο λειμου αρτου και διψης υδατος [πρω]τα μεν ηκεις ταλα[ι]να
κα[ι π]αλιν εκ δευτερου[42]

Most of this text agrees verbatim with both Latin recensions, which are not highly divergent in this section; thus the Latin translation of these three verses appears to be quite faithful.

The Greek does, however, present several distinctive elements. First, in 15:58, where the Latin reads *et qui sunt in montibus fame peribunt*, the Greek has και οι εν τοις ορεσι και μετεωροις εν λειμω διαφθαρησονται. εν τοις ορεσι και μετεωροις ("in the mountains and highlands") forms a doublet that is not present in the Latin. The same phenomenon occurs in 15:59, where the Latin has *propter priora misera venies et iterum . . .* and the Greek [πρω]τα μεν ηκεις ταλα[ι]να κα[ι π]αλιν εκ δευτερου. Again, [π]αλιν εκ δευτερου is a doublet, of which only one element appears in the Latin. It is difficult to decide whether these two doublets stood in the Greek *Vorlage* of the Latin and were abbreviated in translation, or whether they were later, secondary additions within the Greek tradition. The latter alternative seems more probable.[43]

With regard to the readings in these three verses where the two Latin recensions differ, the Greek tends to favor the French. This is the case in six readings. (1 and 2) In 15:57, where Fr has *et tu romphea cades* and Sp *et tu ipsa gladio cades*, Greek reads και συ εν ρομφαια πεση. This indicates that Fr *romphea* is more original than Sp *gladio*, and that Sp *ipsa* is secondary. (3) In 15:57, Fr *conterentur* is a more literal rendering of συντριβησονται than is Sp *subvertentur*. (4) In 15:58, Fr *et manducabunt carnes suas* replicates the word order of και εδονται τας σαρκας αυτων better than does Sp *et carnes suas manducabunt*. (5 and 6) In 15:59, Fr *propter priora misera es* is closer to the Greek order πρωτα μεν ηκεις ταλαινα than is Sp *infelix primaria venies*, and *misera* is a closer rendering of ταλαινα than is *infelix*.

There are, on the other hand, two readings where the Greek favors the Spanish text. The first is in 15:58, where Sp *et sanguinem suum bibent* agrees with Greek και το αιμα αυτων πιονται against Fr *et sanguinem bibent*. The second, and probably the most dramatic, occurs in 15:59, where the Greek has πρωτα μεν ηκεις ταλαινα, Sp *infelix primaria venies*, and Fr *propter priora misera es*. Only Sp *venies* replicates the Greek ηκεις.

Comparison of the Greek text with the two Latin recensions, then, indicates a mixed situation in which the Greek supports the French text six times and the Spanish twice.

This situation, which is not unlike what will be found in our comparative study of the two Latin recensions in chapter 4, suggests that, although the French recension is closer to the more original text of 6 Ezra, neither recension embodies a "pure" form of that text. Rather, both recensions have undergone corruption and editorial modification in the process of transmission.

Another issue that should be addressed here is whether the Oxyrhynchus text sheds any light on the question whether the two Latin recensions represent independent translations of a Greek original or originals, or whether they result from editing within a Latin context. Unfortunately, the Greek fragment is short enough that none of the Latin recensional variations that it covers can help to answer this question definitively. Each of the eight recensional differences discussed here could theoretically derive either from independent translation of a Greek original or from intra-Latin recension.

SECONDARY WITNESSES TO THE TEXT:
QUOTATIONS AND THE EPITOME IN MANUSCRIPT L

The three sources that quote 6 Ezra were introduced in chapter 2. The lengthy and relatively literal quotations of Gildas are of major text-critical importance. The citations in the Mozarabic and Roman liturgies, however, due to their brevity and rather free wording, have a more limited significance. The same is true of the epitome of 6 Ezra in the León manuscript.

Gildas's "De excidio Britanniae"

Gildas quotes 6 Ezra 15:21–27 (*Haec dicit . . . mala multa*) and 16:3–12 (*Inmissus est . . . fluctuantur de profundo*). (The texts of the quotations are given in Appendix 1.) These quotations represent the French recension and, as Bensly noted long ago, tend to ally with manuscript A rather than S.[44] The present analysis treats the citations individually.

In 15:21–27, Gildas's text (G) manifests two separative errors, *meus* 15:21 and *mea* 15:23. Manuscript S has separative errors at *peccantes* 15:22, *apostatae* 15:25, and *Deus* 15:26. Although manuscript A exhibits no separative errors in this section, the unique readings *cessabit* 15:22 and *in* 15:26, together with the fact that this manuscript is so much later than Gildas, suggest that Gildas is not dependent on it. Thus, it seems that none of these three French witnesses is dependent on any other.

G agrees with A against S as follows:

In readings that are almost surely correct: 4 times

In readings that are apparently correct: 5 times

In uncertain readings: never

In probable or certain errors: never.

G agrees with S against A as follows:

In readings that are almost surely correct: twice

In readings that are apparently correct: once

In uncertain readings: never

In probable or certain errors: never

In this section, it is difficult to make a judgment about the interrelationships among the three French witnesses because there are no conjunctive errors. One may note, however, that 15:26, in which G agrees with A five times against S, is one of the passages noted in the description of manuscript S ("The Readings of the Latin Manuscripts, Sangermanensis"), in which S seems to have been assimilated to the Spanish recension. Thus, if G shares an ancestor with S, it was at a level before this assimilation took place. Furthermore, the relatively higher frequency of agreement between G and A suggests that these witnesses could have a common ancestor exclusive of S. Certainty, however, is impossible.

In this section, A is the most reliable witness (two errors), S is next (four errors), and G is the most erratic (seven errors).

Chapter 16, verses 3–12 are part of the text section in which manuscript S exhibits a Spanish text (see "The Readings of the Latin Manuscripts, Sangermanensis). Thus, G and A are the only witnesses to the French recension. The eight-word omission in 16:7 is a separative error for G, and *et* 16:9 and *a fundamento* 16:12 serve the same function for A. Thus, neither witness is dependent on the other. Simple comparison between the texts indicates that A is by far the more reliable: besides the strongly abbreviated text of G in 16:3–5 and its omission of 16:7, G has ten other probable errors, while A has a total of only six.

The Mozarabic Liturgy

The Mozarabic liturgy, as preserved in a tenth-century antiphonary from León, quotes 6 Ezra as follows:

> Sanguis innocens et iustus clamat ad me et anime innocentum suspirant vehementer. Iam non feram dicit Dominus sed faciam vindictam illorum cito. Effuderunt sanguinem eorum.

Sixth Ezra 15:8–9 has:

> Ecce sanguis innoxius et iustus clamat [Sp: proclamat] ad me et animae iustorum clamant [Sp: proclamant] perseveranter. Vindicans vindicabo illos dicit Dominus et accipiam omnem sanguinem innocuum ex illis ad me.

As noted in chapter 2, the first parts of these pericopae are very close, while the second vary. The main text-critical significance of the quotation is that, in the two places where the French and Spanish recensions differ, it supports the French in the first and neither in the second. On the whole, the citation probably represents a free adaptation or quotation from memory of 6 Ezra.

There is, however, one additional connection between the liturgical quotation and the manuscript tradition of 6 Ezra that may be of interest. In 15:8, where the main text of 6 Ezra reads *et animae iustorum clamant* [*Sp: proclamant*] *perseveranter*, and the liturgy *et anime innocentum suspirant vehementer*, manuscript L has *et animae eorum suspirant proclamantes perseveranter*. That is, L combines the verbal elements of the other two versions in a doublet. This could be considered a coincidence were it not for the facts that (1) L and the antiphonary were both written in León in roughly the same era, and (2) L is known to draw from other text versions, and indeed to display unique parallels to the León antiphonary, in other parts of the 2 Esdras corpus.[45] Thus, the shared reading *suspirant* probably indicates a textual connection of some sort between L and the antiphonary. Although the antiphonary predates L by about two centuries, one cannot be certain about the direction of influence, since each work had a long prehistory. Still, it is inherently more likely that readings passed from the manuscript tradition into the liturgy than vice versa.

The Roman Liturgy

The Roman liturgy quotes 6 Ezra once:

> Crastina die delebitur iniquitas terrae, et regnabit super nos salvator mundi.

> On the next day the iniquity of the earth will be wiped out, and the savior of the world will rule over us.

Sixth Ezra 16:52 reads:

> Quoniam ecce [om. Sp] adhuc pusillum et tolletur iniquitas a terra et iustitia regnabit in nos [Sp nobis].

> Because behold, a little longer and iniquity will be taken away from the earth, and righteousness will rule over us.

This citation, like the one in the Mozarabic liturgy, has little text-critical value for 6 Ezra besides the fact that it may reflect a variant written form of the work. In its reading of *nos* instead of *nobis* it supports the French over the Spanish recension.

The Epitome of 6 Ezra in the León Manuscript

The epitome of 6 Ezra in the León manuscript is printed by Klijn in *Der lateinishe Text der Apokalypse des Esra* (p. 100).

This text has little text-critical value for several reasons. First, it agrees in virtually every regard with the Spanish over the French manuscript tradition; the sole exception, *remanebunt* for *relinquentur* 16:31, must be counted a coincidence.[46] Second, it features no significant departures from the text of manuscript L itself besides a few orthographic variants. Thus, unlike the epitome of 5 Ezra in L,[47] that of 6 Ezra could easily have been based on the text of manuscript L itself.

One phenomenon of some interest is that the León epitome of 6 Ezra agrees with the León antiphonary, against all other witnesses, in reading *innocens* in 15:8. The geographical connection here is possibly of significance, especially in view of the fact that the epitome of 5 Ezra in manuscript L also has an important point of contact with the León antiphonary.[48]

CONCLUSION

This chapter has intended to evaluate the relative merits of the witnesses to the text of 6 Ezra and to defend the stemma presented at the chapter's beginning. On the basis of this study, informed text-critical judgments can be made about the readings of t and u, the hyparchetypes of the French and Spanish families, respectively. The results of this deliberative process are presented in Appendix 1. In the left column, which represents the French recension, words presented in the far left margin, without parentheses, generally represent this author's estimation of the original text of t. (Where this is not the case, the hyparchetype of French is represented by the siglum "!f.") The same applies for the Spanish text (u), which is presented in the right column. In the next chapter, the relationship between the recensions will be analyzed and an attempt made to reconstruct their common ancestor.

Several brief points should be made here. First, no evidence has been found in our investigation that challenges the stemma proposed at the beginning of the chapter. That is, the tradition of extant manuscripts does not seem to have undergone cross-fertilization. Second, no reason has been found to question the integrity of the two recensions. Third, no demonstrable evidence has so far been found of influence of the Greek text on the Latin manuscript tradition below the level of the original translation(s). Finally, each of the four witnesses to the text of 6 Ezra outside the Latin manuscript tradition (viz., the Greek fragment and the three quotations) tends to support the French over the Spanish recension. Since at least two of these witnesses clearly predate the Latin manuscript tradition, this latter factor would prima facie support the priority of the French recension. This issue will be addressed again in the next chapter.

FOUR

The Relationship between
the Two Recensions

METHODOLOGICAL CONSIDERATIONS

The analysis in chapter 3 established the interrelationships of the manuscripts and other witnesses to the text of 6 Ezra up to the point of t and u, the two main hyparchetypes of the stemma.

It has been shown that for 4 and 5 Ezra, these two hyparchetypes manifest two distinct textual recensions, usually labeled the "French" and "Spanish," respectively.[1] Given what is known about the transmission history of 6 Ezra, it would not be surprising were it found that, here too, the two hyparchetypes are textually distinct enough to represent two different editorial recensions. Indeed, even a cursory examination of these two texts indicates that this is the case. The purpose of this chapter, then, is to examine the relationship between these texts in order to discern the nature and origin of this relationship.

There are a number of means by which to evaluate the relationship between the texts of 6 Ezra manifested in the French and Spanish hyparchetypes. Perhaps the most objective is to analyze statistically the verbal correlations between t and u. Such an analysis reveals several interesting patterns. First, the two texts agree exactly in their wording, including in word sequence and orthography, in about 72 percent of all cases.[2] This may be compared with figures of 93 percent for 4 Ezra 11–12 and 62 percent for 5 Ezra.[3] Second, the level of verbal correlation between the hyparchetypes starts rather high, at 87 percent in 15:1–18, but then seems progressively to decrease, reaching a level of only 65 percent in the final section of the book (16:48–78). This phenomenon is discussed in the section "Additional Considerations" in this chapter.

The main point, however, is that the two hyparchetypes agree in their wording in only 72 percent of all cases over the whole of 6 Ezra. What we have, then, are two similar texts with significant differences. This situation, prima facie, leads one to suspect either that one or both hyparchetypes underwent extensive unintentional textual corruption, that major intentional editorial activity underlies one or both texts, or that the textual differences resulted from the process of translation from Greek into Latin. There are, of course, other possibilities, such as a combination of these factors (see further below).

A survey of the *types* of textual differences between the hyparchetypes may help to resolve the question. An analysis of the discrepancies between the two texts in chapter 15, for example, yields some interesting data. In this chapter there are 303 differences in wording between the two hyparchetypes. Many of these (109) are differences in synonyms: that is, the two versions say the same thing using different words. Fifty-one of the differences are additions or deletions of individual words in one of the texts. There are nine added or deleted phrases, ranging from two to sixteen words; these account for 48 verbal differences. There are twenty transpositions, thirteen orthographic variations, and only ten cases of different words with different meanings. The rest of the variants (52) are divergences in verbal forms or endings, or in case, number, or gender of nouns and adjectives.

This situation, especially the large preponderance of differences in synonyms, strongly suggests that the variation between the two hyparchetypes is not due primarily to textual corruption. In the case of corruption, one would expect either long stretches of text where one version is preserved without the other, or many places in which the two versions differ in meaning. This, however, is not the case. Rather, the high proportion of synonymous words—together with the fact that many other of the differences, such as those in verbal forms and in added or deleted words, can be accounted for as stylistic variations—indicates a situation in which the discrepancies between the two texts arose intentionally, either through editing or in the process of translation.

Having established this point, it may be helpful now to envisage, for the sake of hypothesis, a more complete range of possibilities as to how the differences between the two versions might have arisen. Perhaps the simplest situation—and in some respects the most likely, since it seems to characterize both 4 and 5 Ezra[4]—is that the differences between the two texts of 6 Ezra arose mainly from editorial recension within a Latin medium. In the simplest form of this scenario, one hyparchetype represents or approximates the "more original" form of the Latin text, whereas the other arose as a deliberate editorial revision of it (in one or more stages). There are, of course, numerous, more complicated possibilities for intra-Latin recension: both extant versions could be revised forms of an original which stood somewhere between them; either a "more original" form or an "edited" form could subsequently have been corrected toward the other; one of the two versions could have been corrected toward a third Latin text, now unknown; and so on.[5] In addition, textual corruption could have played a role at any stage of the transmission process.

The fact that the Latin text of 6 Ezra was almost certainly translated from a Greek *Vorlage*[6] extends the range of possibilities even further. The two Latin text versions could represent independent, somewhat adaptative translations of the same Greek original. (This possibility is especially recommended by the large number of parallel synonyms in the Latin texts.) There could have existed two divergent Greek texts of 6 Ezra, of which the extant Latin versions are faithful translations. Two original Greek texts might have been even more different than the present Latin versions, with one or both translators correcting their version toward the other. One translation could have been carried out first, and the other made, or altered, with reference to it. A Latin translation could have been made and then corrected or altered at a later time with reference to a Greek text, giving rise to a second Latin version.[7] It is also conceivable that the actual situation behind the two versions of 6 Ezra combines several of the options indicated here.

Given this rather daunting range of possibilities, it seems logical first to address the question whether the differences between the two hyparchetypes are more likely to have arisen as a result of translation or are more probably a product of recension within a Latin medium.

In answering this question, several criteria will prove useful. First, if the Latin versions represent independent translations of a Greek text (or texts), and have not been corrected toward one another, one would expect to find numerous instances where the two versions use, at like points in the text, different but synonymous Latin words or expressions to render the same (or a similar) Greek text. Ideally, one would hope to find instances where the two Latin versions feature, at the same textual location, words whose meanings differ, but which can be accounted for as renderings of the same, or a graphically or phonetically similar, Greek term (these would be alternate translations, or translational errors). Identification of several such cases would indicate strongly that the differences between the Latin versions stem, at least in part, from translation.

Similarly, if the Latin versions represent independent translations of a Greek original, they would almost certainly feature longer text units—whole phrases and sentences—that express similar ideas with different syntactical construction, phraseology, word order, and so forth. Also, the identification of larger sections of Latin text that differ substantially in the two versions, but whose differences can be accounted for by appeal to lexical interchange, wordplay, or confusion in Greek, would indicate that the Latin versions derive independently from a Greek *Vorlage*.

On the other hand, if the two Latin versions contain a high proportion of identical readings, or feature lengthy identical sections of text, one would suspect that they derive from a single or similar texts in Latin (unless, of course, they had been assimilated). That is, one would not expect independent translators to produce renderings that are verbally exact at many points, or that contain long sections of identical text.

Likewise, the identification of individual words or larger text units, in which substantial differences between the Latin versions can most easily be explained on the basis of intra-Latin adaptation or corruption, would also point toward recensional activity in a Latin medium.

Finally, as indicated earlier, the two possibilities at issue here are not mutually exclusive. It is possible that the differences between the Latin versions derive from a combination of translational factors and intra-Latin recension.

At this point we may begin to apply some of the criteria that have been outlined above to the problem at hand. We begin with the criterion of synonymous Latin words or phrases that stand at like points in the two texts. The following synonyms, near synonyms, or translational equivalents appear in the two versions.[8] (A tilde [~] placed between two expressions indicates that, although they are functionally equivalent, they stand at different places in the verse.)

	French	Spanish
15:1	plebi	populi
15:3	conturbent	turbent
15:6	operationes	opera nociva
	eorum	illorum
15:8	clamat	proclamat
	clamant	proclamant
15:11	eum	illum
15:12	verberati	verberum
	mastigati	castigationis
	Dominus	Deus
15:13	eorum	illorum
	uredine	aurugine
15:15	ext(e)ritio	contritio
15:16	supervalescentes	invalescentes
15:19	eorum	illorum
15:20	Deus	Dominus Deus
	noto	austro
15:23	eius	illius
15:24	eis	his
	observant	custodiunt
	Dominus	Dominus Deus
15:26	Deus	Dominus
	peccant	delinqunt
	eum	illum
	propterea	propter hoc
15:27	iam	ecce
	super	in
	Deus	Dominus
	eum	illum
15:28	illius	eius
15:29	ut	sicut
	trepidentur	formident
15:30	advenient	venient
	portionem	partem
15:31	supervalescet	convalescet
	eos	illos
15:32	virtute	vim
15:33	territorio	terra
	subsessor	obsessor
	subsedebit	obsidebit
	eos	illos
	illis	ipsis
	inconstabilitio	inconstantia
	regno	reges
	illorum	ipsorum
15:36	suffraginem	poplites

	French	Spanish
15:39	recludent	repellent
	eum	illum
	exteritionem	strages
	orientalem	oriente
15:40	sidus	cataginis
	exterant	exterminent
	inhabitantes	qui inhabitant
	eam	illa
	eminentem	excelsum
15:41	rompheas	gladios
	etiam	~ ita
	plenitudine	multitudine
15:42	fena	herbas
	pratorum	camporum
	frumenta	triticum
	eorum	ipsorum
15:43	transibunt	pertransient
	exterent	exterrent
	eam	illam
15:44	ad ipsam	in unum
	circuibunt	circumcingent
	eam	illam
	subibit	ascendet
15:45	subremanserint	remanserint
	servientes	servient
	his	illis
15:47	propter quod	quia
	adsimilasti	similis facta es
	ei	illius
	in fornicatione	ad quaestum
	ad placiendum et gloriandum	ut placeas et sis gloriosa
	in	penes
	fornicari	fornicariam
15:48	Deus	Dominus
15:49	pestem	pestilentiam
15:50	emissus	missus
15:51	mastigata	~ flagellis
15:53	in omni tempore	semper
	super	in
	eorum	ipsorum
	cum inebriata es	ebria facta
15:55	redditionem	~ in sinus tuos
	percipies	recipies
15:57	nati	filii
	romphea	gladio
	conterentur	subvertentur
15:58	peribunt	disperient
15:59	misera	infelix
	propter priora	primaria
	iterum	rursum
	excipies	accipies

French		Spanish
15:60	oditam	odiosam
	territorii	terrae
	dum revertuntur	rursum revertentes
15:61	extrita	demolita
	in	pro
	stramine	stipula
15:62	comedunt	devorabunt
	territoria	terram
	pomifera	fructiferum
	consument	conburent
15:63	natos	filios
	captivabunt	captivos ducent
	honestatem	censum
	spoliabunt	praeda habebunt
16:2	his	eos
	quia	quoniam
16:3	inmissus	missus
	eum	illum
16:4	inmissus	missus
	eum	illum
16:5	inmissa	missa
	recutiet	repellet
16:6	recutiet	repellet
	cum stramen incensum fuerit	in stipula mox coeperit ardere
16:7	recutiet	repellet
	inmissam	missam
16:8	recutiet	repellet
16:11	eius	ipsius
16:13	eo	~ ipso
	dimissa est	mittuntur
	super	in
16:15	incendetur	succenditur
	excomedat	consumat
16:16	quomodo	quemadmodum
	revertitur	redit
	emissa	missa
16:18	gemitus	dolorum
	copiosi suspirantium	multi gemitus
	disperient	interient
	timebunt	formidabunt
	eis	his
16:19	dimissa	~ missa
	mastix	flagella
	disciplina	emendatione
16:20	super	in
	avertent	convertent
	nec	neque
	plagas	flagellorum
	memorantur	memores erunt
	sempiterna	semper

	French	Spanish
16:21	ut	sicut
	superflorescent	germinabunt
16:22	aporiant [vitam]	interient
16:23	quasi	tamquam
	et	enim
	demolientur	deicientur
16:25	fructiferabunt	dabunt fructus
16:26	tradet se ad vindemiam	matura fiet
	eam	illam
	multa	~ magna
16:27	concupiscet	cupiet
16:28	silva	densis nemoribus
16:30	subremanet	relinquentur
	ab scrutantibus	ab his qui scrutantur
	vindemiam	vineam
16:31	remanebunt	relinquentur
	ab scrutantibus	ab his qui . . . scrutantur
	in	a
	rompheam	gladio
16:32	transient	sint transiturae
16:33	earum	ipsarum
16:34	earum	ipsarum
	earum	illarum
	exterentur	interient
16:35	vero	igitur
	ista	haec
	cognoscite	intelligite
16:36	verbum	sermo
	excipite	sumite
	eum	illum
	ne discredatis de quibus	ne discredatis a Domino et nolite increduli esse his
16:37	adpropinquant	protinus venient
16:38	filium	~ infantem
	nono	novem
	in adpropinquante	ubi coeperit . . . adpropinquare
	gementes	patitur
	circum	circa
16:39	gemet	parturit
	circumtenent	circumcingunt
16:40	plebs	populus
	parate vos	parati estote
	pugnam	bellum
	in	ad
	advenae	incolae
16:43	messem facturus	metat
16:44	nubunt	nuptias faciunt
	facturi	habituri
	non nubunt	nuptias non faciunt
	vidui	viduitatem servaturi

	French	Spanish
16:46	alienigenae	exteri
	metent	manducabunt
	eorum	ipsorum
	captivabunt	captivos ducent
	natos	~ filios
16:47	negotiantur	mercantur
	negotiantur	~ mercantur
	quamdiu	in quantum
	exornant	ornant
	personas	facies
16:48	adzelabor	zelabo
	eos	illos
	super	in
16:49	quomodo	quemadmodum
16:50	eam	illam
	exquirentem	querens
	super	in
16:51	propterea	ideo
	similari	similes esse
	eam	~ illius
	nec	neque
	operibus	factis
16:53	quoniam	quia
	eius	suum
	Deo	Domino
	ipsius	eius
16:54	Dominus	Dominus Deus
	cognoscit	novit
	opera	facta
	cogitatum	cogitationes
	illorum	ipsorum
	illorum	~ eorum
16:56	verbo	sermone
	illius	eius
16:57	illorum	eorum
	conceptum	fundamenta
16:58	in medio aquarum	inter aquas et aquas
16:59	quasi	ut
	eum	illum
16:60	eminenti	cacumine
16:61	posuit	~ inposuit
	misit	dedit
	ei	illi
	et vitam et intellectum	et intellectum vitae
16:62	spiramentum	adspirationem
	Dei	Dominus
	scrutinat	scrutatur
	certe	certa
16:63	peccantibus	omnibus qui peccant
	volentibus	qui volunt
	occultare	~ celare

	French	*Spanish*
16:64	scrutinando scrutinavit	scrutans scrutavit
	opera	facta
	eorum	ipsorum
16:66	aut	et
	coram	ante
16:67	Deus	Dominus
	eum	illum
	iam agere	et non faciatis
	eas	haec
	sempiterno	semper
	Deus	Dominus
	educavit	deducet
	de	ab
	tribulatione	pressura
16:68	incendetur	succendetur
	turbae copiosae	et turbabunt vos multi populi
	rapient	diripient res vestras et sument
	cibabunt idolis occisam	cibabunt vos de sacrificio
16:70	in	per
	exsurrectio	insurrectio
	super	supra
	timentes	hos qui timent
	Dominum	Deum
16:71	quasi	tanquam
	devastandum	exportandum
	timentes	horum metuentes
	Dominum	Deum
16:72	substantias	res
	eos	~ illos
	eicient	expellent
16:73	ut	quemadmodum
	ab	per
16:74	his	ipsis
16:75	haesitemini	formidetis
	Deus	Dominus
16:76	Dominus Deus	Dominus
	superelevent	extollant
16:77	obteguntur	cooperiuntur
	constringitur	conclusus
	tegitur	cooperitur
16:78	ad	in

This is, obviously, a rather substantial collection of lexical equivalences. As noted, a preponderance of textually equivalent synonyms in two versions of a translated document may indicate that the versions represent independent translations of a source text. This extensive list clearly establishes this possibility for the two Latin versions of 6 Ezra. It is also, however, possible in theory that these synonyms result from editorial activity within a Latin medium (this seems to be the case, for example, in 5 Ezra).[9]

To pursue the question in greater depth, let us compare the preceding listing to similar lists drawn from two other Latin texts that feature two versions or recensions.

The following list is based on the same principles as that given above and gives synonyms in the French and Spanish versions of two randomly selected chapters of 4 Ezra, chapters 11–12.

Synonyms in the Two Recensions of 4 Ezra 11–12

	French	*Spanish*
11:6	neque	nec
11:10	eius	suis
11:16	parere	apparere
11:20	comparescebant	conparebant
11:29	evigilabat	vigilabat
11:33	conparuit	apparuit
11:35	illud	istud
11:37	mugiens	rugiens
11:39	eos	haec
11:46	revertetur (?)	relevetur
	eam	illam
12:1	dum	cum
12:3	apparescebant	apparebat
12:5	timore	terrore
12:6	orabo	rogabo
12:13	timoratior	timor
12:17	exientem	exeuntem
12:24	hos	eos
12:25	recapitulabunt	recapitabunt
12:26	apparescentem	apparens
	tamen	quidem
12:29	treicientes	crescentes
12:32	ipsorum	eorum
12:33	eos	illos
	eos	illos
12:36	ergo	autem
12:38	ea	illa
12:44	succensi	incensi
12:46	tristari	contristari
12:50	in	ad

The next list of lexical equivalents is drawn from the "Vulgate"[10] and "Palatine"[11] Latin versions of the *Shepherd of Hermas*, Vis. 1.1.

Synonyms in the Two Versions of *Hermas, Vision* 1.1

	Vulgate	*Palatine*
1.1.1	enutrierat	nutrivit
	puellam	feminae
	annos	temporis
	hanc	eam
	recognovi	cognovi

Vulgate	*Palatine*
	ut	quasi
	diligere	~ amare
1.1.2	post tempus aliquod	postea
	eduxi	produxi
	vidissem	considerans
	cogitabam	coepi cogitare
	corde	animo
	felix	beatus
1.1.3	post tempus aliquod	postea
	proficiscens	venissem
	honorificans	gratularer
	magnifica	magnae
	pulcherrima	ornatae
	dum ambulassem	ambulans
	rapuit	sustulit
	iter facere	ambulare
	autem	enim
	planitiem	locis mollibus
1.1.4	mulierem	feminam
	concupieram	desideraveram
1.1.5	prospiciens	respiciens
	et	~ autem
	illam	eam
	at illa	quae
	recepta	sublata
	arguam	redarguam
1.1.6	inquam	dico ego
	nunc	ergo
	arguis	accusas
	inquit	ait
	verba	sermones
	condidit	fecit
	multiplicavit	crescere
1.1.7	turpe	impudicum
	nonne	non
	veritus	verecundatus
	velut	quomodo
	mei	in me
	commentiris	mentiris
	nefanda	iniqua et immunda
1.1.8	tunc	~ autem
	arridens	ridens
	ait	dixit
	nequitiae	iniqua
	viro	homini
	saevam	iniqua
	illius	eius
	mala	iniqua
	cogitante . . . illo	quando . . . cogitat
	ergo	autem
	nefanda	iniqua

Vulgate	*Palatine*
assumunt	adquirent
hi	illi
diligunt	sibi vindicant
gloriantur	luxoriantes
non expectant	negligunt
futura	~ venturam
1.1.9 et	enim
negligunt	desperant
sed	autem
sanabit	dimittet tibi
totiusque	et totius

On the one hand, even though it is virtually certain that the Latin text of 4 Ezra is based on a Greek *Vorlage*,[12] it seems highly unlikely that the French and Spanish versions of 4 Ezra 11–12[13] represent independent translations of a Greek text (or texts). In these chapters, the two families agree verbatim (including in word order and orthography) in 93 percent of all readings, often featuring sequences of forty to one hundred words of identical text. As the list of synonyms in 4 Ezra 11–12 shows, they display in ninety-seven verses (1,605 words) only thirty cases of synonyms or near synonyms (2 percent of the total text), many of which are variations on the same root. As a rule, in 4 Ezra, the French and Spanish families are so close that they cannot justifiably be called distinct "recensions" or "editions" of the Latin text. Rather, here the "editing" certainly took place within a Latin medium and was relatively superficial in nature.

The two versions of *Hermas, Vis.* 1.1, on the other hand, present a different aspect. Extending our survey to the whole of *Vision* 1 in order to gain a larger text sample, the two texts agree verbatim in only 48 percent of all readings, and the longest sequence where they are identical is only eleven words (1.1.6). Furthermore, in *Vis.* 1.1, which contains 392 words, they exhibit sixty-seven synonyms or near synonyms (17 percent of the total text). Based on these indicators alone, there seems to be a strong possibility that these two texts represent independent translations of Greek versions of *Hermas*; indeed, this is normally taken for granted by scholars.

The situation in 6 Ezra may be considered in relation to these points of reference. The first listing of synonyms showed 287 cases of synonyms or near synonyms in the 141 verses (2,092 words) of 6 Ezra, equal to 14 percent of the total text. This figure is almost as high as in *Hermas, Vis.* 1.1, indicating a real possibility that the two texts of 6 Ezra could represent independent translations of a Greek original or originals.

Other measures, however, present the situation in a somewhat different aspect. First, as noted, the French and Spanish versions of 6 Ezra agree verbatim, including in orthography, in 72 percent of all readings (as compared with only 48 percent in *Hermas, Vision* 1). Although it is theoretically possible that such closely related renderings were produced by different translators, this figure seems to me to be somewhat high for independent translations (unless, of course, the two Latin versions were later assimilated).

One other factor is, in my view, even more telling. The longest sequence of text in 6 Ezra where the two versions are identical is of thirty-seven words (15:20–22). There are also identical passages of thirty-one (15:8–10), twenty-nine (15:37–39), twenty-seven (15:16–19), twenty-six (16:9–11), and twenty-two words (16:41–43). This may be compared with the situation in *Hermas, Vision* 1, almost half as long as 6 Ezra, in which the longest sequences are eleven (1.1.6), nine (1.1.8), and nine words (1.3.4). It seems highly unlikely that independent translators would have produced with such frequency such long sections of identical text as are found in the two versions of 6 Ezra.

In summary, although the proportion of textually equivalent synonyms in the two versions of 6 Ezra is high enough to suggest that these may be independent translations of a Greek *Vorlage*, the simple measure of overall verbal agreement between the two texts and especially the length and number of sequences of identical text argue against that possibility. These indicators make it more likely, in my opinion, that the versions come from one translation and that the differences between them derive from intra-Latin editing. If this is the case, however, one is compelled to wonder why an editor would have chosen to substitute synonyms so frequently. This issue is addressed later in this chapter ("Synonymous Lexical Variants").

Another criterion for determining whether the two versions are independent translations or whether they result from intra-Latin recension is to examine the places where they *diverge* significantly at similar points in the text. If textual differences are found that can be understood as renderings of the same, or a graphically or phonetically similar, Greek word or expression, there is a strong chance that the recensions were translated independently from a Greek original. Textual differences that are explicable on a Latin level, on the other hand, would suggest intra-Latin recension or corruption.

The following list of lexical elements appear at equivalent points in the French and Spanish texts of 6 Ezra, but their meanings diverge significantly.[14] Below each word or phrase is a Greek translational equivalent that could have stood in a *Vorlage*.

Nonsynonymous Equivalents in the Two Recensions of 6 Ezra

	French	*Spanish*
15:16	megestanorum	egestanorum
	μεγιστᾶνες	[meaningless]
15:20	a borea	ab oriente
	ἐκ, ἀπό, βορέου	. . . ἀνατολή
15:32	silebunt	timebunt
	ἡσυχάζω, σιωπάω	φοβέομαι, θροέομαι
15:39	recludent	repellent
	ἀφανίζω, ἀφορίζω, ἀποτίθημι, ἀπάγω	ἀπωθέομαι, ἐκβάλλω
15:43	exterent	exterrent
	ἐκτρίβω, κατατρίβω	σείω, φοβέω
15:44	ad ipsam	in unum
	πρός, εἰς, ἐπί αὐτήν, ἐκείνην	ἐν, εἰς, ἐπί ἑνί, ἕνα, ἕν
15:47	(in) fornicatione	(ad) qu(a)estum
	πορνεία	ἐργασία, πορισμός, ὠφέλεια
15:50	virtutis	vultus
	ἀρετή, δύναμις, ἰσχύς	πρόσωπον

	French	Spanish

French   *Spanish*

15:53	dicens	deridens
	λέγων	ἐκμυκτηρίζω, καταγελάω
15:59	es	venies
	εἶ	ἥκεις, ἥξεις
15:63	honestatem	censum
	εὐσχημοσύνη	κῆνσος
16:11	conterretur	conteretur
	φοβέω (or a compound)	συντρίβω, λικμάω
16:13	gloriae	dextera
	δόξα, καύχημα, καύχησις	δεξιός, μέρος
	sagittam	arcum
	βέλος, τόξευμα, ὀϊστός	τόξον
	acumen	sagittae
	ἀκίς, ἀκμή, κέντρον	[see above]
16:15	frumenta	fundamenta
	σιτίον, σῖτος	θεμέλιος
16:18	ab	in
	ἐκ, ἀπό	ἐν, εἰς, ἐπί
16:22	dispersit	disperdet
	σκορπίζω, διασκορπίζω	φθείρω, ἀφανίζω
16:23	habent	erit
	ἔχουσι	ἔσται
16:26	adligabit	calcabit
	δεσμεύω, δέω, καταδέω	πατέω
16:32	inveteraverunt	in vepre erunt
	παλαιόω	ἄκανθα, καλάμη, χόρτος
16:36	discredatis	discedatis a Domino et nolite increduli esse
	ἀπιστέω	ἀπέρχομαι, ἀποβαίνω, ἀπαλλάσσω
16:38	gementes	patitur
	στενάζω	ἀνέχομαι, ἐάω, πάσχω, ὑπομένω
16:40	in	ad
	ἐν, εἰς, ἐπί	εἰς, πρός, ἐπί
16:46	metent	manducabunt
	ἀμάω, θερίζω	ἐσθίω, φαγ-
	quia	qui
	γάρ	ὅς, οἵ, etc.
16:56	stellarum	ipsarum
	ἀστήρ, ἄστρον	αὐτῶν, ἐκείνων
16:57	conceptum	fundamenta
	καταβολή, σύλληψις	θεμέλιος
16:58	mare	saeculum
	θάλασσα	αἰών, κόσμος
16:61	misit	dedit
	πέμπω, ἵημι	δίδωμι
16:65	erint quae	tanquam
	ἔσονται αἳ (?)	ὡς
16:67	educavit	deducet
	ἐκτρέφω	κατάγω, προπέμπω
16:68	turbae	turbabunt
	λαός, ὄχλος, πλῆθος	θορυβέω, θροέομαι, διαταράσσομαι

	French	Spanish
16:70	lociis	locis
	Λοχεία (?)	τόπος, χωρίον
	in	per
	ἐν, εἰς, ἐπί	διά, ὑπέρ
16:71	devastandum	exportandum
	λυμαίνομαι, διαφθείρω	ἐκφέρω, ἐκβαστάζω, ἐκφορέω,
		ἐκκομίζω
16:75	haesitemini	formidetis
	ἀπορέω, διακρίνω, διαπορέω	δειλιάω, φοβέομαι
16:78	mittitur	fit
	πέμπω, ἵημι	γίνομαι

This list shows several cases where differences in Latin could plausibly be traced to a Greek original. First, in 15:39, ἀποτίθημι (for *recludent*) is close to ἀπωθέομαι (for *repellent*). In 15:47, πορνεία (for *fornicatione*) resembles πορισμός (for *qu[a]estum*). Perhaps the most striking example is in 16:13, where δόξα (for *gloriae*) stands with δεξιός (for *dextera*). Finally, again in 16:13, τόξευμα (for *sagittam*) is close to τόξον (for *arcum*) (this similarity derives from the obvious fact that these Greek words for "bow" and "arrow" are cognate).

Clearly, then, there are several possibilities for divergence in Latin based on a Greek *Vorlage*. It should be noted, however, that each of these cases, like the bulk of the other nonsynonymous lexical equivalences, can also be explained by appeal to intra-Latin recension. In 15:39, while the French *recludo* can mean to "remove" or "lead away," it more commonly has other meanings (viz., to "open," "reveal") that would seem out of place here and that could have prompted emendation. Spanish *quaestum* in 15:47 could be a euphemism for the more direct French *fornicatio*. The French version of 16:13a, which reads literally "For strong of glory (is) the one who stretches the arrow," is so awkward that it almost calls for the words found in the Spanish text.[15]

On the other hand, there are numerous examples in the above list (the last one) that seem most probably to derive from intra-Latin corruption. These include: *megestanorum* and *egestanorum* (15:16); *a borea* and *ab oriente* (15:20); *exterent* and *exterrent* (15:43); *virtutis* and *vultus* (15:50); *conterretur* and *conteretur* (16:11); *frumenta* and *fundamenta* (16:15); *dispersit* and *disperdet* (16:22); *inveteraverunt* and *in vepre erunt* (16:32); *discredatis* and *discedatis* (16:36); and *lociis* and *locis* (16:70). In addition one may add, from the list of synonyms given in the first list, *mastigati* and *castigationes* (15:12); *inconstabilitio* and *inconstantia* (15:33); *exterant* and *exterminent* (15:40); and *certe* and *certa* (16:62). Taken together, these examples suggest that a significant number of the differences between the recensions arose within a Latin medium.

It should be pointed out, however, that the variants listed in the previous paragraph actually prove little, since they could as easily represent corruptions that occurred after the two recensions had been made as variants or errors that arose in the *process* of recension.[16]

In order to argue conclusively that the two recensions derive from a Latin original, it will be necessary to point out variants between them that appear to reflect intra-

Latin editing or confusion *and* that are integrally related to a textual modification that is characteristic of the recension in 6 Ezra as a whole (e.g., additions or omissions of text). Even then the proof will not be definite, since the textual modification associated with the variants could have arisen to adjust the text to one or the other variant, but at least this situation will go further toward indicating a Latin basis for the two versions than do the isolated Latin variants cited here.

There are, in fact, several variants between the two versions that satisfy this requirement. First, in 16:36, Fr reads *ne discredatis de quibus* (Do not disbelieve these things), while Sp has *ne discedatis a Domino et nolite increduli esse his* (Do not swerve away from the Lord, and do not disbelieve these things). The point of origin of this textual variation is clearly the pair *discredatis/discedatis*. It is important to note not only that these graphically similar words have completely different meanings but also that the second part of the phrase in the Spanish text actually replicates the meaning of French *discredatis*, itself a very unusual word. A Spanish copyist or editor might have first misread the uncommon word and substituted a more expected alternative, but then, realizing the error, inserted the additional phrase (*et nolite increduli esse his*) to cover the original meaning. It is also possible that the second phrase in the Spanish text entered as a gloss in the margin or between the lines, based on the correct (French) text.[17] At any rate, this is an example of variation between the recensions that not only is clearly based on intra-Latin confusion but also exemplifies the type of textual difference (in this case, textual expansion) that is typical of the fundamental discrepancies between the two Latin texts.

A second, similar example appears in 16:68, where Fr has *turbae copiosae* ([the burning wrath] of a great crowd [will be kindled over you]), and Sp *et turbabunt vos multi populi* (and many people will trouble you [or: throw you into disarray]). The textual variation is based on the pair *turbae/turbabunt*. Although these words derive from the same root, and *turba* can mean "tumult" or "disturbance," the words in their present contexts clearly differ in signification. Once again, an extra element in Sp ([*multi*] *populi*) covers the true meaning of Fr *turbae*. A Spanish editor might have misread (or deliberately adapted) *turbae* as the verb *turbo*, adjusted the tense, and then added the element *multi populi* to reflect the actual sense of *turbae copiosae*.[18] Again, the textual variation not only reflects intra-Latin interchange but also represents the type of broader textual adaptation that typifies the differences between the versions.

A third example of a similar phenomenon occurs only a few words later in 16:68. Where Fr has *rapient* (they will seize [certain of you]), Sp reads *diripient res vestras et sument* (they will pillage your property and take [certain of you]). The situation is similar to that seen in the two previous passages. The variation seems to be based on the pair *rapient/diripient*. These words are close in meaning, but, whereas the simplex means to "seize" or "snatch," the compound carries the additional sense to "pillage," "lay waste," or "despoil." Just as above, the extra element in Sp (*sument*) reprises the basic meaning of Fr *rapient*. The variation here may well have been deliberate: the Spanish scribe took up the complex verb in an effort to embellish the meaning of the text.[19] This passage again indicates that recensional activity of the style typical of 6 Ezra as a whole took place within a Latin medium.

These three examples show that at least some of the versional variation in 6 Ezra, and that of a type characteristic of the book as a whole, occurred on the basis of a

Latin original. This evidence is corroborated by the several synonymous and non-synonymous variants between the versions that seem to have arisen, through either corruption or association, within a Latin context. This evidence for a Latin basis of the two versions coincides, in turn, with the relatively high degree of verbal similarity that was noted to exist between them and the numerous places at which they offer lengthy sections of identical text. On the other hand, a few lexical differences between the versions were found that could possibly derive from an original in Greek; none of these, however, was judged sufficient to prove the existence of a Greek *Vorlage.*

The bulk of the evidence examined so far, therefore, suggests that the differences between the two versions of 6 Ezra arose within a Latin medium, on the basis of a Latin original. These differences seem to have resulted both from conscious processes of redaction and from textual corruption. The fact that a large proportion of the textual modifications are clearly intentional means that it is justifiable, at our present stage of investigation, to refer to the two Latin versions of 6 Ezra as separate "recensions" of the text.

As already pointed out, the tentative judgment that the two recensions of 6 Ezra derive from a Latin original does not preclude the possibility that some of the differences between them may ultimately stem from recourse to a Greek text or texts. Indeed, the high proportion of synonyms between the recensions may seem difficult to explain on the basis of recensional activity alone and could still be interpreted as indicating some influence of independent translations from Greek. On the other hand, such translational influence should not be assumed until unambiguous evidence for it is located. Indeed, it is argued in what follows that many, if not all, of the differences in synonyms between the recensions can be accounted for by appeal to intra-Latin editing.

In summary, given the present author's predilection for Occam's razor in dealing with textual matters, we will proceed on the assumption that the differences between the two versions of 6 Ezra arose in a Latin medium. It is important, nevertheless, to realize that the more complex situation is often the more accurate historically, and to acknowledge the possibility that at least some of the differences between the Latin recensions may derive ultimately from the influence of a Greek original or originals.

ANALYSIS OF THE DIFFERENCES BETWEEN THE RECENSIONS

It remains now to consider the relationship between the two recensions, that is, the origin of the differences between them. In theory, there are numerous possibilities for this relationship; a sample survey of these was given in the preceding discussion. As noted there, probably the simplest situation is that one recension represents or approximates the "more original" form of the text and the other is a revision of that form. There are many additional, more complex scenarios.

The main object of the present study is to determine whether either of the two recensions can be identified as being, on the whole, superior (i.e., temporally prior) to the other. If one recension seems consistently to manifest superior (primary) readings, and the other to offer a revised (secondary) text, we may assume that the second text is an editorial redaction of the first. If, however, the textual evidence suggests a more complex situation, further analysis must be undertaken.

In the following, an attempt is made first to identify criteria that can be used to address the question of recensional priority. We then seek to apply these criteria, to judge where and how often each recension seems to offer a superior text.[20] The analysis has been organized under categories, according to the apparent motive underlying the recensional variation.

Grammatical and Stylistic Features

One criterion that may prove useful in addressing the question of recensional priority is that of grammar and style. If one recension features many passages that are grammatically inelegant or stylistically rough, while the other consistently has in their place more polished or "correct" readings, the latter recension is more likely to be a secondary revision (unless, of course, the "more difficult" readings are textual corruptions).[21] In the case of 6 Ezra, this criterion would be especially relevant if one recension uses grammatical constructions or word sequence that would be more natural in Greek and the other has in their place more typical Latin ones.

There are numerous passages in 6 Ezra where this criterion can fruitfully be applied. In the vast majority of cases, the French recension presents the more "difficult," awkward, or grammatically tenuous reading, and the Spanish the more elegant and grammatically polished. Many of these cases concern relatively simple grammatical features. In the first words of 6 Ezra (15:1), for example, Fr reads *ecce loquere in aures plebi meae*, whereas Sp has *ecce loquere in auribus populi mei*. The Fr use of the dative *plebi* is extremely awkward and may even be a grammatical error for the genitive, whereas the Sp version is more correct.

In 15:13, where Fr has *quoniam deficiet semina eorum*, Sp reads the verb as *deficient*. Since the most likely Greek equivalent for *semina* is σπέρματα, this seems to be a case where a Greek neuter plural subject with singular verb was unthinkingly replicated by a Latin translator. In any case, the Spanish verb is correct, and is therefore more probably a secondary correction.

In 15:19, Fr reads *non miserebitur homo proximum suum*, where Sp has . . . *proximi sui*. Greek ἐλεέω, the most likely basis for *misereor*, takes the accusative, whereas the Latin verb governs the genitive. Thus, Fr is probably an unthinkingly literal rendition of the Greek text, whereas Sp is a corrected version.

In 15:30, Fr *in dentibus suis* expresses an ablative of means improperly with the preposition; Sp improves the grammar by dropping the preposition. In 15:31, Fr *supervalescet draco nativitatis memores suae* makes little apparent sense, while the Sp reading of *memor* for *memores* ameliorates the situation. Later in the same verse, however, Sp *si converterint se conspirantur in virtute magna* is problematic, whereas Fr *conspirantes* better fits the sense of the passage. In 15:43, Fr reads *usque Babilonem* (probably based on the Greek simplex ἕως), while Sp has the grammatically more correct *usque in Babilonem* (*usque* rarely appears without an accompanying preposition or adverb in the Latin of this period).

The extremely awkward clause *et qui subremanserint servientes his* in Fr 15:45 seems to be based on an extended use of participles that characterizes Hellenistic Greek. Sp *et ceteri qui remanserint servient illis* expresses the thought in proper Latin.

In 15:51, where Fr reads *et infirmaberis et paupera*, Sp has . . . *pauper*. Since *pauper* is a third declension adjective, the Fr form is grammatically impossible. πτωχός, on the other hand, the most likely Greek basis, has a regular feminine form (e.g., Mark 12:42), which perhaps underlies the French text.

In 16:2, Fr *praecingite vos saccos* is clearly grammatically more "primitive" than Sp . . . *saccis*, which properly uses the ablative of means. In 16:7, for Fr *sagittam inmissam a sagittario forte*, Sp has *sagittam a sagittario forti missam*; the latter not only offers the correct spelling of *forti* but also positions *missam* in a more stylized manner, suggesting secondary editing.

In 16:30, Sp *ab his qui . . . scrutantur* uses the more correct deponent form of the verb, whereas Fr *ab scrutantibus* is grammatically doubtful. In 16:38 and 16:39, the incorrect Fr participle *prodiente* (16:39 *prodiendum*) is replaced in Sp by the proper *prodeunte* (16:39 *prodeundum*).

In 16:60, where Fr reads *posuit . . . lacus ad emittendum flumina*, Sp has the grammatically more correct . . . *ad emittenda flumina*, the gerundive now agreeing with its governing noun. Fr 16:71 offers the ungrammatical phrase *neminem parcentes*, whereas Sp uses the correct dative form *nemini parcentes*.

In 16:76, a passage is presented where, contrary to the normal situation, the French version is grammatically more correct. Sp reads *non preponderent vos peccata vestra*, while Fr has *ne . . .* , which is the proper negation of a hortatory subjunctive. Here the French seems to be secondary.

In several passages, a variation in the use of nominal case after the preposition *in* provides evidence of stylistic revision. In 15:14, for example, Fr has *Vae saeculo et qui habitant in eum*, whereas Sp reads . . . *in eo*. The Spanish choice of the ablative here seems grammatically preferable and is thus probably secondary. Exactly the same principle applies in several other passages: 15:33 Fr *erit timor et tremor in exercitum*, Sp . . . *in exercitu*; 15:55 Fr *merces fornicariae in sinus tuos*, Sp . . . *in sinu tuo*; 16:28 Fr *absconderint se . . . in fissuras petrarum*, Sp . . . *in fissuris petrarum*; and 16:52 Fr *et justitia regnabit in nos*, Sp . . . *in nobis*.

In 15:56, where Fr has *et tradet te in malis*, Sp reads . . . *in mala*. The Spanish choice of the accusative seems more appropriate and is thus probably secondary.

In numerous other cases, textual differences between the French and Spanish versions seem to have arisen on the basis of considerations of style rather than of simple grammatical correctness. There are many passages, for example, in which the French text, although relatively clear in meaning, is extremely cumbersome stylistically. Almost invariably, the Spanish forms of these same passages, while conveying the same sense, are far more graceful in expression.

A simple example occurs in 15:53, where Fr reads *exultans percussionem manuum*, Sp *exultans in percussione manuum*. The French reading, while clear enough, is barbarous Latin; the Spanish is properly phrased, and thus seems more likely to be a secondary revision.

In a longer passage in 15:60, Fr has *allident civitatem oditam et exterent eam portionem aliquam gloriae tuae et territorii tui dum revertuntur a Babylonia*, Sp *allident civitatem odiosam et exterent aliquam portionem terrae tuae et partem gloriae tuae exterminabunt rursum revertentes a Babilonia subversa*. The French is extremely awkward (see the translation in Appendix 3). The Spanish, while similar in sense, provides a much smoother and more elegant reading.

In 15:61, Fr *extrita illis eris in stramine* parallels Sp *demolita eris illis pro stipula*. Both the pronoun placement and the choice of preposition in Fr seem more primitive, and thus are more likely to be primary.

In 16:13, Fr reads *fortis gloriae qui tendit sagittam et acumen eius acutum quae dimissa est ab eo non deficiet missa super fines terrae*, Sp *fortis dextera eius quae arcum tendit et sagittae eius acutae quae ab ipso mittuntur non deficient cum coeperint mitti in fines terrae*. The Spanish version makes more sense, has a more stylish word order, and is smoother and stylistically superior in every regard; thus, it probably represents a secondary reworking of the text.

In 16:18, Fr contains the almost nonsensical phrase *initium gemitus et copiosi suspirantium*. Sp has in its place *initium dolorum et multi gemitus*. The Spanish is more logical and thus more probably secondary.

Fr 16:22 *et aporiant vitam super terram, et gladius dispersit quae superaverint a fame* is impenetrable at best, while Sp *a fame enim plurimi qui inhabitant terram interient, et gladius disperdet ceteros qui superaverint a fame* puts the same expression in an elegant and comprehensible form.

The same can be said for the parallel passages in 16:38: Fr *quemadmodum praegnans in nono mense filium suum, in adpropinquante hora partus eius, ante horas duas vel tres gementes dolores circum ventrem eius, et prodiente infante de ventre*; Sp *quemadmodum mulier pregnans infantem suum in utero mensibus novem habens ubi coeperit hora partus eius adpropinquare, ante duas horas vel tres dolores circa ventrem patitur, et prodeunte infante de ventre*. The French is a grammatical, stylistic, and logical disaster, whereas the Spanish is eminently correct and readable. Furthermore, Fr *in adpropinquante hora partus eius* shows the influence of a Greek temporal constuction with ἐν, while the Spanish expresses the phrase in proper Latin.

In the sequence of rhetorically parallel phrases in 16:41–44, the Spanish consistently conforms to a strictly defined pattern of verb tense and adverbial and pronominal usage, whereas the French in several instances departs from the pattern (e.g., *vidui* 16:44). It is easier to explain the consistent Spanish patterning as the work of a later editor than to suppose that the French suffered corruption or deliberately broke the pattern.

In 16:46, the Fr clause *quia in captivitate et fame generant natos suos* at the end of the verse makes no sense in its context, whereas Sp *qui nubunt in captivitate et fame filios generabunt* provides an element that fits nicely. Although *quia* could be seen as a corruption of *qui nubent*, the stylistic emendations at the end of the clause make it clear that the Spanish is secondary.

The Fr correlative set *quamdiu . . . tanto magis* in 16:47–48 is extremely awkward, whereas Sp *in quantum . . . in tanto magis* provides the stylistically more graceful, and more probably revised, pairing.

Still in 16:48, Sp features a phrase with a repeated object that is characteristic of Semitic style—*zelabo illos zelo*—where Fr has simply *adzelabor eos*. The Spanish seems here to be more "primitive," and the French a stylistic improvement.

In 16:67, there is also a clause in which Spanish appears primary. Sp *. . . et non faciatis haec semper* is quite awkward, whereas Fr *. . . iam agere eas sempiterno* reads smoothly and makes sense, thus appearing to be a revision.

There are numerous passages in 6 Ezra in which the finite verb stands in the middle of the clause in one recension and at or near the end in the other. The latter positioning is, of course, the more stylized Latin word order. Given a choice, one would expect the more stylized word order to reflect secondary editorial redaction. In these passages in 6 Ezra, it is far more common for the Spanish to show the more stylized verb placement. Examples are: 15:58 *manducabunt* (here Fr priority is borne out by the Greek fragment); 16:13 *dimissa est/mittuntur;* 16:32 *germinabunt;* 16:46 *generant/generabunt;* 16:47 *negotiantur/mercantur;* 16:51 *similari/similes esse;* 16:56 *novit;* 16:61 *posuit/inposuit;* 16:62 *fecit;* 16:63 *occultare/celare;* 16:67 *educabit/deducet;* and 16:73 *probatur.* The opposite recensional situation (wherein Fr has the more stylized verb placement), however, obtains in 15:29 *audient/audiunt;* 15:45 *exteruerunt/exterrent;* and 16:72 *eicient/expellent.* Thus, by a margin of twelve to three, the factor of verb placement again supports the priority of French, indicating Spanish to be a secondary redaction.

In several passages, French participial phrases, typical of biblical Greek, stand in parallel with Spanish pronoun-finite verb constructions that express the same thought in a more characteristically Latin fashion.[22] These are: 15:40 Fr *inhabitantes* Sp *qui inhabitant;* 15:45 Fr *servientes* Sp *servient;* 16:30 Fr *ab scrutantibus* Sp *ab his qui scrutantur;* 16:31 Fr *ab scrutantibus* Sp *ab his qui . . . scrutabunt;* 16:63 Fr *peccantibus* Sp *omnibus qui peccant;* 16:63 Fr *volentibus* Sp *qui volunt;* and 16:70 Fr *timentes* Sp *hos qui timent.* There are, to my knowledge, no cases wherein the recensional situation is reversed. This grammatical phenomenon can again be interpreted as an attempt by a Spanish editor to improve the Latin style of the text.

There are, then, numerous passages in 6 Ezra in which one of the two recensions displays a text that is grammatically or stylistically superior to the other. In very few of these passages can the textual differences be explained as resulting from textual corruption. Rather, in almost every case, the differences seem to be attributable to conscious processes of redaction: an editor (or editors) has intentionally altered the text grammatically or stylistically. In the vast majority of cases, it is the Spanish text that is the more stylish or grammatically "correct," and the French that is rougher or more grammatically tenuous.

These data can, in fact, be interpreted in two ways. One is that the less refined French text represents the more primitive, more original text of 6 Ezra, and the more elegant Spanish a revised, secondary form. Another is that a French editor has, for some reason, deliberately made the text of that recension coarser and more grammatically idiosyncratic, perhaps to convey an impression of "authenticity" through archaism and a primitive, in some cases biblicizing, style.

Although the latter scenario is theoretically possible, and may actually have occurred in some cases, it seems rather far-fetched when compared with the more expected, more conventional notion of editing being carried out for stylistic *improvement.* Thus, unless there arise compelling reasons to think otherwise, it seems most reasonable to surmise that the grammatically and stylistically superior Spanish text is secondary.

Synonymous Lexical Variants

A second criterion that might be of value in assessing recensional priority concerns the numerous (almost three hundred) synonymous or near synonymous lexical variants that exist between the two recensions (see the preceding listing). Let us suppose, for example, that one recension frequently features highly unusual, idiosyncratic, or "primitive" Latin words[23]—for example, unusual Greek loanwords—and that the other consistently has in their place more idiomatic, expected, or elegant Latin synonyms. This situation would suggest that an editor had modified the wording of the former recension on stylistic grounds. It is rather more difficult to imagine a situation wherein conventional Latin lexemes were intentionally changed to more "primitive," idiosyncratic, or exotic ones.

Actually, the situation in 6 Ezra is very much like this. The French recension features a plenitude of Greek calques and other words that are extremely rare in standard Latin usage (including three *hapax legomena*). In virtually every case, the Spanish version has in their place more conventional Latin equivalents. Some examples are as follow:

Noteworthy Lexical Equivalents between the Recensions

15:12   Fr *verberati*, Sp *verberum*. Fr shows a highly unusual substantive use of the participial form of *verbero* (*lugeat Aegyptus . . . a plaga verberati et mastigati*), whereas Sp has the more expected nominal form.

15:12   Fr *mastigati*, Sp *castigationis*. Besides repeating the situation just described, Fr is a Greek loanword (cf. μαστιγόω) that is attested only twice in Latin, both occurring in Fr 6 Ezra (cf. 15:51, where Sp also differs). Sp is common.

15:15   Fr *ext(e)ritio*, Sp *contritio*. Fr is attested only thrice in Latin: twice in 6 Ezra (cf. 15:39) and once in an OL version of Num 15:31 (Augustine, *Quaestiones in heptateuchum* 4, 25). Sp, while not common, is far better attested.

15:16   Fr *supervalescentes*, Sp *invalescentes*. Fr is extremely rare; in its *-esco* form, it is attested in the lexica only in 6 Ezra (here and in 15:31). Sp is common.

15:20   Fr *noto*, Sp *austro*. Fr, while well attested in Latin, is a Greek loanword (cf. νότος). Sp supplies the more common native Latin equivalent.

15:31   Fr *supervalescet*, Sp *convalescet*. For Fr, see 15:16. Sp is common.

15:33   Fr *subsedebit*, Sp *obsidebit*. Fr is very rare; it does not occur in Latin before about 200 c.e., and in the Vg is a *hapax legomenon*. Fr is common.

15:33   Fr *inconstabilitio*, Sp *inconstantia*. Fr is a *dis legomenon* in Latin; both occurrences are in 6 Ezra (see also 15:16, where Sp retains the word). Sp is common.

15:39   Fr *exteritionem*, Sp *strages*. For Fr, see 15:15. Sp is common.

15:39   Fr *orientalem*, Sp *oriente*. Fr is unusual, and its (apparent) use here as a noun is striking. Sp is, of course, common.

15:40   Fr *sidus*, Sp *cataginis*. Fr is common. Sp *cata(e)gis* is a Greek loanword (cf. καταιγίς) that is very rare in Latin; *TLL* lists only five occurrences (for details, see chapter 5, "The Vocabulary of the Secondary Recension").

15:41   Fr *rompheas*, Sp *gladios*. Fr is a Greek calque (cf. ῥομφαία) which, although it does occur in native Latin texts, is quite rare. Fr is the usual Latin form. (See also 15:57 and 16:31.)

15:45   Fr *subremanserint*, Sp *remanserint*. Fr is rare: it occurs in the Vg only in 6 Ezra (here and at 16:30) and is attested in only a few other texts (for details, see chapter 5, "The Vocabulary of the Earliest Text"). Sp is common.

15:51   Fr *mastigata*, Sp *flagellis*. For Fr, see 15:12. Sp is common.

15:57   Fr *romphea*, Sp *gladio*. See 15:41 and 16:31.

15:60   Fr *oditam*, Sp *odiosam*. Fr is a highly unusual element that seems to be a rare participial form of *odi* or *odio*. It is not listed in *TLL* and does not seem to occur elsewhere in the Vg. Sp is standard.

16:15   Fr *excomedat*, Sp *consumat*. Fr is attested, according to *TLL*, only here and in four other Latin authors (for details, see chapter 5). Sp is common.

16:19   Fr *mastix*, Sp *flagella*. Fr is a Greek loanword (cf. μάστιξ) that is attested only twice in Latin, here and in the *Scholia in Terentium*, p. 160, 1, v. 1, 31 (pre–tenth century). Sp is common.

16:22   Fr *aporiant [vitam]*, Sp *interient*. Fr is highly unusual (for details, see chapter 5). It is probably a Greek loanword (cf. ἀπορέω), and its usage in this context is problematic (see the translation). See also 16:71. Sp is, of course, common.

16:25   Fr *fructiferabunt*, Sp *dabunt fructus*. Fr is attested only thrice in Latin: here, in an OL manuscript of Col 1:6 (cod. g), and in 1 Clement 20:4. Sp uses standard elements.

16:30   Fr *subremanet*, Sp *relinquentur*. For Fr, see 15:45. Sp is common.

16:31   Fr *romphea*, Sp *gladio*. See 15:41 and 57.

16:36   Fr *discredatis*, Sp *increduli esse*. Fr is an unusual element, possibly a Christian neologism, that does not appear in Latin before the fourth century C.E., and that occurs in the Vg only here. Sp is standard.

16:39   Fr *circumtenent*, Sp *circumcingunt*. Fr is an unusual word which occurs, according to *TLL*, in only seven other Latin authors. Sp is more common.

16:46   Fr *captivabunt*, Sp *captivos ducent*. Fr is an unusual element and is a Christian neologism. Sp uses standard lexemes.

16:48   Fr *adzelabor*, Sp *zelabo*. Fr, a Greek loanword (cf. παραζηλόω?), is a *hapax legomenon* in Latin. Sp, while also a Greek calque, is far more common in Latin.

16:62   Fr *scrutinat*, Sp *scrutatur*. Fr is a rare Christian neologism that is attested only in a few Old Latin biblical texts, in 4 Ezra 13:52, in 6 Ezra, and in two early Christian authors, Lucifer of Cagliari and Benedict (for details, see chapter 5, "The Vocabulary of the Earliest Text"). Sp is common.

16:64   Fr *scrutinando scrutinavit*, Sp *scrutans scrutavit*. See 16:62.

16:76   Fr *superelevent*, Sp *extollant*. Fr is very rare; the lexica list it only here and in one of Jerome's commentaries (for details, see chapter 5). Sp is common.

The evidence of this list is highly compelling, as much as that presented in the section on style and grammar. In virtually every case (save one) where the two recensions feature synonymous variants of which one is rare or exotic and the other standard Latin, it is the French that has the *hapax legomenon*, the stylistically "primitive" Latin lexeme, or the Greek loanword, and the Spanish the standard element. Only in the pair cited in 15:40 does the opposite situation occur.

Although, as mentioned, it is theoretically possible that a French editor has deliberately altered vocabulary to convey the impression of a more "primitive," archaic, and therefore authentic text, this scenario is prima facie far less likely than the opposite situation. The weight of the evidence strongly suggests that the French recension is more primary, and that a Spanish editor has systematically excised Greek calques,

Latin neologisms, and unusual or awkward cases of translation Latin, replacing them with more standard or elegant native Latin words.[24]

Differences in Meaning, Including Theological Factors and Apparent Corruptions

Another method for judging recensional priority is simply to compare the readings of the two recensions where they differ in meaning. It is possible that an editor, in revising the text, has not only modified style, grammar, and vocabulary but also "improved upon" substantive elements of the text. It may be found that some of the differences in content between the recensions can be explained by appeal to commonly known principles of redaction (e.g., hyperbole [theological or otherwise], heightening of theological impact, conformity to "orthodox" theological norms, or adherence to biblical textual models). It is also possible that a reading in one recension can be identified as a corruption of the other. In either case, judgments about recensional priority can be made.

Sixth Ezra has several examples of both of these types of textual difference. In 15:24 and 16:54, for example, where Fr reads *Dominus*, Sp has *Dominus Deus*. Likewise, in 15:20, for Fr *Deus*, Sp has *Dominus Deus*. In 16:76, however, the situation is reversed: Fr reads *Dominus Deus*, while Sp simply has *Dominus*. An analogous phenomenon occurs in 16:40, where Fr has *Audite verbum, plebs mea*, Sp *Audite verbum Domini, populus meus*. In every case except 16:76, the Spanish reading is theologically more elaborate and is therefore more likely to be a product of editorial revision.[25]

An interesting case is presented in 15:11. Fr reads *et percutiam Aegyptum plaga sicut prius*; Sp has *. . . plagis. . . .* Since the biblical plagues (Exodus 7–11) were plural (ten), the Spanish seems more likely to be an editorial emendation and the French the more original text.

In 15:20, Fr has *a borea et a noto et ab euro et a libano*, Sp *ab oriente et austro et ab euro et libano*. Fr, then, reads "from north, south, east, and west," Sp "from east, south, east, and west." It is true that Spanish is, in a sense, the "more difficult" reading. It is also, however, difficult to imagine that the author of 6 Ezra actually intended the Spanish meaning rather than the French. Furthermore, Sp *ab oriente*, the problematic element, is easily read as a corruption of the more unusual Fr Greek loanword *a borea* (cf. βορέας). The Spanish here seems to be a corruption of a more primary French text.

Fr 15:39 reads *et superinvalescent venti ab oriente, et recludent eum*, whereas Sp has *. . . et repellent illum*. As noted earlier, the French is prima facie difficult, since *recludo* means primarily "to open up, reveal, disclose," which makes little sense here. There is, however, an additional meaning of the word, "to remove, lead away," which seems more appropriate. In any event, the Spanish is by far the "easier" reading and can thus be viewed as a secondary revision.

In 16:55, where Fr states that God said first *fiat terra* and then *fiat caelum*, Sp has the opposite order. The Spanish version accords with the Masoretic, Old Greek, and Vulgate Gen 1:6–10. Spanish is thus likely to be a secondary correction on the basis of the biblical text.

A final example is a lexical variant in 15:16: Fr *megestanorum*; Sp *egestanorum*. Since the French is a rather unusual loanword from a Greek technical term (μεγιστᾶνες) and the Spanish is meaningless, it appears that the French is primary and the Spanish a corruption of it.

In every case examined here save one, it seems that, where there are differences in meaning between the French and Spanish recensions, and where a rationale for the difference can be identified, the French is more liable to be primary and the Spanish to be a secondary revision.

Quantitative Differences (Additions and Deletions)

The text of 6 Ezra features a number of passages in which one recension is shorter or longer than the other. The Spanish text is, on the whole, the fuller: in total it has 102 more words than the French (2,194 to 2,092 words). Our survey of 6 Ezra 15 mentioned earlier in this chapter reveals that most of the additions or deletions are of one word; in addition, the two recensions have in chapter 15 nine added or deleted phrases of two or more words (six of the nine are extra elements in the Spanish text).

In several cases, it seems possible to make judgments about recensional priority on the basis of these quantitative differences. In 15:4, for example, after the phrase *quoniam omnis incredulus in incredulitate sua morietur*, common to both texts, Sp has *et omnis qui credit fide sua salvus erit*. Whereas it is easy to interpret this as an exegetical expansion by a Spanish editor, it is difficult to imagine a rationale for its deletion (unless, of course, it fell out unintentionally). This element seems to support French priority.

In several cases, an extra word in the Spanish text can be explained as an expansionary or pleonastic touch. In 15:26, Fr has *novit Deus qui peccant in eum*, whereas Sp reads *quoniam novit Dominus omnes qui delinqunt in illum*. Both *quoniam* and *omnes* in Sp could be judged expansionary (and thus secondary). Special occurrences of *omnes* in the Spanish text, apparently for similar, pleonastic purposes, appear in three additional passages: 15:37 Fr *et horrebunt qui videbunt iram illam*, Sp . . . *horrebunt omnes qui . . .* ; 16:18 Fr *et trepidabunt ab eis*, Sp *et trepidabunt omnes in his*; and 16:63 Fr *vae peccantibus*, Sp *vae omnibus qui peccant*. In each case, the pleonastic element seems to be secondary.

A similar argument can be made for a secondary, expansionary Spanish use of the adjective *ceterus* in two passages. In 15:45, Fr has *et qui subremanserint servientes his*, whereas Sp reads *et ceteri qui remanserint servient illis*; in 16:22, Fr has *et gladius dispersit quae superaverint*, Sp *et gladius disperdet ceteros qui superaverint*. A Spanish editor seems to have been in the habit of supplying *omnes* or *ceteri* before substantive relative clauses, in order to provide a nominal base for the substantive. The added words lend emphasis to the text and cause it to read more smoothly.

An analogous case appears in 16:38: Fr *praegnans* (used substantively); Sp *mulier praegnans*. Since *praegnans* does not seem normally to be used as a substantive, Sp can be viewed as a pleonastic stylistic revision.

An expansionary tendency in Sp appears again in 15:27, where Fr reads *mala*, Sp *mala multa*; the latter seems intended to enhance the text's dramatic effect. Compare 16:11: Fr *et quis non conterretur*, Sp *et quis non funditus conteretur*.

In 15:34, Fr reads *Ecce nubs ab oriente et a septentrione usque ad meridianum*, while Sp has the extra element *et ab occidente* after Fr *ab oriente*. Thus, while the French reads "from the east, and from the north across to the south," the Spanish has "from the east and from the west, and from the north across to the south." While it is theoretically possible that the French has lost the extra element, it seems much more likely, given the stereotypical quality of the material, that the extra phrase was added in Spanish to cover all the directions.

In the next verse the Fr phrase *et sidus illorum*, which is unexpected and quite out of place (see the translation in Appendix 3), is lacking in the Spanish. Again, although one could interpret its presence in the French as a corruption or dittography, it seems more likely that a Spanish editor has eliminated it as an intrusive and apparently meaningless element.

A similar situation obtains in 15:51. The phrase *a vulneribus* in Fr *infirmaberis . . . a plaga et mastigata a vulneribus* is extremely awkward, while Sp *infirmeris . . . a flagellis et plaga* lacks the intrusive element, causing the text to read more smoothly and make sense.

The extra phrase *et magna confusio* in Sp 16:21 seems to be a secondary addition for dramatic effect. Similarly, in 16:29, the unique Sp element *in singulis arboribus* is probably an exegetical expansion: it is more logical to suppose that three or four olives were left behind on every tree than in the grove as a whole.

In two cases of quantitative difference, however, it is a longer Spanish text that seems primary, whereas the French seems to have dropped elements, by either accident or design. In 15:55, for example, Sp reads *merces fornicariae in sinu tuo est; propterea secundum facta tua recipies in sinus tuos*, while Fr has *merces fornicariae in sinus tuos; propterea redditionem percipies*. The Spanish is awkward and redundant, reiterating the element *in sinus tuos*, whereas the French reads more smoothly, appearing to be a stylistic revision (Sp *est*, however, does appear secondary).

Again, in 16:71, Sp has the unique phrase *aporiati enim homines a malis suis*. Unlike several examples cited previously, there is no obvious rationale for a Spanish editor having added this phrase. Furthermore, it is rather primitive stylistically (thus apparently characteristic of the original text of 6 Ezra) and contains the highly unusual word *aporior* (which also appears in 6 Ezra Fr 16:22, being there, apparently, excised by a Spanish editor). Also, the phrase contains as many letters (twenty-nine) as one might expect to find in a typical line of a medieval Latin manuscript. This suggests the possibility that a line might have dropped out of a manuscript accidentally. For all these reasons, it seems probable that this phrase was part of the original text of 6 Ezra.

There is a whole range of passages where the presence or absence of simple conjunctions or prepositions, such as *et* and *ab*, can also serve as indicators of literary style. In most cases, an expansive, pleonastic use of such elements, such as sometimes characterizes Semitic biblical style, manifests a certain stylistic crudeness, whereas a more restrained use results in a smoother and more elegant text. This phenomenon occurs especially between the successive elements in series of clauses or nouns, and (for *et*) at the beginning of clauses.

In 15:5, for example, Fr reads *induco . . . super orbem terrarum mala: gladium et famem et mortem et interitum*, Sp *. . . : gladium, famem, mortem et interitum*. The Spanish is plainly more elegant. An almost identical case appears in 15:49. Again, in 15:62, Fr has *comedunt te et civitates tuas et territoria tua et montes et omnem silvam* *tuam et ligna pomifera igne consument,* Sp *devorabunt te et civitates tuas, terram tuam et montes tuos, omnes silvas tuas et lignum fructiferum igni conburent.* Again, the Spanish is far more refined.

A similar principle, this time with *ab,* can be applied in 15:20, where Fr has *a borea et a noto et ab euro et a libano,* Sp *ab oriente et austro et ab euro et libano.* The Spanish text here clearly shows better style. In 16:23, Fr *et derelinquetur deserta terra* stands parallel to Sp *derelinquetur enim terra deserta;* the latter is plainly stylistically preferable and is thus probably secondary.

Other examples of French pleonastic use of *et* to link clauses or elements in a series, where the conjunction lacks in Spanish, occur in 15:32, 41, 42; 16:46, 47, 54. A similar situation with *ab* appears in 16:12. On the other hand, the opposite situation (Sp pleonastic *et* lacking in Fr) obtains in 16:2, 21.

In 15:63; 16:9, 15, 26, 76, 77, the French has but Spanish lacks an initial *et* in a clause that is characterisic of Semitic biblical style but that is stylistically barbarous in Greek or Latin. The opposite recensional situation, however, appears in 15:55, 61, 62; 16:73. As in the examples cited, the lack of the pleonastic *et* can be interpreted as a sign of secondary stylistic editing.

Furthermore, it was noted in the first part of this chapter that in two passages where intra-Latin corruption or interchange is accompanied by a quantitative textual change (viz., 16:36, 68), the textual variation is more easily explained on the assumption that the (shorter) French version is primary and serves as the source of the variation, and that the (longer) Spanish version is a secondary elaboration.

Again, then, analysis of the quantitative differences between the French and Spanish texts suggests that, in the vast majority of cases, the French is more original and the Spanish a secondary revision of it made on grounds of style or content. In certain passages, as noted, the logic for this assessment could be hypothetically reversed, and the French recension argued to be a revision designed deliberately to make the text seem more obscure, archaic, and therefore "authentic." Again, however, the probability of this seems rather remote in comparison with the more conventional and expected situation of revision intended to improve the text.

It should also be pointed out that, although Fr seems to offer the superior text in the vast majority of cases, there are, as in each of the other categories examined previously, a number of passages in which the Spanish seems to have the less refined and more primary reading. The implications of this will be addressed later in this chapter.

CONCLUSIONS

In the foregoing survey we have examined virtually every passage in 6 Ezra in which cogent arguments can be advanced for preferring the reading of one recension over the other. In every category of variants examined—grammatical and stylistic differences, synonymous lexical variants, differences in meaning, and quantitative differences—it was determined that the vast majority of the differences between the recensions could be best explained by assuming the French text to be more original and the Spanish to be a secondary revision. Based on the evidence so far, the Spanish revision seems to have been made primarily on the grounds of grammatical and stylistic (including lexical) improvement, although in several passages emendation also took place on the basis of theology or other matters of content. In sum, then, this evidence clearly suggests that the French text is on the whole superior to, that is, temporally prior to, the Spanish. On the other hand, in each of the categories examined, there were always a few cases in which the reverse recensional situation obtained—where the Spanish text seemed the more original and the French secondary.

Interestingly, this double-edged assessment mirrors our evaluation of the relationship of the Greek Oxyrhynchus fragment of 15:57–59 to the two Latin recensions (see chapter 3). There it was found that, in this brief section of text, the Greek agrees with the French recension against the Spanish six times, and with the Spanish against the French twice.

Each of the three known citations of 6 Ezra—in Gildas and the Hispanic and Roman liturgies—also tends to align with the French recension, supporting its priority; however, in none of these cases is there evidence of influence from the Spanish text.

This combination of results, obtained in (1) internal comparative analysis of the Latin recensions and (2) evaluation of the relationship of the Greek fragment to the Latin recensions, seems to indicate a slightly more complex recensional situation in 6 Ezra than has been admitted thus far. Although the French recension is preferable in the vast majority of readings, there are clearly a certain number of cases in which the Spanish seems superior. This suggests that neither the French nor the Spanish represents the "more original" text of 6 Ezra in its pure form, but rather that each recension has suffered some degree of editorial interference, besides undergoing, undoubtedly, unintentional textual corruption. In terms of the manuscript stemma presented at the beginning of chapter 3, these processes of redaction and corruption would have occurred between the level of x, the archetype (earliest recoverable form) of the text, and t and u, the hyparchetypes of the French and Spanish texts, respectively. The fact remains, however, that the French recension seems far closer to the earliest recoverable form of the text than does the Spanish, based on every criterion examined thus far.[26]

In practical text-critical terms, this means that the French text must be preferred wherever there is not an excellent reason for choosing the Spanish. In my opinion, it would be an arbitrary and methodologically treacherous editorial policy simply to pick and choose between the readings of the two recensions, taking whichever seems preferable in any given instance. Rather, I have taken the course of accepting the French reading in every case where there is not, in my view, a compelling reason for choosing the Spanish. This latter situation occurs in only a few cases: (1) the two readings in 15:57–59 where the Oxyrhynchus fragment supports Spanish over French; (2) the Sp phrase *aporiati enim homines a malis suis* 16:71 which is lacking in the Fr text; (3) the Sp reading *alii* (in preference to Fr *alios/aliis*) in 15:16; and (4) Sp *fundamenta* (over Fr *frumenta*) in 16:15.

The results of this text-critical process are presented in Appendix 1. In this arrangement, the left column represents the French recension, and the right the Spanish. The reading on the far left of each column, without parentheses, normally represents my best estimate of the hyparchetype of that recension. Since the French is judged superior in every instance except the four cases cited here, the reading occupying the place of the French hyparchetype (far left column) also normally represents my estimate of the earliest recoverable text of 6 Ezra. In the cases where the Spanish is judged superior, that reading is placed in the far left position of the left column, marked by "!a," and is followed by my estimate of the reading of the French hyparchetype (marked with "!f"). Thus, in every case, the reading at the far left of the left column signifies the earliest recoverable text. This preferred text is also presented in running fashion in Appendix 2 and is translated in Appendix 3.

These findings about the recensional situation in 6 Ezra have wider implications for the situation in the 2 Esdras corpus as a whole. As noted in chapter 1, most critics assume the French text (Φ) to be superior to the Spanish (ψ) in 4 Ezra, although the degree of variation between the two texts here is rather small. Investigation of 5 Ezra, on the other hand, shows the Spanish recension to be clearly superior, and the degree of variance between the two recensions to be even more dramatic than in 6 Ezra. Thus, in terms of apparent recensional priority, the situation in 6 Ezra conforms to that in 4 Ezra, while contravening that in 5 Ezra.

This situation, while surprising, is rendered more comprehensible by the fact that the codicological links between 4 and 6 Ezra are much stronger than those between either of these units and 5 Ezra.[27] Still, the exact relationship between the two recensions of 4, 5, and 6 Ezra, and the fact that the recensions differ in their value between the three works, have yet to be explained satisfactorily.[28] Also, the high degree of variation between the verbal relationships of the recensions in each of the three works (93 percent verbal correlation in a sample of 4 Ezra, 72 percent in 6 Ezra, and 62 percent in 5 Ezra) has not been adequately accounted for.

ADDITIONAL CONSIDERATIONS

Having determined provisionally that the differences between the two recensions of 6 Ezra arose within a Latin medium, and that the French recension seems in the vast majority of cases to represent the more original form of the text, we now turn to some additional issues. One is the question of the motivations that guided the editor or editors responsible for producing the Spanish text.

The primary concern that seems to underlie the Spanish recension is a thorough revision of grammar and style. It is as difficult to separate these two factors as it is to give priority to one over the other. The earliest recoverable text of 6 Ezra, as represented mainly in the French recension, is plainly a rather "primitive" piece of Latin translation prose! It contains numerous grammatical aberrations, syntactical constructions and lexical elements influenced by the Greek text from which it was translated, phrases and clauses that are stylistically abominable, and textual elements that simply do not make sense. The main concern of the Spanish recenseur was to rectify these literary infelicities, correcting grammatical flaws, transforming awkward and barbarous "translation" Latin into readable and natural prose, replacing exotic and strange-sounding words, and, at times, simply eliminating nonsense phrases. These types of changes account for about 95 percent of the activity of the Spanish editor.[29]

A second motive that seems to have guided the recension, though in a far less dramatic way, is reflected in changes in the content of the text. There are several cases in which theological elements (e.g., *nomina sacra*) are inserted or made more pronounced in the Spanish text (especially in 15:4), and two instances (15:11; 16:55) in which that text seems to have been adapted to conform to a biblical model. There are also several passages (15:27, 34; 16:11, 21, 29) in which a Spanish editor added short words or phrases to enhance the effect of the text or to make it more consistent.

Also, following our provisional conclusions about recensional priority, it may be possible to identify a few further redactional traits of the Spanish editor(s), ones that are important but have not been mentioned thus far because they did not actually contribute to a decision on recensional superiority.

First, the Spanish has a tendency to replace certain complex or other transitive verbs in the French with expressions that combine a verb and another word (usually a noun or adjective). Examples are: 15:47 Fr *adsimilasti* Sp *similis facta es* (cf. 16:51); 15:63 Fr *captivabunt* Sp *captivos ducent* (cf. 16:46); Fr *spoliabunt* Sp *praeda habebunt*; 16:20 Fr *memorantur* Sp *memores erunt*; 16:25 Fr *fructiferabunt* Sp *dabunt fructus*; 16:44 Fr *nubunt* Sp *nuptias faciunt*; Fr *non nubunt* Sp *nuptias non faciunt*; 16:46 Fr *captivabunt* Sp *captivos ducent* (cf. 15:63); and 16:51 Fr *similari* Sp *similes esse* (cf. 15:47). As above, this practice was probably motivated by stylistic concerns.[30]

Second, a Spanish editor frequently interchanges third-person pronouns (mainly *is, hic, ille,* and *ipse*). Most dominant is the alteration of forms of *is* to forms of *ille*, which occurs no less than twenty-six times. Likewise, forms of *is* are changed to forms of *ipse* eight times. A survey of the distribution of pronominal alteration in the Spanish recension is revealing: a Spanish editor changes forms of *is* to another pronoun thirty-eight times, *ille* to another pronoun seven times, *hic* three times, and *ipse* only once. Conversely, in the Spanish, other pronouns are changed to *is* six times, to *ille* twenty-seven times, to *hic* four times, and to *ipse* twelve times. Thus, the Spanish displays a marked tendency to change pronouns away from forms of *is*, and toward *ille* and *ipse*. Again, these tendencies probably arise from stylistic considerations.

One final issue concerning recensional relationship is the point, noted at the beginning of this chapter, that the level of verbal correlation between the two recensions, while registering 72 percent for the text as a whole, actually starts much higher (87 percent in 15:1–18) but then seems progressively to diminish, dropping to only 65 percent in the book's final section (16:48–78).[31] The reason for this can only be surmised. It is possible that a Spanish editor started the redactional task with a light hand but for some reason began to modify the text more heavily as the work progressed.[32] There are, of course, other ways to account for the situation (e.g., multiple redactors who worked on different portions of the book). I am not aware of textual situations in other works from antiquity where precisely this phenomenon occurs.

FIVE

Vocabulary

Although the Latin version of 6 Ezra was almost certainly translated from Greek, and thus represents a secondary witness to the text, there are several reasons for studying the Latin vocabulary of the book.[1] First, since the vocabulary of 6 Ezra is extremely idiosyncratic, the subject is of substantial interest in itself. Second, study of the Latin text may give some indication as to the date and provenance of the translation. Third, study of the Latin vocabulary could shed light on the question whether the Greek version is itself a translation from some other language. Finally, lexical study can give additional insight into the book's recensional situation.

Sixth Ezra was almost certainly translated into Latin by a Christian[2] and was probably regarded by that translator as being of or close to "scriptural" status.[3] Discussion of early Christian Latin translation literature of a biblicizing type is invariably tied to the issue of early Latin translation of the Greek Bible. Certain terms and ideas employed in the following analysis presuppose a basic knowledge of this area.[4]

The label "Old Latin" (also "Vetus Latina," "Veteres Latinae," "Itala") is generally used to designate Latin translations of the Bible that were made before, or independently of the influence of, the "Vulgate" translation of Jerome and his school (ca. 380 C.E.).[5] It is generally acknowledged that the earliest reliable information available to us about Old Latin biblical texts derives from North Africa.[6] This is the provenance of Tertullian (fl. 195–220) and Cyprian (fl. 246–58), the two earliest datable witnesses to Latin texts of the Bible. Furthermore, certain early Old Latin gospel manuscripts exhibit a text that is close to the citations of Cyprian, leading scholars to designate this text type as "African." This name does not necessarily denote the origin or delimit the circulation of this text type; it is simply a convenient label.

The biblical citations of certain other patristic writers, and the majority Latin texts of Ben Sira and the Wisdom of Solomon, also manifest this text type.[7] The African text type is characterized by (1) a highly literalistic mode of translation (including retention of many "Graecisms"); (2) frequent Greek calques and Latin neologisms; and (3) a generally unpolished Latin style and colloquial phraseology.

The next historically attested stage of development in the Old Latin text tradition is the "European" text type, so-called mainly to distinguish it from the African. This is found, for example, in authors like Novatian (fl. 250–57) and Lucifer of Cagliari (fl. 354–71), and in biblical manuscripts that are textually related to these authors' citations of Scripture. This text is somewhat more stylistically refined and grammatically sound than the African but nonetheless seems to have developed from it.

A further stage of development, and of stylistic and grammatical refinement, of the European Old Latin text is found in authors such as Ambrose (fl. 374–97) and Ambrosiaster (date unknown), and in cognate biblical manuscripts.

Finally, beginning around 380 C.E., Jerome and his school revised a current (European) Old Latin text of the New Testament, and Jerome further translated the Jewish Scriptures into Latin anew on the basis of a Hebrew text. These translations form the "Vulgate." Since Jerome for theological reasons did not translate or revise the texts of most of the "apocrypha," these writings survive even in the "Vulgate" version in Old Latin text forms. Although the Vulgate text became normative within a few centuries, Old Latin texts continued to be used and copied.[8]

THE VOCABULARY OF THE EARLIEST RECOVERABLE (FRENCH) TEXT OF 6 EZRA

As noted earlier, the earliest recoverable Latin text of 6 Ezra is lexically rather idiosyncratic. Among its main features are (1) many Greek loanwords, which presumably derive from the Greek *Vorlage* of the Latin translation, and (2) numerous "primitive" and/or highly unusual Latin words, many of which are compounds formed with *super-* (from Greek ὑπερ-) and other prepositional prefixes. Sixth Ezra contains three Latin *hapax legomena* of this latter type (see below).

The earliest recoverable text of 6 Ezra has no Hebrew loanwords. The Greek calques are as follows (an asterisk marks passages in which the loanword is altered or omitted in the secondary Spanish recension): *abyssum*[9] (ἄβυσσος) 16:57; *adzelor* (παραζηλόω?) 16:48*; *aporior*[10] (ἀπορέω) 16:22*, 71; *apostata*[11] (ἀποστάτης) 15:25; *boreas* (βορέας) 15:20*; *brachium* (βραχίων) 15:11; *camera* (καμάρα) 16:59; *c(h)arta* (χάρτης) 15:2; *draco* (δράκων) 15:29*; *eurus* (εὖρος) 15:20; *idolum* (εἴδωλον) 16:68*; *libanus* (λίψ, λιβός; or λίβανος) 15:20; *mastigo* (μαστιγόω) 15:12*, 51*; *mastix* (μάστιξ) 16:19*; *megestanes* (μεγιστάνες) 15:16*; *notus* (νότος) 15:20*; *plaga* (πληγή) 15:11, 12, 51; 16:19, 20*; *prophetia*[12] (προφητεία) 15:1; *romphea*[13] (ῥομφαία) 15:15, 22, 41*, 57*; 16:31*; *thesaurus*[14] (θησαυρός) 16:57; and *zelo(r)* (ζηλόω) 15:52; 16:49, 50. Thus, of thirty-three Greek loanwords, the Spanish text alters or omits fourteen.

Sixth Ezra also features a number of Christian neologisms, most of which are attested first in Latin in authors like Tertullian or Cyprian or in Old Latin biblical texts, and which then appear subsequently in later Christian (and sometimes pagan) writers.[15] Many of these are Greek loanwords and other words that entered Latin through the medium of Greek biblical translation. A listing of these neologisms follows (in this list, the Greek equivalent of the word is provided if it is accessible and not already indicated; words that do not appear in, or are modified in, the Spanish recension are again marked with an asterisk): *abyssum* 16:57; *adinventio*[16] 15:48; 16:54, 63; *aporior*

16:22*, 71; *apostata* 15:25; *captivo*[17] 15:63*; 16:46* (for αἰχμαλωτίζω or αἰχμαλωτεύω); *circumteneo*[18] 16:39* (for περιέχω or περιβάλλω); *conculcatio*[19] 16:69 (for καταπατέω); *devoratio* 16:78 (for κατάβρωμα); *ext(e)ritio* 15:15*, 39* (for ἐκτρίβω); *fornicaria*[20] 15:55; 16:49 (for πόρνη); *fornicor*[21] 15:47* (for πορνεύω); *fructifero*[22] 16:25* (for καρποφορέω); *inconstabilitio*[23] 15:16, 33* (for ἀστασία); *inproperium*[24] 16:69 (for ὄνειδος); *mastigo* 15:12*, 51*; *mastix* 16:19*; *peccator*[25] 15:23; 16:53 (for ἁμαρτωλός); *sanctificatio*[26] 15:25 (for ἁγιασμός); *scrutino*[27] 16:62*, 64 (bis)** (for ἐξερευνάω); *sibilatus* 15:29 (for συριγμός or συρισμός); *subremaneo*[28] 15:45*; 16:30* (for ὑπολείπω); *superelevo*[29] 16:76* (for ὑπεραίρω); *superinvalesco* 15:39 (for ὑπερισχύω); *supervalesco* 15:16*, 31* (for ὑπερισχύω or ὑπερέχω); and *tribulatio*[30] 15:19; 16:19, 67*, 74 (for θλῖψις). Thus, of forty neologisms, twenty-one are altered or omitted in the Spanish recension, including seventeen that are not Greek loanwords.

Another important category of words for our study includes ones that are attested only rarely, or only in 6 Ezra, in the text of the Vulgate.[31] These include (words altered or omitted in the Spanish recension are again marked with an asterisk): *adzelor* 16:48* (hapax in the Vulgate); *apostata* 15:25 (ter: here; Job 34:18; Prov 6:12); *circumteneo* 16:39* (hapax); *desertio* 16:26 (ter: here; 1 Esdr 1:58; 4 Ezra 3:2); *discredo* 16:36* (hapax); *excomedo*[32] 16:15* (hapax); *exsurrectio* 16:70* (hapax); *ext(e)ritio* 15:15*, 39* (bis [i.e., only in 6 Ezra]); *fissura* 16:28 (bis: here and Isa 2:21); *fructifero* 16:25* (hapax); *horridus* 15:34 (hapax); *inconstabilitio* 15:16, 33* (bis [i.e., only in 6 Ezra]); *invetero* 16:32* (ter: here; PsG 17:46; Isa 65:22); *mastigo* 15:12*, 51* (bis [i.e., only in 6 Ezra]); *mastix* 16:19* (hapax); *megestanes* 15:16* (hapax); *redditio* 15:55* (quaterni: here and thrice in Ben Sira); *romphea* 15:15, 22, 41*, 57*; 16:31* (here, five times in Ben Sira and once in Revelation); *scrutino* 16:62*, 64 (bis)** (quaterni: here and 4 Ezra 13:52); *sibilatus* 15:29 (hapax); *subremaneo* 15:45*; 16:30* (bis [i.e., only in 6 Ezra]); *suffrago*[33] 15:36* (hapax); *superelevo* 16:76* (hapax); *superfloresco* 16:21* (hapax); *superinvalesco* 15:39 (hapax); and *supervalesco* 15:16*, 31* (ter: here and Sir 43:32 [Gk 43:30]). Thus, of thirty-nine occurrences of words that are rare in the Vulgate, twenty-eight are altered or omitted in the Spanish recension.

The following lexemes in the earliest recoverable text of 6 Ezra are especially unusual or noteworthy and therefore merit special attention:

Catalogue of Unusual Lexemes

adzelor   16:48   [Sp *zelo*] (cf. παραζηλόω?). This Greek calque is a *hapax legomenon* in Latin.

aporior[34]   16:22   [Sp *intereo*], 71 [Sp =] (cf. ἀπορέω). An unusual Greek loanword, this is attested in Latin (besides here) only: thrice in OL sources; thrice in the Vg; in four Christian authors (from Laurentius Novae); and in one pagan source (the *Historia Apollonii*, 5–6th c.).

circumteneo[35]   16:39   [Sp *circumcingo*] (cf. περιέχω, περιβάλλω). This Christian neologism appears in Latin in only seven other authors, from 1 Clement.

excomedo[36]   16:15   [Sp *consumo*] (cf. ἐξεσθίω, κατεσθίω). This word is attested elsewhere in Latin only four times: Chiron, 901 (4th c.); Ps.-Apuleius, *Herbarium* 8, l. 4 (4th c.); Jerome, *Epistle* 78, 3, 2; and Gildas, *De excidio* 85 (6th c.).

exsurrectio   16:70   [Sp *insurrectio*] (cf. ἐπανάστασις?). This occurs in only three other Latin authors: Hippocrates, *Prognosticum* 11 (5th c.); Cassius Felix, *De medicina* 72 (447 C.E.); and Eusebius of Emesa, *Homilies* 3 and 9 (4th c.).

ext(e)ritio   15:15   [Sp *contritio*], 39 [Sp *strages*] (cf. ἐκτρίβω). This is attested in Latin only here and in an OL version of Num 15:31 quoted by Augustine (*Quaestiones in heptateuchum* 4, 25; 419 C.E.).

fructifero[37] 16:25 [Sp *dabunt fructus*] (cf. καρποφορέω). Attested in Latin thrice: here, in an OL manuscript of Col 1:6 (cod. g), and in 1 Clement 20:4.

inconstabilitio[38]   15:16   [Sp =], 33 [Sp *inconstantia*] (cf. ἀστασία). This Latin word is attested only in 6 Ezra.

libanus (-*um*) 15:20 [Sp =]. This word is significant mainly because it is a Greek loanword written in error for another. Latin *libanus* (-*um*), like Greek λίβανος (from Hebrew לבנה: white resin), means mainly "frankincense." (As proper nouns, both the Latin and Greek forms denote "Lebanon" or "Mount Lebanon" [Hebrew לבנון: the white mountain].) Its use in 6 Ezra 15:20 is apparently an error for *lips*, *libos* (from Greek λίψ, λιβός), the southwest (wind) (so called because it brought λίψ or λιβάς, "moisture"). The context in 15:20 clearly calls for a direction, almost certainly "west." Manuscripts C and V correctly emend to *lib(i)a*.[39]

mastigo 15:12 [Sp *castigatio*], 51 [Sp *flagellum*] (cf. μαστιγόω). This Greek calque is attested in Latin only in 6 Ezra.

mastix 16:19 [Sp *flagellum*] (cf. μάστιξ). This loanword is attested only here and in the *Scholia in Terentium*, p. 160, 1, v. 1, 31 (pre-10th c.). Thus, 6 Ezra is probably the earliest known use of the word in Latin.

[Since publication of *TLL* ceases here, the lexical information available for the following items is more limited than for those listed here. The lexica and concordances used are *OLD*, Forcellini, Souter, Blaise, Fischer, Rönsch, and Lechner-Schmidt (see n. 1).]

scrutino[40] 16:62 [Sp *scrutor*], 64 [bis] [Sp *scruto* bis] (cf. ἐρευνάω, ἐξερευνάω). This word is rare; besides here and 4 Ezra 13:52, the lexica list only OL forms of Zeph 1:12 (Lucifer Cagliari, *De sancto Athanasius* 1, 72); Joel 1:7 (Augustine, *Speculum* [Patr. n. bibl. I. 2. p. 99]); and John 7:52 (Cant.); and Benedict, *Regula* 55 (6th c.).

sibilatus 15:29 [Sp =] (cf. συριγμός, συρισμός). This does not occur elsewhere in the Vg. The lexica list only Probus *Instituta artium* 4, 47 (4th c.) and Caelius Aurelianus *Acutae passiones* 2, 27, 144 (fifth c.).

subremaneo[41] 15:45 [Sp *remaneo*]; 16:30 [Sp *relinquo*] (cf. ὑπολείπω). The lexica attest this Christian neologism only here and in: Tertullian, *De anima* 18 (210 C.E.); OL Gen 32:24 (codex Lugdunensis); Iulianus Romanus [?] apud Charisius, 249, 5 (4th c.); and Marius Mercator, *Cyrilli Alexandrini scholia de incarnatione* c. 1032 B (5th c.).

superelevo[42] 16:76 [Sp *extollo*] (cf. ὑπεραίρω). This word is attested only here and in Jerome, *In Isaiam* 13, 49.24 f. p. 574.

superinvalesco 15:39 [Sp =] (cf. ὑπερισχύω). The lexica list only this passage and OL Gen 49:26 (codex Lugdunensis).

supervalesco 15:16 [Sp *invalesco*], 31 [Sp *convalesco*] (cf. ὑπερισχύω, ὑπερέχω). Sixth Ezra comprises the only attestations in the lexica for the -*esco* form. *Supervaleo* occurs in Vg Sir 43:32 [Gk 43:30] and in the anonymous *De genealogiis patriarcharum* (PL 59, col. 534 C).

These data, together with those presented earlier, make it clear that the vocabulary of 6 Ezra lacks affinity with that of the Vulgate but has strong relations with that of Old Latin Bible translations (see further below). A further avenue of investigation within this sphere is to study the precise lexical affinities of 6 Ezra with regard to the Old Latin texts.

Several scholars have collected data on the lexical relationships between the African and European Old Latin text types in the New Testament, focusing on different Latin synonyms used to translate the same Greek word. Especially active in this area have been H. F. Von Soden[43] and E. Valgiglio,[44] both of whom have formulated extensive listings of synonymous lexemes that characterize the two Old Latin text forms.[45] These data, then, may be applied to the earliest recoverable text of 6 Ezra to determine whether its vocabulary seems closer to the earlier and more "primitive" African text type or to the later and more developed European.

The following words in the earliest recoverable text of 6 Ezra are more characteristic of the earlier African text type (the European alternative is given in parentheses). (In cases where variants between the French and Spanish recensions of 6 Ezra mirror African/European variations, this is also noted.)

Words Typical of the "African" (vs. "European") Text

absconsus (vs. *occultus*)   16:62 (bis)

adesse (vs. *instare*)   16:74

altus (vs. *excelsus*)   15:40

ardor (vs. *fervor*)   15:50; 16:68

bellum (vs. *proelium*)   16:18, 34

cogitare (vs. *sollicitus esse*)   16:63

cognoscere (vs. *scire*)   16:35, 54

dicere (vs. *aio*) passim (nineteen times)
   [*Aio* never occurs in 6 Ezra.]

discedere (vs. *se subtrahere*)   15:25

excludere (vs. *eicere*)   16:78

exire (vs. *egredi*)   15:23, 29, 30; 16:9

frumentum (vs. *triticum*)   15:42 [The
   Spanish text has *triticum*, the European
   equivalent.]

germinare (vs. *nasci*)   16:32

implere (vs. *plere*)   15:41

liberare (vs. *salvare*)   15:27; 16:17, 67, 74

locus (vs. *praedium*)   16:26

mandatum (vs. *praeceptum*)   15:24; 16:76

manducare (vs. *edere*)   15:58

metuere (vs. *timere*)   15:18

natio (vs. *gens*)   15:29

observare (vs. *custodire*)   15:24
   [The Spanish text has *custodire*,
   the European equivalent.]

occidere (vs. *mortificare*)   15:53

populus (vs. *plebs, turba*)   15:10

potare (vs. *potum dare*)   16:60

potestates (vs. *praeses*)   16:18

prodire (vs. *procedere*)   16:38, 39

quoniam (vs. *quia*)   15:2, 4, 13; 16:13,
   52, 53, 75 [In 16:53, the Spanish
   text has *quia*, the European
   equivalent.]

rapere (vs. *educere*)   16:46, 68

saeculum (vs. *mundus*)   15:14; 16:39

sermo (vs. *verbum*)   15:1

similare (vs. *adsimilare*)   16:51

spina (vs. *lumbus*)   16:32, 77

suspendi (vs. *circumdari*)   16:58

tegere (vs. *operire*)   16:77

transire (vs. *praecedere*)   15:43; 16:32, 77

turbari (vs. *certare*)   15:18, 32; 16:12

Thus there are thirty-six characteristically African words in the earliest recoverable text of 6 Ezra, with seventy-nine total occurrences of these words. In three cases, the Spanish recension converts the African word to a European equivalent.

The following words in the earliest recoverable text of 6 Ezra are typical of the "European" Bible versions (the African equivalent is given in parentheses):

Words Typical of the "European" (vs. "African") Text

accipere (vs. *adsumere*)   15:9

adsimilare (vs. *similare*)   15:47

advena (vs. *hospes*)   16:40

agricola (vs. *rusticus*)   16:24

ante (vs. *in conspectu*)   16:38
brevis (vs. *collectus*)   16:21
capere (vs. *circumvenire*)   16:42
comburere (vs. *exurere*)   16:53
comminari (vs. *corripere*)   16:11
convenire (vs. *colligere*)   15:44
copiosus (vs. *multus*)   15:35, 38; 16:18, 68
    [In 16:18, 68, the Spanish text has
    multus, the African equivalent.]
coram (vs. *in conspectu*)   16:53, 65, 66
desertum (vs. *solitudo*)   16:60
dimittere (vs. *remittere*)   16:13, 19
dolor (vs. *parturitio*)   16:38, 39
dux (vs. *ducator*)   16:75
educere (vs. *inponere*)   15:11
effundere (vs. *perfundere*)   15:22, 35, 44
eicere (vs. *expellere*)   16:72 [The Spanish
    text has *expellere*, the African equivalent.]
excelsus (vs. *altus*)   15:11
ferre (vs. *baiulare*)   15:29
gens (vs. *natio*)   15:15 (bis)
gloria (vs. *claritas*)   15:46, 47, 50, 60, 63;
    16:12, 13, 53, 66
haesitare (vs. *dubitare*)   16:75
irritum facere (vs. *reprobare*)   15:19
lacus (vs. *torcular*)   16:60
lugere (vs. *plangere*)   15:12, 13, 44; 16:33 (ter)
magis (vs. *vehementius*)   16:48
misereri (vs. *contristari*)   15:19
opus (vs. *factum*)   15:48; 16:51, 54, 64
    [In 16:51, 54, 64, the Spanish text has
    factum, the "African" equivalent.]
ornare (vs. *componere*)   15:47
pauper (vs. *egenus*)   15:51

plebs (vs. *populus*)   15:1;   16:40 [In
    both instances, the Spanish text has
    populus, the African equivalent.]
possessiones (vs. *divitiae*)   16:47
praeceptum (vs. *mandatum*)   16:76
propter (vs. *causa*)   15:6, 18, 19, 27, 47,
    59; 16:45, 64
quia (vs. *quoniam*)   15:15; 16:2, 46, 72
    [In 16:2, the Spanish text has *quoniam*,
    the African equivalent.]
semen (vs. *seminatio*)   15:13
species (vs. *deformatio*)   15:46, 54
spiritus (vs. *flatus*)   16:61
superare (vs. *supervincere*)   16:22
superbia (vs. *ambitio*)   15:18
suscitare (vs. *excitare*)   15:39
timere (vs. *metuere*)   15:3, 29; 16:10, 18,
    67, 70, 71, 75 [In 16:71, the Spanish
    text has *metuere*, the African
    equivalent.]
tollere (vs. *auferre*)   16:52
traducere (vs. *divulgare*)   16:64
tribulatio (vs. *pressura*)   15:19; 16:19, 67,
    74 [In 16:67, the Spanish text has
    pressura, the African equivalent.]
turba (vs. *populus*)   16:68 [The Spanish
    text has *populus*, the African
    equivalent.]
valde (vs. *nimis*)   15:34; 16:49
verbum (vs. *sermo*)   16:36, 40, 56, 58 [In
    16:36, 56, the Spanish text has *sermo*,
    the African equivalent.]
violare (vs. *profanare*)   15:39

Thus there are fifty-two characteristically European words in the text of 6 Ezra, with 104 total occurrences of these words. For nine words, representing 14 total occurrences, the Spanish text converts the European lexeme to an African equivalent.

Several striking features emerge from the data presented so far in this chapter. Perhaps most dramatic is the idiosyncracy of the lexical usage in 6 Ezra, that is, the large number of rare words that occur here. Many of these are Greek calques that presumably derive from the Greek *Vorlage*. Moreover, even many unusual Latin lexemes that are not loanwords can be accounted for by recourse to the Greek original, especially the compounds with *super-*, which render Greek forms with ὑπερ-. A second feature, implicit in the first, is the large number of Greek loanwords in the text. A third point is the close affinity between the vocabulary of 6 Ezra and early Christian lexical usage. This is indicated by the large number (twenty-five) of Christian neologisms in the text, and by the patterns of attestation of the individual lexemes discussed above. Fourth is the strong tendency of the vocabulary of 6 Ezra to conform more closely to "Old Latin" than to "Vulgate" lexical usage. Not only does 6 Ezra feature seventeen words that are *hapax legomena* in the Vulgate, but a number of the elements discussed above (viz., *desertio, ext(e)ritio, fornicaria, fructifero, invetero, redditio, romphea, subremaneo, superinvalesco,* and *supervalesco*), besides being rare in the Vulgate, show close connections with "Old Latin" biblical texts. Furthermore, several other lexemes not mentioned here have close ties to apocrypha that, not having been revised by Jerome, are present in the Vulgate in "Old Latin" text forms: namely, *captivo* 15:63; 16:46; *cogitatus* 16:54; and *odibilis* 15:48. Fifth, these data dramatically confirm the conclusions reached in chapter 4 regarding the priority of the French recension. Of the seventeen unusual lexemes discussed individually, all except three are represented at least once by different, more common synonyms in the Spanish version. This indicates that the Spanish reviser(s) of 6 Ezra strove consistently to bring the text into conformity with more conventional Latin lexical usage.

Indeed, as noted, a large proportion even of the Greek loanwords and Christian neologisms in the text are modified by the Spanish reviser(s). Furthermore, many of the lexemes that are *hapax legomena*, or at least are extremely rare, in the Vulgage are revised in the Spanish recension: namely, *cogitatus* 16:54 (Sp *cogitatio*); *redditio* 15:55 (Sp *in sinus tuos*); *suffrago* 15:36 (Sp *poples*); and *superfloresco* 16:21 (Sp *germino*). Thus, not only was the Spanish reviser sensitive to foreign words and neologisms in the text but he also may have been motivated by lexical sensibilities similar to those of Jerome and his school.

Sixth, the proportion between typically African and typically European lexemes is approximately equal in 6 Ezra, the measure standing slightly in favor of the European (by a proportion of 1.0 to .76). This fact in itself is not significant except to show that 6 Ezra was not translated in a setting where one or the other text type was dominant. Interestingly, roughly the same proportion obtains in the earliest recoverable text of 5 Ezra.[46]

Unfortunately, the data gathered here do not contribute significantly to our knowledge of the original language of 6 Ezra or of the time or place of its translation into Latin. It is true that the abundance of Greek loanwords does confirm the existence of the Greek *Vorlage*, but that *Vorlage* was already virtually assured by the Oxyrhynchus fragment. The absence of Semitic loanwords cannot, of course, prove that the book never had a Semitic form. The dates and provenances of the authors who use some of the idiosyncratic lexemes found in 6 Ezra are too scattered to be useful in determining the time or place of the Latin translation. Likewise, the almost equal mixture of typically African and European lexemes does not lend assistance in this area.

THE VOCABULARY OF THE SECONDARY (SPANISH) RECENSION OF 6 EZRA

The vocabulary that is unique to the Spanish recension of 6 Ezra, judged by us to be a secondary revision of the text, is not nearly as idiosyncratic as that of the French. Indeed, this is one of the main criteria for regarding the French recension as superior. Another factor influencing the relatively lesser lexical idiosyncracy of the Spanish text is that the pool of words that is unique to the Spanish is not nearly as large as that contained in the French as a whole, since many French words are retained by the Spanish reviser.

The sole Greek calque unique to Sp is *cata(e)gis* 15:40 (from καταιγίς). Likewise, there is only one Christian neologism unique to Sp: *insurrectio* 16:70 (for ἐπανάστασις). Several words unique to Sp are attested rarely or never in the Vulgate: *cata(e)gis* 15:40 (never); *circumcingo* 15:44; 16:39 (only in Sir 45:9); and *insurrectio* 16:70 (never).

Two lexemes unique to Spanish merit special comment:

cata(e)gis 15:40 [Fr *sidus*] (cf. καταιγίς). This word is attested in Latin in only five other authors: Seneca, *Naturales quaestiones* 5, 17, 5 (first c.); Apuleius, *De mundo* 12 (2nd c.); *Liber genealogus* 1 p. 164, 58 (5th c.); *Notae Tironianae* 110, 78 (date uncertain); and *Glossarius de Eusebius* 5, 423, 8 [in the *Corpus glossariorum Latinorum*] (date uncertain).

insurrectio 16:70 [Fr *exsurrectio*] (cf. ἐπανάστασις, ἐπίθεσις). This is attested in an OL citation of 2 Chr 25:27 (cod. Complutensis), and in four authors of the fourth to the sixth century: Ambrose, *De Abraham* 2, 3, 11 (4th c.); Cassius Felix, *De medicina* 43; 76 (5th c.); Origen, *In Matthaeum* 69.9, 13; 71.6 (5–6th c.); and Rusticus, *Synodicon* 1, 4 (6th c.).

The following words that are unique to the Spanish recension are shown, by comparison of African and European New Testament texts, to be characteristic of the African version (the European alternative is given in parentheses). (In cases where variants between the French and Spanish recensions echo African/European alternatives, this is also noted.)

Words Typical of the "African" (vs. "European") Text

bellum (vs. *proelium*) 16:40

discedere (vs. *se subtrahere*) 16:36

expellere (vs. *eicere*) 16:72 [The French text has *eicere*, the European equivalent.]

factum (vs. *opus*) 15:55; 16:51, 54, 64 [In 16:51, 54, 64, the French text has *opus*, the European equivalent.]

germinare (vs. *nasci*) 16:21

inponere (vs. *educere*) 16:61

locus (vs. *praedium*) 16:70

manducare (vs. *edere*) 16:46

metuere (vs. *timere*) 16:71 [The French text has *timere*, the European equivalent.]

multus (vs. *copiosus*) 15:35, 38; 16:18, 68 [In 16:18, 68, the French text has *copiosus*, the African equivalent.]

populus (vs. *plebs, turba*) 15:1; 16:40, 68 [In 15:1 and 16:40, the French text has *plebs*, one "European" equivalent; in 16:68, the French text has *turba*, the other European equivalent.]

pressura (vs. *tribulatio*) 16:67 [The French text has *tribulatio*, the European equivalent.]

quoniam (vs. *quia*) 15:26; 16:2 [In 16:2, the French text has *quia*, the European equivalent.]

sacrificium (vs. *idolothytum*) 16:68

saeculum (vs. *mundus*) 16:58

sermo (vs. *verbum*) 16:36, 56 [In both passages, the French text has *verbum*, the European equivalent.]

stipula (vs. *festuca*) 15:61; 16:6

turbari (vs. *certare*) 15:3; 16:68

Thus there are eighteen characteristically "African" words in the Spanish recension, with thirty total occurrences of these words. For nine words, representing fourteen total occurrences, the more original French text had the "European" lexical equivalent.

The following words unique to the Spanish recension are more typical of the European text type (African equivalents are placed in parentheses):

Words Typical of the "European" (vs. "African") Text

accipere (vs. *adsumere*)   15:59

advena (vs. *hospes*)   15:10

captivum ducere (vs. *praedari*)   15:63;
    16:46

comburere (vs. *exurere*)   15:62

custodire (vs. *observare*)   15:24 [The
    French text has *observare*, the African
    equivalent.]

dolor (vs. *parturitio*)   16:18

excelsus (vs. *altus*)   15:40

igitur (vs. *nempe*)   16:35

opus (vs. *factum*)   15:6

ornare (vs. *componere*)   16:47

propter (vs. *causa*)   15:26

quia (vs. *quoniam*)   15:47; 16:53 [In
    16:53, the French text has *quoniam*, the
    African equivalent.]

salvus esse (vs. *salvare*)   15:4

secundum (vs. *cata*)   15:55

timere (vs. *metuere*)   15:32

triticum (vs. *frumentum*)   15:42 [The
    French text has *frumentum*, the African
    equivalent.]

zelus (vs. *aemulatio*)   16:48

Thus there are seventeen characteristically European words in the Spanish recension, with nineteen total occurrences of these words. In three cases, the more original French text had the "African" lexical equivalent.

The main conclusions to be drawn from the data presented here are negative. The vocabulary unique to the Spanish recension is not unusual, nor is it typified by Greek loanwords. There are a few Christian neologisms and words that are not characteristic of the Vulgate, but in several cases these replace words in the French text that are even more exotic (e.g., Sp *circumcingo* for Fr *circumteneo* 16:39, and Sp *insurrectio* for Fr *exsurrectio* 16:70). Only *cata(e)gis* 15:40 [Fr *sidus*] is highly idiosyncratic, in addition to being rarer than its French counterpart.

In sum, then, study of the vocabulary unique to the Spanish recension tends to confirm the conclusion reached in chapter 4 and also in the first part of this chapter—that the Spanish recension is secondary.

One remarkable feature of the Spanish recension that is indicated by the above data, however, is that the reviser had a distinct tendency to prefer African to European lexemes. First, in the vocabulary that is unique to the Spanish text, African elements outnumber European by a margin of 30 to 19, a proportion of 1.0 to .63. In the French text, by contrast, the European elements had prevailed by a proportion of 1.0 to .76. Second, as indicated here, in only three of seventy-nine occurrences of African words in the French text (4 percent) does the Spanish reviser choose to alter the word to a European equivalent. On the other hand, the reviser changes 14 of 104 European elements (13 percent) to their African equivalent. Thus, of the 30 characteristically African elements that are unique to the Spanish recension, a full 14 (47 percent) stood in a European form in the more original French text and were altered by the reviser to the African form.

These data suggest that the Spanish reviser(s) not only had an affinity for African lexemes but also tended to substitute them for European counterparts. Apparently the reviser(s) worked in a context where the African text type was favored, or at least where its lexical proclivities were current. Unfortunately, however, since little definite is known about the circulation of this text type, and since the date of the Spanish revision is uncertain, one cannot be more specific than this. It seems odd that the reviser(s), who obviously worked later than the more original translation, would tend to replace its later, European text elements with earlier, African ones; yet this does seem to have occurred. The evidence for the priority of the French recension on other grounds is so overwhelming (see chapter 4), however, that this small factor cannot lead us to question that judgment.

The vocabulary that is typical of the Spanish recension seems to indicate that it, like the more original French text, originated in a context outside the influence of the Vulgate. Otherwise, the few unique or unusual lexemes in the Spanish text do not provide any striking insights into the time or place at which the recension was made.

SIX

The Religious Affiliation
of the Author

The contents and style of 6 Ezra—above all, its strong affinities with the literary tradition of the Hebrew Bible—make it almost certain that the book was written by a Jew or a Christian. These two categories, furthermore, need not be mutually exclusive: the lines of demarcation between Judaism and Christianity in the first centuries C.E. were often rather fluid. I will argue in this chapter that the author of 6 Ezra was a "Christian," in the commonly understood sense of the term. There do not seem to be sure grounds for assessing his attitude toward the Judaism of his day.

Assertion of Christian authorship rests on two main factors. One is that 6 Ezra seems clearly to know and imitate the Book of Revelation. The second lies in the book's alleged predictions about the persecutions that await its audience. The descriptions of these persecutions fit closely with what is known about pagan persecution of Christians in the second and third centuries (the apparent date of 6 Ezra), whereas little evidence exists for persecution of Jews during this period.

The literary parallels between 6 Ezra and Revelation occur mainly in 6 Ezra 15:43–16:1, with parallels in Rev 14:8; 16:19–19:3. The two documents describe in a strikingly similar way the characteristics and fate of a city called "Babylon." Both books attribute to Babylon certain negative features that they associate with femininity, namely, prostitution, fornication, and vanity. In 6 Ezra these features are extended also to "Asia," an imitator of Babylon "in all her [Babylon's] deeds and designs" (15:48), and a "consort in the beauty of Babylon and the glory of her person" (15:46). Both books attribute to Babylon (or Asia) the persecution and murder of God's elect, and both describe Babylon's violent, cataclysmic overthrow and the subsequent mourning of those around her. (Sixth Ezra goes on to describe the destruction of Asia by the same forces that devastated Babylon.)

Let us examine some of these parallels in more detail. First, as noted, 6 Ezra describes Asia as a "consort in the beauty of Babylon and the glory of her person" (15:46). In 15:54, Asia is enjoined bitterly to "make up the beauty of your face." The forces that will eventually destroy Asia will "remove the glory of your face" (15:63). In Revelation, by the same token, the "great whore" (17:1) is "clothed in purple and scarlet, and adorned with gold and jewels and pearls" (17:4; cf. 18:16). She had "glorified herself" (18:7); however, in her destruction, "all your dainties and your splendor are lost to you" (18:14).

The glorious, beauteous woman to whom Babylon or Asia is compared is, more-over, according to both books, a fornicator and a whore. In 6 Ezra, Asia has "made yourself like" Babylon by "adorn[ing] your daughters in fornication in order to please and glory in your lovers, who have always wanted you to fornicate" (15:47). "The wages of a whore are in your [Asia's] bosom" (15:55). Revelation, as noted earlier, describes Babylon as "the great whore" (17:1). "All the nations have drunk of the wine of the wrath of her fornication, and the kings of the earth have committed fornication with her" (18:3; cf. 17:2; 18:9). The woman sitting on the beast "hold[s] in her hand a golden cup full of abominations and the impurities of her fornication; and on her forehead was written a name . . . 'Babylon the great, mother of whores and of earth's abomina-tions'" (17:4–5; for the idea specifically of a "mother" of whores, see 6 Ezra 15:47). Babylon has "corrupted the earth with her fornication" (19:2).

In both 6 Ezra and Revelation, the "whore" is depicted also as infecting others through her corruption. In 6 Ezra, the pernicious Babylon has been imitated by Asia, who in turn has "adorned your daughters in fornication in order to please and glory in your lovers" (15:47). According to Revelation, in the same way, Babylon has "made all nations drink of the wine of the wrath of her fornication" (14:8; cf. 18:3). Again, "the inhabitants of the earth have become drunk" with "the wine of [Babylon's] for-nication" (17:2). "All nations were deceived by your sorcery" (18:23); Babylon has "corrupted the earth with her fornication" (19:2).

Another feature shared by the two books is that Babylon or Asia has killed God's elect. Furthermore, this act is connected in both sources with drunkenness. In 6 Ezra, God asks Asia, "Would I have acted so zealously against you . . . if you had not killed my elect, always exulting with clapping of hands and talking about their death when you were drunk?" (15:52–53). "Just as you will do to my elect, says the Lord, so God will do to you . . ." (15:56). According to Revelation, John "saw that the woman was drunk with the blood of the saints and the blood of the witnesses to Jesus" (17:6). "In [Babylon] was found the blood of prophets and of saints, and of all who have been slaughtered on earth" (18:24). God has "judged the great whore . . . he has avenged on her the blood of his servants" (19:2).

Furthermore, both books use similar language and imagery to describe the destruc-tion of Babylon or Asia. In both cases, the destruction is a punishment for the evil acts committed by the personified locale. Sixth Ezra states that "the glory of your [Asia's] strength will be dried up like a flower, when the heat that has been sent upon you rises up" (15:50). The destroyers will "despoil your honor, and remove the glory of your face" (15:63). According to Revelation, by the same token, the ten horns and the beast will "make [the whore] desolate and naked; they will devour her flesh and burn her up with fire" (17:16). "All your dainties and your splendor are lost to you" (18:14).

With special reference to the "harlot" imagery, 6 Ezra goes on to state that "you [Asia] will be weakened and made poor from the blows . . . so that it is impossible for you to receive powerful ones and lovers" (15:51). In Revelation, "the kings of the earth,

who committed fornication and lived in luxury with her, will weep and wail over her
... they will stand far off ... and say, 'Alas, alas, the great city, Babylon, the mighty
city! ...'" (18:9–10).

Furthermore, the two books use similar terminology to depict the actual, physical
destruction of Babylon. Sixth Ezra states that destructive storm clouds will "go steadily
across to Babylon, and will destroy her. They will ... pour out a storm and every wrath
upon her, and the dust [or: ashes] and smoke will rise up to the sky" (15:43–44). "In
passing they will strike the hateful city and destroy her" (15:60). According to Revelation, in the same way, "then a mighty angel took up a stone ... and threw it into
the sea, saying, 'With such violence Babylon the great city will be thrown down, and
will be found no more'" (18:21). "God remembered great Babylon and gave her the
wine-cup of the fury of his wrath" (16:19). "The kings of the earth ... see the smoke
of her burning" (18:9; cf. 18:18); "the smoke goes up from her forever and ever" (19:3;
cf. esp. 6 Ezra 15:44).

Again, with reference to Asia, 6 Ezra states that "[God] will unleash evils upon you—
want, poverty, and famine, and the sword, and pestilence—in order to destroy your
houses for injury and death" (15:49). "You will be destroyed by [the storm clouds]
like straw, and they will be fire to you. All of them will devour you ..., and all of your
forests ... they will consume with fire" (15:61–62). Revelation says, on the other hand,
with reference to Babylon, that "her plagues will come in a single day—pestilence and
mourning and famine—and she will be burned with fire" (18:8). "The kings of the
earth ... see the smoke of her burning" (18:9; cf. 18:18); "in one hour she has been
laid waste" (18:19; cf. 18:17).

Finally, both books record the reactions of surrounding witnesses to the destruction of Babylon. According to 6 Ezra, "[the storm clouds] will converge on her and
surround her ... and the dust [or: ashes] and smoke will rise up to the sky, and everyone around will mourn her" (15:44). Revelation states that "the kings of the earth ...
will weep and wail over her when they see the smoke of her burning; they will stand
far off ... and say, 'Alas, alas, the great city, Babylon, the mighty city! ...'" (18:9–10;
cf. 18:17–19). "The merchants of these wares ... will stand far off, in fear of her tor-
ment, weeping and mourning aloud" (18:15; cf. 18:11).

This remarkable series of parallels, all of which occur within relatively short text
spans in the two books, is too extensive and detailed to be coincidence. There is no
evidence, or reason to suppose, that the two books had a common source. Thus it
seems most probable that one book is dependent on the other. Whereas Revelation is
widely attested, and known to have been considered scripturally authoritative in some
Christian circles, at an early period,[1] the evidence for 6 Ezra is much later and more
sketchy. There is absolutely no historically defensible reason to suppose that 6 Ezra
was used as a source by the author of Revelation, whereas dependence in the other
direction is entirely plausible. We therefore conclude that the author of 6 Ezra knew
and used Revelation in composing his book.

Since Revelation is in its present form clearly a (Jewish-)Christian document, allusions to it by a Christian or Jewish-Christian author would be understandable,
whereas its use by a non-Christian Jewish author would not.

Further comment may be made about the *way* in which the author of 6 Ezra adapted
Revelation for his own purposes. It was noted previously that many of the points and

much of the language that describe Babylon in Revelation are taken up and applied to Asia in 6 Ezra. Furthermore, Revelation makes it a point that Babylon has corrupted all the *other* nations of the earth with its impurity. The author of 6 Ezra, on the other hand, evinces relatively little interest in "Babylon" itself; the book's main concern is with how *Asia* has imitated and thereby replicated the vices of Babylon.

The narrative in 6 Ezra 15:43–16:1 may, then, be viewed as an extension and *reapplication* of the polemical social, political, and cultural concerns that were originally directed against Rome in the Book of Revelation, to the entirely new context of Asia Minor.[2] The author of 6 Ezra reappropriates the negative symbolism and imagery of Revelation for his own purposes, namely, as invective against Asia Minor. This process, besides having important cultural and sociological ramifications, is also a telling indicator as to the provenance of 6 Ezra. It is difficult to imagine why an author living in any other area of the empire than Asia Minor would have exercised such elaborate literary measures to prove that this particular region was heir to the abominations previously practiced by Babylon/Rome.

It is also worth noting that, in reappropriating the language and imagery of Revelation, the author of 6 Ezra worked in a relatively fluid way: there are no actual quotations of Revelation, only allusions. This mode of intertextual reference through allusion rather than quotation is typical of eschatological and apocalyptic literature in general.

A second indicator that 6 Ezra is a Christian rather than a Jewish document lies in its descriptions of the impending persecution to be experienced by God's elect. I argue above (chapter 1, "Goals and Conclusions, *Sitz im Leben*") and below (chapter 7) that these descriptions refer not to abstract models or "ideal types" of persecution but to actual life situations that existed in the community of 6 Ezra or in its immediate social context. The persecution is described in detail in 6 Ezra 16:68–74:

> For behold, the burning (wrath) of a great crowd will be kindled over you, and they will seize certain of you, and will feed (them) what was killed for [or: to] idols. And those who consent to them will be held by them in derision and disgrace and will be trampled under foot.
>
> For there will be in (various) places [or: in Lociis/Locii/Lociae] and in neighboring cities a great [or: many an] insurrection against those who fear the Lord. For people pressed by their own evils will be like madmen, sparing no one, in order to pillage and destroy those who still fear the Lord. For they will destroy and pillage their property, and will drive them out of their house(s). Then the proving of my elect will become manifest, like gold that is proven by fire.
>
> Listen, my elect, says the Lord. Behold, (the) days of tribulation are here, and I will deliver you from them.

This description manifests a number of important points. First, the persecution is a pogrom, or mob action. There is no explicit reference to any official edict, measures, or trials (although such clearly could stand in the background).

The actions of the incensed mob take several forms. Those who "fear the Lord"[3] are pillaged, destroyed, and driven from their houses, and their property is destroyed and pillaged (16:71–72). Some people are seized and fed "what was killed for idols" (16:68). Those who accede to this measure are "held . . . in derision" by the mob (16:69).

Furthermore, the mob action seems to take place in a number of contiguous localities (16:70).[4]

In order to focus our investigation of this description, it will be necessary to consider in what parts of the empire, and in what periods, the events depicted here are most likely to have taken place. Our study of the provenance of 6 Ezra (chapter 1, "Goals and Conclusions, Provenance") indicated that Asia Minor and Egypt are the two most plausible locales for the book. Consideration of the date of 6 Ezra (chapter 7) suggests that the book was almost certainly written between 95 and 313 C.E.[5] The comments that follow assume these basic guidelines.

We begin by asking whether the actions described in 6 Ezra 16:68–74 could plausibly have been directed against Jews. Probably the most relevant historical phenomena to be taken into consideration here are the great Jewish revolts against the Romans in 66–70 (Israel), 115–117 (Egypt, Cyrenaica, Cyprus, and Mesopotamia), and 132–135 (Israel). These revolts provide the most dramatic instances of conflict between Jews and Gentiles in our period of interest and furnish primary historical axes around which persecutions such as those described in 6 Ezra could have revolved.

Prima facie, it seems unlikely that the types of mob actions described in 6 Ezra would have taken place in connection with or in the aftermath of one of these revolts. The Roman suppressions of these revolts were military actions, not affairs of religious practice or scruple. It seems unlikely that retaliatory measures meted out by the Romans, or even by angry mobs in various Greek cities, would have included such practices as forced eating of sacrificial meat. This is the sort of persecutory action that, since it involves an aspect of religious praxis, would be expected in a religious persecution in a relatively stable political situation, not in a state of war or its aftermath.

Furthermore, the Romans seem after the revolts generally to have adopted (or, perhaps more accurately, to have continued) relatively benign policies toward the conquered Jews, especially in the Diaspora, rather than pressing the sorts of measures indicated in 6 Ezra.[6] In the case of Asia Minor in particular, there is no evidence either for Jews of that region being involved in any of the revolts or for the revolts having influenced Roman policy toward Jews in the area.[7] Also there is no evidence for, or particular reason for, Greek citizens of cities affected by the revolts pursuing vindictive measures against the Jews in the aftermath of the warfare. As stated earlier, the practices apparently reflected in 6 Ezra are what one would expect to be directed against a persecuted minority religious community in a relatively stable social situation, not against an enemy that had just been decimated in a brutal war.

When we move to historical contexts outside the three revolts, again there is remarkably little evidence for pagan persecution of Jews in the regions and period on which our investigation focuses. In Asia Minor, the second and third centuries C.E. seem generally to have been a peaceful and prosperous period for Jews.[8] Epigraphic and archaeological evidence from various cities gives evidence of large, flourishing, wealthy, and influential Jewish communities.[9] There is literally no evidence during this period for the types of anti-Jewish activity (on the part mainly of local Greek citizens, not Romans) that Josephus attests for Asia Minor in, for example, the latter half of the first century B.C.E.[10] This had been a time of pronounced anti-Jewish sentiment among the Greeks in Asia Minor, with the Romans (who, on the whole, were pro-Jewish) being compelled to produce numerous edicts to reaffirm Jewish rights there.[11]

Even then, however, the main issues at stake had been (1) the rights of Jews to practice their "ancestral customs" (e.g., Sabbath observance) and (2) their right to send contributions to the temple in Jerusalem.[12] (The latter seems to have been an especially controverted issue.)[13] As important as these rights of freedom of religious action are within a Jewish context, they are far from the types of violent, persecutory activity to which 6 Ezra refers.[14] Indeed Josephus, to my knowledge, records no incidence of anti-Jewish pogroms in Asia Minor even during the turbulent first century B.C.E.; thus, they would be even less expected in the more stable second and third centuries C.E.

On the whole, the Jews of Asia Minor seem in the latter period to have been accorded a high level of tolerance, respect, and autonomy in the realms of political governance and religious practice. The evidence indicates that they took active social and political roles in their cities.[15] There are numerous indications that Judaism in Asia Minor was extremely attractive to Gentiles and that many of the latter adopted affiliations of some sort with Jewish communities or institutions.[16] Indeed, it is argued by some that the hostility formerly directed against the Jews by Greeks in various parts of Asia Minor in the first century B.C.E. now, in the first centuries C.E., begins to soften, and even to take on a new focus against the Christians.[17]

> Among the sentiments the pagans express [viz., toward the Jews] it is even possible to detect a new and more positive note. Little by little the old anti-Semitic spirit gives way, especially among the educated classes, to a distinct sympathy, nourished by a common hostility to the common enemy [viz., the Christians].[18]

P. W. van der Horst further maintains that the vitality of the Jewish communities in Aphrodisias and certain other Asia Minor cities actually inhibited the growth of Christianity in these locales.[19]

The situation regarding persecution of Jews in Asia Minor may well have changed as Christianity began to exert increasing influence in the upper levels of the imperial administration in the fourth century, but by this era we are moving outside the time range of 6 Ezra. Besides, there is no plausible reason why Christians would have enforced against Jews such measures as the forced eating of sacrificial meat.

In Egypt the situation is different, but no more suggestive of the likelihood of pagan persecution of Jews in the second or third centuries than in Asia. Egypt had, of course, been a major center of the Jewish revolt of 115–117 and was also the site of the infamous anti-Jewish riots in Alexandria during 38–41 C.E. In fact, in reading Philo's account of the latter events, one cannot help but be struck by the similarities between the actual situation in Alexandria and that envisioned in 6 Ezra. In *In Flaccum* 56–65, Philo describes Jews being driven from their homes and divested of their property, angry Greek mobs looting Jewish houses and workshops, and some Jews being put to death. "And then, being immediately seized by those who had excited the seditious multitude against them, they were treacherously put to death. . . . Their enemies . . . in their savage madness had become transformed into the nature of wild beasts . . ." (*In Flaccum* 65–66; cf. especially 6 Ezra 16:71). "And if [the people gathered as suspects] appeared to belong to our nation, then [the Greeks] . . . laid cruel commands on them, bringing them swine's flesh, and enjoining them to eat it . . ." (*In Flaccum*

96; cf. 6 Ezra 16:68). Indeed, Josephus informs us that anti-Jewish sentiment among the Greeks of Alexandria was "perpetual" (*J.W.* 2.487 [2.18.7]).

Philo furthermore worries that reports about the pagan destruction of synagogues in Alexandria could spread through the cities of the east, inciting persecution of Jews there as well (*In Flaccum* 45–47). In fact, in *Legatio* 371, he despairs of the latent anti-Jewish enmity that characterizes the empire at large:

> For if [the emperor] were to give us up to our enemies, what other city could enjoy tranquility? What city would there be in which the citizens would not attack the Jews living in it? What synagogue would be left uninjured? What state would not overturn every principle of justice in respect of those of their countrymen who arrayed themselves in opposition to the national laws and customs of the Jews?[20]

Josephus for his part reports that, besides the events under Flaccus, there was an eruption of Greek-Jewish violence in Alexandria during the reign of Nero, which had to be resolved by the city's governor Tiberius Julius Alexander (*J.W.* 2.490–93 [2.18.7]).

Despite the marked incidence of enmity and violence between Greeks and Jews in Alexandria in the first century C.E. and previously, however, there is little evidence for similar activity taking place in a later period. Smallwood argues that in Alexandria,

> racial tension seems to have subsided after the holocaust of 115–17 for well over a century at least. With the drastic reduction in the size of the Jewish community there, as elsewhere in Egypt, the Greeks had less reason for jealousy, suspicion and fear. . . .[21]

Indeed, the revolt of 115–117 seems to have decimated the Jewish population of Egypt. Papyrus evidence indicates a dramatic waning of the Jewish population there between 115 and 200 C.E.; during the third century, furthermore, there is practically no evidence for Judaism in Egypt.[22] Attestation begins to increase again after 300,[23] but by this time we are moving outside the time frame of 6 Ezra.

With reference specifically to the second and third centuries C.E., the most plausible time of composition of 6 Ezra, one would not expect the types of persecutory activity indicated in 6 Ezra 16:68–74 to have been leveled against a people that had recently been decimated in a war and whose population was declining almost to the point of nonexistence. Pagan persecution of Jews does not seem likely to have been a significant issue in Egypt during the second and third centuries C.E., and indeed we have no evidence for such persecution.

There is, it must be acknowledged, evidence for persecutory measures and violent actions being directed by pagans against Jews in areas other than Asia Minor and Egypt during the first several centuries C.E. One of the most noteworthy, described by Josephus in *J.W.* 7.43–62 (7.3.3–4), took place in 67 C.E. in Antioch. A certain Jew named Antiochus, whose father was "governor" of the Antiochene Jews, for some reason accused his father and other Jews of conspiring to set fire to the city. Antiochus, moreover, took the step of voluntarily sacrificing "in the manner of the Greeks," and persuaded the Antiochenes to compel other Jews to do the same, "because they would by that means discover who they were that had plotted against them, since they would not do so." When, some time later, a fire actually did break out in the city, the suspicions of the Antiochenes fastened upon the Jews: "all fell violently upon those that were accused; and this, like madmen, in a very furious rage . . ." (cf. 6 Ezra 16:71).

This incident, which reflects a high level of anti-Jewish sentiment in Antioch during the early years of the revolt of 66–70 in the land of Israel, is especially noteworthy in that it attests the use of the "sacrifice test" that was practiced against the Jews during the Maccabean revolt and that would later be used regularly by the Romans against the Christians (see the Trajan/Pliny correspondence, and further comments below). Although this incident is relevant to the question of pagan persecution of Jews in the Roman Empire, it falls outside both the time frame and the geographical scope of our investigation.[24]

WHEN WE CONSIDER the narrative of 6 Ezra 16:68–74 in light of the experiences of *Christians* in Asia Minor and Egypt during the second and third centuries, however, a rather different picture emerges. It should first be noted that Asia Minor and Egypt, besides being perhaps the two main centers of Christianity during the early and middle empire, were also the two main focal points of Christian persecution.[25] Persecution of Christians is, of course, widely attested in many areas of the empire during the first three centuries C.E. This, moreover, is not the place to enter the debate concerning the rationales or legal bases for these persecutions. The main points in this context are first that Christians were persecuted during the second and third centuries consistently and in many areas of the empire, especially Asia Minor and Egypt, and second that, in many cases, the recorded details of these persecutions fit remarkably well with the accounts of 6 Ezra.

It may be useful first to set a brief historical background for the discussion. The most significant and widely known instances of Roman persecution of Christians were the empirewide efforts mounted by Septimius Severus in 202–203, Decius in 249–251, Valerian in 257–260, and Diocletian and his colleagues and successors in 303–313. Each of these persecutions had its own rationale, each featured its own goals and measures for achieving those goals, and each was brought to an end by a decision, usually by a new emperor, to restore toleration. The main literary evidence for persecution of Christians in the first three centuries C.E. derives from these empirewide actions, particularly those under Decius and Diocletian.

Besides these major, imperially sanctioned efforts, there is also abundant evidence for scattered, local persecutions, sometimes of an ad hoc nature, in various times and places.[26] Whatever legal bases were perceived as obtaining for these persecutions, the practice of Christianity was commonly viewed as a capital offense, and local governors and authorities could decide to prosecute it at any time.[27] In many instances, pressure to do so came from the local populace, whose main concern was that the Christians were atheists who, especially by virtue of their increasing numbers, invoked the displeasure of the gods. One striking demonstration of this attitude is the fact that, in Asia Minor, local persecutions often followed directly upon natural disasters such as earthquakes.[28]

One main feature that characterized especially the smaller scale persecutions, but one that also obtained at times in the "official," empirewide efforts, is that of mob actions or pogroms. In such actions, angry bands of citizens took it into their own hands to force Christians from their residences, loot and destroy their property, and in some cases bring them to local authorities for trial. Often, especially in local incidents, such actions were ad hoc, not taking impetus specifically from official edicts or higher authorities. It is this type of impromptu mob violence that seems to be reflected in 6 Ezra 16:68–72:

For behold, the burning (wrath) of a great crowd will be kindled over you, and they will seize certain of you. . . . For there will be in (various) places and in neighboring cities a great insurrection against those who fear the Lord. For people pressed by their own evils will be like madmen, sparing no one, in order to pillage and destroy those who still fear the Lord. For they will destroy and pillage their property, and will drive them out of their house(s).

There is abundant evidence for precisely this kind of persecutory activity being directed against Christians in many parts of Asia Minor, Egypt, and other provinces during the second and third centuries. Eusebius, for example, paraphrases Justin's reference to a letter written to Hadrian by Serennius Granianus, a Roman proconsul of Asia, to the effect that "it was not just to put [Christians] to death, without accusation or trial, to appease popular clamor" (*Hist. eccl.* 4.8.6).

The *Martydom of Polycarp* attests mob participation in the proceedings against the bishop of Smyrna during the reign of Marcus Aurelius (ca. 155–156). "When [the fact that Polycarp had confessed Christianity] was said by the herald, the entire crowd . . . shouted with uncontrollable anger and a great cry, 'This one is . . . the destroyer of our gods'" (12:2). According to the same document, ". . . the crowds [were] in so great a hurry to gather wood and faggots from the workshops and the baths [for the burning of Polycarp]" (13:1).

Eusebius, writing of the period toward the end of the reign of Marcus Aurelius, states that "the persecution of us in some parts of the world was rekindled more violently by popular violence in the cities" (*Hist. eccl.* 5.1.1). Eusebius quotes Melito, writing in an apology to Marcus Aurelius, as follows:

The race of [our] religion [is] persecuted and driven about by new decrees throughout Asia. For shameless informers and lovers of other people's property have taken advantage of the decrees, and pillage us openly, harrying [us] night and day. . . . We beseech you . . . not to neglect us in this brigandage by a mob. (*Hist. eccl.* 4.26.5–6)

The account of the martyrs of Lyons and Vienne in France (177 C.E.) preserved in Eusebius's *Historia ecclesiastica* 5.1.3–63 states that these Christians

endured nobly all that was heaped upon them by the mob, howls and stripes, . . . at the hands of an infuriated populace against its supposed enemies. . . . Then they were dragged into the market-place by the tribune. . . . (*Hist. eccl.* 5.1.7)

The same account speaks of mob action in: 5.1.15 "all men turned like beasts against us . . . they then became furious and raged against us"; 5.1.17 "all the fury of the mob . . . was raised beyond measure"; 5.1.38 "[all the punishments] which the maddened public . . . were howling for and commanding"; 5.1.43 Attalus was "loudly called for by the crowd"; 5.1.50 "to please the mob the governor had given Attalus back to the beasts"; and 5.1.30–31:

the local authorities accompanied him [Pothinus, bishop of Lyons], and all the populace, uttering all kinds of howls at him. . . . Then he was dragged about without mercy, and suffered many blows; for those who were near ill-treated him with feet and hands and in every way. . . .

Further evidence of mob violence in the Lyons/Vienne persecution is preserved in *Hist. eccl.* 5.1.57–60.

In recording persecutions in Alexandria during the time of Origen, around 206, Eusebius says that "many a time the heathen multitude round about in its fury went near to stoning [Origen]" (*Hist. eccl.* 6.3.4). As one of Origen's associates was being led away, "the crowd tried to annoy her, and insult her with shameful words" (*Hist. eccl.* 6.5.3).

Tertullian, in *Ad Scapulam* 4.6–7, speaks of the emperor Septimius Severus (193–211) publicly saving Christians "from the hands of a raging populace."

With reference to the Decian persecution (249–251), Dionysius's letter to Fabius of Antioch concerning events in Alexandria states that outbursts of persecution actually preceded the imperial edict by a full year: "That prophet and creator of evils for this city, whoever he was, was beforehand in stirring and inciting the masses of the heathen against us, fanning anew the flame of their native superstition" (*Hist. eccl.* 6.41.1). Specific incidents of mob violence in Alexandria during this period are described in *Hist. eccl.* 6.41.3–8. Especially relevant to 6 Ezra is the following:

> Then with one accord they all rushed to the houses of the godly, and, falling each upon those . . . , they harried, spoiled and plundered them, appropriating the more valuable of their treasures." (*Hist. eccl.* 6.41.5; cf. 6 Ezra 16:70–72)

All of this occurred before the promulgation of the imperial edict. After the edict had been issued, "many others throughout the cities and villages [of Egypt] were torn in pieces by the heathen" (*Hist. eccl.* 6.42.1).

The *Passion of James and Marianus*, which records events in Cirta, Numidia (northern Africa), in 259, under Valerian, speaks of the persecution that raged "through the blind fury of the heathen and the action of the miltary officials" (2.2). "The fury of a bloodstained and blinded governor . . . was hunting out with bands of soldiers all the beloved of God" (2.4). James and Marian were arrested when "a furious bevy of centurions and a disorderly crowd . . . flocked to the country-house where [they] lived" (4.3). Finally, the *Martyrdom of Pionius*, documenting events in Smyrna during the Decian persecution, states that when Pionius and his companions refused to sacrifice, "the crowd mocked and beat them" (18.6). All of these descriptions attest to the fact that mob violence akin to that described in 6 Ezra 16:68–72 was commonplace in various contexts of persecution of Christians in the empire in the second and third centuries.

A second aspect of the persecution envisaged in 6 Ezra, perhaps even more significant for our purposes since it is so specific, is that some of those who are seized by the mob will be forced to eat "what was killed for idols" (16:68). This description has several potential ramifications. First, Jews, and many early Christian groups, observed a biblical prohibition against eating meat from which the blood had not been drained (cf. Lev 3:17; 17:10–14; Acts 15:29). Second, several sources attest that in persecutions during the Maccabean revolt, Jews had been forced by the Greeks to eat pork, also forbidden by the Torah (2 Macc 6:18; 7:1; 4 Macc 5:2, 6; 6:15). Third, many Jews and early Christians observed a general prohibition against eating meat that had been sacrificed to a pagan god, by reason of religious scruple (cf. Exod 34:15; 4 Macc 5:2; Acts 15:20, 29; 21:25; 1 Cor 8:1–13; 10:7, 14–22; Rev 2:14, 20; Gregory Thaumaturgus, *Canonical Epistle* 1). Finally, and probably having the greatest relevance in the present case, a common injunction in those imperial edicts that required sacrifice to the emperor and the gods of the Roman state was that some of the sacrificial meat be ingested by the sacrificer.[29] The exact rationale for this requirement is uncertain. It might have been intended to confirm the sincerity and thus strengthen the efficacy of the sacrificial act. Alternatively, it might have been directed specifically against Jews and Christians, with the thought that even those who might manage somehow to scruple or feign offering the sacrifice would nonetheless blanch at the necessity of eating it.

Whatever its motivation, the measure of forcing people to eat sacrificial meat that is attested in 6 Ezra 16:68 also has widespread attribution in records of Roman persecution of Christians, especially in the major, empirewide persecutions.

To my knowledge, the first time such a practice is attested in the context of a persecution of Christians is under Decius. First, each of the forty-one extant *libelli* from this persecution, all of which come from Egypt, exhibits a standard form, of which the ingestion of the sacrifice is a regular component.[30] J. R. Knipfing reconstructs a composite form of the relevant section of the *libelli* as follows:

> I have always and (all my life) without interruption sacrificed and poured libations and manifested piety toward the gods . . . , and now (again) in your presence in accordance with the edict, I have made sacrifice and poured a libation *and partaken of the sacred victims.* I request you to certify this below. . . . (emphasis mine)[31]

The provision of "partak[ing] of the sacred victims" (τῶν ἱερείων ἐγευσάμην) is attested in thirty-one of the forty-one *libelli*; the only ones that do not have it are fragmentary and lack the section in which it would have occurred. Thus, during the Decian persecution in Egypt, ingestion of the sacrificial animal was a standard part of the required sacrifice to the emperor and the gods of the Roman state.

The same practice is recorded during the Decian persecution in Asia Minor (Smyrna), in the *Martyrdom of Pionius*. This document first records Pionius symbolically placing chains on himself and two companions "lest any be given to suspect that they were being induced to eat forbidden foods" (2.4; cf. 6.3). The temple verger then arrives to "seek out the Christians and drag them off to offer sacrifice and to taste forbidden meats" (3.1). When sacrifice is demanded of Pionius and his associates, "[t]he public servant [assisting in the sacrifice] stood holding the sacrificed meat. He did not however dare to approach anyone, but simply ate it in the sight of everyone" (18.5). The Christians refuse to partake.

The practice of requiring Christians to eat sacrificial meat is also attested during the Great (Diocletianic) Persecution, this time in Palestine. Eusebius, in *The Martyrs of Palestine*, records measures enforced in 309–310 by Maximin Daia, Caesar of the eastern provinces and one of the most notorious Christian persecutors of the era:

> They were urging the curators of the cities . . . that all the men with their wives and children and slaves . . . should offer sacrifice and libations to demons and that they should compel them even to taste the sacrifices; and it was ordered that every article which was bought in the market was to be defiled by libations and sprinkling of the blood of the sacrifices. (*De mart. Pal.* 9.2, recension L)

> This [edict] ordered that . . . men with their wives and households . . . should offer sacrifice and libations and taste with scrupulous care the accursed sacrifices themselves;

that the articles for sale in the market-place should be defiled by the libations from the sacrifices, and that guards should be posted before the baths in order to defile with the abominable sacrifices those whose custom it was to cleanse themselves therein. (Ibid., recension S)[32]

We can probably assume that similar measures were put into force in other areas of the empire, including Asia Minor and Egypt, during the Great Persecution.

Although all of these examples come from the empirewide persecutions of Decius and Diocletian, there is no reason why the practice of compelling Christians to eat sacrifical meat could not also have been enforced in smaller-scale, local persecutions. When the practice became familiar as part of the standard "apparatus" of Christian persecution, it could, conceivably, have been applied in almost any context, including ad hoc situations of persecution.

Finally, a third aspect of the persecution envisaged in 6 Ezra is that "those who consent to [eat the meat] will be held by [the mob] in derision and disgrace and will be trampled under foot" (16:69).

This sociological phenomenon is also attested in several sources documenting Roman persecution of Christianity. Eusebius's account of the martyrs of Lyons and Vienne, for example, states that even those who had denied being Christians were nevertheless imprisoned, and "in addition were insulted by the heathen as ignoble and cowardly" (*Hist. eccl.* 5.1.35).

The same author's description of the Decian persecution in Alexandria states that certain Christians who held public positions "approached the impure and unholy sacrifices, some pale and trembling, as if they were . . . themselves the sacrifices and victims to the idols, so that the large crowd that stood around heaped mockery upon them, and it was evident that they were by nature cowards" (*Hist. eccl.* 6.41.11). Again during the Decian persecution, this time in Smyrna, the hero of the *Martyrdom of Pionius* is portrayed as stating that the pagan citizens of the city "laughed and rejoiced at those [Christians] who deserted, and considered as a joke the error of those who voluntarily offered sacrifice" (4.3). Pionius reproves his pagan audience by pointing out that even Homer "counsels that it is not a holy thing to gloat over those who are to die" (4.4).

In describing the persecutions under Diocletian in his own time, Eusebius speaks of "the pastors of the churches, some shamefully hiding themselves here and there, while others were ignominiously captured and made a mockery of by their enemies" (*Hist. eccl.* 8.2.1).

In each of these cases, pagan mockery was precipitated by the fact that certain Christians strove in some way to escape the full brunt of responsibility for their faith. The same phenomenon, specifically in the situation of consenting to eat sacrificial meat, is envisioned in the scenario of 6 Ezra 16:69.

It is evident from this survey not only that persecution of Christianity was widespread in Asia Minor and Egypt during the second and third centuries c.e. but also that many details of the persecutory activity envisaged in 6 Ezra are actually attested in a concrete and highly vivid fashion in literary descriptions of Roman persecution of Christians in the second and third centuries. Especially noteworthy are the correlations between the forced eating of sacrificial meat that was shown to have been required during the Decian and Diocletianic persecutions and the similar measures envisioned in 6 Ezra 16:68. On the other hand, there is extremely scant evidence for persecution of Jews in the same period in either Asia Minor or Egypt, and good reason to believe that such persecutions not only are absent from the literary records but also rarely, if ever, occurred.

This evidence confirms the supposition that 6 Ezra is a Christian rather than a Jewish document. Assuming that the details of the persecution described in 6 Ezra 16:68–74 have at least some relationship to what is being experienced, has been heard about, or is expected by the community within which the book emerged, it is relatively easy to imagine this as a Christian community but difficult to envisage it as a Jewish one. While it is still possible *in theory* that the persecution language in 6 Ezra 16:68–74 derives from a Jewish milieu, the combination of the observations made just above with the parallels between 6 Ezra and Revelation outlined in the first section of this chapter, in my view, effectively clinches the case for Christian authorship of 6 Ezra.

SEVEN

Date

Sixth Ezra was probably composed between 95 and 313 C.E. The *terminus post quem* is set by the apparent date of the Book of Revelation, which book 6 Ezra almost certainly knows.[1] Even if 6 Ezra's dependence on Revelation is not admitted, 6 Ezra cannot have been written before 70 C.E., since the book's allusions to "Babylon" (15:43, 46, 60; 16:1) almost certainly denote Rome,[2] and since the identification between Rome and Babylon in Jewish and Christian circles most likely postdated the Roman destruction of the Jerusalem temple.[3]

A *terminus ante quem* of 313 C.E. assumes that the many allusions in 6 Ezra to religious persecution (1) refer to persecution of Christians and (2) reflect a *Sitz im Leben* in which such persecution is still a live issue. The first point presumes that 6 Ezra is of Christian origin, a thesis argued in chapter 6. The second is, in my opinion, indicated by the length and tone of the passages in 6 Ezra that speak of persecution. 16:68–74 is especially telling:

> For behold, the burning (wrath) of a great crowd will be kindled over you, and they will seize certain of you, and will feed (them) what was killed for [or: to] idols. And those who consent to them will be held by them in derision and disgrace and will be trampled under foot.
>
> For there will be in (various) places [or: in Lociis/Locii/Lociae] and in neighboring cities a great [or: many an] insurrection against those who fear the Lord. For people pressed by their own evils will be like madmen, sparing no one, in order to pillage and destroy those who still fear the Lord. For they will destroy and pillage their property, and will drive them out of their house(s). Then the proving of my elect will become manifest, like gold that is proven by fire.
>
> Listen, my elect, says the Lord. Behold, (the) days of tribulation are here, and I will deliver you from them.

In my view, a description of such a vivid and urgent character probably does not derive from fixed literary *topoi* but reflects a situation in which persecution is an immediate issue, a real and present danger: it is either occurring in the present, has taken place in the near past, or is expected in the future. It is unlikely that such a situation obtained in any part of the empire after 313, when Licinius issued an edict restoring Christian property throughout the empire. This marked, for all intents and purposes, the end of imperial persecution of the church.[4]

The only compelling arguments for a dating of 6 Ezra that is more precise than this are those advanced by A. von Gutschmid in his 1860 article, "Die Apokalypse des Esra und ihre spätern Bearbeitungen."[5] The main outlines of von Gutschmid's thesis have been accepted by virtually every subsequent commentator except H. Weinel and H. Duensing, who argue that it is not possible to date 6 Ezra more precisely than in the general range of 120–300 C.E.[6] Due to the originality, convincing nature, and pervasive influence of von Gutschmid's arguments, it seems reasonable first to describe his position in detail, then to evaluate it. Von Gutschmid begins by assuming that 6 Ezra was written by a Christian in Egypt (p. 2), apparently because that is the first locale mentioned in the book (15:10–15). Strangely, however, he never explains or justifies this assumption as to provenance.[7]

Von Gutschmid claims to be able to date 6 Ezra precisely in 263 C.E. on the basis of a coincidence of three types of internal evidence: (1) a passage allegedly describing the military activities of Odaenathus of Palmyra against Shapur and the Persians (15:28–33); (2) material allegedly treating the movements of various Germanic tribes in the Roman Empire (15:34–63); and (3) information allegedly describing persecution of Christians in Egypt (16:68–73). Unfortunately, as von Gutschmid himself admits, the period in which he dates 6 Ezra is "one of the most obscure in world history" (p. 2). This judgment, moreover, which is based on a marked paucity of primary sources for the period, is as valid today as it was in von Gutschmid's time.[8]

Von Gutschmid claims that the key to dating 6 Ezra is the *visio horribilis* in 15:28–33, which describes a fearful battle in the "east" between "the nations of the Arabian dragons" and the "Carmonians." The description runs as follows:

> (28) Behold, a terrible vision and its appearance from the east, (29) and the nations of the Arabian serpents will come out in many chariots, and their hissing is borne over the earth from the day of (their) march, so that all who hear them will also be afraid and tremble. (30) The Carmonians, raging in wrath, will go out of the woods [MSS SMNE add: like wild boars] and (they) will arrive in great strength and will stand in battle with them, and (they) [the Carmonians] will destroy a portion of the land of the Assyrians with their teeth.
>
> (31) And after these things the serpent, remembering its origin, will become still stronger, and if they turn back [or: flee], agreeing in great strength to pursue them, (32) those [or: the former] [the Carmonians] also will be thrown into turmoil and will be silent because of their strength, and they will turn their feet in flight. (33) And from the territory of the Assyrians, an ambusher will lie in ambush for them [presumably the Carmonians], and will destroy one of them, and there will be fear and trembling in their army and turmoil in their kingdom.

In the opinion of von Gutschmid, this is a *vaticinatio ex eventu* that can refer to only one historical event: the battles between Odaenathus and Shapur on the eastern borders of the Roman Empire around 260–267 C.E.

> The Arabians have advanced in conquest beyond the borders of Arabia and come into the area of Assyria only once before the time of Islam, namely in the time of Palmyrene

rule. Odaenathus, the founder of [the Palmyrene kingdom], . . . was the one prince who allied with the Romans the Arabian nomadic tribes along the Euphrates; he himself was an Arab, and Arabs formed the main power of his rule. (p. 2)[9]

The "Carmonians," von Gutschmid goes on to claim, are actually (as the result of an orthographic slip) "Carmanians," a reference to the province of Carman (Kerman, Kirman), which lay on the Indian Ocean and Persian Gulf (in modern Iran), southeast of the main power center of the Sassanian Empire in Ctesiphon and eastern Mesopotamia.

> Carmania was at that time in the possession of the Sassanids, whose first conquest was this land; it belonged to them already before the complete overthrow of the Arsacids. Carmania thus can only be a designation of the Sassanids, after what was one of the original seats of their power. (pp. 10–11)[10]

Thus, von Gutschmid concludes that the conflict between "the nations of the Arabian dragons" and the "Carmonians" in 6 Ezra 15:28–33 refers specifically to the battles between Odaenathus of Palmyra, fighting on behalf of the Romans, and Shapur I, Persian king of the Sassanians, which took place in Syria and Mesopotamia between 260 and 267 C.E.[11]

Let us consider for a moment what (little) is known about these conflicts, independently of von Gutschmid's attempt to link them to 6 Ezra. Although the actual, reconstructable historical details of these engagements are not altogether clear, the following scenario seems roughly accurate. After capturing the Roman emperor Valerian in 260, Shapur and the Persians launched a major offensive into Roman territory, reaching central Asia Minor before turning back with substantial plunder. In the course of their return, however, they suffered several losses to the Romans, one of which was at the hands of Odaenathus of Palmyra, who struck them several times near Carrhae as they passed through Syria on their way to Ctesiphon. The Roman emperor Gallienus, grateful to Odaenathus, conferred on him numerous honors, and it was arranged that he would lead a Roman counteroffensive against the Persians.

In 262, Odaenathus, with a combined force of imperial Roman and native Syrian (Palmyrene) troops, first recaptured Carrhae and Nisibis, then defeated Shapur near the latter city, and finally pursued him all the way to his capital Ctesiphon, which he besieged for some time before withdrawing. Apparently Odaenathus marched on and besieged Ctesiphon again in 266/267; some sources state that he captured the city on this occasion.[12] He was then, however, called away to fight the Goths in Asia Minor, and was assassinated shortly thereafter, in either Emesa or Cappadocia.[13]

In attempting to correlate the details of 6 Ezra 15:28–33 with this historical scenario, von Gutschmid first acknowledges the possibility that the *eos* of 15:33 ("an ambusher will lie in ambush for *them*") represents the Arabs, that the "ambusher" is the murderer of Odaenathus, that the *unum ex illis* ("and destroy *one of them*"; 15:33) is Odaenathus himself, and that the "turmoil in their kingdom" (*inconstabilitio in regno illorum*; 15:33) represents the consequences of Odaenathus's assassination (the assassin himself was killed soon afterward).[14] He himself prefers, however, what he considers a more natural reading, also accepted by the present author, that the *eos* of 15:33 refers not to the Arabs but to the "Carmonians" mentioned in the previous verse. The *unum ex illis* would then, according to von Gutschmid, be a Persian general, the "ambusher" an enemy of Shapur and the Persians (presumably one of the troops of Odaenathus), and "the whole passage an allusion to an episode of the war between Shapur and Odaenathus not known to us in further detail" (p. 13).[15]

With regard to the geographical setting of the battle in "the land (territory) of the Assyrians" (15:30, 33), von Gutschmid argues that Assyria proper cannot be meant, since that was already Sassanid territory, and it would be illogical for the Persians ("Carmonians") to "destroy a portion of" their own territory (v. 30). He posits instead that "Assyria" refers to southwestern Mesopotamia, specifically the Hatra, a territory lying roughly between the Roman and Persian spheres of influence.[16] He correlates 15:29 ("the Arabian serpents will come out in many chariots") with the first major advance of Odaenathus in 262, 15:30 ("the Carmonians . . . will stand in battle with them") with the counteroffensive of the Persians that would have occurred when Odaenathus withdrew from Ctesiphon, and 15:31 ("the serpent . . . will become still stronger . . . agreeing in great strength to pursue them") with the beginning of the second major campaign of Odaenathus, which he dates in 263/64.

Von Gutschmid continues:

> Of the uprisings in the Persian army to which the seer alludes [15:33], we know, it is true, nothing; however, even without this, it would be necessary to surmise inner disturbances in the Persian regime for this period, since otherwise the weakness of the Sassanids in the last years of Shapur and under the following kings is inexplicable. (p. 15)

According to von Gutschmid, then, 15:28–33 cannot have been written before 263 C.E. since it refers to Odaenathus's second campaign. He assumes that the pericope reflects a fresh knowledge of the events, and therefore places it between 263 and 266 (p. 15).

Von Gutschmid proceeds to take the "firm ground" won by this interpretation as a key for interpreting what he takes to be other historical allusions in the book. The details of 15:5–27, he claims, describe the plight of Christians in Egypt during the early 260s; the "prophecy" "is, through numerous allusions, grounded in events that have visibly happened . . . since here everything bears a very concrete, vivid color" (p. 3). The political and social turmoil described in 15:15–19 alludes to several phenomena: the Gothic invasions of 253–270; the Roman-Persian wars of 256–266; internal conflict in Egypt between various aspirants to the imperium in 261–264 and 268–273; social disturbances due to political instability; and the persecution of Christians that continued in the wake of the empirewide movements initiated by Decius (249–251) and Valerian (257–260).

Moving to the visions in 15:34–45, von Gutschmid proposes that the vivid descriptions of storm clouds arising from various quarters, clashing with one another, and pouring out destruction on the earth represent different barbarian invasions, especially by the Goths, that plagued the empire in the third century. He identifies the "clouds from the east and from the north" in 15:34–37 as Gothic incursions into Asia Minor and Greece between 255 and 263 C.E. In the same period, he says, between 260 and 263, "another Germanic horde ravaged Illyrium and Italy and threatened even Rome" (p. 16); Gallienus managed to rescue the city in 263. It is in 15:37, he claims, that the *vaticinatio ex eventu* finally breaks off and the true present of the prophecy becomes apparent. Sixth Ezra was written, according to von Gutschmid, precisely at the time when a number of barbarian tribes had joined together in a venture directed against Italy itself, around 263 C.E. Thus,

> The prophet is writing at a time when Rome was so beset from all sides that everyone expected her speedy ruin. Rome was in such a situation, in fact, under the reign of Gallienus. (pp. 4–5)

> The situation now passed . . . to the picture of our prophet of the advances of all the enemy powers all around against Rome; [6 Ezra] must have been written when the danger of destruction was still hovering over Rome. (p. 17)

It may be useful here briefly to summarize what is known from independent sources about the incursions of barbarian tribes into various parts of the empire in the period with which von Gutschmid is concerned.[17] These incursions and the peoples who launched them are traditionally divided into two groups: movements of east Germanic and Asian tribes (the Goths, Marcomanni, Quadi, Sarmatae, Carpi, Borani, Heruli, Maeotidae, etc.) across the Danube and the Black Sea into the provinces of Pannonia, Moesia, Dacia, Greece, and Asia Minor; and movements of west Germanic peoples (the Alemanni, Juthungi, etc.) across the Rhine and into the provinces of Germany, Raetia, Gaul, and even into Italy itself.

Dexippus of Athens dates the beginnings of significant incursions of east Germanic tribes into the empire in 238 C.E.[18] Already by that time, however, the Goths were receiving subsidies from Rome, indicating that problems had certainly existed previously. In 237–238, in fact, Goths had plundered Greek cities on the Black Sea. The Goths continued to present major problems between 245 and 249, during the reign of Philip, and again under Decius, around 250, when Illyrium and the Balkans were devastated. Between 251 and 257, the Goths, together with certain other tribes (e.g., Borani and Carpi), apparently ran almost free in various parts of Asia Minor, Greece, and the Balkans, causing significant devastation; this seems to have been an especially difficult time for Rome. In 254, the Marcomanni and Quadi penetrated Pannonia, and the former moved into Italy, reaching as far as Ravenna.[19]

Apparently, the waves of Gothic invasion subsided somewhat between 257 and 267, at least in Asia Minor, due in part to the efforts of Gallienus and Odaenathus. In 267, however, near the end of Gallienus's reign, new and even more violent incursions began; Asia Minor was completely overrun by the Goths and Heruli, who then moved into Greece and the Balkans in 268. Alföldi calls this force "probably the strongest German army that trod the soil of the Empire in the third century" (*CAH* 12:149). Gallienus and Claudius had success against these forces in 268 and 269, as did Aurelian in 270–271. Although there was trouble from the Carpi on the Danube in 272 and 274 that was dealt with by Aurelian, and some movement by the Goths across the Black Sea into Asia Minor in 275–276, it seems that by the early 270s the most dangerous incursions had come to an end. Aurelian's withdrawal from Dacia in 271 also seems to have helped establish the Danube frontier against further invasions (*CAH* 12:153).

Other, less pressing problems with invading eastern tribes did occur before the accession of Constantine: in 282, Carus crushed an incursion across the Danube by Quadi and Sarmatae; in 286, Diocletian had to deal with Germanic forces in Pannonia and Moesia; in 289 and 292, the same emperor engaged the Sarmatae; and in 294–

297, Galerian fought the Goths and other tribes along the Danube. It is generally recognized, however, that the peace established by Diocletian ca. 298 C.E. virtually signaled the end of further disturbances from outside the empire for the period with which we are concerned as a time frame for 6 Ezra.

Considering now the situation in western Europe, the earliest significant movements of west Germanic tribes into the empire seem to have come in 253, when the Alemanni took advantage of a withdrawal of Roman forces to raid Gaul and move into Italy itself; according to Zosimus (1.37–38), even Rome was at risk. Between 254 and 259, Gallienus was constantly engaged in wars against Germanic tribes invading from the north. In 258, the Alemanni staged another major incursion into Italy; Gallienus moved south across the Alps and crushed them near Milan in 259. In 268, the same tribe advanced over the Brenner Pass as far as Lake Garda (between Milan and Verona, just north of the Po), where they were defeated by Claudius. In 269, when the imperial armies were drawn to the Balkans to deal with invasions of the Goths, the Alemanni and Juthungi invaded Italy again, plundering Milan and Placentia. They had nearly reached Rome when Aurelian returned from Pannonia to defeat them decisively, decimating the invaders. Eventually, Aurelian was able to quell the threat of barbarian invasion even as far north as Raetia. Aurelian also built new walls around Rome in 271 as a precaution against further attacks.

Probus had to deal with Germanic invasions into Gaul in 276, but by 278 this danger had ended. From the accession of Carus in 282, "[t]he moods of depression and uncertain hope are over. As the forces inimical to the Empire ebb, the forces of recovery flow in an ever increasing tide" (*CAH* 12:320). Although some further problems with the Alemanni were experienced under Diocletian in 286–289 in the upper Rhineland and under Constantius in 298 in Gaul, these were relatively isolated instances. In general the same precept obtains here as in the east: the peace established by Diocletian seems to have signaled the end of problems with the barbarians for some time.

In overview, then, the most serious threats of barbarian invasion in both east and west seem to have occurred between 251 and 271 C.E. Not surprisingly, this period coincides with a time of crisis in other aspects of the empire as well. (See further below—e.g., an empirewide plague in 252–267; major Persian offensives in 253–263; empirewide persecution of Christians in 249–260; and numerous internal rebellions and revolts, especially in 260–262. According to Alföldi, 260 was a year of "catastrophes unexampled in Roman history"; "the whole Empire was in confusion, and conditions moved rapidly toward anarchy" [*CAH* 12:182]. *CAH* labels the period between 249 and 270 C.E. as "The Crisis of the Empire" [xv]; likewise Potter speaks of the political "crisis" of the mid–third century [e.g., p. 18]. According to Olmstead ["The Mid–Third Century," 242], the mid–third century was a period "when the Roman Empire was in far more danger of complete collapse, in east as in west, than at the conventional date of 476.")

This period of significant barbarian activity in 251–271, then, fits well with the *general* time frame in which von Gutschmid wishes to date 6 Ezra. The apparent lull in activity in the east between 257 and 267 and in the west between 259 and 267, however, dramatically calls into question his contention that the period around 263 was one of special threat from barbarian forces. The period between 263 and

267 especially seems to have been one of relative quiet and stability in all parts of the empire.

Let us, then, return to von Gutschmid's survey of 6 Ezra. Moving to 15:46–63, he claims that this section, with its bitter invective against Asia Minor and its "kill[ing of God's] chosen people" (15:53), reflects first the persecutions of Decius (249–251) and Valerian (257–260), which would have been especially strong in that region. "The prophet seems to write under the fresh impression" of these persecutions (p. 18). Also, according to von Gutschmid, 15:60–63, which describes the devastation of Asia by forces or "storm-clouds" returning from "Babylon," reflects incursions of Goths into Asia Minor in 255–263.

Finally, in 6 Ezra 16, von Gutschmid again sees reflected persecution of Christians in Egypt, which would have begun under Valerian in 257 and continued under Macrianus and Aemilianus until 263/264,[20] when the tolerant Gallienus again gained the upper hand in Egypt. "The situation in which the seer writes best corresponds . . . to the beginnings of Aemilianus" (according to von Gutschmid, this is around 262–263) (p. 21).

Von Gutschmid concludes:

> When we review the historical allusions of the two final chapters [6 Ezra 15–16], they lead us without exception to the beginning of the 260s; an exact designation of the time arises from the fact that the renewal of war between Odaenathus and the Persians cannot have occurred before 263, and that the danger to Rome and Asia from the Goths ended in 263. To the year 263, so found, fits now also without exception the situation of the Egyptian Christians, which the seer presupposes. . . . He writes under the fresh impression of a violent persecution of Christians . . . and in the expectation of new persecutions. . . . This [viz., the beginning of the revolt of Aemilianus, and of his conflicts with the forces of Gallienus] is now, I think, the point in time when the last two chapters were composed. We know from the history of the bishop Dionysius that the mood which is expressed in them was one that prevailed at that time among Egyptian Christians. (pp. 22–23)

Von Gutschmid's arguments are, in many regards, quite compelling. Sixth Ezra does present the appearance of having been written at a time of significant crisis in the empire, and the larger time frame in which von Gutschmid places the book— namely, generally between 249 and 270, and specifically during the reign of Gallienus (253–268)—fits such a situation well. Indeed, there is no other period in the larger time frame in which 6 Ezra could plausibly have been written—namely, between 95 and 313 c.e.—when the empire stood in such a severe state of chaos and instability, and when the types of social situation that 6 Ezra *seems* to reflect were so regnant. The reign of Gallienus, as described earlier, witnessed in combination devastating sweeps of barbarian invasion from the north, serious instances of internal rebellion within the empire, and periods of severe persecution of Christianity, all of which seem to be reflected in some measure in 6 Ezra.

Perhaps the most convincing element in von Gutschmid's argument, however, and that which he himself recognizes to be its cornerstone, is his hypothesis about the historical background of the vision of conflict between "Arabs" and "Carmonians" in 15:28–33. Odaenathus and his troops could, in fact, be considered "Arabs,"[21] and they did fight against the army of an empire that included "Carmania," in a region that could plausibly be called "Assyria."[22] Von Gutschmid is also accurate in noting that at no time during the second or third century did any other force that could plausibly be called "Arabs" carry out activities remotely similar to what is described in 6 Ezra 15:28–33. Therefore, it seems reasonable to conclude that, *if 6 Ezra 15:28–33 is in fact intended to describe a concrete situation that can be located in history*, it probably refers to the battles between Odaenathus and Shapur between 262 and 267.

Presuming, in addition, that 6 Ezra was written during a period when persecution of Christians was still a live issue, as is implied at many points in the book, this would place its composition between 262 and 313 C.E. Indeed, as noted earlier, this is the range of dating accepted by most commentators.[23]

Is it possible, as von Gutschmid maintains, to narrow this range still further, even, as he does, fixing 6 Ezra precisely in the year 263? I think this may be somewhat more problematic. Let us consider some of the criteria used by von Gutschmid to establish this date.

One of the main assumptions underlying von Gutschmid's dating is that the period immediately preceding 263 was a time of significant threat from the Goths in Asia Minor and the west. This contention, however, seems debatable. Alföldi, for his part, comments as follows on the situation in the Balkans, Asia Minor, and Italy during the period 257–263:

In the Balkans:

> The usurpations of 260, in which the desperation of the Danube population expressed itself, only made a weak position [viz., of the empire] weaker still. But from 261 onwards there was some relief; the undisturbed activity of the mint of Siscia points to a re-organization beginning in 262. (*CAH* 12:147)

In Asia Minor:

> If in the next decade [viz., 257–267] no further expeditions [of the Goths] by sea followed, the credit must be assigned to the efforts of Gallienus; the reputation of Odaenathus may have contributed something to the result.
> . . . in the years following 260 the restlessness of the East Germans seems to some extent to have died down. . . . (*CAH* 12:148)

And in Italy:

> [The army of Gallienus] inflict[ed] a crushing defeat on the . . . Alemanni near Milan. The exact year is not certain, but it must have been either 258 or 259. . . . The blow thus sustained by the Alemanni certainly weakened them and drove them from Italy. . . . Gallienus did, indeed, refortify Vindonissa in 260, to bar the way southward to the Alemanni, and other forts were built at the same time. . . . [Alföldi's next mention of barbarian activity in the west occurs in 268.] (*CAH* 12:155)

These comments suggest that it may be difficult to find independent confirmation for the types of barbarian activity that von Gutschmid envisages having occurred in Asia Minor, or elsewhere, in the crucial (for him) years 260–263.

The question arises how von Gutschmid, writing in 1860, worked with the impression that the early years of the 260s were fraught with such danger from forces outside the empire. One answer lies in the uniformly negative notices given to Gallienus and his reign by the ancient Roman historical sources, specifically Eutropius,[24] Aurelius

Victor,[25] the *Historia Augusta*,[26] and an important lost source of all of these, the so-called *Kaisergeschichte*.[27]

Gallienus seems to have had an antisenatorial bent, which apparently caused his memory to be damned by the previously mentioned historical sources of the fourth and fifth centuries, most of which have a prosenatorial bias. According to H. W. Bird, one influential document that served as a source for all of these writings, the lost *Kaisergeschichte*, "made Gallienus responsible for all the evils of his times."[28] This can be inferred from the vicious slurs on the personal character and gubernatorial capacities of Gallienus that characterize each of these sources, and that especially dominate the *Historia Augusta*. Eutropius's evaluation of Gallienus is short and relatively innocuous: "For a long time [Gallienus] was peaceful and calm, but subsequently, after abandoning himself to every kind of debauchery, he relaxed the reins of government with cowardly inaction and despair" (*Brev.* 9.8). The *Historia Augusta* goes to far greater lengths. Associated with these generally negative notices in the ancient sources are claims that the entire reign of Gallienus was marked by an endless chain of internal revolts and invasions of outside barbarian tribes, events against which Gallienus was powerless and about which he was unconcerned.[29]

Gallienus's reputation has, in fact, been substantially refurbished by modern historians, who recognize the tendentious nature of the ancient sources.[30] According to one evaluation, the emperor "successfully preserved the essential unity of the Empire in a time of great danger."[31] Von Gutschmid, however, seems still to be working under the influence of the *Historia Augusta* and the other ancient sources, which, it can be shown, actually displaced into Gallienus's reign disastrous events and invasions that in fact occurred in other periods (e.g., under Gallienus's father, Valerian).[32] It is perhaps for this reason that von Gutschmid tends to overstate the dangers to the empire from outside forces in the early 260s. His claim especially that Rome itself was threatened by barbarian tribes in the years immediately preceding 263,[33] and was saved by Gallienus in 263, is not corroborated by independent historical analysis.

Another of the leading assumptions in von Gutschmid's dating of 6 Ezra is that the book was written in Egypt. This is important for him because it indicates a provenance where persecution of Christians might still have been in effect at a time when the conflicts between Odaenathus and Shapur could also have been known. That is, since Gallienus did not gain complete control in Egypt until 262/263, his edict of toleration of Christians, issued in 260, would not have been operative there until the later time. However, as noted previously, von Gutschmid never supports his claim of Egyptian provenance for 6 Ezra with any evidence or argumentation; in fact, this claim does not hold up under scrutiny. Although it is true that Egypt is the first locale mentioned in the book (15:7–19), the key material in this pericope clearly reflects a stylized literary topos drawn from the Exodus account; there is no indication that this should be taken to represent the actual geographical setting of the book. As argued in chapter 1, although it is possible that 6 Ezra was written in Egypt, Asia Minor seems more likely.

On the whole, von Gutschmid seems unduly concerned with locating an exact year and an exact place when all the alleged historical references in 6 Ezra could have coincided in a dramatic way. We have already, however, noted some problems in his attempt to fix that time and place. First, there is no evidence that barbarian activities in either the east or the west were especially strong in the years immediately preceding 263, and no evidence that Rome was under seige in that year. Second, there is no compelling reason to assume that 6 Ezra was written in Egypt.

Another, broader methodological problem inherent in von Gutschmid's approach is his insistence on locating a precise historical referent for every detail in 6 Ezra. Thus, for example, "nation rising up against nation" in 15:15 refers to the Gothico-Roman and Persio-Roman wars (p. 5); in 15:16, the "king" is Gallienus and the "nobles" are the Macriani, Quietus, and Aemilianus (pp. 5–6); the "hunger for bread" in 15:19 signifies the famine during the seige of Brucheion (p. 6); and in 15:20, the "kings . . . from the east" are the Sassanians while the "kings . . . from the south" are the Palmyrenes (p. 8). This highly analytical type of approach to apocalyptic/eschatological texts, which was in vogue at the time von Gutschmid wrote, has since been recognized as being overly mechanical and literalistic, and as not taking adequately into account the free-flowing, free-associative, metaphorical, and even mythopoetic character of eschatological prophecy. To attempt in every case to locate precise historical references and meanings in the imagery that characterizes such texts not only is misleading but also does injustice to the literary character of the documents.

Also, von Gutschmid seems overly insistent that 6 Ezra must have been written at a time and place when all the factors he has identified must be operative *at that very moment*. There is, however, no reason to assume that eschatological prophecy must work in this way. On the contrary, eschatological prophecy assumes, and its themes and motifs are normally drawn from, a long and wide-ranging literary and historical tradition. The prophecy of the book of Daniel, for example, makes extensive use of imagery taken from previous Israelite prophecy, and 4 Ezra and Revelation in turn draw explicitly on Daniel, as well as on other writings of the biblical prophetic tradition.

Thus, we cannot be assured that any of the dire phenomena that typify eschatological prophecy such as that found in 6 Ezra refer to events in the real world of the author at all. Civil unrest, plagues, famine, wars, and natural catastrophes are, so to speak, stock elements of such prophecy, widely known from the biblical prophets, the apocalypses, and works like the *Sibylline Oracles*. The frequent literary parallels that 6 Ezra displays to such earlier writings indicate that its author was self-consciously writing within a literary tradition of eschatological prophecy; much of the allusion and imagery in the book could have been drawn from this tradition without necessarily reflecting current events.[34]

There is another reason it cannot be assumed that the eschatological prophecy of 6 Ezra must refer to events contemporaneous with the author. Simple historical memory may account for actions that occurred in a relatively distant past being included in an eschatological scenario. Invasions of foreign forces, for example, must leave such a terrible and lasting impression on people's minds that the memory of such activities can be appealed to even decades after the events themselves. The same is certainly true of persecution, famine, plague, and other events that characterize eschatological prophecy such as that found in 6 Ezra.

Thus, the type of analytical and rigidly historicist approach adopted by von Gutschmid invariably runs the risk of forcing historical evidence into the mold set by the text. Such an approach also fails to take adequate account either of the free-flowing and literarily allusive quality of eschatological prophecy or of the fact that the envisioned eschatological scenario may be influenced by simple historical memory.

Moreover, even if we suppose that at least some of the narrative elements of 6 Ezra are relevant to the book's actual historical setting, we simply do not know enough about the details of social instability, threat of barbarian invasion, or persecution of Christians in individual parts of the empire during the late third century to make informed judgments about where or when such factors might have been germane. Persecution of Christians must have persisted to some degree in certain areas of the empire from the time of Decius all the way to the edict of tolerance of 313.[35] As noted earlier, incursions of barbarian forces continued in some areas of the empire until the end of the third century. Civil unrest and instability obtained to some degree during the whole of our period, and, in fact, was especially pronounced in some regions in the late third and early fourth century. It is unnecessary, and in many regards futile, to attempt to isolate specific times and areas where certain constellations of social factors could have given rise to a book like 6 Ezra.

In my opinion, then, it is hazardous to be overly specific in dating a book like 6 Ezra. For all of the reasons given here, I prefer a more flexible approach to the problem than that adopted by von Gutschmid. Operating for the moment under the supposition that the events described in 15:28–33 are in fact intended to describe a concrete historical situation, it seems most reasonable to allow the broader period of 262 to 313 as the probable time of composition of the book. It is true, moreover, that the social climate in the empire was far more tense and uncertain during the earlier part of this period, and this might push our dating toward the early end of the spectrum.

A further consideration is that, in 283, the emperor Carus marched against Persia, which had declined while Rome had staged a recovery in the 270s, and captured Ctesiphon; all of Mesopotamia now fell for some time under Roman control. It is possible that this conquest could have made the earlier conflicts between Odaenathus and Shapur seem anticlimactic and passé, in the eyes of eschatologically minded observers of world events like the author of 6 Ezra. Thus, if the vision in 15:28–33 does in fact narrate the conflict between Odaenathus and Shapur, it seems more likely to have been written before 283 than after.[36] This may be another factor indicating that 6 Ezra was written in the earlier rather than the later part of the period 262–313.

In the preceding analysis, I was careful to state that *if 6 Ezra 15:28–33 is in fact intended to describe a concrete situation that can be located in history*, it probably refers to the battles between Odaenathus and Shapur in 262 to 267. There is, however, another possibility. It is entirely conceivable that 15:28–33 is not a *vaticinatio ex eventu* at all but an imaginative scenario of eschatological prophecy arising from the mind of an author.

What are the grounds for this hypothesis? An initial consideration is the simple fact that the vision arises "from the east." For inhabitants of the Roman Empire, "the east" was in certain respects an unknown and mysterious land, sometimes associated with unseen and potential danger. In political terms, this view resulted from the fact that the empires that inhabited modern-day Iraq and Iran, first the Parthians/ Achmaenids and then the Sassanids, were notorious, potent, and long-standing enemies of the empire.

In Jewish and Christian ideology, which perspective would have been particularly relevant to the author of 6 Ezra, the idea of the "east" as a place of mystery and potential danger (sometimes with apocalyptic implications) is manifested most clearly first in various Hebrew biblical prophecies (especially the visions of Gog and Magog in Ezekiel 38–39) and then in early Jewish and Christian circles in the widespread notion that potent eschatological foes of the biblical peoples would arise from the east. The latter idea is evident, for example, in the widely attested myth of *Nero redivivus,* the idea that Nero was not dead but in hiding in the east (in Parthia), and would from there lead an eschatological invasion of the land of Israel.[37] The notion of hostile eschatological forces arriving from the east is especially evident in the Book of Revelation (cf. 16:12–16; 20:7–10). The idea of the east as a place of mystery, if not necessarily of danger, is also reflected in the popular legend of the ten lost tribes of Israel, which were thought to reside in some unknown area in the east; according to some sources, this group also would return to Israel at the eschaton.[38]

The main point here is that the vision "from the east" in 6 Ezra 15:28–33 could be intended to evoke deep-seated archetypal imagery in the minds of readers rather than necessarily referring to a real, identifiable geographical situation.

A second indication that 15:28–33 may be an imaginative eschatological construction is the reference in 15:29 to "Arabian dragons" whose "hissing is borne over the earth . . . so that all who hear them will also be afraid and tremble." This image recalls a passage in Herodotus's *History:*[39]

> Not far from the town of Buto, there is a place in Arabia to which I went to learn about the winged serpents. When I came thither, I saw innumerable bones and backbones of serpents; many heaps of backbones there were, great and small and smaller still. This place . . . is where a narrow mountain pass opens into a great plain, which is joined to the plain of Egypt. Winged serpents are said to fly at the beginning of spring, from Arabia, making for Egypt; but the ibis birds encounter the invaders in this pass and kill them. The Arabians say that the ibis is greatly honored by the Egyptians for this service, and the Egyptians give the same reason for honoring these birds.
>
> . . . The serpents are like water-snakes. Their wings are not feathered but most like the wings of a bat. (2.75–76)

This description indicates that "Arabian dragons" or "serpents" were one of a number of archetypal, mythological images that were available in antiquity to inhabitants of the Greco-Roman *oikoumene.* In the passage in Herodotus, moreover, this image has a distinctly threatening character, similar to its usage in 6 Ezra. It is, I would argue, possible that the author of 6 Ezra employed the image of "Arabian serpents" not because he had in mind any concrete historical referent but simply because the image was known in antiquity as part of a repertoire of sinister and threatening, and hence potentially eschatological, creatures. In fact, a situation could even be imagined where both of these possibilities obtain: the "Arabian[s]" could refer to the forces of Odaenathus, with the image of "dragons/serpents" being drawn from mythology. Also, in view of the reference by Herodotus, it should be noted that the "Arabian dragons" in 6 Ezra 15:29–33 could be construed as evidence for an Egyptian provenance of the book.

A third indication that 15:28–33 might be an imaginative eschatological construction rather than referring to a concrete historical situation lies in the designation of one of the two opposing parties as "Carmonians." As noted previously, Carmania (or: Carman, Kerman, Kirman) was part of the Sassanian Empire. In fact, it was the first province outside Persis to have been conquered (ca. 208 C.E.) by Ardashir, father of

Shapur and founder of the Sassanian Empire. Still, despite von Gutschmid's assertion that the association between the Sassanians and "Carmonians" was a natural one, it seems odd to me that the author of 6 Ezra would choose to designate the Sassanian Empire as "Carmonians/Carmanians." This would be rather like an apocalypse labeling the Romans as "Carthaginians" or "Gauls"! It is conceivable but not likely.

I would suggest that the *Carmonii* in 15:28–33 might have been chosen not because of their association with the Sassanids but because they represent a people living in one of the remote and exotic reaches of the known world. If 15:28–33 is a mythological rather than a historical conflict scenario, it would be natural to include in that scenario forces that would have a potentially mythological valence. I argued earlier that the "Arabian dragons" clearly have this valence. It is possible that "Carmanians," inhabitants of a remote district on the far side even of the distant Sassanian Empire itself, also possessed in the Greco-Roman popular imagination an aura of mystery that might account for their inclusion in a mythical eschatological scenario. Of course, as above, both possibilities could obtain: the "Carmanians" could have been chosen to represent the Sassanids in 15:28–33 precisely because of their potentially mythological associations. Indeed, this would be similar in some regards to the way in which "Babylon" represents Rome in 4 Ezra, 1 Peter, Revelation, 6 Ezra, *Sibylline Oracle* 5, and rabbinic literature.[40]

The idea that Carmania might have possessed a mysterious or mythological valence in the popular mind in the Greco-Roman world does have support in the literary evidence. Strabo,[41] Pliny,[42] Lucan,[43] Quintus Curtius,[44] and Arrian[45] all mention Carmania consistently in connection with India, Ceylon, Arabia, Bactria, Ethiopia, and other exotic lands. The entire tone of Pliny's description of Carmania in *Nat. Hist.* 6.96–99, 109, 149 is extraordinarily exotic: the Carmanians live in association with the "fish-eaters,"[46] the "Isle of the Sun," the "Couch of the Nymphs," the "turtle-eaters" (who are covered with shaggy hair and wear clothes made of fish skin), and thirty-foot-long sea serpents. Their land is a trove of exotic plants and minerals.[47] A description of the Carmanians by Strabo is especially revealing:

> They sacrifice an ass to Ares, the only god they worship, and they are a warlike people. No one marries before he has cut off the head of an enemy and brought it to the king; and the king stores the skull in the royal palace; and he then minces the tongue, mixes it with flour, tastes it himself, and gives it to the man who brought it to him, to be eaten by himself and his family; and that king is held in the highest repute to whom the most heads have been brought. (*Geog.* 15.2.14 [sect. 727])

These descriptions suggest that the "Carmonians" could have been used by the author of 6 Ezra deliberately to evoke an image of the exotic, mythical, and obscure rather than necessarily being intended with a fixed historical reference.[48]

Three further considerations call into question the theory that 6 Ezra 15:28–33 is a *vaticinatio ex eventu* of the Palmyrene-Persian wars. One is the remarkable fact that the use of the image of "dragons" or "serpents" for the "Arabian" as opposed to the "Carmonian" forces seems, according to one important source, to be reversed! *Sibylline Oracle* 13 represents a unique and invaluable source of evidence for the present study in that it not only depicts in detailed and allegorical fashion precisely the same sequence of historical events that is at issue in von Gutschmid's theory, but also can be shown to have been written shortly before the death of Odaenathus in 267.[49] It is, therefore, a detailed and strictly contemporary account.

It happens that *Sibylline Oracle* 13, in which animal imagery is actually the normal mode of representing historical figures, consistently depicts the *Sassanids* as "serpents":

> When two war-swift lordly men will rule the mighty Romans, one will show forth the number seventy [Valerian], while the other will be of the third number [Gallienus]; and the high-necked bull [probably Valerian] digging the earth with his hoofs and rousing the dust on his double horns will do much harm to the dark-hued serpent [Shapur and the Persians] cutting a furrow with its scales; then he [Valerian] will be destroyed. After him again another will come, a well-horned hungry stag in the mountains [Macrianus] desiring to feed his stomach with the venom-spitting beasts [Persians]; then will come the sun-sent, dreadful, fearful lion [Odaenathus], breathing much fire. With great and reckless courage he will destroy the well-horned swift stag [Macrianus] and the great, venom-spitting, fearsome beast[50] [Shapur and the Persians] discharging many shafts and the bow-footed goat [Callistus?]; fame will attend him; perfect, unblemished, and awesome, he will rule the Romans and the Persians will be feeble. [13.155–71; this is the end of *Sibylline Oracle* 13, except for the epilogue in ll. 172–73][51]

According to this contemporary account, then, the *Persians* are the "dark-hued serpent" and "venom-spitting beast(s)." In his commentary on this passage, D. Potter notes that

> the identification of the Persians with serpents may be particularly appropriate in view of their famous dragon banners and the play in lines 164 and 168 upon two meanings of ἰοβόλος: "arrow-shooting" (see also l. 120) and "venom-spitting."[52]

> As the lion is presented as coming from the sun, the use of the serpent for the Persian army may take on an added significance. A lion coming from on high might be seen as especially connected with Bel, and Bel was often represented as conquering a snake-footed demon: the imagery is particularly appropriate. The struggle between Bel and this demon recalled the cosmogonic myth in which the sky-god defeated the forces of Chaos, represented by a sea monster. . . . [Potter here gives several bibliographical references][53]

These considerations suggest that in the representation of empires as animals in the context of popular, allegedly prophetic historical reviews (for this phenomenon see especially Daniel 7 and the "Animal Apocalypse" of 1 Enoch 85–90),[54] the Persians could commonly be depicted as "serpents." This challenges the theory, implicit in von Gutschmid's interpretation of 15:28–33, that the "serpents" in this passage actually represent the Palmyrenes.[55]

A second reason why it may be unjustifiable to take 15:28–33 as a reference to the Palmyrene-Persian wars is simply that what (little) is known of the particulars of these wars does not cohere particularly well with the details of the account in 6 Ezra. The historical accounts for this period, which are notoriously weak,[56] tell us only that Odaenathus in 262 marched against the Persians, took Carrhae, defeated Shapur at Nisibis, and then pursued the Sassanid king to the capital at Cteisphon, which he besieged. Odaenathus, the sources continue, advanced again to Ctesiphon around 267 and beseiged the city a second time; some sources claim that he captured the city before being called back to Syria, where he was later murdered.[57]

Besides the potentially valid representation of the Palmyrenes as "Arabian serpents" and the Persians as "Carmonians," and the fact that the conflicts between Odaenathus and Shapur did take place in an area that could conceivably be called "Assyria," there is little else in 6 Ezra 15:28–33 that relates with certainty to what we know of the Palmyrene-Persian wars. The sources give no indication that Shapur enjoyed success in these conflicts, as would seem to be implied by the phrase "and (they [presumably the Persians]) will destroy a portion of the land of the Assyrians with their teeth" (15:30).[58] Furthermore, since "Assyria" here would most likely be reckoned as Persian territory,[59] it is difficult to explain, as von Gutschmid admits,[60] why the Persians would have "destroy[ed]" their own land. It is true that the renewed offensive of the "dragon" in 15:31 could reflect the second campaign of Odaenathus, but, since this offensive probably took place in 266/67 c.e., this would in turn invalidate von Gutschmid's thesis that 6 Ezra was written in 263, when Egyptian Christians were still under threat of persecution.[61]

Finally, there is the episode described in 15:33: "from the territory of the Assyrians an ambusher will lie in ambush for them, and destroy one of them, and there will be fear and trembling in their army and turmoil in their kingdom." The context here suggests that the "them" upon whom fear and trembling will come are the "Carmonians." Nothing is known, however, from historical sources of such an event having taken place with reference to either army. While this does not, of course, preclude the possibility that such an event could have occurred, it does not add support to the theory that 15:28–33 is a *vaticinatio ex eventu* of the Palmyrene-Persian wars, which is the issue under discussion. Also, the idea of an ambusher lying in wait for the Carmonians would make most sense as occurring in some territory other than their own; in 15:33, however, the ambusher comes from "Assyria," part of the Persian holdings.

A third factor that calls into question the theory that 15:28–33 describes the Palmyrene-Persian wars is the fact that one natural reading of this pericope is that the "Arabian dragons" are *also* called "Assyrians." This identification is suggested in 15:30, where, in response to the Arabian offensive, the Carmonians come out to confront them in battle, and proceed to "destroy a portion of the land of the Assyrians with their teeth." Again in 15:31–33, where (apparently) the "dragon" pursues the fleeing Carmonians, "from the territory of the Assyrians, an ambusher will lie in ambush for them [apparently the Carmonians]" (v. 33). Although it does seem odd that "Arabian dragons" would *also* be called "Assyrians," the readings suggested here are in all other respects the most natural understandings of these passages. If this is true, the identification of the "Arabian dragons/Assyrians" with the Palmyrenes becomes questionable, since "Assyria" would not normally be considered a part of Palmyrene territory. Furthermore, in *Sibylline Oracle* 13, "Assyrians" and "the land of the Assyrians" seem clearly to refer to the Persians and Persia.[62]

Several considerations, then, call into question the theory that 6 Ezra 15:28–33 is intended to describe the concrete historical situation of the Palmyrene-Persian wars. If this theory were to be abandoned, how would it affect our evaluation of the other potential historical indicators in 6 Ezra—namely, persecution of Christians, general social and political unrest, and incursions of barbarian forces—and the impact of such indicators on the book's dating?

Let us begin by considering the factor of persecution of Christians. While the first official, empirewide persecution was that under Decius in 249–251, there is abundant evidence that sporadic, local persecution of Christians occurred with some frequency before that time.[63] These, of course, began as early as the time of Nero.[64] Assuming that 6 Ezra does reflect a persecution that has occurred in the recent past or is expected in the near future, there is no reason the book could not have been written before 249, in an area where persecution was especially problematic at some given time. The Book of Revelation, which seems clearly to reflect a situation of intense persecution and martyrdom,[65] and which comes from the late first century, provides a useful source of comparison.

Sixth Ezra also seems to reflect a situation of social and political unrest. The empire was, in general, relatively stable during the second and early third centuries. There were, however, periods of crisis, such as the problems with barbarians under Marcus Aurelius and other emperors described below, and the civil wars under Septimius Severus; 6 Ezra could have been composed within such contexts. Indeed, to a minority community in the throes of persecution, even a sociopolitical situation that looked stable from the outside could be perceived as being in a desperate condition. Again, the Book of Revelation provides a useful frame of reference. Furthermore, as noted earlier, it is possible that the elements in 6 Ezra that point to a situation of social unrest do not reflect events in the real world at all but are literary topoi used in an eschatological context.

It is also possible, though by no means certain, that the social unrest envisioned in 6 Ezra, especially in 15:34–45, 60–63, includes the movement of foreign peoples (i.e., "barbarians") into the empire. Although, as pointed out, such incursions were most serious between 251 and 271, they began much earlier. The first signs of serious trouble seem to have occurred under Marcus Aurelius, when in 167 Cimbric forces, including Marcomanni, Quadi, Vandals, Charii, and Langobardi, swept into northern Italy and penetrated to Verona, where they were turned back by Marcus in 170. (This event could, in fact, have given rise to the imagined threat of an advance to Rome depicted in 6 Ezra 15:43–45.) The same emperor experienced further problems with barbarians in Germany, Dacia, and other areas; the situation in the north seems to have been especially severe (*CAH* 12:354).

During the early third century, the Carpi, from around Dacia, seem to have presented serious difficulties for the Romans. Maximinus (235–238) and the Gordians (238–244) also had problems with Germanic tribes. The incursions of the Goths and Carpi during the time of Philip the Arab (244–49), and certain other events of the 230s and 240s, are described here. Finally, it should again be kept in mind that the events described in 15:34–45 and 60–63 could potentially represent eschatological literary topoi that have little relation to actual historical circumstances.

These considerations suggest that, if 15:28–33 does *not* depict a historical event but rather is an imaginative eschatological scenario, 6 Ezra could conceivably have been written at almost any time between 95 and 313 c.e. One might argue that considerations of historical probability incline us toward a date in the late second or especially the third century, when general social and political instability, and the persecution of Christians, were most widespread. At the same time, however, we should remember that the Book of Revelation envisages the violent downfall of Rome at a time when, historically, such an event would have been almost inconceivable. This is to say that the potential influence of psychological, mythological, and eschatological topoi, as opposed to purely "historical" factors, upon the contents of eschatological prophecy must not be underestimated. Furthermore, Revelation suggests severe persecution of Christianity in a period when such persecution is otherwise virtually unknown. We must be careful not to assume that the actual setting of a book like 6 Ezra must necessarily cohere with our sketchy knowledge of early imperial history.

We are faced, then, with a dilemma. Is 6 Ezra 15:28–33 a *vaticinatio ex eventu* that refers to the Palmyrene-Persian wars, in which case 6 Ezra should be dated between 262 and 313? Or is it an imaginative construction of eschatological prophecy, in which case 6 Ezra could have been written at almost any time between 95 and 313?

In my opinion, it is impossible to resolve this dilemma conclusively. There is, however, one consideration that may lead us toward a tentative judgment. As von Gutschmid points out, the author of 6 Ezra is, in general, reluctant to speak in specifics. Besides the references to Egypt, Assyria, "Babylon," and Asia (the four-part schema that constitutes the organizing framework for chapter 15), the mention of Arabians and Carmonians in 15:28–33, and the possible place-name "Lociis/Locris" in 16:70, the book contains no references of a concrete nature. The fact that the scenario in 15:28–33 *is* so specific, that the combatants are identified by country of origin rather than simply by direction of the compass, and that the details of conflict between the two forces are drawn in such concrete terms, suggests the possibility that here the author has set aside his normal practice of prophesying about the future in general terms, and decided to include an actual scenario from the historical past. Thus, given the necessity of making a choice, I would judge that 6 Ezra 15:28–33 does in fact allude to the Palmyrene-Persian wars. The exact mechanics of how this literary scenario came into being, and how it came to be incorporated into 6 Ezra, are, of course, unknown.

In conclusion, 6 Ezra is almost certainly to be dated between 95 C.E., the approximate date of the Book of Revelation, which it knows, and 313 C.E., the end of persecution of Christians in the Roman Empire. Within these limits, the period between 262 and 313 (notably the earlier part of this period) seems especially likely since this was a time of substantial political instability and severe persecution of Christians, and since 15:28–33 may refer to events that took place in 262–267. The interpretation of 15:28–33 is, however, uncertain, and situations of political unrest and Christian persecution obtained at many times and in many places during the second and third centuries. Furthermore, the character of eschatological prophecy does not require that the social setting envisioned in the prophecy necessarily reflect actual historical events at all. Thus, in theory, 6 Ezra could have been written at almost any time within the broader limits suggested previously, namely, 95–313 C.E.

Notes

Chapter One

1. How 6 Ezra came to be associated with "Ezra" is discussed in what follows.

2. For example, the *Sibylline Oracles*, the Book of Revelation, certain parts of *1 Enoch*, *2 Enoch*, 4 Ezra, *2 Baruch*, and the *Assumption of Moses*, and various other Jewish and Christian "apocalypses."

3. The classic term for this genre is *Drohrede* (or *Drohwort*), "threat discourse." For discussion of the genre see G. M. Tucker, *Form Criticism of the Old Testament* (Philadelphia: Fortress, 1971) 59–65; idem, "Prophecy and the Prophetic Literature," *The Hebrew Bible and its Modern Interpreters* (ed. D. A. Knight and G. M. Tucker; Philadelphia: Fortress, 1985) 325–68, esp. pp. 335–37; idem, "Prophetic Speech," *Int* 32 (1978) 31–45, esp. pp. 38–44; C. Westermann, *Basic Forms of Prophetic Speech* (trans. H. C. White; Philadelphia: Westminster, 1967) passim, esp. pp. 129–89; J. H. Hayes, "The History of the Form-Critical Study of Prophecy," *Society of Biblical Literature 1973 Seminar Papers* (2 vols.; ed. G. MacRae; Cambridge: Society of Biblical Literature, 1973) 1.60–99, esp. pp. 67–69, 71–72, 79–80; R. R. Wilson, "Form-Critical Investigation of the Prophetic Literature: The Present Situation," *Society of Biblical Literature 1973 Seminar Papers*, 1.100–127, esp. pp. 102–3, 106–11, 118–20; W. E. March, "Prophecy," *Old Testament Form Criticism* (ed. J. H. Hayes; San Antonio: Trinity University Press, 1974) 141–77, esp. pp. 141–69; and K. Koch, *The Growth of the Biblical Tradition: The Form Critical Method* (trans. S. M. Cupitt; New York: Scribner, 1969).

4. Despite its categorization as such in the various editions of Hennecke-Schneemelcher's *New Testament Apocrypha*, 6 Ezra is not an "apocalypse" in the proper sense of the term, as defined in modern scholarship (see esp. J. J. Collins, ed., *Apocalypse: The Morphology of a Genre* [*Semeia* 14 (1979)]). A. Y. Collins, writing on "The Early Christian Apocalypses" in *Semeia* 14 (pp. 61–121), characterizes 6 Ezra as a "related work" or "related type" to the apocalypse (pp. 98–99, 105). In my view, the work should be labeled "eschatological prophecy."

5. See chapter 7 and, for a summary, chapter 1, "Date of Composition."

6. Further attention is given to this issue, including the question of whether 6 Ezra is Jewish or Christian, in chapter 6.

7. This literary unit is also sometimes known as "4 Ezra."

8. For a description of the book's origin, see esp. M. E. Stone, *Fourth Ezra* (Hermeneia; Minneapolis: Fortress, 1990) 9–11.

9. The citations are in Clement of Alexandria, *Stromateis* 1.22.149.3; 3.16.100.3; and *Apostolic Constitutions* 2.14.9; 8.7.6. Consult A.-M. Denis, *Fragmenta Pseudepigraphorum quae supersunt Graeca* (PVTG 3; Leiden: Brill, 1970) 130–32.

10. Viz., Latin, Syriac, Ethiopic, Georgian, two independent Arabic versions, Armenian, and Coptic.

11. Tertullian and Cyprian may also have known a Latin text of 4 Ezra; however, in neither case is this certain.

For quotations of 4 Ezra in Latin sources, see B. Violet, *Die Esra-Apokalypse* (Teil 1: Die Überlieferung; GCS 18; Leipzig: Hinrichs, 1910) 433–38; and A. F. J. Klijn, ed., *Der lateinische Text der Apokalypse des Esra* (TU 131; Berlin: Akademie, 1983) 93–97.

12. The *editio princeps* of the fragment is by A. S. Hunt, ed., *The Oxyrhynchus Papyri* (London: Egyptian Exploration Fund, 1910) 7.11–15.

13. Sixth Ezra does also survive in several other language versions that derive from a late form of the Latin: e.g., the "second" Armenian, "second" Georgian, Slavonic, and medieval Hebrew versions, and possibly a Rumanian version. See Stone, *Fourth Ezra*, 5. Since all these versions of 2 Esdras lack the "missing fragment" in 4 Ezra 7, they can be presumed to have been translated from a Latin manuscript that was dependent on MS S. See below on Bensly ("History of Scholarship") and chapter 2, "Primary Evidence: The Manuscripts," for further discussion.

14. Gildas, *De conquestu Britanniae* 60.1 (M. Winterbottom, ed. and trans., *Gildas: The Ruin of Britain and Other Works* [History from the Sources; London and Chichester: Phillimore, 1978] 48, 115).

15. See L. Brou and J. Vives, eds., *Antifonario visigotico mozarabe de la Catedral de León* (2 vols.; Monumenta Hispaniae Sacra, Serie Liturgica 5,1–2; Barcelona-Madrid: Viader, 1959) 1.126 (MS f. 91v, 16–92r, 2).

16. See C. Marbach, *Carmina scripturarum* (*scilicet antiphonas et responsoria ex sacro scripturae fonte in libros liturgicos sanctae ecclesiae Romanae derivata*) (Strasbourg: Le Roux, 1907; reprint ed., Hildesheim: Olms, 1963) 538.

17. For the Roman liturgy, this statement is based both on a general consensus of scholarly opinion and on the fact that manuscripts that are relevant to the rite survive from the seventh century. For the Hispanic liturgy, although the citation of 6 Ezra given earlier comes from a tenth-century León antiphonary, that antiphonary is judged by its editor, L. Brou, to represent the liturgical situation current in Spain in the fifth to the sixth century. See chapter 2, "The Mozarabic Liturgy," for documentation of and additional comments on this issue.

18. See, e.g., M. R. James, introduction to R. L. Bensly, *The Fourth Book of Ezra* (TextsS 3,2; Cambridge: Cambridge University Press, 1895) xlii–xliii. If Ambrose really did know 6 Ezra, this would place the book's translation into Latin before 375.

19. See the remarks in chapter 2, "Secondary Evidence." B. Violet and H. Gressmann (*Die Apokalypsen des Esra und des Baruch in deutscher Gestalt* [GCS 32; Leipzig: Hinrichs, 1924] lii n. 5) point out a parallel between Tertullian's *Adv. Marc.* 4.16.1 (*loquere in aures audientium*) and 6 Ezra 1:1 (*loquere in aures plebi meae*); this, however, is not strong enough to suggest literary dependency.

20. Hunt, *The Oxyrhynchus Papyri*, 7.11–15.

21. This is suggested by the fact that three of the eight significant manuscripts of 4/6 Ezra, MSS S, A, and C, ascribe different titles to the two works. It is improbable that the two books would have been textually conjoined at an early stage, and then separated and differently titled at a later stage in the manuscript tradition.

22. Fourth and Sixth Ezra are textually joined, with no indication of a separation between them, in MSS M, N, E, V, and L.

23. See Violet, *Die Esra-Apokalypse*, 428–32. Both manuscripts of the Arabic2 text, however, end at 14:44, somewhat before the Latin ending.

24. Unfortunately, the evidence of the Greek fragment of 6 Ezra, while tending to confirm the originally independent existence of the work, leaves it uncertain whether the book in Greek had a longer beginning than it has now in Latin. See Hunt, *The Oxyrhynchus Papyri*, 7.13, and the comments in chapter 2, "Description of the Significant Manuscripts, Oxyrhynchus Fragment 1010."

25. This manuscript also represents the earliest witness to a full Latin text of each of the three works—4, 5, and 6 Ezra.

26. *De excidio Britanniae* 60.1 (Winterbottom, *Gildas*, 115).

27. It is worth noting, however, that Gildas nowhere quotes 4 Ezra.

28. See T. A. Bergren, *Fifth Ezra: The Text, Origin and Early History* (SBLSCS 25; Atlanta: Scholars Press, 1990) chaps. 1 and 7.

29. See Bergren, *Fifth Ezra*, chap. 2.

30. This manuscript is a witness to the revised order of texts in 2 Esdras, in which 5 Ezra stands at the beginning of the corpus.

31. See Bergren, *Fifth Ezra*, 76–78, 140.

32. See Bergren, *Fifth Ezra*, chaps. 2–3.

33. Although the designations "French" and "Spanish" were probably originally intended to reflect the geographical distribution, or origin, of the recensions, subsequent discoveries concerning the history of the text have proven them inaccurate in this regard. Nevertheless, the names have become standard and are retained here for the sake of convenience.

34. As noted, the Latin texts of both 4 and 5 Ezra also survive in two distinct recensions, which divide along the lines of the same manuscripts as in 6 Ezra. Fourth Ezra seems to be similar to 6 Ezra in that the French recension is primary; in 5 Ezra, however, the Spanish text seems the more original. For a detailed study of the recensional situation in 5 Ezra, see Bergren, *Fifth Ezra*, chap. 4. The recensional situation in 4 Ezra has never been studied in depth; preliminary remarks are, however, provided by Violet in *Die Esra-Apokalypse*, pp. xxiv–xxvii. A detailed attempt to construct and evaluate the possible scenarios for the interrelationships between the French and Spanish recensions of 4, 5, and 6 Ezra is made by the present author in "Christian Influence on the Transmission History of 4, 5, and 6 Ezra," *The Jewish Apocalyptic Heritage in Early Christianity* (ed. J. C. VanderKam and W. Adler; CRINT 3, 4; Assen: Van Gorcum; Minneapolis, MN: Fortress, 1996) 102–27.

35. The citations of 6 Ezra that predate MS S, notably those by Gildas, all attest the more original, French recension of the book.

36. Gildas seems to have written his history of Britain in South Wales: see J. Morris's introduction to Winterbottom, *Gildas*, 3. The reference to Italy alludes to the apparent citation of 6 Ezra in the Roman liturgy (see n. 16) and to the fact that 4 and 5 Ezra are also cited in this liturgy.

37. The label "significant" manuscript or "significant" version is used here to denote a manuscript of 6 Ezra that can be proven not to derive exclusively from any other known manuscript.

Latin texts of 6 Ezra in fact appear in many more manuscripts than these eight; the reason the others are not considered "significant" for text-critical purposes is outlined in chapter 2, "Primary Evidence."

38. It should be noted, however, that there are partial or fragmentary Latin manuscripts of both 4 and 5 Ezra that do not include 6 Ezra. See D. de Bruyne, "Quelques nouveaux docu-

ments pour la critique textuelle de l'Apocalypse d'Esdras," *RBén* 32 (1920) 43–47; Violet and Gressmann, *Die Apokalypsen*, xvii–xxi; Klijn, *Der lateinische Text*, 13–17; Bergren, *Fifth Ezra*, 39, 43–44, 55–57; and idem, "Christian Influence." R. L. Bensly (*The Missing Fragment of the Fourth Book of Ezra* [Cambridge: Cambridge University Press, 1875] 42) lists several "non-significant" manuscripts that contain only 5 Ezra and one that has only 4 and 6 Ezra. There are also numerous liturgical manuscript witnesses that feature 4 Ezra 8:20–36 as a separate unit (see the previous references to Violet/Gressmann and Klijn).

39. For details see Bensly, *The Missing Fragment*, 6 (n. 1), 42, 82–85; Violet, *Die Esra-Apokalypse*, xxvii; de Bruyne, "Quelques nouveaux documents," 43 and n. 2; and idem, "Un manuscrit complet du 4ᵉ livre d'Esdras," *RBén* 24 (1907) 254–57, esp. pp. 256–57, which together list some sixty of these manuscripts. S. Berger (*Histoire de la Vulgate pendant les premiers siècles du Moyen Age* [Paris: Hachette, 1893; reprint ed., New York: B. Franklin, 1958] 94) counts eighty-four. For further information see Bergren, *Fifth Ezra*, 5 and nn. 16–18.

40. R. Weber, ed., "Liber Ezrae Quartus," *Biblia Sacra Iuxta Vulgatam Versionem* (2 vols.; Stuttgart: Deutsche Bibelgesellschaft, 1969; 3rd ed. 1983) 1931–74.

41. Witness, e.g., the fact that the two most recent original studies of 6 Ezra (A. von Gutschmid, "Die Apokalypse des Esra und ihre spätern Bearbeitungen" *ZWT* 3 [1860] 1–81; and James's introduction to Bensly, *The Fourth Book* [1895]) both date from the nineteenth century!

42. P. Sabatier, *Bibliorum sacrorum latinae versiones antiquae seu vetus Italica* (3 vols.; Rheims: Florentain, 1743; reprint ed., Munich: Ziffer, 1976). Second Esdras appears on 3.1069–84, 6 Ezra on 1082–84.

Sixth Ezra is also printed by J. A. Fabricius, *Codex pseudepigraphus Veteris Testamenti* (2nd ed.; 2 vols.; Hamburg: Felginer, 1722–41) 2:294–307; Fabricius, however, only reproduces the Clementine text.

43. F. Lücke, *Versuch einer vollständingen Einleitung in die Offenbarung des Johannes oder allgemeine Untersuchung über die apokalyptische Literatur überhaupt* (2nd ed.; 2 vols.; Bonn: Weber, 1852) 184–87, 212.

44. See n. 41. Sixth Ezra is treated on pp. 1–24.

45. *Das vierte Buch Esrae* (*"Esdra Propheta"*) (Handbuch der Einleitung in die Apokryphen 2; Tübingen: Fues, 1863). Comments pertinent to 6 Ezra appear on pp. 276–84.

46. Aurelian ruled from 270 to 275.

47. A. Hilgenfeld, *Messias Judaeorum* (Leipzig: Reisland, 1869). Comments, text, and notes on 6 Ezra are found on pp. xxx–xxxi, xlvi–xlix, 191–205, and 208–11.

The manuscripts are "St. Germain" (ninth century; Paris B.N. 11504–11505); "Turin" (thirteenth century; Turin C.16.5); and "Dresden" (fifteenth century; Bibliothecae regiae A. fol. 47).

48. Hilgenfeld believed that 5 and 6 Ezra were originally continuous but that 5 Ezra 2:48 offered a natural point at which to insert the earlier prophecies of 4 Ezra, resulting in the present "French" order of the book.

49. This dating is conditioned mainly by material found in 6 Ezra.

50. A.-M. Le Hir, "Une livre apocryphe—du 4ᵉ Livre d'Esdras," *Etudes bibliques* (2 vols.; Paris: Albanel, 1869) 1. 139–250, esp. pp. 240–50.

51. Le Hir's arguments for this position are discussed in chapter 1, "Goals and Conclusions, Original Language," of the present volume.

52. O. F. Fritzsche, ed., *Libri apocryphi Veteris Testamenti graece* (Leipzig: Brockhaus, 1871). The Latin text of 6 Ezra is found on pp. 645–53; comments on dating, etc., appear on p. xxx. Fritzsche published his text of 2 Esdras again in the same year in *Libri Veteris Testamenti pseudepigraphi selecti* (Leipzig: Brockhaus, 1871) 22–85.

53. See n. 38.

54. According to Berger (*Histoire de la Vulgate*, 103), this excision probably took place at St. Riquier.

55. This is not surprising, since Gildas's entire second quotation (of 6 Ezra 16:3–12) falls in that part of 6 Ezra in which MS S switches allegiance to the Spanish text. Even the first quotation (of 15:21–27), however, shows distinct affinities to A as opposed to S.

56. J. S. Wood, "The Missing Fragment of the Fourth Book of Esdras," *Journal of Philology* 7 (1877) 264–78.

57. This manuscript, now known as Complutensis 1, is presently in Madrid, Biblioteca de la Universidad Central, no. 31 (MS C in the present edition).

58. The manuscript is in Paris, Bibliothèque Mazarine (3–)4; MS M in the present edition. See S. Berger, "Un manuscrit complet du 4ᵉ livre d'Esdras," *RTP* 1885, 414–19.

59. See n. 39.

60. Now in Madrid, Biblioteca Nacional, vitr. 15-1; MS V in the present edition.

61. Legionensis 2: León, Real Colegiata de San Isidoro 1,3; MS L in the present edition.

62. R. L. Bensly, *The Fourth Book of Ezra*, with an introduction by M. R. James (TextsS 3,2; Cambridge: Cambridge University Press, 1895).

63. According to James's introduction to the edition, Bensly (through Berger) knew of both the Ávila and León manuscripts. The former he believed in 2 Esdras to be a copy of the Complutum manuscript, while circumstances prevented him from examining the latter.

64. H. Weinel, "Das sechste Buch Esra," *Neutestamentliche Apokryphen* (2nd ed.; ed. E. Hennecke; Tübingen: J. C. B. Mohr, 1924) 394–99.

65. H. Weinel, "Das sechste Buch Esra," *Handbuch zu den neutestamentlichen Apokryphen* (ed. E. Hennecke; Tübingen: J. C. B. Mohr, 1904) 336–39.

66. De Bruyne, "Un manuscrit complet." The manuscript is Brussels, Bibliothèque Royale, 1er Série (9107–)9109(–9110); MS N in the present edition.

67. Marbach, *Carmina scripturarum*, 538.

68. Violet, *Die Esra-Apokalypse* (GCS 18).

69. See Hunt, *The Oxyrhynchus Papyri*, 7.11–15.

70. "Original Language" of this chapter shows why it is most probable that the presently attested Latin version of 6 Ezra is based on a Greek text, as exemplified by the Oxyrhynchus fragment, and not vice versa.

71. De Bruyne, "Quelques nouveaux documents."

72. The manuscript is now in Luxembourg, Bibliothèque Nationale, 264; MS E in the present edition.

73. Violet and Gressmann, *Die Apokalypsen des Esra und des Baruch*.

74. P. Riessler, ed., *Altjüdisches Schrifttum ausserhalb der Bibel* (Augsburg: Filser, 1928) 318–27 (translation), 1286–87 (discussion).

75. W. O. E. Oesterley, *2 Esdras* (*The Ezra Apocalypse*) (Westminster Commentaries; London: Methuen, 1933).

76. Hunt pointed out that the evidence of the Oxyrhynchus Greek fragment of 6 Ezra indicates that 6 Ezra circulated in Greek independently of 4 Ezra. For further details, see the earlier discussion and chapter 2, "Description of the Significant Manuscripts."

77. Brou and Vives, *Antifonario visigotico mozarabe*.

78. See chapter 2, "The Mozarabic Liturgy," and chapter 3, "The Mozarabic Liturgy," of the present volume.

79. H. Duensing, "Das fünfte und sechste Buch Esra," *Neutestamentliche Apokryphen* (3rd ed.; 2 vols.; ed. E. Hennecke and W. Schneemelcher; Tübingen: Mohr [Paul Siebeck], 1959–64) 2.488–98. English translation by D. Hill, "The Fifth and Sixth Books of Ezra," *New Testa-*

ment Apocrypha (2 vols.; ed. E. Hennecke, W. Schneemelcher, and R. McL. Wilson; Philadelphia: Westminster, 1963–65) 2.689–703.

80. Weber, *Biblia Sacra*. "Liber Ezrae Quartus," pp. 1931–74.

81. As the editors note, "in chapters 15 and 16 [MSS] CME display a different recension of the text" (p. 1967).

82. J. M. Myers, *1 and 2 Esdras* (AB 42; Garden City, NY: Doubleday, 1974). Sixth Ezra is treated on pp. 330–54.

83. M. A. Knibb, "The Second Book of Esdras," *The First and Second Books of Esdras* (R. J. Coggins and M. A. Knibb; Cambridge Bible Commentary; Cambridge: Cambridge University Press, 1979). Sixth Ezra is discussed on pp. 283–305.

84. H. Duensing and A. de Santos Otero, "Das fünfte und sechste Buch Esra," *Neutestamentliche Apokryphen in deutscher Übersetzung* (ed. W. Schneemelcher; 5th ed.; 2 vols.; Tübingen: J. C. B. Mohr [Paul Siebeck], 1987–89) 2.581–90.

85. See Bergren, *Fifth Ezra*, 300 n. 24.

86. A.-M. Le Hir, in his article on 6 Ezra in *Etudes bibliques* (Article cinquième, 1.249–50, n. 1), discusses a number of features in the Latin text of 6 Ezra that he interprets as mistranslations of a Hebrew original. The first is in 15:20, where, however, he (with the majority text) mistakenly reads *ab oriente* for *a borea*; in the same verse he misinterprets *libano* as meaning "north." The second is in 15:29, where he advances an overly literal interpretation of a phrase that is intended figuratively, objecting that "the Arabs have never fought" in chariots (*in curribus multis*). The third is in 15:36, where he mistakenly accepts a corrupted reading of the second hand of MS S (*fimus*) rather than the true reading of *femur*. The fourth is in 15:53, where he unnecessarily insists that Latin *dicens* must rest on the Hebrew אמר, which can carry the connotation of "to sing hymns of joy"; the Latin term, however, makes perfectly good sense on its own. The fifth is in 16:70, where he again adopts the corrupted (majority) reading of the Clementine Vulgate, *erit locis locus*, rather than the true reading *erit lociis*.

Thus, in no case can Le Hir's hypothesis of corruption of the Latin text of 6 Ezra on the basis of a Hebrew *Vorlage* be proven convincing.

87. For discussion of this issue, see chapter 7.

88. With reference to Asia, I have in mind such expressions as "woe to you, miserable one" (15:47); "you have adorned your daughters in fornication" (15:47); "it is impossible for you to receive powerful ones and lovers" (15:51); and "the wages of a whore are in your bosom" (15:55).

89. See esp. PW 13, 1, cols. 1135–1288; 13, 2, cols. 1289–1363.

90. See Pliny, *Nat.* 4.7.12 (sec. 27).

91. See Pliny, *Nat.* 4.3.4 (sec. 7).

92. See esp. PW 13, 2, cols. 1289–1363.

93. PW 13, 1, col. 946.

94. PW 13, 1, col. 946. Although it seems logical to postulate that this epithet was connected with the naming of the piece of land in Ptolemaic Alexandria on which the royal palace and temple of Artemis were located, Pauly-Wissowa does not make this connection explicit.

95. Hunt, *The Oxyrhynchus Papyri*, 7.11.

96. For a summary of the evidence, see chapter 6 of the present volume. On the Diocletianic persecution, see *CAH* 12.671.

97. Note the parallel injunctions to "Write!," or parallel accounts of writing, in many pieces of Jewish and Christian literature: e.g., Exod 17:4; Deut 17:18; 27:3; 31:19; Isa 30:8; Jer 30:2; 51:60–64; Ezek 24:2; 43:10–12; Dan 7:1; 8:26; 12:4; 4 Ezra 12:36–38; 14:4–6, 20–48; Tob 12:20; 13:1; *1 Enoch* 68:1; 81:6; 82:1–3; 93:1–3; *2 Enoch* passim; *Jub.* 23:32; and *Par. Jer.* 6:19.

Chapter Two

1. See esp. Bensly, *The Missing Fragment*. See also B. M. Metzger, "The 'Lost' Section of 2 Esdras (= 4 Ezra)," *Historical and Literary Studies: Pagan, Jewish and Christian* (NTTS 8; Grand Rapids, MI: Eerdmans, 1968) 48–51; and Wood, "The Missing Fragment."

2. Several further important observations concerning this point are made by Berger in *Histoire de la Vulgate*, 94–95.

3. A. Hilgenfeld, in a review of Bensly-James, *The Fourth Book* (*ZWT* N.F. 4 [1896] 478–80), censured Bensly for having ignored certain manuscripts having the gap in chapter 7 that had been used by himself and Fritzsche in their editions of the Latin 4 Ezra. Hilgenfeld maintained that even manuscripts lacking the "missing fragment" could still have valuable readings due to possible influence on them by other manuscripts that were independent of S. Bensly took account of this possibility, and took great pains to disprove it, in *The Missing Fragment* (pp. 19–24).

4. Violet, *Die Esra-Apokalypse*, xxvi–xxvii.

5. L. Gry, however, in *Les dires prophétiques d'Esdras* (2 vols.; Paris: Geuthner, 1938), included in his edition of the Latin 4 Ezra several manuscripts that lack the missing section.

6. To my knowledge, this uncertainty in the cases of 5 and 6 Ezra has not previously been voiced. Most commentators on these books assume that the textual situation in the Latin 4 Ezra must also extend to them.

7. See, however, the points made by Berger, *Histoire de la Vulgate*, 95.

8. Violet, *Die Esra-Apokalypse*, xxvi–xxvii.

9. These editions, which include most notably the "Clementine Vulgate" and critical texts by Hilgenfeld and Fritzsche, are discussed, with bibliographic detail, in chapter 1.

10. See Bergren, *Fifth Ezra*, 42.

11. Unfortunately, the strength of this observation is diluted somewhat by the fact that S, in 5 Ezra, contains very few errors that could not be corrected by emendation. Perhaps the most significant is *sacramentum* (for *testamentum*) in 2:7, which is also found in the manuscripts containing the gap. There are several errors in S that appear in their correct form in the other manuscripts (e.g. *creavi* [other MSS] for *crevi* [S] [2:14]), but all these could have been emended.

12. Bensly, *The Missing Fragment*, 19–24 and passim. Bensly focused especially on errors, such as omissions, that were not liable to independent emendation.

13. Violet, *Die Esra-Apokalypse*, xv–xxvii; Violet and Gressmann, *Die Apokalypsen des Esra und des Baruch*, xiii–xvii.

14. Klijn, *Der lateinische Text*, 13–17.

15. Hunt, *The Oxyrhynchus Papyri*, 7.11–15.

16. Hunt's *editio princeps* (n. 15) is the only extended discussion of this fragment known to me.

17. Hunt points out that "if the figure 40 is the number of the leaf, this would point to the existence of some prefatory matter no longer represented in the Latin" (p. 13). It is tempting to connect this possibility with the theory, mentioned in chapter 1, that the beginning of the original form of 6 Ezra might have been modified, i.e., compressed, when it was joined to 4 Ezra in the Latin tradition (see chapter 1, "Transmission History").

18. L. Delisle, *Inventaire des manuscrits de Saint-Germain-des-Prés conservés a la bibliothèque impériale, sous les numéros 11504–14231 du fonds latin* (Paris: Durand, 1868) 1; Berger, *Histoire de la Vulgate*, 93–96, 157, 326–27, 332, 341, 344, 363–64, 407; Bensly, *The Missing Fragment*, passim; Bensly-James, *The Fourth Book*, xii-xiii; Violet, *Die Esra-Apokalypse*, xvi–xvii; Klijn, *Der lateinische Text*, 13–14.

19. The note places the manuscript in the eighth year of Louis le Débonnaire (see Bensly-James, *The Fourth Book*, xii).

20. Berger, *Histoire de la Vulgate*, 96. In other places Berger maintains that the manuscript came from Corbie (pp. 93, 407).

21. Berger, *Histoire de la Vulgate*, 93.

22. Violet, *Die Esra-Apokalypse*, xvii.

23. This section appears to be in a different hand because its writing is extremely compressed in comparison with the material around it. However, it is theoretically possible that it is the work of the same scribe, who wished for some reason to fit the section onto one page of the manuscript. First Esdr 3:1–5:3 makes up a distinct narrative unit that is discussed further in n. 39. It is also possible that f. 60v was originally left blank and was filled in later by the same or a different scribe.

24. This is not the end of 1 Esdras 2, which has thirty-one verses.

25. Folio 72 is skipped in the numeration of the manuscript.

26. B. Fischer, *Verzeichnis der Sigel für Handschriften und Kirchenschriftsteller* (Vetus Latina: Die Reste der altlateinische Bibel 1; Freiburg: Herder, 1949) 20. The "Vetus Latina" siglum for the manuscript is 150.

Although all of the "apocrypha" except Judith and Tobit survive in Latin, technically speaking, only in "Old Latin" (i.e., pre- or non-Hieronymian) texts, the present discussion will refer to the forms of these books normally found in the "Vulgate" as "Vulgate" texts and to other forms as "Old Latin" texts.

27. Berger, *Histoire de la Vulgate*, 332.

28. *Der lateinische Text*, 14.

29. This is the case except for 6 Ezra 15:59–16:31, which unexpectedly exhibits a Spanish text. For further discussion, see chapter 3, "Readings of the Latin Manuscripts, Sangermanensis."

30. E. Coyecque, *Catalogue général des manuscrits des bibliothèques publiques de France. Départements*, vol. 19: *Amiens* (Paris: Plon, 1893) 6–7; Berger, *Histoire de la Vulgate*, 103, 374; Bensly, *The Missing Fragment*, passim; Bensly-James, *The Fourth Book*, xiii–xiv; Violet, *Die Esra-Apokalypse*, xvii; Klijn, *Der lateinische Text*, 14.

31. James notes that the manuscript was probably moved to Amiens proper in 1791 (Bensly-James, *The Fourth Book*, xiii).

32. Klijn, *Der lateinische Text*, 14.

33. Wood, "The Missing Fragment," passim; Berger, *Histoire de la Vulgate*, 22–23, 62, 157, 331, 341–42, 343, 363, 392; Bensly-James, *The Fourth Book*, xiv; Violet, *Die Esra-Apokalypse*, xvii–xviii; Klijn, *Der lateinische Text*, 14–15.

Klijn lists "Complutensis 1" as "lost" and available only in a photographic copy at the Abbazia San Girolamo in Rome. Dr. A. Thibaut of the Abbazia San Girolamo has, however, informed me that this manuscript is still preserved in Madrid, and that it is "Complutensis 2" that was destroyed during the Spanish civil war.

34. B. Fischer, *Lateinische Bibelhandschriften im frühen Mittelalter* (AGLB 11; Freiburg: Herder, 1985) 72.

35. Fischer, *Verzeichnis der Sigel*, 18. The "Vetus Latina" siglum for this manuscript is 109.

36. Berger, *Histoire de la Vulgate*, 331.

37. Klijn, *Der lateinische Text*, 15.

38. A. Molinier, *Catalogue des manuscrits de la Bibliothèque Mazarine* (Paris: Plon, 1885) 1:2; Berger, "Un manuscrit complet"; idem, *Histoire de la Vulgate*, 94, 103, 334, 341, 345, 411; Bensly-James, *The Fourth Book*, xiv–xv; Violet, *Die Esra-Apokalypse*, xviii–xix; Klijn, *Der lateinische Text*, 14.

39. Since a copy of this manuscript was not available to me, I do not know whether 1 Esdr 3:1–5:3 appears here in the same hand as the other material. It is natural to attempt to account for the identical fragments of 1 Esdras (3:1–5:3) found here and in MS S. This section of 1 Esdras forms a distinct narrative unit, the story of the three young bodyguards in the court

of Darius, which, unlike most of the rest of 1 Esdras, is not paralleled in the "canonical" books of Ezra and Nehemiah. On the basis of the evidence of MSS S and M, it seems reasonable to conclude that this unit had an independent textual history in Latin. It does not seem necessary to posit a direct textual connection between MSS S and M in this regard.

40. Berger, *Histoire de la Vulgate*, 334. Presumably this manuscript also contains the NT Gospels, although Berger does not list them. They probably stand either before or after Acts.

41. Klijn, *Der lateinische Text*, 14.

42. J. van den Gheyn, *Catalogue des manuscrits de la Bibliothèque Royale de Belgique*, vol. 1: *Ecriture sainte et Liturgie* (Brussels: Lamertin, 1901) 1–2; de Bruyne, "Un manuscrit complet"; Violet, *Die Esra-Apokalypse*, xix; Klijn, *Der lateinische Text*, 14.

43. Van den Gheyn, *Catalogue des manuscrits*, 1. It seems likely that the label "1 Esdras" in this list is intended to include the canonical Ezra-Nehemiah.

44. De Bruyne, "Quelques nouveaux documents"; Violet and Gressmann, *Die Apokalypsen des Esra und des Baruch*, xiii–xvii; Klijn, *Der lateinische Text*, 14.

45. De Bruyne, "Quelques nouveaux documents," 43.

46. Berger, *Histoire de la Vulgate*, 23–24, 142–43, 332, 341, 345, 392; Bensly-James, *The Fourth Book*, xv; Violet, *Die Esra-Apokalypse*, xx–xxi; M. de la Torre and P. Longás, *Catálogo de Códices Latinos de la Biblioteca Nacional*, vol. 1: *Bíblicos* (Madrid: Biblioteca Nacional, 1935) 31–39; Klijn, *Der lateinische Text*, 15.

47. According to de Bruyne ("Quelques nouveaux documents," 47), in the original form of the manuscript, 2 Esdras was added to the end of the manuscript, after the NT, in a second hand.

48. Berger, *Histoire de la Vulgate*, 332. The order of the books in the manuscript's original form, aside from what is given above, is not known to me.

49. Berger, *Histoire de la Vulgate*, 21, 334, 341, 385; Bensly-James, *The Fourth Book*, xv–xx; Violet, *Die Esra-Apokalypse*, xxi–xxiv; Klijn, *Der lateinische Text*, 15.

50. Violet, *Die Esra-Apokalypse*, xxi–xxiv.

51. E.g., Fischer, *Verzeichnis der Sigel*, 17; idem, *Lateinische Bibelhandschriften*, 73; Klijn, *Der lateinische Text*, 15; J. Williams, "A Model for the León Bibles" (*Madrider Mitteilungen des Deutschen Archäologischen Instituts Madrid* 8 [1967] 281–86) passim; and idem, "A Contribution to the History of the Castilian Monastery of Valeranica and the Scribe Florentius" (*Madrider Mitteilungen des Deutschen Archäologischen Instituts Madrid* 11 [1970] 231–48) 236.

52. Berger, *Histoire de la Vulgate*, 21; Williams, "Contribution," 236; Fischer, *Lateinische Bibelhandschriften*, 73.

53. For this view, see Berger, *Histoire de la Vulgate*, 21; Fischer, *Verzeichnis der Sigel*, 17; idem, *Lateinische Bibelhandschriften*, 73; and P. Galindo, "La 'biblia de León' del 960" (*Gesammelte Aufsätze zur Kulturgeschichte Spaniens* 16 [1960] 37–76) 75 (*apud* Williams, "Model," 281 n. 4).

54. Williams, "Model."

55. Williams, "Model," 283. A set of four handsome illuminated plates of Legionensis 1 of 960 is reproduced in N. Fernández Marcos, *Scribes and Translators: Septuagint and Old Latin in the Books of Kings* (VTSup 54; Leiden: Brill, 1994) fig. 2, a–d.

56. Both Florentius's Bible of 943 and Codex Gothicus Legionensis of 960 were written at the Castilian monastery/scriptorium of Valeranica, where Florentius was the leading scribe. The 960 Bible is a skillful replica of the 943 Bible and was copied by Florentius's student Sanctius. Williams, in "A Contribution to the History of the Castilian Monastery of Valeranica and the Scribe Florentius" (n. 51), attempts to reconstruct the history of Florentius and the monastery of Valeranica. See also the same author's *Frühe spanische Buchmalerei* (Munich: Prestel, 1977).

57. The possibility that Legionensis 2 was a copy of Florentius's Bible of 943 rather than of Legionensis 1 is now acknowledged in the new edition of B. Fischer's essay "Bibelausgaben

des frühen Mittelalters," edited by H. J. Frede (Fischer, *Lateinische Bibelhandschriften*, 73 n. 85b).

58. If the extremely idiosyncratic version of 4 Ezra in the Bible of 1162 was in fact copied from the Bible of 943, it is worthwhile briefly to consider the history of the 943 manuscript. Williams judges its model to have been "a peninsular manuscript of the early Christian period," thus "a venerable relic" ("Contribution," 236).

Although Williams's overall thesis about the relationships between these three Bibles is carefully argued and seems generally convincing, there is one obvious question that he has not addressed. His argument is based primarily on the *differences* between the Bibles of 960 and 1162. However, precisely the same question can now be raised regarding the presumed differences between the Bibles of 943 and 960: whence did these differences arise?

59. Violet, *Die Esra-Apokalypse*, xxii n. 1.

60. Violet, *Die Esra-Apokalypse*, 439; Klijn, *Der lateinische Text*, 97–98.

61. For a description and bibliography of the *Inventiones Nominum*, and a discussion of the parallels between it and the Legionensis 2 preface, see Bergren, *Fifth Ezra*, 76–78, 140.

62. The epitome for 4/6 Ezra is printed by Violet in *Die Esra-Apokalypse*, 439–42, and by Klijn in *Der lateinische Text*, 98–100.

63. Bergren, *Fifth Ezra*, Appendix 6, pp. 413–14.

64. Fischer, *Verzeichnis der Sigel*, 17. The "Vetus Latina" siglum for Legionensis 1 is 91; Legionensis 2 is 92. In fact, it was largely the differences between the glosses in the two Bibles that led Williams to conclude that Legionensis 2 was not dependent on Legionensis 1.

65. Berger, *Histoire de la Vulgate*, 334.

66. The text of 5 Ezra, however, shows some interesting connections with the French recension; see Bergren, *Fifth Ezra*, 112–13.

67. The same hesitancy is evident in the deliberations of the Council of Trent, which in 1546 placed 1 and 2 Esdras and the Prayer of Manasseh in an "appendix" at the end of the Vulgate; see chapter 1, "Transmission History."

68. E.g., James's introduction to Bensly, *The Fourth Book*, xlii.

69. Several Old Latin forms of Isa 40:22 approximate Ambrose's citation. Jerome's commentary on Isaiah reads *qui statuit quasi cameram caelum, et extendit quasi tabernaculum.* . . . Ambrose himself, in *Hexaemeron* 6.2, has *qui statuit caelum ut cameram*. Although James interprets the latter quotation as proving that Ambrose is not referring to Isa 40:22 in Ep. 11 (*The Fourth Book*, xlii), there is no reason why the same author cannot cite the same passage with two wordings. Furthermore, the *Hexaemeron* reference shows that Ambrose was in the habit of citing the passage.

As noted previously, if Ambrose does in fact quote 6 Ezra here, it would mean that the book would have been translated into Latin by about 375, as well as (probably) having been joined to 4 Ezra by that date.

70. See J. Morris's "Historical Introduction" to Winterbottom, *Gildas*, 1 and 3.

71. Critical editions of this treatise, listed in chronological order, are: J. Stevenson, ed., *Gildas, De excidio Britanniae* (London: Sumptibus Societatis, 1838) (quotations from 6 Ezra on p. 67); T. Mommsen, ed., *Gildae Sapientis de excidio et conquestu Britanniae* (*Monumenta Germaniae Historica* Auctores Antiquissimi 13 [Chronica minora 3]; Berlin: Weidmannos, 1898; reprint ed., 1961) 1–85 (quotations from 6 Ezra on p. 59); H. Williams, ed., *Gildae de excidio Britanniae* (Cymmrodorion Record Series 3; London: Society of Cymmrodorion, 1899–1901) (with English translation) (quotations from 6 Ezra on pp. 138–41); and M. Winterbottom, ed., *Gildas: The Ruin of Britain and Other Works* (with English translation) (quotations from 6 Ezra on pp. 48–49 [English] and 115–116 [Latin]). J. Morris, in the introduction to Winterbottom's edition, dates the *De excidio* around 540 or just before (p. 1).

72. J. Morris calls the preface to the *De excidio* "the only surviving narrative history of fifth century Britain" (Winterbottom, *Gildas*, 1).

73. Winterbottom, *Gildas*, 48.

74. See chapter 1, nn. 9 and 11.

75. No fewer than eight language versions of 4 Ezra survive today; see chapter 1, n. 10.

76. 4 Ezra 12:42. See also Clement of Alexandria's attribution of his quotation of 4 Ezra 5:35 in *Stromateis* 3, 16.100, 3: Ἔσδρας ὁ προφήτης λέγει.

77. Brou and Vives, *Antifonario visigotico mozarabe*, 126–27 (ff. 91v–92).

78. This is the primary (French) text; the secondary (Spanish) recension differs only in substituting *proclamat* for *clamat* and *proclamant* for *clamant*.

79. For 4 Ezra, see Klijn, *Der lateinische Text*, 93–97, and chapter 1, n. 9, of this volume; for 5 Ezra, Bergren, *Fifth Ezra*, chapter 2.

80. See esp. L. Brou's article "Le 4ᵉ Livre d'Esdras dans la Liturgie Hispanique et le Graduel Romain 'Locus iste' de la Messe de la Dédicace," *Sacris Eruditi* 9 (1957) 75–109. For 5 Ezra, see Bergren, *Fifth Ezra*, 66–70 and 133–38.

81. See chapter 1, "Transmission History"; and Bergren, "Christian Influence."

82. See also Bergren, *Fifth Ezra*, 66–75.

83. Brou, "Le 4ᵉ Livre d'Esdras," 76.

84. Brou, "Le 4ᵉ Livre d'Esdras," 75.

85. See Bergren, *Fifth Ezra*, 66–75.

86. Marbach, *Carmina scripturarum*, 538.

87. For the place of the antiphon in the Roman liturgy, see *Breviarium Romano-Seraphicum*, vol. 1, pars hiemalis (Patersonius: Societatis Sancti Antonii, 1943) 360.

88. Marbach, *Carmina scripturarum*, 538, lists a second occurrence of this phrase in the same *Vigilia* (see *Breviarium Romano-Seraphicum*, p. 360: *Ad matutinum*, Lectio 3). Additionally he points out the similarity of the phrase to Dan 9:24, which reads in the Vulgate . . . *et deleatur iniquitas et adducatur iustitia sempiterna*.

89. Compare Ps 37(36):10: *et adhuc pusillum et non erit peccator* . . . (quoted from the Vulgate's *Psalmi iuxta LXX*).

90. See Klijn, *Der lateinische Text*, 15–16, 93–97; Bensly-James, *The Fourth Book*, xl–xli; and Bergren, *Fifth Ezra*, 70–76, 138–39.

91. See Klijn, *Der lateinische Text*, 15–16, 93–97; Bensly-James, *The Fourth Book*, xl–xli; Brou, "Le 4ᵉ Livre d'Esdras," passim; and Bergren, *Fifth Ezra*, 66–76, 133–39.

92. See Klijn, *Der lateinische Text*, 15–16, 93–97; Bensly-James, *The Fourth Book*, xl–xli; Brou, "Le 4ᵉ Livre d'Esdras," passim; and Bergren, *Fifth Ezra*, 70–76, 138–39.

Chapter Three

1. As a rule, the procedures of textual criticism followed here are those laid out in the handbooks of P. Maas (*Textual Criticism* [Oxford: Oxford University Press, 1958]) and M. L. West (*Textual Criticism and Editorial Technique* [Stuttgart: Teubner, 1973]).

2. These orthographic peculiarities and scribal errors pertain, of course, not only to the individual manuscripts but also to the chain of manuscripts that lie between the manuscript's hyparchetype and the manuscript itself; the latter records the residue of all scribal activity between these two points.

3. Violet, *Die Esra-Apokalypse*, xxv; Violet and Gressmann, *Die Apokalypsen des Esra und des Baruch*, xxii; and de Bruyne, "Quelques nouveaux documents," passim. The only real difference between the Latin stemmata of 4 and 6 Ezra is that 4 Ezra has several additional fragmentary manuscript witnesses (viz., P and G, described by Klijn in *Der lateinische Text*, 13–14).

4. Bergren, *Fifth Ezra*, chapter 3.

5. Since both representatives of the French family, S and A, come from northern France, it seems reasonable to locate the transmission history of the family in this region.

6. The number of "unique readings" recorded in this chapter for each manuscript represents exactly that: the number of times the manuscript shows a reading that is not present in any other known significant manuscript. These were counted by a computer program. A "unique reading" is, of course, not *necessarily* an error, but scribal errors committed in the period between a manuscript's hyparchetype and the manuscript itself tend to be unique readings, and manuscripts that have been copied carelessly (or frequently) within this period tend to have a higher number of unique readings. The number of "unique readings" in a manuscript, then, tends to be inversely proportional to the care taken in copying between the hyparchetype and the manuscript, and thus an objective and relatively reliable measure of the manuscript's accuracy.

Two corrective factors should be noted here. First, manuscripts in a family with fewer representatives (e.g., S and A) will tend by nature to have more unique readings than those in families with more representation (e.g., CMNEVL). Second, since orthographic variants are often unique readings, manuscripts with unusual orthography will tend to show relatively more unique readings.

7. By "orthographic traits" I denote readings in the manuscript that differ from "classical" orthography. This is not intended as a value judgment, since the Latin "autograph" of 6 Ezra itself undoubtedly contained many "nonclassical" spellings. However, since most of the readings listed in these sections are unique to particular manuscripts, it is presumed that they are the work of a scribe in the manuscript's immediate line of transmission. A few of the orthographic variants listed for various manuscripts are not "unique readings" in the strict sense, being found also in manuscripts in other branches of the stemma.

Although recording the orthographic traits of the manuscripts may seem superfluous, a number of writers on "late Latin" have remarked on the difficulty of finding data documenting such characteristics. Thus, this material is provided in the hope that it may prove useful not only in the study of the manuscripts of 6 Ezra but also in that of late Latin orthography in general.

8. The corrections in MS S are discussed by Bensly in *The Missing Fragment*, 18–21.

9. Berger, *Histoire de la Vulgate*, 95–96.

10. Bensly, *The Missing Fragment*, 18–20.

11. Where Bensly's (*The Fourth Book*, 1–6) and Weber's (*Biblia Sacra Vulgata*, 1931–34) collations of this manuscript agree (at least the former was made from the manuscript itself), such agreement is taken to be sufficient verification of its readings. Where they disagree, the reading has been checked in a microfilm of the manuscript.

12. The correcting hands are discussed below.

13. Confusion of verbal endings is characteristic of late Latin: cf. C. H. Grandgent, *An Introduction to Vulgar Latin* (Boston: Heath, 1907) sec. 125.

14. The corrections in MS A are discussed by Bensly in *The Missing Fragment*, 18–19.

15. This manuscript was collated by the present author from a microfilm. The collation in Bensly-James, *The Fourth Book* (pp. 87–92) was found faulty in several regards, some significant.

16. Grandgent, *Introduction*, secs. 316–18, 322–23.

17. See Grandgent, *Introduction*, sec. 282.

18. See chapter 4, "Additional Considerations," of the present volume.

19. This manuscript was collated by the present author from the original.

20. This manuscript was collated by the present author from the original. De Bruyne's list of deviations between MSS M and N in 5 and 6 Ezra and several chapters of 4 Ezra ("Un

manuscrit complet," 255–56) is basically accurate but is incomplete, especially in points of orthography, and contains some printing errors.

21. This may indicate that there was not a very long chain of transmission between p and MSS M and N.

22. Note that, in principle, it is necessary to demonstrate separative errors for only one of the three MSS M, N, and E; see Bergren, *Fifth Ezra*, 104.

23. This manuscript was collated by the present author from a microfilm print.

24. See Bergren, *Fifth Ezra*, 106–8.

25. *Die Apokalypsen des Esra und des Baruch*, xvii. The "scribe" in question, of course, was not necessarily the scribe of this manuscript but rather of some manuscript between p and E.

26. This illustrates the late Latin tendency to prefer compound to simplex verbs; see Grandgent, *Introduction*, secs. 25–27.

27. See chapter 4, "Additional Considerations," of the present volume.

28. This manuscript was collated by the present author from a microfilm. Unclear readings were checked against the original.

29. This substitution exemplifies the late Latin tendency toward use of the preposition *de*; see Grandgent, *Introduction*, sec. 77.

30. This manuscript was collated by the present author from a microfilm.

31. Cf. James's introduction to Bensly-James, *The Fourth Book*, xv–xx; and Violet's comments in *Die Esra-Apokalypse*, xxi–xxiv.

32. The texts of both 4 and 5 Ezra in this manuscript actually feature much longer additions than this.

33. Bergren, *Fifth Ezra*, 112–16.

34. N. Fernández Marcos, *Scribes and Translators*, chaps. 4–6. Fernández Marcos studies the Latin manuscripts ranging from 91–95 in the Beuron Vetus Latina numbering system; MS L is 92 in this series. These manuscripts date from the tenth to the sixteenth century, and all come from the same general region of central Spain. Some of Fernández Marcos's data derive from previous publications of others; see especially *Scribes and Translators*, 44 n. 12.

Fernández Marcos has determined that the Latin used in the marginal glosses in Samuel-Kings is typical of the third century C.E. (p. 72). It would be interesting to compare the Latin in the additions in 2 Esdras.

35. Fernández Marcos notes that the closest equivalents are found in the Targums and in some "biblical paraphrases" from Qumran, but he points out that the expansions in the Old Latin manuscripts are of quite a different character from those in these other categories (pp. 45–46).

36. Violet, *Die Esra-Apokalypse*, xxii–xxiii.

37. Grandgent, *Introduction*, secs. 25–27.

38. Maas, *Textual Criticism*, esp. pp. 42–49.

39. Grandgent, *Introduction*, secs. 25–27.

40. The transition from forms of *is* to forms of *ille* is the most common pronominal emendational tendency in the Spanish revision as a whole (text u); see chapter 4, "Additional Considerations."

41. See chapter 4, "Additional Considerations," of the present volume.

42. I am entirely dependent here on the transcription and restorations given by Hunt in *The Oxyrhynchus Papyri*, 7.13–14.

43. For extensive discussion of the phenomenon of doublets in Greek and Latin translation biblical literature, see Fernández Marcos, *Scribes and Translators*, 34–35, 53–63 and the notes thereto.

44. Bensly, *The Missing Fragment*, 36–40.

45. See Bergren, *Fifth Ezra*, 112–16, 140–42. In 5 Ezra, L, especially in its textual expansions, clearly reflects knowledge of the other (French) recension, which is secondary in 5 Ezra (*Fifth Ezra*, 112–16). Interestingly, some of these expansions could be considered doublets, combining elements of the two recensions. Also, the text of L in 4 Ezra 13:3 displays unique parallels to the quotation of this passage in the León antiphonary (see Brou, "Le 4ᵉ Livre d'Esdras," 90–91; Klijn, *Der lateinische Text*, 81 [on 13:3]; Bergren, *Fifth Ezra*, 69–70). (It seems probable that further examination of the citations of 4 and 5 Ezra in the León antiphonary would reveal additional parallels with L.) Finally, the epitome of 5 Ezra in MS L has one textual element that is unique in the Spanish manuscript tradition but is paralleled by a quotation of that passage in the León antiphonary (see Bergren, *Fifth Ezra*, 140–42).

46. That the text of the epitome should follow the Spanish tradition is not in itself remarkable, since L is a Spanish manuscript. The phenomenon becomes noteworthy, however, in comparison with the epitome of 5 Ezra in MS L; this epitome does display several clear contacts with the French tradition (see Bergren, *Fifth Ezra*, 140–42). This situation is undoubtedly related to the fact, noted in "Readings of the Latin Manuscripts, Legionensis," that, whereas the main text of 5 Ezra in MS L also contains several points of correlation with the French tradition, that of 6 Ezra does not. The difference between the two books and their epitomes in this regard may be related to the difference in value of the respective recensions of the two books: in 5 Ezra, the Spanish tradition is almost certainly primary, while in 6 Ezra the French is superior.

47. See Bergren, *Fifth Ezra*, 140–42.

48. See n. 45 and Bergren, *Fifth Ezra*, 141.

Chapter Four

1. For 4 Ezra, see esp. the text editions of Bensly-James (*The Fourth Book*), Violet (*Die Esra-Apokalypse*, and Klijn (*Der lateinische Text*). For 5 Ezra, see Bensly-James (*The Fourth Book*) and Bergren (*Fifth Ezra*).
In 4 Ezra, the French recension is normally labeled Φ, the Spanish ψ.

2. This means that, in 72 percent of all readings, a word in one recension is matched by the identical word, with identical spelling, in the identical order, in the other recension. The total number of cases ("all cases") is established by counting the words in either recension and adding to that the number of "additions," relative to the text of the first recension, made in the other recension. This will be understood more easily by referring to the arrangement of the recensions in Appendix 1. The number of identical matches between the two texts is determined by counting the "equal signs" (=) in the left margin of the right (Spanish) column.

3. See Bergren, *Fifth Ezra*, 153–61.

4. See Bergren, *Fifth Ezra*, chap. 4.

5. For additional discussion of possibilities, see Bergren, *Fifth Ezra*, 153–54.

6. See chapter 1, "Goals and Conclusions, Original Language."

7. To complicate matters still further, it is possible in theory that a text of 6 Ezra in Hebrew, Aramaic, or some other language underlay the Greek version. This possibility, however, is argued against in chapter 1, "Goals and Conclusions, Original Language."

8. Some of the translational equivalences listed here are not true synonyms but can be construed as approximately similar in meaning.

9. See Bergren, *Fifth Ezra*, chap. 4, esp. pp. 157–59.

10. A. Hilgenfeld, ed., *Hermae Pastor veterem latinam interpretationem e codicibus* (Lipsiae: Fues [Reisland], 1873).

11. O. Gebhardt and A. Harnack, eds., *Hermae Pastor graece addita versione latina recentiore e codice Palatino* (Patrum Apostolicorum Opera 3; Lipsiae: Hinrichs, 1877).

12. See esp. Violet, *Die Esra-Apokalypse*, xiii–iv; Violet and Gressmann, *Die Apokalypsen des Esra und des Baruch*, xxix–xxxi; G. H. Box, *The Ezra-Apocalypse* (London: Pitman, 1912) xi–xiii; M. E. Stone, "Some Remarks on the Textual Criticism of 4 Ezra," *HTR* 60 (1967) 107–15, esp. pp. 107–8; and G. Mussies, "When Do Graecisms Prove That a Latin Text Is a Translation?" *Vruchten van de Uithof* (H. A. Brongers Festschrift; Utrecht: Theologisch Instituut, 1974) 100–119.

13. As noted earlier, both the manuscripts and stemmata for the Latin text traditions of 4 and 6 Ezra are virtually identical.

14. A few of the variants that were given in the list of synonyms in the two recensions, but whose status is ambiguous, are also included here.

15. Note that in each case, it is the French text that presents the more difficult reading and the Spanish that seems more likely to have arisen from editorial emendation.

16. This possibility is reinforced by the fact that in the pairs of variants noted earlier, the superior reading seems sometimes to be on the French side and sometimes on the Spanish. This suggests that there did, at some stage, occur textual corruption that is reflected in the hyparchetypes of the two recensions.

17. Note that it is much easier to account for this variation if one assumes the French text to be primary and the Spanish secondary.

18. As in the previous case, the variation is more easily explained if the French text is assumed to be primary and the Spanish secondary.

19. It is also possible in theory that the words lacking here in Fr—*res vestras et sument*—represent a dropped line. The parallels with the two passages described previously, however, suggest that deliberate elaboration on the part of a Spanish editor is more likely.

20. Some of the points treated here are also discussed by M. R. James in his introduction to Bensly's text edition (*The Fourth Book*, lxiii–lxxviii), where James argues convincingly for the overall superiority of the French text.

21. Another possible exception to this principle would be a situation wherein an editor deliberately introduced grammatical incongruities or stylistic infelicities into a text in order to make it seem more archaic or primitive, and thus more "authentic." This possibility is addressed below.

22. For discussion of this issue, see B. Fischer, "Limitations of Latin in Representing Greek," in B. M. Metzger, *The Early Versions of the New Testament* (Oxford: Clarendon, 1977) 362–74, esp. pp. 366–67 and the literature cited there.

23. Note, e.g., the many compounded Latin forms found in the French recension in the list that follows, especially forms compounded with "super-." It could be argued that these forms, literal translations of Greek words formed with ὑπερ- (stylistically a more widely accepted category), were regarded by a Latin editor as stylistically suspect and liable for emendation. (Note also the unusual Latin forms compounded with "ex-" and "sub-" in the French list.) Whereas the French recension contains the preposition *super*, or verbal compounds of it, eleven times (15:16, 27, 31, 53; 16:13, 20 [bis], 48, 50, 70, 76), the Spanish lacks these elements in literally every case, always featuring some synonym. In the twenty-one parallel passages where the French and Spanish recensions present verbal synonyms, in which one verb is more heavily compounded than the other, the French is the more heavily compounded by a ratio of 16:5. This again suggests that a more style-conscious Spanish editor tended to remove these compounds.

24. See chapter 5 for additional material and comments relevant to this issue.

25. Analogous situations occur even more frequently in 5 Ezra: see Bergren, *Fifth Ezra*, 193–95. While it is possible that, in 16:40, *Domini* has fallen out of the French text, the probability of a Spanish editorial addition seems slightly higher.

26. A "rough and ready" survey of *all* the textual differences between the French and Spanish recensions reveals that, in those cases where there seems to be a clear reason to prefer one

recension over the other, the French seems primary in 171 cases and the Spanish in only 27. Likewise, in the text passages cited in the analysis above, which represent the more decisive cases, the French seem preferable 122 times, the Spanish only 17.

27. Data detailing the codicological situation in each of the eight significant manuscripts of the 2 Esdras corpus are presented in chapter 2, "Primary Evidence." These data first show that 5 Ezra is placed sometimes before the 4/6 Ezra unit (as in the French manuscripts) and sometimes after it (as in the Spanish manuscripts). Second, there are five manuscripts (MNEVL) in which absolutely no textual division is indicated between 4 and 6 Ezra, as opposed to only three (CMN) where the same situation obtains for 5 Ezra. The link perceived between 4 and 6 Ezra is especially evident in MS L, where the same epitome covers both books.

28. A detailed attempt to address these issues is made in Bergren, "Christian Influence."

29. Interestingly, these types of editorial changes are similar to those noted by N. Fernández Marcos to characterize the edited "Antiochene" text of the books of Samuel-Kings, in comparison with the "Old Greek" (Septuagint) version: see *Scribes and Translators*, 31–34.

30. This may be related to the pronounced Spanish tendency, noted earlier (n. 23), to replace compound verbs with simplex forms.

31. Besides the statistical indicator of simple percentage of agreement between the two texts, another factor that strikingly indicates this phenomenon is the way in which the same French lexemes are treated in the Spanish recension in the beginning and end of the text. The Greek loanword *romphea*, for example, occurs five times in the French text, at 15:15, 22, 41, 57, and 16:31. In the first two instances, the loanword is retained in the Spanish recension, whereas in the latter three it is modified to read *gladius*. Likewise, the Latin *dis legomenon inconstabilitio* occurs in the French text at 15:16 and 15:33. In the former case, the word is retained in the Spanish, whereas in the latter it is changed to the more common *inconstantia*.

32. For further reflection on this phenomenon, see Bergren, "Christian Influence."

Chapter Five

1. The data presented in this chapter derive mainly from the following reference tools: B. Fischer, ed., *Novae concordantiae bibliorum sacrorum iuxta vulgatam versionem critice editam* (5 vols.; Stuttgart: Frommann-Holzboog, 1977); P. G. W. Glare, ed., *Oxford Latin Dictionary* (Oxford: Clarendon, 1982); and the *Thesaurus Linguae Latinae* (ed. Consilium ab academiis societatibusque diversarum nationum electi; Leipzig: Teubner, 1900–). *OLD* sets its *terminus ante quem* at about 180 C.E., while *TLL* is intended to be exhaustive to around 500 C.E.

TLL is still incomplete; where it fails (after "P") the following works have been consulted: A. Blaise, *Dictionnaire latin-français des auteurs chrétiens* (Strasbourg: Le Latin Chrétien, 1954); A. Forcellini, *Lexicon totius latinitatis opera et studio* (Prati, 1858–75); W. Lechner-Schmidt, *Wortindex der lateinisch erhaltenen Pseudepigraphen zum Alten Testament* (Tübingen: Franke, 1990); H. Rönsch, *Itala und Vulgata: Das Sprachidiom der urchristlichen Itala und der katholischen Vulgata unter Berücksichtigung der römischen Volkssprache* (2nd ed.: Marburg: Elwert, 1875); and A. Souter, *A Glossary of Later Latin to 600 A.D.* (Oxford: Clarendon, 1949).

Since it is virtually certain that the Latin text of 6 Ezra predates 400 C.E., it has been deemed unnecessary in most instances to consult standard dictionaries of "medieval Latin" such as D. du Cange's *Glossarium Mediae et Infimae Latinitatis*, the *Mittellateinisches Wörterbuch* newly edited by two German academies, F. Blatt and Y. Lefèvre's *Novum Glossarium Mediae Latinitatis*, J. H. Baxter and C. Johnson's *Medieval Latin Word-List from British and Irish Sources*, and J. F. Niermeyer's *Mediae Latinitatis Lexicon Minus*. All these works have *termini a quo* in the fifth century C.E. or later.

2. We argue in chapter 6 that 6 Ezra is itself a Christian piece; it is inherently improbable that a Jew or pagan would have translated such a document into Latin. Furthermore, almost

nothing is known of Jewish translational activity from Greek to Latin in the ancient world, whereas such activity was commonplace among Christians (on this issue, and for some exceptions, see Bergren, *Fifth Ezra*, 165–66, 285–86).

3. Note that all of the extant Latin manuscripts of 6 Ezra occur either in Bibles (MSS SCMNEVL) or in collections of biblical materials (MS A). Note also that each of the surviving Latin citations of 6 Ezra (in Gildas, the Mozarabic liturgy, and the Roman liturgy) clearly implies a "biblical" or "canonical" status for the text (see further chapter 2 and chapter 3).

4. The following treatment is an abbreviated version of the more detailed description given in Bergren, *Fifth Ezra*, 225–29.

5. There is, of course, a vast amount of literature on the OL versions of the Bible. For an excellent recent bibliographical survey, see N. Fernández Marcos, *Scribes and Translators*, 42–43 n. 6, 84 n. 29, and 86 nn. 33–34. Fernández Marcos also provides an outstanding examination of the significance of a certain select group of Spanish OL manuscripts for the textual criticism of the books of Samuel-Kings: *Scribes and Translators*, 41–87.

6. This statement does not imply that North Africa is the first place where a Jewish or Christian Latin idiom developed. Although the latter theory has traditionally been accepted in scholarship on Latin Christianity, some recent investigations have called it into question. See esp. C. Mohrmann, "Les origines de la latinité chrétienne à Rome," *VC* 3 (1949) 67–106, 163–83. L. R. Palmer (*The Latin Language* [London: Faber & Faber, 1954] 199–200) supports Mohrmann's position that Christian Latin did not originate in North Africa, pointing out that "this thesis [that the Latin spoken by Roman Christians derived from North Africa] had in any case little *a priori* probability."

Although Judaism in the West is relatively well documented in the Greco-Roman period, little is known about Jewish literary activity in Latin (see Bergren, *Fifth Ezra*, 165–66 and notes). N. Fernández Marcos, however, in a recent study of a group of five Spanish OL manuscripts in the books of Samuel-Kings, points out a number of indisputable points of contact between certain OL readings and a Hebrew *Vorlage* that indicate that there was some manner of connection between these two text levels (*Scribes and Translators*, esp. pp. 82–87 and notes). Fernández Marcos acknowledges that there is no actual evidence for pre-Christian Latin biblical translations made from Hebrew (p. 86).

7. Since Jerome, who had a manifest distaste for the "apocryphal" books, translated only Tobit and Judith of this group, the "Vulgate" versions of the other apocryphal books are actually OL texts. For further discussion, see Bergren, *Fifth Ezra*, 226 n. 7.

8. The sixth century seems to have been the transitional point when the majority of biblical manuscripts being copied switched from an OL to the Vulgate text type. See J. Gribomont, "L'Église et les versions bibliques," *Maison-Dieu* 62 (1960) 41–68, esp. p. 58.

9. See C. Mohrmann, *Etudes sur le latin des chrétiens* (4 vols.; Storia e Letteratura 65, 87, 103, 143; Rome: Edizioni di Storia e Letteratura, 1958–77) 1:45; 2:121; 3:61, 105, 144, 205–6, 208.

10. See Mohrmann, *Etudes*, 2:239; 3:190; Rönsch, *Itala und Vulgata*, 252.

11. See Mohrmann, *Etudes*, 1:62, 89; 3:60, 130, 134; M. A. Sainio, *Semasiologische Untersuchungen über die Entstehung der christlichen Latinität* (Helsinki: Finnischen Literaturgesellschaft, 1940) 16, 23–25.

12. See Mohrmann, *Etudes*, 2:238; 3:60–61, 104, 113.

13. See Rönsch, *Itala und Vulgata*, 245.

14. See Rönsch, *Itala und Vulgata*, 271.

15. In the strict sense it is probably inaccurate to call these "Christian" neologisms, since Christian biblical Latin clearly was not unique in its idiom and vocabulary. On the one hand, Christian Latin must have been strongly influenced by, and in some senses indistinguishable from, Jewish biblical usage. The problem here is that, as indicated earlier, there is practically

no evidence for identifiably Jewish translations of the Bible into Latin, and little evidence for identifiably Jewish literary Latin of any kind.

On the other hand, Christian biblical Latin must have participated in the literary world of, and shared many features of, contemporary "pagan" (religious) usage.

The fact remains, however, that there is a distinct body of Latin vocabulary that is inextricably linked with early Latin biblical usage, almost all of the evidence for which derives from Christian (usually NT) biblical manuscripts and early Christian authors.

16. See Rönsch, *Itala und Vulgata*, 69–70.

17. See Rönsch, *Itala und Vulgata*, 164.

18. See Rönsch, *Itala und Vulgata*, 183.

19. See Rönsch, *Itala und Vulgata*, 70.

20. See Mohrmann, *Etudes*, 2:16; 3:105; Rönsch, *Itala und Vulgata*, 101; E. Valgiglio, *Le Antiche Versioni Latine del Nuovo Testamento* (Koinonia 11; Naples: D'Auria, 1985) 93, 314.

21. See Mohrmann, *Etudes*, 1:59, 93; 2:16, 238; 3:38, 61–62; Rönsch, *Itala und Vulgata*, 155; Valgiglio, *Le Antiche Versioni*, 84.

22. See Rönsch, *Itala und Vulgata*, 174.

23. See Rönsch, *Itala und Vulgata*, 216.

24. See Rönsch, *Itala und Vulgata*, 32–33.

25. See Mohrmann, *Etudes*, 4:315; Valgiglio, *Le Antiche Versioni*, 70.

26. See Mohrmann, *Etudes*, 1:25; 2:238; 3:60, 113; 4:14; Rönsch, *Itala und Vulgata*, 77; W. Matzkow, *De vocabulis quibusdam italae et vulgatae christianis: Quaestiones lexicographae* (Berlin: Pilz & Noack, 1933) 37–38.

27. See Rönsch, *Itala und Vulgata*, 158.

28. See Rönsch, *Itala und Vulgata*, 212.

29. See Rönsch, *Itala und Vulgata*, 210.

30. See Mohrmann, *Etudes*, 1:34, 91, 184; 2:121–22; 3:43, 62, 202, 206–7; 4:337; Rönsch, *Itala und Vulgata*, 79.

31. In discussions in this and following chapters, the label "Vulgate" generally signifies the text as it appears in the Stuttgart edition of 1969 (3rd ed., 1983). This text includes both Jerome's "Gallican" Psalter ("iuxta Septuaginta") and his Psalter "iuxta Hebraicum," as well as an "Appendix" to the Vulgate comprising the Prayer of Manasseh, 3, 4, 5, and 6 Ezra, Psalm 151, and the Letter to the Laodiceans. The numerical figures given in the present discussions include all these works and are based on the concordance to the Stuttgart second edition that was produced by B. Fischer (see n. 1). Since this concordance includes all the variants listed in the Stuttgart edition, the figures given here also include variants, unless otherwise noted.

32. See Rönsch, *Itala und Vulgata*, 211.

33. See Rönsch, *Itala und Vulgata*, 68, 299.

34. See Mohrmann, *Etudes*, 2:239; 3:190; Rönsch, *Itala und Vulgata*, 252.

35. See Rönsch, *Itala und Vulgata*, p. 183.

36. See Rönsch, *Itala und Vulgata*, 211.

37. See Rönsch, *Itala und Vulgata*, 174.

38. See Rönsch, *Itala und Vulgata*, 216.

39. It is true that this word could potentially be taken as evidence for a Greek or even a Hebrew stage of the text. Since, however, the interchange between *libos* and *libanus* could as easily have taken place on a Latin as on a Greek level, principles of economy in textual criticism require that we not add an extra, unnecessary stage to our theorizing about the text.

40. See Rönsch, *Itala und Vulgata*, 158.

41. See Rönsch, *Itala und Vulgata*, 212.

42. See Rönsch, *Itala und Vulgata*, 210.

43. H. F. Von Soden, *Das lateinische Neue Testament in Afrika zur Zeit Cyprians* (TU 3,3; Leipzig: Hinrichs, 1909).

44. Valgiglio, *Le Antiche Versioni.*

45. In the studies of these scholars, the Vulgate is normally also included as an example of a more developed form of the European text.

Von Soden's and Valgiglio's results are collated and presented in an easily accessible, alphabetized form in an appendix to T. A. Bergren, *A Latin-Greek Index of the Vulgate New Testament* (SBLRBS 26; Atlanta: Scholars Press, 1991) 175–207.

46. See Bergren, *Fifth Ezra,* 238–42.

Chapter Six

1. Revelation was known to Papias (see W. G. Kümmel, *Introduction to the New Testament* [rev. ed.; trans. H. C. Kee; Nashville: Abingdon, 1975] 470 and n. 41); Justin (*Dial.* 81.4); Marcion (cf. Tertullian, *Adv. Marc.* 4.5); Irenaeus (*Adv. haer.* 5.30.3); Melito of Sardis (*apud* Eusebius, *Hist. eccl.* 4.26.2); Clement of Alexandria (*Quis dives salvetur* 42); Tertullian (*Praescr. haer.* 36); and numerous other early Christian authors. See Kümmel, *Introduction,* sec. 34; R. H. Mounce, *The Book of Revelation* (NICNT; Grand Rapids, MI: Eerdmans, 1977) 36–39. For the status of Revelation as "scripturally authoritative," see Kümmel, *Introduction,* 470–71.

2. In this connection it is ironic that Revelation, while apparently directing most of its invective against Rome, is, of course, written in an Asian context.

3. It is tempting to connect this expression (Latin *timentes Dominum*) not only with the general biblical injunction to "fear the Lord" but also with the "God-fearers" known from Acts, the Aphrodisias inscription, and other sources. On "God-fearers," see J. M. Reynolds and R. Tannenbaum, *Jews and Godfearers at Aphrodisias: Greek Inscriptions with Commentary* (Cambridge: Cambridge University Press, 1987); L. H. Feldman, *Jew and Gentile in the Ancient World: Attitudes and Interactions from Alexander to Justinian* (Princeton, NJ: Princeton University Press, 1993) chap. 10 and passim; S. Mitchell, *Anatolia: Land, Men, and Gods in Asia Minor* (2 vols.; Oxford: Clarendon, 1993) 2.8–9, 31–32; E. Schürer, *The History of the Jewish People in the Age of Jesus Christ* [new English version rev. and ed. G. Vermes, F. Millar, and M. Goodman; 3 vols.; Edinburgh: T. & T. Clark, 1973–87] 3.1:150–76; and P. W. van der Horst, "Jews and Christians in Aphrodisias in the Light of Their Relations in Other Cities of Asia Minor" (*Nederlands Theologisch Tijdschrift* 43 [1989] 106–21) 109–11 and the literature cited there, esp. p. 110 n. 22. See also n. 16 of the present chapter.

4. The question whether *lociis* in 16:70 should be read *locis* ("places") or taken as the name of a particular locale, is discussed in chapter 1, "Goals and Conclusions, Provenance."

5. The *terminus post quem* is indicated by the use of "Babylon" for Rome, which suggests a date after 70 C.E., and specifically by 6 Ezra's apparent knowledge of the Book of Revelation, probably written around 95 C.E. The *terminus ante quem* is established generally by the fourth-century Oxyrhynchus fragment, and specifically by the fact that 6 Ezra seems almost certainly to reflect persecution of its Christian audience, a phenomenon that had ceased by 313 C.E.

6. Perhaps a noteworthy indicator of this is the speech, quoted by Josephus, that was allegedly delivered by Titus to the conquered Jews in the outer temple court after the burning of the temple in 70 C.E.; see *J.W.* 6.323–50, esp. sec. 350. (This speech could, of course, have been fabricated by Josephus, but it still indicates the tone the Romans wished to project.) See also M. Simon, *Verus Israel: A Study of the Relations between Christians and Jews in the Roman Empire* (*135–425*) (trans. H. McKeating; Oxford: Oxford University Press, 1986) 41.

Especially relevant for our consideration of 6 Ezra, which was most likely written in Asia Minor, is the fact, stressed by P. R. Trebilco, that none of the three Jewish revolts seems to have affected Roman policy toward the Jews in Asia Minor. See P. R. Trebilco, *Jewish Communities in Asia Minor* (SNTSMS 69; Cambridge: Cambridge University Press, 1991) 32–35.

It is true that drastic measures were enforced by Hadrian in Jerusalem and Judea after the suppression of the revolt of 132–135, but these measures were not long-lived, and furthermore did not directly affect Asia Minor or Egypt, our two main areas of concern.

7. See esp. Trebilco, *Jewish Communities*, 32–33; Mitchell, *Anatolia*, 2.36.

8. See esp. Trebilco, *Jewish Communities*, 33–35, 57, 83, 103, 165, 183–89; and Feldman, *Jew and Gentile*, chap. 2. For this period in Asia Minor in general, see E. M. Smallwood, *The Jews under Roman Rule: From Pompey to Diocletian* (SJLA 20; Leiden: Brill, 1976) chap. 19. See also Simon, *Verus Israel*, chap. 2.

9. An especially useful survey of the evidence is provided by Trebilco, *Jewish Communities*: Sardis and Priene are treated in chap. 2; Acmonia in chap. 3; and Apamea in chap. 4. P. W. van der Horst, in "Jews and Christians in Aphrodisias," discusses the Jewish communities of Aphrodisias (pp. 107–13), Sardis (pp. 113–15), Acmonia (pp. 115–17), Eumenia (pp. 115–17), and Smyrna (pp. 116–17). Mitchell, *Anatolia*, 2.31–37, also gives an outstanding and detailed treatment.

Van der Horst estimates the Jewish population of Asia Minor during the early empire to have been about one million (pp. 106–7). The new edition of Schürer (*History of the Jewish People*, 3.1:17–36) lists some fifty locales where Jewish presence in Asia Minor is attested during this period.

On the substantial level of influence of the Jewish communities of Aphrodisias and Sardis, e.g., see van der Horst, "Jews and Christians in Aphrodisias," 109–15.

10. See Trebilco, *Jewish Communities*, 183–85. Van der Horst notes, e.g., that there are no signs of pagan anti-Semitism in Sardis during the imperial period ("Jews and Christians in Aphrodisias," 114).

11. Many of these are listed in serial fashion by Josephus in *Ant.* 14.185–267 (14.10), which records events under Julius Caesar and shortly thereafter, and 16.160–73 (16.6.1), which treats the era of Augustus. See also Trebilco, *Jewish Communities*, 34, 183.

12. See *Ant.* 14.213–67 (14.10.8–26); 16.160–73 (16.6.1–3).

13. *Ant.* 16.160 (16.6.1); 16.162 (16.6.2); 16.166, 168, 170, 171 (16.6.3).

14. Josephus does describe Jews being "injured" in Laodicea (*Ant.* 14.242 [14.10]) and people "ill-treat[ing] the Jews" in Asia and Cyrene (*Ant.* 16.160 [16.6.1]), but he is not explicit about the incidence of bodily injury.

15. See esp. Trebilco, *Jewish Communities*, 57, 83, 103, 165, 183–89; van der Horst, "Jews and Christians in Aphrodisias," passim. For privileges granted by the Romans to the Jews of Asia Minor, see T. Rajak, "Was There a Roman Charter for the Jews?," *JRS* 74 (1984) 107–23.

16. I refer to, among others, proselytes and "God-fearers." On these categories of persons in Aphrodisias and elsewhere, see the references given in n. 3 of the present chapter. Note esp. Feldman, *Jew and Gentile*, chaps. 9–11 and passim.

That Judaism in Asia Minor was attractive not only to pagans but also to Christians is evident from the strong anti-Jewish polemic of many Christian authors there, who evidently felt that Judaizing activities and potential conversion to Judaism were threats to the Christian communities. See esp. Simon, *Verus Israel*, chap. 11; and van der Horst, "Jews and Christians in Aphrodisias," 115–19, and the literature cited there.

17. See W. H. C. Frend, *Martyrdom and Persecution in the Early Church* (New York: University Press, 1967) 194–95; Simon, *Verus Israel*, 41 (and the literature cited there), 103–4.

18. Simon, *Verus Israel*, 41.

19. "Jews and Christians in Aphrodisias," 113, 115–20.

20. These claims are difficult to assess, given the relative lack of evidence for pagan persecution of Jews in the empire after the first century C.E. It is true that Philo had in this piece

certain rhetorical reasons for arguing these points, but it is difficult to believe that his claims would be entirely without basis.

21. Smallwood, *The Jews*, 516.

22. See esp. V. A. Tcherikover, "Prolegomena," *Corpus Papyrorum Judaicarum* (3 vols.; ed. V. A. Tcherikover, A. Fuks, and M. Stern; Cambridge, MA: Harvard University Press, 1957–64) 1.92–96.

23. Smallwood, *The Jews*, 516–19; Tcherikover, "Prolegomena," 96.

24. Josephus, in *J.W.* 2.457–93 (2.18.1–7), records a number of other occurrences of anti-Jewish violence in various parts of the eastern empire prior to 70 C.E. Additionally, the incident in 40 C.E. wherein Caligula threatened to erect a statue of himself in the Jerusalem temple was apparently instigated by a case of Jewish-Greek conflict in Jamnia, where, according to Philo, Greeks "cause [the Jews] a great deal of trouble, and . . . do them a great deal of injury" (*Legatio* 200). This incident, however, again had to do with challenges to the "ancestral customs" of the Jews rather than with attacks on their persons or property. Josephus records Greek-Jewish flare-ups in Caesarea under Felix (*J.W.* 2.266–70 [2.13.7], 2.284–96 [2.14.4–6]) but does not mention mob violence against the Jews. For analysis of several of these incidents, see Feldman, *Jew and Gentile*, chap. 4. All of these cases, however, again fall outside the chronological and geographical range of our study.

25. See Eusebius, *Praeparatio Evangelium* 3.5; 6.20.9; 9.2.4; 9.2.6; Frend, *Martyrdom and Persecution*, 393; and L. H. Canfield, *The Early Persecutions of the Christians* (Columbia University Studies in History, Economics and Public Law 55.2; New York: Columbia University Press, 1913) 103–4.

26. Eusebius, e.g., in *Hist. eccl.* 3.33.2, describing the situation under Trajan, states that "sometimes the populace, sometimes even the local authorities contrived plots against us, so that with no open persecution, partial attacks broke out in various provinces, and many . . . endured martyrdom." Canfield maintains that the state of affairs in Asia Minor was that "certainly, sometimes in one city, sometimes in another, persecution must have been almost continuous and permanent" (*Early Persecutions*, 103).

27. See Frend, *Martyrdom and Persecution*, 251.

28. Frend, *Martyrdom and Persecution*, 177, 287.

29. It should be noted that this practice is attested already in 4 Maccabees (5:2), a Jewish work of the mid–first century C.E. Thus, it could be argued in theory that the description of such a practice in 6 Ezra derives not necessarily from known practices of Roman persecution, but from a literary model such as 4 Maccabees.

30. These *libelli* are collected, translated, and commented on by J. R. Knipfing, "The Libelli of the Decian Persecution," *HTR* 16 (1923) 345–90.

31. Knipfing, "Libelli," 346–47.

32. Translated by H. J. Lawlor and J. E. L. Oulton, *Eusebius, The Ecclesiastical History and Martyrs of Palestine* (2 vols.; London: SPCK, 1928) 372.

Chapter Seven

1. For the date of the Book of Revelation, see A. Y. Collins, *Crisis and Catharsis: The Power of the Apocalypse* (Philadelphia: Fortress, 1984) 54–83, and the literature cited there; and, for a briefer treatment, her "Revelation, Book of" (*ABD* 5:694–708, esp. pp. 700–701). See also Kümmel, *Introduction*, 466–69; L. L. Thompson, *The Book of Revelation: Apocalypse and Empire* (New York: Oxford University Press, 1990) 13–17, 95–116; G. R. Beasley-Murray, *Revelation* (NCBC; Grand Rapids, MI: Eerdmans, 1974) 37–38; and Mounce, *Revelation*, 31–36.

The claim that the author of 6 Ezra knew and used the Book of Revelation is defended in detail in chapter 6.

2. As is the case in the Book of Revelation, it is difficult to imagine that the references to "Babylon" in 6 Ezra actually refer to the historical Babylon (for this idea in Revelation, see Collins, "Revelation, Book of," 5:700; eadem, *Crisis and Catharsis*, 57). Since it was common practice in early Jewish and Christian literature to refer to Rome as "Babylon" (see *Sib. Or.* 5:143, 159; 4 Ezra 3:1, 2, 28, 31; often in rabbinic literature; 1 Pet 5:13; and Revelation 14–18, passim), and since 6 Ezra seems to know and use Revelation, which does so, it is most logical to suppose that the references to "Babylon" in 6 Ezra also refer to Rome. This is supported by the statement in 15:46 that Asia is "consort in the beauty of Babylon and the glory of her person"; Asia was during the imperial period, of course, part of the Roman Empire. Sixth Ezra's references to Babylon as "that hateful one" (15:48) and "the hateful city" (15:60) also suggest this identification, since for a Jewish or Christian author Rome would have been the most likely referent for such appellations.

It is also possible in theory that "Babylon" refers to Constantinople. This identification occurs, e.g., in the *Apocalypse of Daniel* (7:2, 5, 11), a ninth-century Christian pseudepigraphon. Such a reference, though, implies a situation in which the imperial government was centered in Constantinople, i.e., after 330 C.E., whereas 6 Ezra seems to date from before this time.

3. See esp. the comments by Collins in "Revelation, Book of," 5:700; eadem, *Crisis and Catharsis*, 57–58.

4. Even before this time, in 311 C.E., Galerius had issued an edict of toleration recognizing Christianity as a lawful corporation; this decree was also an important step in ending Christian persecution. For both the edicts of 311 and 313, see *CAH* 12.671–77, 689–91; D. S. Potter, "Persecution of the Early Church" (*ABD* 5:231–35) 234; and Frend, *Martyrdom and Persecution*, 384–92.

One further consideration that should be raised here is the possibility that 6 Ezra stems from the brief period between 361 and 363 when the emperor Julian attempted to suppress Christianity and promote paganism. Several points, however, argue against this theory. Most important, there is no evidence for outright persecution of Christians under Julian. This would make 6 Ezra 16:68–74 specifically, and the eschatological intensity of the work generally, difficult to account for. Second, the fact that the Oxyrhynchus fragment of 6 Ezra is dated to the fourth century weakens (but admittedly does not preclude) a late-fourth-century date for the book.

5. *ZWT* 3 (1860) 1–81.

6. Weinel first advanced this position in "Das sechste Buch Esra," *Handbuch zu den neu-testamentlichen Apokryphen*, 336; and "Das sechste Buch Esra," *Neutestamentliche Apokryphen*, 394–95. Weinel's position was followed by Duensing in subsequent editions of Hennecke's collection: first, H. Duensing, "The Fifth and Sixth Books of Ezra," *New Testament Apocrypha*, 2:689–703 (= "Das fünfte und sechste Buch Esra," *Neutestamentliche Apokryphen*, 3rd ed., 2.488–98). The most recent edition is H. Duensing and A. de Santos Otero, "Das fünfte und sechste Buch Esra," *Neutestamentliche Apokryphen in deutscher Übersetzung*, 5th ed., 2.581–82. (For full bibliographic references to all of these works, see the notes to chapter 1.)

7. The same assumption was made earlier by Lücke, *Versuch*, 186, 212, again without justification.

8. See, e.g., D. S. Potter, *Prophecy and History in the Crisis of the Roman Empire: A Historical Commentary on the Thirteenth Sibylline Oracle* (Oxford Classical Monographs; Oxford: Clarendon, 1990) 51; F. Paschoud, ed., *Zosime, Histoire Nouvelle*, Tome 1 (Collection Budé; Paris: Les Belles Lettres, 1971) 157–58; and A. T. Olmstead, "The Mid–Third Century of the Christian Era," *CP* 37 (1942) 241–62, 398–420, esp. pp. 242–43. A statement made by Olmstead is especially telling: "The period which follows [from 238 to the end of the third century] is the most obscure portion of all imperial Roman history" (p. 242).

9. With reference to the "Arabian[s]" in 6 Ezra 15:29, one notes also that Philip, the Roman emperor from 244 to 249, was an Arabian who lavished attention on his home prov-

ince. Also, *Sibylline Oracle* 13, which idealizes Syria and its native heroes Uranius Antoninus and Odaenathus, inveighs against both Arabia (13.64–73) and Persia (13.155–171; see also below). According to D. S. Potter (*Prophecy and History*, 153), for the authors of *Sibylline Oracle* 13, "[t]he treaty that [Philip] made was resented, and so was the wealth that poured into the cities of *Provincia Arabia*." See also Olmstead, "The Mid–Third Century," 262.

10. Interestingly, Olmstead ("The Mid–Third Century," 259), on the basis of the Kaaba inscription, argues that the reference to wars among the Persians in *Sib. Or.* 13:33, written in 253 C.E. and describing the period around 248, alludes to "a revolt of Kerman" (presumably against the Sassanids). The inscription mentions "'Artaxir, king of Kerman,' also 'Artaxaros, king of Kirmanzene'" (Greek section, ll. 39ff.).

It is also worth noting that, in describing the route taken by Shapur in his incursion into Asia Minor in 260, the Pahlavik portion of the Kaaba inscription has confused the Asian city Comana "with homeland Kerman" (Olmstead, "The Mid–Third Century," 416).

11. Cf. *Sib. Or.* 13:13–16, which describes "an uprising of the evil Persians, Indians, Armenians, and Arabs at the same time" against Rome; "the Roman king . . . will draw near to them, driving warriors against the Assyrians . . ." (quotations from *Sibylline Oracle* 13 are drawn from D. S. Potter, *Prophecy and History*, 167–77). Again, in 13:31–34, "and then there will be the lawless strife of arrogant kings, in wars the Syrians will perish terribly, Indians, Armenians, Arabs, Persians, and Babylonians will ruin each other in mighty battles."

12. See esp. Syncellus, *Ecloga Chronographica* 716–17.

13. As noted earlier (n. 8), reconstruction of these events rests on extremely slim evidence. For this reason, the date of both of Odaenathus's campaigns, the reason for his initial withdrawal from Ctesiphon, and the events of the period between the two campaigns are tentative or unknown.

The main primary sources for this historical reconstruction are: Zosimus, *Historia Nova* 1.39; *Historia Augusta*, V. *Gall.* 3.1–5; 10.1–8; 12.1; 13.1–3; *Tyr. Trig.* 15–17; 30.6; *Sib. Or.* 13:155–71; Syncellus, *Ecloga Chronographica* 716–17; Zonaras, *Epitome Historiarum* 12.24; and G. A. Cooke, *A Text-Book of North-Semitic Inscriptions* (Oxford: Clarendon, 1903) nos. 126–130.

With reference to the *Historia Augusta*, we should perhaps note that, according to Olmstead, these writings are "perhaps the worst source material the historian has attempted to utilize. . . . most of their documents and many of their sources are fakes" ("The Mid–Third Century," 242).

Important secondary treatments of this period include: Olmstead, "The Mid–Third Century"; Potter, *Prophecy and History*, 51–58, 338–47; *CAH* vol. 12, esp. pp. 112, 135–37, 148, 172–80; von Gutschmid, "Die Apokalypse," 11–13; Paschoud, *Zosime, Histoire Nouvelle*, 1.37 (n. 67), 157–58; M. Besnier, *L'Empire romain de l'avènement des Sévères au Concile de Nicée* (Histoire Ancienne, troisième partie; Histoire Romaine, Tome 4; première partie; Paris: Les Presses Universitaires de France, 1937) 212–17; W. Ensslin, *Zu den Kriegen des Sassaniden Schapur 1* (Sitzungsberichte der Bayerischen Akademie der Wissenschaften, Philosophisch-historische Klasse, Jahrgang 1947, Heft 5; Munich: Verlag der Bayerischen Akademie der Wissenschaften, 1949) 69–85; and A. Alföldi, *Studien zur Geschichte der Weltkrise des 3. Jahrhunderts nach Christus* (Darmstadt: Wissenschaftliche Buchgesellschaft, 1967) 190–201.

14. This is the interpretation suggested by Lücke, *Versuch*, 185.

15. To 6 Ezra 15:33, compare *Sib. Or.* 13:17–20.

16. For the Hatra, see Potter, *Prophecy and History*, 19–21, 35, 190, 377–79; Olmstead, "The Mid–Third Century," 251.

17. The main sources for this historical survey are: *CAH*, vols. 11 and 12, passim; Potter, *Prophecy and History*, chap. 1; Olmstead, "The Mid–Third Century"; and von Gutschmid, "Die Apokalypse," 1–24.

18. *Hist. Aug., Max. et Balb.* 16.3.

19. *CAH* 12.139, 154. If 6 Ezra 15:34–63 actually refers to a historical event, this is a likely candidate. Sixth Ezra describes destructive storm clouds that are "driven violently west" (15:39), "go steadily across to Babylon and destroy her" (v. 43), and ravage Asia "while they are returning from Babylon" (v. 60). If the "clouds" are understood as referring to barbarian tribes, this would signify an invasion through the Balkans into Italy and then back east into Asia Minor. The present episode is probably the one in our period that best fits this scenario.

20. For persecution continuing in the east after the death of Valerian under Macrianus and, in Egypt, even longer under Aemilianus, see Eusebius, *Hist. eccl.* 7.10.9; 7.11. See also the comments of von Gutschmid, "Die Apokalypse," 9, 23.

21. See esp. G. W. Bowersock, *Roman Arabia* (Cambridge, MA: Harvard University Press, 1983) 118, 128–39, 142, 155. See also the *Encyclopedia Britannica* (11th ed.), "Palmyra," 20.652. Procopius, *Persian War* 2.5.5, states that Odaenathus was "ruler of the Saracens" in the region of Palmyra; "Saracens" and "Arabs" are usually understood as being equivalent in the literature of this period.

22. The exact signification of "Assyria" in the context of 15:28–33 is problematic. The term traditionally designates the land on the upper Tigris, south of Armenia. This had been conquered by Ardashir (Artakhshatr), founder of the Sassanid Empire and father of Shapur, at some time before 226, and apparently remained under Sassanid control at least until the time of Odaenathus. Thus, the "land (territory) of the Assyrians" in 15:30, 33, taken in this traditional sense, would designate Sassanid holdings. Moreover, Odaenathus, after taking Carrhae and Nisibis in 262, would have moved through this area in his approach to Ctesiphon; in fact, his battle with Shapur referred to in *Hist. Aug., Tyr. Trig.* 15.3; 30.6 could have taken place here. Thus, the conflict between Arabs and Carmonians in "Assyria" in 15:30, 33 fits well with this reconstructed history.

Von Gutschmid, however, noting that the "Carmonians" (= Persians) *destroy* part of Assyria in 15:30, argues that "Assyria" here cannot be part of Sassanid territory, but must designate the Hatra in southwest Mesopotamia, an area lying between the Roman and Persian holdings. Unfortunately, there is no evidence that Odaenathus ever fought the Persians in this region.

According to D. S. Potter (*Prophecy and History*, 130), the "land of the Assyrians" in *Sib. Or.* 12:155 (cf. 12:191, 256–61; 13:16, 105) actually designates Persia. (See also *Prophecy and History*, 197–99.) This interpretation is confirmed to some degree by the *Res gestae* of Shapur, preserved in the Kaaba inscription near Persepolis:

> All these [Roman] cities, with their surrounding territories, thirty-six, and men who were from the peoples of the Romans, from the non-Aryans, in captivity we led, and among our own peoples of the Aryans, in Persis, and in Parthia, and in Uzene, and in Assyria and among the other peoples by eparchies, where were foundations both of our father and grandfathers and our ancestors, there we settled them. (Greek section, ll. 33ff; quoted by Olmstead, "The Mid–Third Century," 417–18)

From this inscription, it is clear that Shapur not only considered "Assyria" part of his "Aryan" ancestral domain but also settled captives there after his campaign of 260.

In any case, von Gutschmid's interpretation seems strained: "Assyria" in this period would almost certainly have been part of Sassanid territory. Thus, the facts that the "Carmonians" destroy part of Assyria in 15:30, and that an ambusher from Assyria snares them in 15:33, remain problematic for von Gutschmid's interpretation. See also n. 11.

23. See esp. the conclusions of the various interpreters surveyed in chapter 1, "History of Scholarship."

24. See H. W. Bird, ed., *The Breviarium ab urbe condita of Eutropius* (Liverpool: Liverpool University Press, 1993).

25. See F. Pichlmayr and R. Gruendel, eds., *Sexti Aurelii Victoris Liber de Caesaribus* (2nd ed.; Leipzig: Teubner, 1970).

26. See D. Magie, ed., *The Scriptores Historiae Augustae* (3 vols.; LCL; Cambridge, MA: Harvard University Press, 1932).

27. See Bird, *Breviarium*, xliv–xlix; T. D. Barnes, "The Lost *Kaisergeschichte* and the Latin Historical Tradition," *BHAC* 1968/69 (1970) 13ff.

28. Bird, *Breviarium*, 139.

29. See, e.g., Eutropius, *Brev.* 9.8–9; Aurelius Victor, *De Caes.* 33.3–6, 15; *Hist. Aug.*, *V. Gall.* 1.2–4; 2.5–7; 3.1–2, 6–8; 4.3, 7–9; 5.6–7; 6.1–9; 7.1; 11.1–2; 12.6; 13.6–10; 16.1.

30. For convenient summaries of this view, see Magie, *The Scriptores Historiae Augustae*, 3.16–17 n. 1; and *OCD* 456.

31. *OCD* 456.

32. See, e.g., Eutropius, *Brev.* 9.8 and Bird's nn. 20–21 (pp. 139–40); Aurelius Victor, *De Caes.* 33.3–6 (compare with Eutropius, *Brev.* 9.8); *Hist. Aug.*, *V. Gall.* 4.7–8 (and n. 5); 5.6–7 (and n. 3); and 6.1–9 (the destruction of the Artemision occurred under Valerian).

33. Even the *Historia Augusta*, which takes great pains to vitiate Gallienus's competence in every possible way, does not mention a direct barbarian threat to Rome under his rule.

34. One likely exception to this principle lies in the book's descriptions of persecution of "the elect." As noted previously, these descriptions seem so vivid and immediate, and are presented in such dramatic detail, that, in my view, it can be assumed that the author or community of 6 Ezra had either heard of or experienced such persecutions, or expected them in the future. This, in fact, is the principal reason for dating 6 Ezra prior to 313.

35. There was, e.g., on the death of Gallienus (268) a reaction against his policy of toleration, and persecution occurred under his successor, Claudius II. Aurelian (ruled 270–75) also seems to have been hostile toward Christianity, especially at the end of his life. Even after Galerius's edict of toleration in 311, Maximin Daia renewed persecution briefly until 313.

36. The pericope 15:28–33 could also, of course, be a separate unit of tradition that was composed before 283 but was incorporated into 6 Ezra at a later date. D. S. Potter (*Prophecy and History*, 125–32) notes that several of the *Sibylline Oracles* were composed in a piecemeal and imitative fashion, often relying heavily for their material on a common body of oracular sources and on other, separately known oracles. In theory, it is possible that 6 Ezra was composed in a similar fashion, and that various individual vignettes within the work, including 15:28–33, originally circulated independently or were copied from other sources.

37. See, e.g., *Sib. Or.* 3:63–74; 4:119–24, 138–39; 5:28–34, 99–110, 138–53, 215–24, 363–70; 8:70–72, 140–47; 13:122–36; Rev 13:3, 18; 17:8, 11; *Asc. Isa.* 4:1–4. For an evaluation of the *Sibylline Oracles* materials, see J. J. Collins, *The Sibylline Oracles of Egyptian Judaism* (SBLDS 13; Missoula, MT: Scholars Press, 1974) 80–87.

38. See, e.g., 4 Ezra 13:12–13, 39–50; 14:33; *Assumption of Moses* 2–4; Josephus, *Ant.* 11.133; *2 Apoc. Bar.* 1:2–3; chaps. 62–87; *Sib. Or.* 2:168–76; *Asc. Isa.* 3:2; *T. Jos.* 19:1–7; *Testament of Naphtali* 6; Commodian, *Carmen apologeticum* 941–73; idem, *Instructiones* 1.42; *m. Sanh.* 10:3.

39. I owe this reference to Professor David S. Potter.

40. See n. 2.

41. *Geog.* 15.2.8–14 (secs. 724–26).

42. *Nat. hist.* 6.84, 95, 108, 212; 12.56; 36.61; 37.39, 110, 131, 132.

43. *Bell. civ.* 3.205–65, esp. 3.250.

44. *Hist. Alex.* 9.10.20.

45. *Anabasis of Alexander* 6.17, 27–28.

46. See also Arrian, *Indica* 32.1–5; idem, *Anabasis* 6.28.5; Strabo, *Geog.* 15.2.14 (sec. 726).

47. See Pliny, *Nat. hist.* 12.56, 79; 36.61; 37.21, 39, 110, 131–35.

48. An additional point may be made based on the types of evidence cited earlier. Sixth Ezra 15:30 states that "the Carmonians, raging in wrath, will go out of the woods. . . ." The warlike (therefore presumably "wrathful") nature of the Carmanians was stressed in the quotation from Strabo's *Geography* (15.2.14) cited previously. The same attribute is implied in Arrian's *Indica* 36.8. With regard to "go[ing] out of the woods," Strabo states explicitly that Carmania is "full of large trees" and is especially noted for its vines (*Geog.* 15.2.14). Arrian likewise emphasizes that Carmania "is better wooded than the country of the Fish-eaters and the Oritans and bears more fruits" (*Indica* 32.4; cf. 32.5. For the fruits, see also Strabo, *Geog.* 15.2.14 [sec. 726]). Thus, descriptions of Carmania and the Carmanians that presumably are independent of 6 Ezra tend to stress the same attributes that are found there.

This fact indicates the possibility that the author of 6 Ezra, besides being familiar with the general reputation of Carmania as an exotic land, also knew some particulars about it. At the same time this argues against the assumption that the "Carmonians" are simply a cipher for the Persians; on the contrary, attributes specifically connected with Carmania are adduced to describe them.

49. See Potter, *Prophecy and History*, 141–54.

50. To this use of the singular noun, which Potter takes to refer to Shapur personally (*Prophecy and History*, 342–43), compare 6 Ezra 15:31, which speaks of "the dragon."

51. Potter (*Prophecy and History*, 141–42) argues that this pericope was written between 261 and 267 C.E., about ten years after the rest of *Sibylline Oracle* 13 had been completed, with the intention of bringing the prophecy up to date.

52. Potter, *Prophecy and History*, 331.

53. Potter, *Prophecy and History*, 343.

54. On this practice see D. Bryan, *Cosmos, Chaos and the Kosher Mentality* (JSPSup 12; Sheffield: Sheffield Academic Press, 1996).

55. On this point see also n. 62, which suggests that the Persians would be more likely to have been called "Assyrians" (15:30, 33) than the Palmyrenes. It should be noted that the depiction of the Persians as "serpents" and "venom-spitting beasts" in *Sibylline Oracle* 13 was probably due at least in part to the fact that the author(s) of this piece had a strong pro-Syrian and anti-Persian bias. See Potter, *Prophecy and History*, 151–54. Note also that in *Sib. Or.* 5:29, it is Nero who is referred to as a "terrible snake."

56. See von Gutschmid, "Die Apokalypse," 2, and the comments made at the beginning of this chapter, including n. 8.

57. A more detailed version of this brief historical sketch, with full documentation from primary and secondary sources, is provided earlier in this chapter.

58. As von Gutschmid notes, it is technically possible that the "(they)" in 15:30 refers to the "Arabian dragons"; however, the "Carmonians" are the more natural subject.

59. See n. 22.

60. Von Gutschmid, "Die Apokalypse," 14.

61. There is a strange internal contradiction in von Gutschmid's argument here. On page 12 he states that "Gallienus acknowledged [Odaenathus] in 264 as Caesar of the East, and Odaenathus seized anew the offensive against the Persians, this time conquering even Ctesiphon." He then says, "it is this second campaign of Odaenathus against the Persians that is alluded to in [6 Ezra 15] v. 31" (p. 15). On page 22, however, he states:

an exact designation of time [for the composition of 6 Ezra] results from the fact that the renewal of the war between Odaenathus and the Persians cannot have happened before 263 and that the danger to Rome and Asia from the Goths ended in 263. To the year 263, so found, fits also without exception the situation of the Egyptian Christians. . . .

Von Gutschmid is claiming explicitly, then, that 6 Ezra, written in 263, refers to an event that did not happen until 264 or thereafter.

In any event, it seems clear from the historical sources surveyed earlier that Odaenathus's two offensives against the Persians took place in 262 and 266/67, not 261 and 263/64, as von Gutschmid claims.

62. Potter, *Prophecy and History*, 130, referring to *Sib. Or.* 12:155, 191, 256–61; 13:16, 105. See also nn. 22 and 55; Potter, *Prophecy and History*, 197–99.

63. See *CAH* 12.203, 515–20, 654–61.

64. See the accounts of Tacitus (*Annals* 15.44) and Suetonius (*Nero* 16).

65. See esp. 1:9; 2:10, 13; 6:9–11; 7:14; 12:11; 13:7, 15; 17:6; 18:24; 19:2; 20:4.

The Text of 6 Ezra

Parallel Alignment of the French and Spanish Recensions, with All Textual Witnesses

SIGLA

Manuscripts

A	Ambianensis: Amiens, Bibliothèque Communale 10
A	Uncorrected readings
A+	First hand (only where corrected)
A++..	Correcting hands
C	Complutensis 1: Madrid, Biblioteca de la Universidad Central 31
E	Epternacensis: Luxembourg, Bibliothèque Nationale 264
L	Legionensis 2: León, Real Colegiate de San Isidoro I,3
L . . .	Introductory material in Legionensis text
L1	Epitome of 5 Ezra
L2	Incipits of the epitome and 2 Esdras preface
L3	Preface to 2 Esdras
L4	Epitome of 4/6 Ezra
M	Mazarinaeus: Paris, Bibliothèque Mazarine (3–)4
N	Bruxellensis: Brussels, Bibliothèque Royale 1er Série (9107–)9109(–9110)
S	Sangermanensis: Paris, Bibliothèque Nationale latin (11504–)11505
S	Uncorrected readings
S+	First hand (only where corrected)
S++..	Correcting hands
V	Abulensis: Madrid, Biblioteca Nacional vitr. 15–1
W	Marginal notes and corrections of MS C (Cmg)
X	Oxyrhynchus Greek fragment of 6 Ezra

Quotations, References

@g	Gildas's *De excidio Britanniae*
@g0	Consensus of all witnesses to Gildas (= editor's estimation of the original)

@g1	All witnesses to G except those listed (= editor's estimation of the original)
@g2	Consensus of the modern editions of Gildas
@g3	Stevenson's edition
@g4	Josseline's edition (Mommsen's Q)
@g5	Polydore's edition (Mommsen's P)
@g6	Mommsen's MS D (Bensly's B)
@g7	Mommsen's MS D(1) (first hand only)
@g8	Mommsen's MS A
@r	Roman Breviary and Missal
@r	Reading where only one citation
@r0	Reading of all citations, where more than one
@r1,@r2	Reading of individual citations, where more than one differ
@y	Antiphonary of León
@y	Reading where only one citation
@y0	Reading of all citations, where more than one
@y1,@y2..	Reading of individual citations, where more than one differ
@z	Ambrose's "citation" of 6 Ezra

Editions

!a	Editor's estimation of the reading of the 6 Ezra archetype
!b	R. L. Bensly, *The Fourth Book of Ezra*
!c	Clementine Vulgate
!f	Editor's estimation of the reading of the French hyparchetype
!s	Editor's estimation of the reading of the Spanish hyparchetype
!t	R. Weber, *Biblia Sacra iuxta vulgatam versionem*: the right column (alternate text)
!w	R. Weber, *Biblia Sacra iuxta vulgatam versionem* ("Stuttgart Vulgate")

SIGNS USED IN THE PARALLEL TEXT

verbum[XYZ]	MSS X, Y, and Z read "verbum"
(verbum X)	Variant reading of "verbum" in MS X
=	Sp reading same as main Fr reading
=[XY]	Sp MSS X and Y same as main Fr reading
(= X)	Variant Sp MS X same as main Fr reading
+	Element added
(+ verbum XY)	Variant addition of "verbum" in MSS X and Y
~	Different word order [transposition]
verbum{~}	"Verbum" is transposition of an identical Fr reading
verbum{~:}	"Verbum" is transposition of a similar Fr reading
verbum[~XY]	Reading in Sp MSS X and Y is transposed in relation to an identical reading in other MSS
verbum[~:XY]	Reading in Sp MSS X and Y is transposed in relation to a similar reading in other MSS
(verbum ~X)	Variant "verbum" in MS X is transposed in relation to an identical reading in other MSS
(verbum ~:X)	Variant "verbum" in MS X is transposed in relation to a similar reading in other MSS

>	Element lacking ["deletion"]
(>XY)	MSS X and Y lack this reading
(>~XY)	MSS X and Y transpose an identical reading
(>~:XY)	MSS X and Y transpose a similar reading
[>]	Fr reading is lacking in Sp MSS
[>~]	Identical Fr reading is transposed in Sp MSS
[>~:]	Similar Fr reading is transposed in Sp MSS
[>XY]	Fr reading is lacking in Sp MSS X and Y
{comment}	Comment
{>8}	Deleted word is part of an eight-word deletion
{+8}	Added word is part of an eight-word addition
*	Erasure
s.	See
s.a.	See above
s.b.	See below

EXPLANATION OF THE PARALLEL ALIGNMENT

This vertical parallel alignment of 6 Ezra aims to present the textual evidence for the book in an easily understandable format. In general, the left column represents the "French" recension (MSS SA) and the editions based on it (!w!c!b), while the right column represents the "Spanish" recension (MSS CMNEVL). An exception to this occurs in 6 Ezra 15:59–16:31, wherein manuscript S and the editions based on it (!c!b) transfer their allegiance to the Spanish text.

The readings placed, without parentheses, in the far left margin of each column are normally those judged by the editor to have belonged to the hyparchetype of that recension.

The major exception to this latter principle is that the reading in the far left margin of the left column, without parentheses, *always* represents the editor's estimation of the common archetype of the two recensions (!a), even when this differs from the French hyparchetype (!f). In the latter case, the estimated reading of the French hyparchetype is placed second, in parentheses. Also, variant French readings that are identical to the reading of any Spanish witness(es) are represented in both columns.

The principle of the alignment is that only one word is represented on each line. The only exception to this is cases where it is clear that a witness has mistakenly read one word as two; in this case, the two words are placed together, with the sign "_" between them.

When the variants of a particular reading would extend beyond columnar limits, they are continued on the next line and indented.

Although all the manuscripts are punctuated, punctuation is normally omitted in the alignment. It is represented only when the punctuation in some witness causes its text to be read with a different sense than that implied by the word order and verse division of the main French and Spanish texts (the sense of these texts is generally not ambiguous). When punctuation is represented, it is always with a period (.); no attempt is made to distinguish between the various marks of punctuation used in the manuscripts. When a question mark is clearly indicated in a manuscript, it is represented in the alignment as a "comment" ({+ ?}).

Capital letters are used for words in the "incipits" and "explicits" of the manuscripts.

French Recension	Spanish Recension
Incipit of the Book	
INCIPIT	[>]
LIBER (>A+) {'L-' inserted by A++}	[>A+MNEVL](= C)
QUINTUS	[>~:C,MNEVL]
EZRAE (>A)	[>AMNEVL](ESDRE C)
	(+ PROPHETE C)
	(+ QUARTUS ~:C)
(+ CUM S)	
(+ VERSIS S)	
(+ II_CCXXX S)	
15:1	
	(+ preceperat L)
	(+ mihi L)
	(+ Dominus LL4)
	(+ et VL)
	(+ dixit VL)(loquitur L4)
	(+ ad L)
	(+ mihi V)(me L)(eo L4)
ecce	=[CMNEV](haec L)
loquere	=
	(+ verba L)
in	=
aures	auribus
plebi (plebis S++A++!c)	populi
meae	mei
	(+ quae L)
sermones	=[CMNEV](sermonibus L)
prophetiae (profetiae A)	=[MNEV](profetie C) (propheciae L)
	(prophecie L4)
quos	=
inmisero (immisero !c)	=[CEVL](immisero MN!c)
in	=
os	=
tuum	=
dicit	=
Dominus	=
15:2	
et	=
fac	=
(+ ut S!c!b){>A!w}	ut[SCMNEVL!c!b]
{points erased over 'ut' -S}	
in	=
{points erased over 'in' -S}	
carta {S++A++} (cartha S+) (cartas A+)(charta !c)	=[CMNEV](cartas A+L)
scribi {A} (scribantur S!c!b)	scribantur[SCMNEVL!c!b]
{final 'i' on erasure -A}	
{points erased over '-an' -S}	
{points erased under '-tur' -S}	
eos {A} (>S!c!b)	[>SCMNEVL!c!b]
	(+ et L)
	(+ in L)
	(+ libro L)
	(+ ponantur L)

French Recension	Spanish Recension
quoniam	=
fideles	=
et	=
veri	=
sunt	=
15:3	
ne	=
timeas	=
a	=[CMNEL](>V)
cogitationibus (gogitationibus A+)	=
{about 9 letters erased -S;}	eorum[CMNVL](>E)
{probably 'eorum quae' =Sp.}	quae[MNEL](que V)(>C)
adversum	=
te	=
	(+ moventur MNE)(agunt L)
nec (ne A+) {for A+, s.b.}	=
conturbent {A!w} (turbent S!c!b)	turbent[SCMNEV!c!b](= L)
te	=
incredulitates	=
dicentium (contradicentium !b)	=[CMNEV](dicencium L)
	(+ quia L)
	(+ hoc L)
	(+ vanum L)
	(+ est L)
15:4	
quoniam	=
omnis	=
incredulus	=
in	=[CMNEL](>V)
incredulitate	=[CVL](incredulitatem MNE)
sua	=[CVL](>MNE)
morietur	=
	et
	omnis
	qui
	credit
	(+ per L)
	fide[CMNEV](fidem L)
	sua[CMNEV](suam L)
	salvus[CMNEL] (salvabitur V)
	erit[CMNEL](>V)
	(+ in L)
	(+ eternum L)
	{+ xxii L}
15:5	
ecce	=[CMNEV] (haec L{s.b.})
	(+ dicit ~CVL)
	(+ Dominus ~CVL,L4)
ego	=[MNE](>CVL)
induco	=[CMNEV](>L) (missurum_esset L4)
dicit	=[MNE](>~CVL)

French Recension	Spanish Recension
Dominus	=[MNE](>~CVL)
	(+ ecce L{s.a.})
super	=[CMNEVL](in L4)
orbem	=[CMNEV](>L)
terrarum	=[CMNEVL](terra L4)
mala	=[CMNEL](male V)
gladium	=[CMNEVLL4]
et	[>CMNEV](= L)
famem	=[CMNEVLL4]
et	[>]
mortem	=[CMNEVLL4]
et	=[CMNEVLL4]
interitum	=[CMNEVLL4]
15:6	
propter	=
quod	=
superposuit (superpolluit !c)	=
iniquitas	=
(+ in S+){apud !w}	
{2–3 letters erased -S; !w reads 'in'}	
omnem	=[CMNE](orbem VL)
terram	=[CMNE](terrae V) (terre L)
et	=
adimpletae {A++!w} (adimpleta SA+!f!c!b)	adimpleta[SA+MNEV!f!c!b] (adinpleta CL)
sunt	=
operationes {A!w} (opera S!c!b)	opera[SCMNEVL!c!b]
(+ nociva S!c!b){>A!w}	nociva[SMNEVL!c!b] (nociba C)
eorum {A!w} (illorum S!c!b)	illorum[SCMNEVL!c!b]
15:7	
propterea	=
dicit	=
Dominus	=
15:8	
iam	=
non	=
silebo	=
(+ in !b)(de !c)	in[CMNEVL!b](de !c)
impietatibus (impietates A!w) {'-es' on erasure -A}	=[MNE](inpietatibus CVL)
eorum	=
quae {S+} (quas S++) (>A{>10})	=[VL](que C)(qui MNE)
inreligiose {S+} (>A{>10}) (irreligiose S++!c)	=
agunt (>A{>10})	=
nec (>A{>10})	=[MNEVL](neque C)
sustinebo (>A{>10})	=
in (>A{>10})	=
his (>A{>10})	=
quae (>A{>10})	=[MNEL](que CV)
inique (>A{>10})	=
exercent (>A{>10})	=[MNE,V{?}] (exercescent C{V?}) (exercerunt L) (+ unusual sign '-rx'{?} V)
ecce	=
{@y begins here}	
sanguis [SA!w!c!b@y]	=[CMNEVLL4]

French Recension	Spanish Recension
innoxius (innoxus A+) (innocens @y) (innocuus A++)	=[MNE](innocuus A++CVL) (innocens L4@y)
et [S!w!c!b@y](>A)	=
iustus [S!w!c!b@y](>A)	=
clamat [SA!w!c!b@y]	proclamat[CMNEL] (proclamant V)
ad [SA!w!c!b@y]	=[CMNEL](>V{>6})
me [SA!w!c!b@y]	=[CMNEL](>V{>6})
et [SA!w!c!b@y]	=[CMNEL](>V{>6})
animae [SA!w!c!b] (anime @y)	=[MNEL](anime C@y) (>V{>6})
iustorum [SA!w!c!b] (innocentum @y)	=[CMNE](eorum L)(>V{>6}) (+ suspirant L{cf. @y})
clamant [SA!w!c!b] (suspirant @y)	proclamant[CMNE](>V{>6}) (proclamantes L)
perseveranter [S!w!c!b] (vehementer @y) (perseverantes A)	=[MNL] (perseverantes ACV) (perseverantur{?} E)
15:9	
(+ iam @y)	
(+ non @y)	
(+ feram @y)	
(+ dicit ~@y)	
(+ Dominus ~@y)	
(+ sed @y)	
vindicans [SA!w!c!b] (faciam @y)	=
vindicabo [SA!w!c!b] (vindictam @y)	=[CMNEVL](vindicetur L4)
illos [SA!w!c!b] (illorum @y)	=
(+ cito @y)	
dicit [SA!w!c!b](>~@y)	=
Dominus [SA!w!c!b] (>~@y)	=
et [SA!w!c!b](>@y)	=
accipiam [SA!w!c!b] (effuderunt @y)	=
omnem [SA!w!c!b](>@y)	=
sanguinem [SA!w!c!b@y]	=
{@y ends here}	
innocuum {S++A} (innoxium S+S+++!c!b)	=
ex	=
illis	=
ad	=
me	=
15:10	
ecce	=
populus	=
meus	=
quasi	=
grex	=
ad	=
occisionem	=
ducitur	=[CMNEV](duitur{?} L)
iam	=
non	=
patiar	=[CMNE](paciar L) (faciam V)
illum	=
habitare	=
in	=

French Recension	Spanish Recension
terra	=
Aegypti	=[E](Egypti CMV) (Aegipti N)(Egipti L)
	advenam
15:11	
sed	=
educam	=[L](aeducam C) (deducam MNE)
	(perducam{?} V)
eum	illum
in	=
manu	=
potenti (potentem S+)	=
et	=
brachio (brahio A) (bracchio !c)	=[MNEVL](bracio C)
excelso	=
et	=
percutiam	=[CMNE](percuciam VL) (percutere L4)
Aegyptum (Aegiptum A) (>!c)	=[CE](Egyptum M) (Aegiptum AN) (Egiptum
	VL)(Egipto L4)
	(+ variis L4)
plaga (plagam S+)	plagis[CMNELL4](= V)
sicut	=[CMNEVL](ut L4)
prius	=[CMNEVLL4]
et	=
corrumpam	=[MNEVL](conrumpam C)
(+ omnem ~S++!c!b)	omnem[~S++CV!c!b](>MNEL)
terram	=
omnem (>~S++!c!b)	[>~S++CV!c!b,MNEL]
eius	=
15:12	
lugeat (lugebit !c)	=
Aegyptus (Aegiptus A)	=[E](Egyptus CM) (Aegiptus AN) (Egiptus
	VL)
et	=
fundamenta	=
eius	=
a (>!c)	=
plaga	=
verberati (verberata !c) (verberationis !b)	verberum
et (in S)	=
mastigati {A} (castigationes S) (castigatione !c)	castigationis[CMNEL!b]
(castigationis !b) {points below and a	(mastigationis V)
letter above 'm'erased -A; 'i' written above 'g'	
in another hand -A}	
	(+ eius E)
quam (quas S!c)	=
inducet {A++!a} (inducit S!f!b) (inducat A+)	=
(+ ei !c)	
Dominus {A!w!b} (Deus S!c)	Deus[SCMNVL!c](= E)
	(+ super L)
	(+ eam L)
15:13	

French Recension	Spanish Recension
lugeant (lugebunt !c)	=
cultores	=
operantes	[>]
terram	terrae[MNEV](terre CL)
quoniam	=
	(+ non V)
deficiet {S+A++} (deficient S++!w!c!b)	deficient[S++CMNEVL!w!c!b]
(deficiat A+)	
semina (semita A)	=
eorum	=
et (>!c{>4})	=[CVL](>MNE!c{>4})
vastabuntur (>!c{>4})	=[CVL](>MNE!c{>4})
ligna (>!c{>4})	=[CVL](>MNE!c{>4})
eorum (>!c{>4})	illorum[CVL](>MNE!c{>4})
ab	=
aurugine {!a(?)}(uredine SA!f!w!c!b)	=[MNE](****gine C) (origine V)
{written on erasure -S} {'-ed-' on erasure -A}	(eruginae L)
et	=
grandine	=[CMNEV](grandinae L)
et (>A++{>4})	=
a (>A++{>4})	=[CMNEV](>A++{>4} ,~L)
sidus (sydus A+!a!f) (>A++{>4})(sidere !c)	sydus[A+C!a!f](sydere MN) (= V)(sidere E!c)
	(assidus L)
terribile (>A++{>4}) (terribili !c)	=[CV](terribili MNE!c) (terribilae L)
15:14	
vae	=[CML](ve NEV)
saeculo	=[MNEV](seculo CL)
et	=
qui	=
habitant {A} (inhabitant S!b)	=[CNVL] (inhabitant SME!b)
in	=
eum (eo A++!c)	eo[A++CMNEVL!c]
15:15	
quia	=[CMNEV](qui L)
adpropinquavit (appropinquavit A++!c)	=[L] (appropinquavit A++MNEV!c)
	(adpropinquabit C)
gladius	=
et	=
extritio {A+} (contritio SA++!c!b)	contritio[SA++CNE!c!b] (contricio MVL)
illorum {A} (eorum S!c!b)	=[CVL](eorum SMNE!c!b)
et	=
exsurget {'-get' added above line - first hand? -A}	exurget[CMEV](= N) (surget L)
gens	=
super {S!b} (contra A!w!c)	=
gentem	=
ad	=
pugnam	=
et	=
romphea {A++!w} (rumphea SA+!f!b)	=[!s](rompheae MNE) (romfea
(rhomphaea !c)	C) (rompheam V) (rorifens L)
in	=
manibus	=

169

French Recension	Spanish Recension
eorum	=[CMNEL](>V)
15:16	
erit	=
enim	=[MNVL](aenim C)(autem E)
inconstabilitio (constabilitio A!w)	=[CME] (inconstabilicio NVL)
	in
hominibus	=[CMNE](omnibus V) (manibus L{s.a., v. 15})
(+ . S++)	
(+ et !c)	
aliis {A+} (alisalios !w) (alii S++A++!c!b) (alius S+)	=[CV](alius S+L)(>MNE)
alii {!a} (alios A+)(>~!w) (aliis SA++!c!b)	=[CMNEV](aliis SA++L!c!b)
supervalescentes {A!w} (invalescentes S!c!b)	invalescentes[SCMNEVL!c!b]
non	=
curabunt	=
regem	=
suum	=
et (>A{>4})	=
principem (>A{>4}) (principes !c)	=
megestanorum {!w} (>A{>4}) (>A{>4})	egestanorum[C]
(me_gestanorum S) (viae_gestorum !c)	(vel_maiestanorum W) (egentes_tenorum MNE) (et_gestanorum V) (gestanorum L)
suorum (>A{>4})	=
in	[>~:]
potentia	inpotentia[CMNEV{1 word}] (inpotencia L) {this could be read as 2 words, e.g. in CM}
sua	=
.	=[CMNEV](>~L)
15:17	
concupiscet (concupiscit A)	=[CMNEV](concupiscit AL)
	(+ . ~L)
enim	=[MNEV](aenim C)(>~L)
homo	=
	(+ enim ~L)
	(+ ire ~MNE)
in	=
civitatem	=
ire (>~A)	=[CV](irae L)(>~AMNE)
et	=
non	=
poterit	=
(+ ire ~A)	
.	=[CMNEV](>~L)
15:18	
propter	=
superbiam	=[MNEVL](supervia C)
enim {on erasure -A}	=[MNE](aenim C)(>VL)
eorum	=
	(+ . ~L)
civitates	=
turbabuntur	=
domus	=[MNEV](domos C) (domusque L)

170

French Recension	Spanish Recension

exterentur   =[MNEV](exterrentur C) (exterretur L)

homines   =

metuent {2nd '-e-' on erasure -A}   =[CMNE](metuunt VL)

15:19

non   =

miserebitur   =

homo   =

proximum (proximi A++) (proximo !w)   proximi[A++MNEVL] (proximo C!w)

suum (sui A++)(suo !w)   sui[A++MNEVL](suo C!w)

ad   =

irritum (impetum !b)   =[CVL](ritum MNE)

faciendum   =

in (>!c)   =

domos (domus A+)   =

eorum   =

in   =[VL](immittam M) (inmittam E)(>C) (mittam N)

gladium (gladio A++)   =

ad   =[CMNEV](a L)

diripiendas   diripiendam[CMNEL] (diripiendum V)

substantias   substantiam[CMNEV] (substanciam L)

eorum   illorum[CMNVL](= E)

propter   =[CVL](>MNE{>6})

famem   =[CL](famen V)(>MNE{>6})

panis   =[CVL](>MNE{>6})

et   =[CVL](>MNE{>6})

tribulationem (tribulatione S)   =[CVL](>MNE{>6})

multam (multa S)   =[CVL](>MNE{>6})

15:20

ecce   =

ego   =

convoco   =[CL](convocabo V) (invoco MNE)

dicit   =

   Dominus

Deus (Dominus A)   =

omnes   =

reges   =

terrae   =[MNE](terre CVL)

ad   =

movendum {A} (me_vendum{?} S) (me_verendum !c!b)   =[MNEVL](mobendum C)

qui (>S+!b)   =[CMNE](quae L)(que V)

sunt (>S+!b)   =

a {A!w} (ab S!c!b)   ab[SCMNEVL!c!b]

borea {A!w} (oriente S!c!b)   oriente[SCMNEL!c!b] (oriento V) (+ et E) (+ occidente E)

et   =

a {A!w} (ab S!c!b)   [>]

noto {!w} (notho A) (austro S!c!b)   austro[SCMNEVL!c!b]

et {A} (>S!b)   =[CL](>SMNEV!b)

ab   =[CMNL](a V)(>E)

euro (auro S)   =[CMNL](ueutro V)(>E)

et	=
a	[>]
libano	=[MNEL](libia C)(liba V)
ad	=[CVL](et MNE)
convertendos	=[CVL](convertendum MNE)
in (>!b)	=
se	=
et	=
reddere	=
quae	=[MNEL](que CV)
dederunt	=
illis	=
15:21	
sicut	=
faciunt	=
usque	=
hodie	=[MNEV](hodiae L)(odie C)
electis {added by 1st hand above line -A}	=
meis	=
sic	=
faciam	=
	(+ illis L)
et	=
reddam	=
	(+ eis L)
	(+ mala L)
in	=
sinum {A} {'i' on erasure -A} (sinu S!c!b)	=[C](sinu SMNEVL!c!b)
ipsorum {A} (eorum S!c!b)	=[CV](eorum SMNEL!c!b)
.	=[CEVL](>M,N{?})
{@g [Gildas] begins here}	
haec	=[CMNE](hec VL)
	(+ . N)
dicit	=
Dominus	=
Deus {SA@g5!w!c!b} (meus @g1)	=
15:22	
non	=
parcet (pareet @g7)	=
dextera	=
mea	=
super {followed by erasure -A}	=
peccantes{A@g0} (peccatores S!c)	=
nec	=
cessabit (cessavit A+)	=[CMNE](cessavit A+VL)
romphea {@g6!w} (romphaea @g1)	rumphea[SAN!a!f!b]
(rumpfea @g8) (rhomphaea !c)	(= MEV)(rumfea C)
(rumphea SA!a!f!b)	(ronfea L) (romphearumque L4)
	mea
super	=
effundentes	=[CVL](fundentes MNE)
sanguinem	=
innocuum (innoxium !c)	=[CMNEV](innocentem L)

French Recension	Spanish Recension
super	=
terram	=
15:23	
et (>@g0!c)	=[CVL](>@g0MNE!c)
exiit (exibit @g1) (exiet @g8)	exiet[@g8CMEVL](= N)
ignis	=
ab	=
ira	=
eius (mea @g0)	illius[CMNV](= E) (mea @g0L)
et	=
devoravit (devorabit @g0)	=[VL](deforabit C) (devorabit @g0MNE)
fundamenta	=
terrae	=[MNEV](terre CL)
et	=
peccatores	=[CMNEVLL4]
quasi	=
stramen	=[CEVL](stamen MN) (vel_paleas W)
	(+ lignorum L)
	(+ viridis L)
incensum	incendentur[CV] (incenduntur L)
	(accendentur MNE)
15:24	
vae	=[CM](ve NEV)(ut L)
eis {S@g1} (hiis A+) (his A++@g8)	his[A++@g8MNEVL](= C)
qui	=
peccant	=
et	=
non	=
observant	custodiunt
mandata	=
mea	=
dicit (ait @g8)	=
Dominus (Deus @g5)	=
	Deus[CMNVL](>E)
15:25	
non	=
parcam	=
illis	=
discedite	=
filii	=[CMNEL](fili V)
apostatae {A@g1} (a_potestate S!c)	=[EL](apostate CMN!s)
(apostestate @g8)	(a_potestate SV!c)
(+ et @g0)	
nolite	=[CMNEV](nolitae L)
contaminare	=
sanctificationem	=
meam	=
15:26	
(+ quoniam S!c!b) {>A@g0!w}	quoniam[SCMNEVL!c!b]
novit	=[MNEVL](nobit C)
Deus {A@g1} (Dominus S@g8!c!b)	Dominus[S@g8CMNEVL!c!b]
(+ omnes S!c!b){>A@g0!w}	omnes[SCMNEVL!c!b]
qui	=

French Recension	Spanish Recension
peccant {A@g1} (peccavit @g6) (derelinqunt S+) (delinqunt S++) (delinquunt !c)	delinqunt[S++!s] (delinqunt MNE!c) (delincunt C) (delinquoduunt V) (diligunt L)
in (>A)	=[CMNE](>AVL)
eum {A@g0} (illum S!c!b)	illum[SCMNEVL!c!b]
propterea	propter hoc[CMNEV](>L)
tradet {A@g0} (tradidit S!c!b)	=
eos (vos @g8)	=[MNE](illos CVL)
(+ Deus S)	
in	=
mortem (occisionem ~@g8)	=[CMNEV](morte L)
et (>@g5)	=
in	=[CMNEL](>V)
occisionem (mortem ~@g8)	=[CMNEV](occisionae L)
15:27	
iam	ecce[CNEVL](et_ce M)
enim	=[MNEVL](aenim C) (+ iam VL{s.a., Fr})
venerunt	=[CVL](venient MNE)
super	in
orbem	=
terrarum	=
(+ multa ~@g8)	(+ multa ~@g8V)
mala	=
(+ multa @g1)	multa[@g1CMNEL](>~@g8V)
{@g ends here}	
et	=[MNEVL](>C)
manebitis	=[MNE](manebit CV) (manebunt L)
in	=
illis	=
non	=
enim	=[MNEVL](aenim C)
liberabit {A++!w!c!b} (liberavit SA+!f)	=[CMNEL] (liberavit SA+V!f)
vos	=
Deus	Dominus
propter (propterea A)	=
quod	=
peccastis	=[MNEVL](peccatis C)
in	=
eum (eo A++)	illum[CMNEL](= V)
15:28	
ecce	=
visio	=
(+ et S)	
horribilis (orribilis !c)	=[MNE](orribilis CL!c) (oribilis V)
et	=
facies	=
illius	eius
ab	=[MNEL4](ad CVL)
oriente	=[MNE](orientem CVL) (aquilone L4)

French Recension	Spanish Recension
15:29	
et	=[MNE](>CV,~:L)
exient	=[CMNEV](exientque L) (exire L4)
	(+ flatus V{s.b., S}) (fluctus L)
nationes	=[CMNEVLL4]
draconum	[>]
	(+ et MNE)
Arabum (Arabam{?} A+) (Arabym A++)	=[CVLL4](arabunt MNE)
in	=
curris (curribus A++!c)	curros[CVL](currus MNE)
multis	multos[CMEVL](= N)
et	=
(+ sic S)(sicut !c)	(+ ibi CVL)(sic S) (sicut !c){>~:MNE}
sibilatus {A} (flatus S!c{s.a., VL})	=[MNE](planctus CVL)
eorum	=[MNEVL](ipsorum C)
a (>!c)	=
die (>!c)	=[CMNEV](diae L)
itineris (numerus !c)	=
fertur	=
super	=
terram	=
ut	sicut[N{sic_ut} EVL{M2}] (sic
	CM{1})
etiam (iam !c)	=[MNVL,E{et_iam?}] (aenim C)
timeant	=[MNEV](timent C) (timeat L)
et	=
trepidentur (trepident !c)	formident[MNEL]
(repetentur A)	(formidant C) (formiderit V)
omnes	=
qui	=
illos	[>~]
audient	audiunt[CMNVL](= E)
	illos{~}
15:30	
Carmonii (Carmini A+) (Carmine A++)	=[C](coronii V) (Caronii L) (Carmine
	A++MNE) (vel_apri_carmeli W)
insanientes (insaniantes A+)	=
in	=
ira	=[MNEVL](iram C)
et {S!c} (>A!w!b)	=[MNE](>CVL)
exient	=
(+ ut S!c!b)	(+ ut SMNE!c!b)
(+ apri S!c!b)	(+ apri SMNE!c!b) {'ri' on erasure -M}
	(+ et ~L)
de	=
silva	=[MNEVL](silba C)
et	=[CMNEV](>~L)
advenient	venient
in (de !c)	=
virtute	=[MNEL](virtutem CV)
magna	=[MNEL](magnam CV)
et	=
constabunt	=

French Recension	Spanish Recension

	(+ cum ~MNE)
	(+ illis ~MNE)
in	=
pugnam	=[MNEV](pugna CL)
cum	=[CVL](>~MNE)
illis	=[CVL](>~MNE)
et	=[CMNEVLL4]
vastabunt	=[CMNEVL](devastare L4)
portionem	partem
terrae	=[MNEV](terre CL) (terras L4)
Assyriorum (Assiriorum A)	=[CMNE](Assuriorum V) (Assirioru L) (Assiriorum AL4)
in (>!c{>3})	[>CMNEVL,!c{>3}]
dentibus (>!c{>3})	=
suis (>!c{>3})	=
15:31	
et	=
post	=
haec	=[MNE](hec CVL)
supervalescet (supervalescent !c!b)	convalescet[CMNEV] (valescet L)
draco (dracones !c!b)	=
	(+ et MNE)
(+ memoriae ~:A)	
nativitatis	=[CMNE](habitantis V) (inhabitans L)
(+ suae ~!c)	(+ suae ~MNE!c)
memores {S!c!b} (>~:A) (memoria !w)	memor[CMNE](memoriae V) (memoris L)
suae (sui S)(>~!c)	=[VL](sue C)(>~MNE!c)
	(+ erit MNE)
et	=[CVL](>MNE)
si (>!c)	=
converterint (converterent A) (convertent !c)	=[CVL](converterit MNE)
se	=
conspirantes	conspirantur[CVL] (conspiranter MNE)
in	=
virtute	=[CMNEVL](fortiter L4)
magna	=
ad	=
persequendos	=[CMNEVL](exterminare L4)
eos	illos
15:32	
et (>!c)	[>CMNEV!c,~:L]
isti	=[CMNEV](istique L)
turbabuntur	=
et	=
silebunt	timebunt
in	[>]
virtute	vim[CMNEL](virorum V)
illorum	=
et	=
convertent	=[MNEV](convertens C) (converterent L)
pedes	=[CVL](>MNE{>5})
suos	=[CVL](>MNE{>5})
in	=[CVL](>MNE{>5})

French Recension	Spanish Recension
fugam	=[CVL](>MNE{>5})
	et[CVL](>MNE{>5})
	faciem
	suam
	ad
	aquilonem
15:33	
et	=
a (>~A)	in
territorio (averterit_orio A)	terra
Assyriorum (Assiriorum A)	=[CMNEL](Assiriorum AV)
subsessor {S++A} (obsessor S+)	obsessor[S+CMNEV] (obsesor L)
subsedebit {A} (obsedebit S+) (obsidebit S++!c!b)	obsidebit[S++MNEVL!c!b] (obsedebit S+C)
eos {A!w!c} (illos S!b)	illos[SCMNL!b](= EV)
et	=
consumet	=[CMNEV](consummet L)
unum	=[CMNEV](vim L)
ex	=
illis	ipsis
et	=
erit	=
timor	=
	(+ magnus L)
et	=
tremor	=
in	=
exercitum (exercitu A{?} !c)	exercitu[A{?} CMNEV!c]
(exercituum S+) {possible erasure over '-u' -A}	(= L) {possible erasure over '-u' -A}
illorum	=
et	=
inconstabilitio {A} (inconstantia !b)	inconstantia[CMNE!b]
(constantia S) (contentio !c)	(inconstancia VL)
{'-ti-' written above line- 1st hand -A}	
in (>A)	=
regno {A} (reges S!c!b)	reges[SCMNEVL!c!b]
illorum {A} (ipsorum S!c!b)	ipsorum[SCMNEVL!c!b]
15:34	
ecce	=
nubs (nubes A++!c)	nubes[A++CMNEVLL4!c]
ab	=
oriente	=
et	
	ab[CVL](>MNE)
	occidente
	{+ xxiii L}
	et
a (>!c)	=
septentrione {S++} (septentrionem S+)	=[CNEV](septemtrione AM)
(septemtrione A)	(septemtrionae L)
usque	=
ad	=
meridianum	=
et	=

French Recension	Spanish Recension
facies	=[CVL](faciem MNE)
illorum (earum !c)	=
horrida	orrida[CV](orridas L) (corrigent MNE)
valde	=[CMNEV](valdae L)
plena	=[CV](plenae MNEL) (plenas L4)
irae	=[MNEL](ire CL4)(ira V)
	(+ Domini L4)
et	=
procellae (procelle S)	=[MNEL](procelle SC) (procella V)
15:35	
et	=
conlident (collident S++A++!c)	=[CL] (collident S++A++MNEV!c)
se	=
	in
invicem (>A)	=
(+ in A)	
(+ se A)	
et	=[CMNEVLL4]
effundent (collident !c)	=[CLL4](effundet V) (fundent MNE)
sidus (sydus A!a!f)	sydus[ACMN!a!f](= EVLL4)
copiosum	=[CMNEVLL4]
super	=[CMNEVLL4]
terram	=[CMNEVL](terras L4)
et	[>]
sidus	[>]
illorum	[>]
et (>A)	=[CMNEVLL4]
erit (>A)	=[CMNEVLL4]
sanguis (sanguinem A+)	=[CMNEVL](sanguinis L4)
a	=[CMNE](>VLL4)
gladio	=[CMNEVL](humano L4)
	(+ ronphearum L)
usque	=[CMNEVLL4]
ad (>A+)	=[CMNEVLL4]
ventrem	=[CMNEVLL4]
	(+ et ~C)
equi (aequi S)(>!c)	=[CMNEVLL4]
15:36	
et	=[MNEL](>~C,V)
	(+ a L)
femur {!w!b} (femus S+) (fimus S++!c)(faemur A)	=[CEL](foemur MN) (femus{?} V)
hominis	=
et (usque !c)	=[MNELL4](in CV)
	(+ usque L)
(+ ad !c)	(+ ad L!c)
suffraginem (substramen !c)	[>~:]
cameli {SA++} (camelli A+)	=[CMNEL](camilli V) (camelis L4)
	poplites[~:MNE] (>V{erased}) (poblites
	~:CL) (poplite L4)
et	=
erit	=
timor	=
et	=

178

French Recension	Spanish Recension

tremor
multus {originally 'multos' -S}
super
(+ ter A)
terram
15:37
et
horrebunt

qui
videbunt
iram
illam
et
tremor

adprehendet {S++} (adprehendit S+A+!f!b)
  (apprehendet A++!c)
illos
15:38
et
post
haec
movebuntur (movebunt !c)
nimbi
copiosi
a
meridiano
et

septentrione (septemtrionem A+)
  (septemtrione A++)
et (>A)
portio
alia
ab
occidente
15:39
et
superinvalescent
venti
ab
oriente
et
recludent
eum (eam !c)

et
nubem
quam (quem S+)
suscitavit (suscitabit A++)
in
ira

Spanish Recension column:

=
=[CMNVL](multitudo E)
=

=

=
=[MNE](orrebunt CVL)
omnes
=
=
=[CMNEL](>V)
=
=[CMNEV](>L)
=[CMNEV](tremore L)
(+ magno L)
=[L] (apprehendet A++MNEV!c)
  (adpreendet C)
=

=[CMNEVLL4]
=
=
=[MNEVL](mobebuntur C)
=[CVLL4](nimphae MNE)
=[CVL](copiosae MNE) (multique L4)
=
=
=
(+ a CVL)
=[CNEL] (septemtrione A++MV)

=
=[CMEL](porcio NV)
=[CVL](illa MNE)
=
=

=
=
=
=
=
=
repellent
illum
(+ retro MNE)
=
=
[>]
suscitabit[A++CMNE](= VL)
=
iram

179

French Recension	Spanish Recension
et	=
sidus (situs A+)	sydus[CMN](= EVL)
	(+ stellam L)
	(+ multam L)
	(+ ruginem L)
	(+ vel L)
	(+ cadavera L)
ad	=
faciendam	faciendas
exteritionem {S} (*extri_tionem A+)	strages
(extricationem A++)	
(exterritationem !c)	
ab (ad !c)	=
orientalem {S} (orientale A+) (orientali A++)	oriente
	vero
natum {S} (notum !w!b) (ventum !c)(natho A+)	=[CVL](>~MNE)
(notho A++) {'-ho' on erasure;	
originally 'nati' -A}	
et	=
	(+ ad V)
occidentem (occidente A++)	occidente[A++CMNEVL]
	(+ natum ~MNE)
violabitur	=[CMNE](molabitur V) (volabitur L)
15:40	
et	=
exaltabuntur	=
nubes	=
magnae (magne S!f)	=[MNE](magne SCVL!f!s)
{possibly A+ = 'magnas', with !w}	
et	=
validae (valida S) (validas A+)	=[MNE](valide CVL)
	(+ et MNE)
	(+ ire ~V)
plenae (plena S)	=[MNE](plene CVL)
irae	=[MNEL](ire C)(>~V)
et	=
sidus	cataginis[C](cathaginis L) (caliginis MNEV)
ut	=
exterant (exterrant A+) (exterreant !c)	exterminent[CMNVL] (examinent E)
omnem	=
terram	=
et	=
	qui
inhabitantes	inhabitant[CE] (inhabitent L) (habitant MNV)
in {A} (>S!w!c!b)	=[MNEVL](>SC!w!c!b)
eam (ea A++)	illa[CMNVL](ea A++E)
et	=
fundent {S+A+} (fundet S++) (infundent !c)	=[MNE](effundent A++CVL)
(effundent A++)	
super	=
omnem	=[MNEVL](omne C)
(+ locum !c)	(+ montem MNE)(locum !c)
altum	={V?}

French Recension	Spanish Recension
et	=
eminentem	excelsum
sidus	sydus[CMN](= EVL)
	(+ . ~V)
terribilem {SA+} (terribile A++!w)	terribile[A++CMNEVL!w]
. (>S)	=[CMNEL](>S,~V)
15:41	
ignem	=
et	=
	(+ aquam E)
	(+ et E)
grandinem	=
et	[>CMNEVL](= L4)
rompheas {A++!w} (rumpheas SA+!a!f!b)	gladios[CVLL4](>MNE)
(rhomphaeas !c)	
volantes	=[CVLL4](>MNE)
et	=
aquas	=
multas	=
	ita{~:}
ut	=
etiam	[>~:]
impleantur	=[MNEV](inpleantur CL)
omnes	=
campi	=
et	=
omnes	=[CMNEL](omnem V)
rivi	=
a {A} (>S!c!b)	=
plenitudine (plenitudinem S+)	multitudine
aquarum	=
illarum (multarum !c)	=[CVL](>MNE)
15:42	
et	=
demolient (demolientur A++!c)	=[CL](demollient V) (demolientur
	A++MNE!c)
civitates	=
et	=
muros (murus A+)	=[CVL](ipsos MNE)
et	[>]
montes	=
et	=
colles	=
et	=
ligna	=
silvarum	=
et	[>CMNEV,~:L]
faena {!w} (fena S!f!b) (foena A)(foenum !c)	herbas[V](erbas C) (erbasque L)(herbam MN)
	(herbarum E)
pratorum	camporum
et	=
frumenta	triticum[MNEVL] (tritticum C)
eorum	ipsorum

French Recension	Spanish Recension

15:43
et	=
transibunt	pertransient[CVL] (pertransiet MNE)
constanter {S{?} A!w!b} (constantes !c) {ambiguous '-es' or '-er' -S+}	=[CMN](constantur V,L{?}) (>E) {'constant~', ambiguous '-ur' or '-er' -L}
usque	=[CMNEV](>L)
(+ ad !c)	in[CMNEVL](ad !c)
Babilonem {S} (Babylonem A!w!c!b)	Babiloniam[CNEVL] (Babyloniam M) (Babilon L4)
et	=
exterent (exterrent A+)	exterrent[A+CL](= V) (exterrebit MNE) (exterminari L4)
eam	illam

15:44
convenient (cum_venient A)	=
	enim[MNEVL](aenim C)
ad	in[CMNE](>VL)
ipsam (ipsum S+)	unum[CMNE](>VL)
et	=
circuibunt (circumibunt A)	circumcingent
eam	illam
et	=[CMNEL](>V{>15})
effundent	=[CL](fundent MNE) (>V{>15})
sidus	[>~CMNEL,V{>15}]
et	[>~CMNEL,V{>15}]
omnem	=[CMNEL](>V{>15})
iram	=[CMNL](terram E)(>V{>15})
	et[~CMNEL](>V{>15})
	sydus[~CMN](sidus ~EL) (>V{>15})
super (in A)	=[CMNEL](>V{>15})
eam	=[CMNEL](>V{>15})
	donec[CMNEL](>V{>15})
	funditus[CMNEL](>V{>15})
	eradicent[CMNEL](>V{>15})
	illam[CMNEL](>V{>15})
et	=
subibit	ascendet
pulvis	=
et	=
fumus	=
	eius
usque	=
ad (in !c)	=
caelum	=[CMNE](celum VL)
et	=
omnes	=
in	=
circuitu {stroke above 'cu' and points above 'itu' erased -A}	=
lugebunt (lugebant S+)	=[CMNEV](lugebant S+L) (+ super L)
eam	=

French Recension	Spanish Recension

15:45

et	=
	ceteri[CVL](caeteri MNE)
qui	=[CMNVL](>E)
(+ sub ~!c)	
(+ ea !c)	
subremanserint (remanserint !c)	remanserint[MNV!c] (remanserunt CL)(>E)
servientes (servient !c!b)	servient[CMNEL!c!b](>V)
his	illis[CMNVL](ei E)
qui	=
eam	(>!c) [>~CMNEVL,!c]
exteruerunt {A++!w!b} (exterruerunt SA+!f!c)	exterrent[CVL] (exterent MNE)
	eam{~}

15:46

et	=[CMNEVLL4]
tu	=[CVL](>MNE)
Asia (Assia A+)	=[CMNEVL4](Esaye L)
consors (concors !c)	=
in	=[CMNE](>VL)
specie (speciae A) (spem !c)	=
Babilonis {S} (Babylonis A!w!c!b)	=[CEVL] (Babylonis AMN!w!c!b)
et	=
gloria	=[CMNEV](gloriae L)
personae	=[MNEL](persone CV)
eius	=[MNEVL](aeius C)

15:47

vae	=[CML](ve NEV)
tibi	=[CMNEL](tu V)
misera	=[CVL](miserae NE) (misere M)
propter	quia
quod	[>]
adsimilasti (assimilasti A++)	similis
(+ te A++)	
	facta
	es
ei	illius[CV](illis MNL) (illi E)
(+ et !c)	
ornasti	ornando
filias	=
tuas	=
in	ad[CMNEV](>L)
fornicatione	questum[CMNE](quos V) (quibus L)
ad	ut[CMNE](tu VL)
placendum	placeas
et	=[CMNEV](ut L)
	sis
gloriandum	gloriosa
in	penes
amatoribus	amatores
tuis	tuos[CMNVL](tuas E)
qui	=
te (tecum !c)	=
(+ cum A++)	

French Recension	Spanish Recension
cupierunt	=[CMN](concupierunt EVL)
	(+ . ~MNEV)
semper	=
(+ . ~!b)	.[CL!b](>~SAMNEV!w!c)
	{15:48}
	imitata[~CMNE] (inmitata ~L) (inita ~:V)
	es{~}
fornicari (fornicare A+) (fornicariam !b)	fornicariam[CMNEVL!b]
. {SA!w!c} (>~!b)	[>~CMNEVL!b]
15:48	{>}
odibilem (odivilem A+)	=[CMNEL](hodibilem V)
imitata	[>~]
es	[>~]
in	=
omnibus	=
operibus {added in margin by 1st hand -A}	=[CMNEVL](opera L4)
	(+ mala L4)
eius	=[CMNVL](>E)
et	=[CMNEV](>L)
(+ in !c)	(+ in CNVL!c)
adinventionibus	=[MNE](adventionibus CL) (adventionem V)
eius	=
	secuta[CMNEV](>L{>5})
	es[CMNEV](>L{>5})
	illam[CMNEV](>L{>5})
	placitura[CV] (placituram MNE) (>L{>5})
	potentibus[CMNEV](>L{>5})
	et
	principibus[CMNE] (principalibus VL)
	eius
	(+ et C)
	ut
	(+ in V)
	gloriosa[CMNEL] (gloriose V)
	fias
	et[CMNEV](>L)
	placeas
	in[CMNEVL](pro L4)
	fornicationibus[CMNEV] (fornificationibus
	L) (fornicatione L4)
	eius[CMNVL](sua L4)(>E)
propterea	=
dicit	=
Deus	Dominus
15:49	
inmittam (immittam !c)	=[CEVL](immittam MN!c)
tibi	=
mala	=
viduitatem	=
paupertatem	=
et	[>]
famem	=[CMNEL](famen V)
et	[>]

French Recension	Spanish Recension

gladium   =
et   =
pestem   pestilentiam[CMNE] (pestilenciam VL)
ad   =
devastandas   =[CMNEVL](devastatas L4)
domos (domus S!b)   =
tuas   =
ad (a S+!c)   [>]
violationem (violatione !c)   [>]
et   [>]
mortem (morte !c)   [>]
15:50
et   =
gloria   =[CMNEV](gloriam L)
virtutis   vultus
tuae   tui
sicut   =
flos   =
siccabitur   =[CMNEV](sicabitur L)
cum   =[MNEVL](quum C)
exsurget   exurget[CMEV](= NL)
ardor   =[CMNEV](>L)
qui   =
emissus   missus
est   =
super   =
te   =
15:51
et (>!c)   =[CVL](ut MNE)
infirmaberis {S++A++} (infirmaveris A+)   infirmeris[CMNE]
     (firmaberis S+)   (infirmes V) (irfirmis L)
et (ut !c)(>A++)   =
paupera (paupercula !c)   pauper[CV] (pauperescas MNE)(= L)
     {originally 'pauperes_eas' -M}
     (+ efficias L)
a (>!c)   =[CMNEL](>~V,!c)
     flagellis[~:CMNEL] (affligis ~:V)
     et{~}
plaga (plagata !c)   =[CMNEL](planga V)
et   [>~]
mastigata (castigata !c)   [>~:]
a   [>]
vulneribus (mulieribus !c)   [>]
     ita[CMNEV](>L)
ut   =
non   =
possit {S} (possitis A+) (possis A+++!w!b)   possis[A+++CMNEVL!w!b]
     (possint A++!c)
vos {SA} (tuos !w!b) (te !c)   [>~:]
suscipere   =
potentes   =[CMNEL](potentis V)
et   =[MNE](>CVL)
amatores   =
     tuos{~:}

15:52
numquid (nunquid !c)   =[CMNVL](nunquid E!c)
ego   =[MNE](ergo CVL)
sic   =[CMNEV](si L)
zelabo (zelabor !c)   zelassem[CMNV](zelatus E) (celassem L)
                                                  (+ esse E)
te   =
dicit   =[CMNEL](>V)
Dominus   =[CMNEV](>L)
15:53
nisi   =
occidisses (occidisset A)   =
electos (electus A+)   =[MNEVL](aelectos C)
meos (meus A+)   =
                                                  {+ ? MNE}
in   [>~:]
omni   [>~:]
tempore   semper[CMNEV](sed_per L)
exultans (exaltans S++!c)   =[CVL](exultasti MNE)
                                                  in
percussionem {SA!c} (percussione !w!b)   percussione[CMNEVL!w!b]
manuum {S++A+++} (manum S+A++!f) (meam A+) =
et   =
dicens   deridens[CMNEV] (derridens L)
super   in
mortem (montem S++)   morte[CMNEV](= L)
eorum   ipsorum
{+ ? S}
cum   [>~:]
inebriata   ebria[CMEVL](aebria N)
                                                  facta
es (esses !c)   [>~:CMNVL](= E)
                                                  (+ de L)
                                                  (+ sanguine L)
                                                  (+ eorum L)

15:54
exorna   exornans
                                                  (+ enim L)
speciem   =
vultus   =
tui   =[CMEVL](sui N)
15:55
                                                  et
merces (mercis S+)   =
fornicariae (fornicaria A) (fornicationis !c)   =[MNEVL](fornicarie C)
(+ tuae !c)
in   =
sinus (sinos S+)(sinu !c)   sinu[CMNEVL!c]
tuos (tuo !c)   tuo[CMNEVL!c]
                                                  est
propterea (propter !c)   =[CMNEL](propter V!c)
(+ hoc !c)

French Recension	Spanish Recension
	secundum
	facta
	tua
redditionem	[>~:]
percipies {A} (recipies S!b) (accipies !c)	recipies[SCMNE!b] (recipias V) (respicies L)
	in{~:}
	sinus[~:CMNEL](sinos ~:V)
	tuos{~:}
15:56	
sicut	=
facies	facis[CMNE](= VL)
electis (electos S)	=[MNEVL](aelectis C)
meis {meos S}	=
dicit	=
Dominus	=
sic	=
faciet (faciat S+)	=
tibi	=
Deus	=
et	=
tradet	=[MNEVL](tradent C)
te	=
in	=
malis (malum !c)	mala[CMNVL](malum E!c)
15:57	
et	=
nati	filii[CMNEL](fillii V)
tui	=
{X begins here}	
fame (famae A)({λει} μω X)	=[CMNEV](famae AL)
interient (διαφθαρησεται X)	=[CMNEVL]
et (και X)	=[CMNEVL]
tu (συ X)	=[CMNE](>~:VL)
	ipsa[MNE](ipse C) (eversa V{?} ,L)
(+ εν X)	
romphea {!w} (rumphea SA!a!f!b) (rhomphaea !c) (ρομφαια X)	gladio[CMNEVL]
cades (πεση X)	=[CMNEL](cadet V)
et (και X)	=[CMNEVL]
civitates (αι_πολεις X)	=[CMNEVL]
tuae (σου X)	=[MNEL](tue CV)
conterentur (συντριβησονται X)	subvertentur[CMNEVL]
et (και X)	=[CMNEVL]
omnes (παντες X)	=[CMNEVL]
	(+ fores L)
tui (tuae A+)(σου X)	=[CMNEVL]
	(+ gladio ~MNE)
	(+ cadent ~MNE)
(+ οι X)	
in (εν X)	=[CMNEVL]
campo (τοισ_πεδιοις X)	=[MNEL](campum CV)
gladio (>~X)	=[CVL](>~MNEX)

French Recension	Spanish Recension
cadent (πεσουνται X)	=[CVL](>~MNE)
(+ εν ~X)	
(+ μαχαιρη ~X)	
15:58	
et (και X)	=
qui (οι X)	=
sunt (>X)	=
in (εν X)	=
montibus (τοισ_ορεσι X)	=
(+ και X)	
(+ μετεωροισ X)	
fame (famae A) (εν_λειμω X)	=
peribunt (διαφθαρησονται X)	disperient
et (και X)	=
manducabunt (εδονται X)	[>~]
{originally -'bant' -S}	
carnes (τασ_σαρκασ X)	=
suas (αυτων X)	=[CMNE](illorum V) (semetipsorum L)
	manducabunt{~}
et (και X)	=
sanguinem (το_αιμα X)	=
suum {!a} (αυτων X) (>SA!f!w!c!b)	=
bibent (bibant S+) (πιονται X)	=
a (απο X)	=
fame (famae A)(λειμου X)	=
panis (αρτου X)	=
et (και X)	=
siti (sitis A+)(διψησ X)	=
aquae (aque S)(υδατοσ X)	=[MNEL](aque SCV)
15:59	
{Only A@g(X)!w in this column}	{SCMNEVL!t!c!b in this column}
	infelix[~:SCMNEVL!t!c!b]
propter	[>SCMNEVL!t!c!b]
priora (priorem A++) ({πρω} τα X)	primaria[SCMNEVL!t!b] (per_maria !c)
(+ μεν X)	
misera {A++!w} (misserat{?} A+)(>~X)	[>~:SCMNEVL!t!c!b]
(miseriam A+++)	
venies {!a} (ηκεισ X) (es A++!w)(>A+{A+++})	=
(+ ταλαινα ~X)	
et (και X)	=
iterum (παλιν X)	rursum[SCMNEV!t!c!b] (sursum L)
(+ εκ X)	
(+ δευτερου X)	
{X ends here}	
excipies	accipies[SCMNEVL!t!c!b]
	(+ tu L)
mala	=
15:60	
et	=
in	=
transitum	=[S+MNE] (transitu S++CVL!t!c!b)
allident	=[S++CMNEVL!c!b] (adlident S+!t)
civitatem	=[SCMNEL!t!c!b] (civitates V)

French Recension	Spanish Recension
oditam	odiosam[CEL!t] (otiosam SM!b) (occisam
	!c)(ociosam N) (hodiosam V)
et	=
exterent {A++!w} (exterrent A+)	=[SMNE!t!c!b] (exterrent A+CVL)
eam	[>SCMNEVL!t!c!b]
	aliquam[~SCMNEVL!t!c!b]
portionem	=[SCMNE!t!c!b] (porcionem VL)
aliquam	[>~SCMNEVL!t!c!b]
	terrae[~:MNEVL!t!c!b] (terre ~:SC)
	tuae[~:SMNEVL!t!c!b] (tue ~:C)
	et[~SMNEL!t!c!b] (>C{>4} V{>4})
	partem[SMNE!t!c!b] (>C{>4} V{>4} L{>3})
gloriae	=[MNE!t!c!b] (>C{>4} V{>4} L{>3}) (glorie S)
tuae	=[SMNE!t!c!b] (>C{>4} V{>4} L{>3})
et	[>~SCMNEVL!t!c!b]
territorii {A++} (terraeturiae A+)	[>~:SCMNEVL!t!c!b]
tui {A++} (tuae A+)	[>~:SCMNEVL!t!c!b]
	exterminabunt[SCMNEVL!t!c!b]
dum	rursum[SCMNEVL!t!c!b]
revertuntur (revertentur A++)	revertentes[SCMNEL!t!c!b] (te V)
a	=[CMNEVL!t!b](ad S!c)
Babylonia	Babilonia[CEVL](= MN!t!b) (Babiloniam S)
	(Babylonem !c)
	(+ . M)
	subversa[CMNEVL!t!b] (subversam S!c)
15:61	
	et[CMNEVL!t!c!b](ut S)
extrita	demolita[SCMNEVL!t!c!b]
	eris[~SCMNEVL!t!c!b]
illis	=
eris	[>~SCMNEVL!t!c!b]
	(+ in MNE)
in	pro[SCVL!t!c!b](>~MNE)
stramine	stipula[SCVL!t!c!b] (prostibulo MNE)
et	=
ipsi	=
	erunt[~SCMNE!t!c!b](>~VL)
tibi	=
erunt	[>~SCMNE!t!c!b](= VL)
ignis	=
15:62	
	et[SCMNEVL!t!c!b]
omnes	[>SCMNEVL!t!c!b]
hii	[>SCMNEVL!t!c!b]
comedunt {A+} (comedent A++)	devorabunt[SMNEVL!t!c!b] (deforabunt C)
te	=
et	=
civitates	=
tuas	=
et	[>SCMNEL,V{>10} ,!t!c!b]
territoria {A++} (terraeturia A+)	terram[SCMNEL!t!c!b] (>V{>10})
tua	tuam[SCMNEL!t!c!b] (>V{>10})
et	=[SCMNEL!t!c!b](>V{>10})

montes	=[SCMNEL!t!c!b](>V{>10})
	tuos[SCMNEL!t!c!b] (>V{>10})
et	[>SCMNE,V{>10} ,!t!c!b] (= L)
omnem	omnes[SCMNL!t!c!b] (>E,V{>10})
	(+ . SMNE)
silvam	silvas[SCMNEL!t!c!b] (>V{>10})
tuam	tuas[SCMNEL!t!c!b] (>V{>10})
et	=
ligna	lignum[SCMNEV!t!c!b] (linum L)
pomifera	fructiferum[SMNEL!t!c!b] (tuum
	C)(fructaferum V)
igne	igni[SCMNEVL!t!c!b]
consument	conburent[SCVL!t!b] (comburent MNE!c)
15:63	
et	[>SCMNEVL!t!c!b]
natos	filios[SCMNEVL!t!c!b]
tuos	=
captivabunt	captivos[SCMNEVL!t!c!b] (captivas L4)
	ducent[~:SCMNEVL!t!c!b]
et	=
honestatem	censum[SCMNEVL!t!c!b] (genus W)
tuam	tuum[SCMNEVL!t!c!b]
	(+ in MNE!c)
spoliabunt	praeda[S!t!b](preda CV) (praedam M!c)
	(predam NE) (predabunt L)
	habebunt[SCMNEV!t!c!b] (>~:L)
et	=
gloriam	=[SCMNEL!t!c!b](gloria V)
faciei	=
tuae	=[SMNEVL!t!c!b](tue C)
exterminabunt	=
	(+ et L)
	(+ tunc L)
	(+ humiliaberis L)
	{+ xxv L}
16:1	
vae	=[SCML!t!c!b](ve NEVL4)
tibi	=[SMNE!t!c!b](vobis CVL)
Babilon {A} (Babylon !w)	=[CEVLL4] (Babylon SMN!w!t!c!b)
et	=[SCMNEVLL4!t!c!b]
Asia {A++} (Assia A+)	=[SCMNEVL4!t!c!b] (Esaye L)
vae	=[SCML!t!c!b](ve N{?} EV)
tibi	=[SMNE!t!c!b](vobis CVL)
Aegypte {!w} (Aegyptae A!f)	=[CE!t!c!b](Egypte M) (Aegyptae SA!f)
	(Aegipte N) (Egypti V) (Egiptum L)
	(Egipte L4)
et	=[SCMNEVLL4!t!c!b]
Syria	=[SCMNEL4!t!c!b](Siria V) (Syrie L)
16:2	
praecingite	precingite[CMNEVL] (= S!t!c!b)(amicte L4)
vos	=
saccos {A+} (sacco A++)	saccis[SCMNEVLL4!t!c!b]
	(+ et SMNE!t!c!b)

French Recension	Spanish Recension

	(+ ciliciis SMNE!t!c!b)
	et[SCMNEVL!t!c!b]
plangite	=[SCMNEVL!t!c!b] (plangere L4)
filios	=
vestros	=
et	=
dolete	=[SCMNEV!t!c!b](doletae L)
de	[>SCMNEVL!t!c!b]
his	eos[SCMNE!t!b](hos VL) (>!c)
quia	quoniam[SCMNEVL!t!c!b]
adpropinquavit {A+!w} (appropinquavit A++)	=[S+!t!b] (appropinquavit S++A++MNE!c) (adpropinquabit CL) (appropinquatur V)
contritio	=[SCNE!t!c!b] (contricio MVL)
vestra	=
16:3	
{@g [Gildas] begins here}	
inmissus {A++@g1} (inmisus A+) (immissus @g3@g6)	missus[S+CMNEVL!t] (= S++!b) (immissus @g3@g6!c)
est	=
	vobis[~SCMNEVL!t!c!b]
gladius	=[SCMNEL!t!c!b] (gladioque L4) (ignis ~V{s.b., v. 4})
vobis	[>~SCMNEVL!t!c!b]
et (>@g0{>9})	=
quis (>@g0{>9})	=
est (>@g0{>9})	=[SCMNE!t!c!b](e{?} L) (>V,@g0{>9})
qui (>@g0{>9})	=[SCMNE!t!c!b] (>VL,@g0{>9})
avertat (>@g0{>9})	=[SCMN!t!c!b](avertet E) (vertat{?} L) (extinguet ~V{see v. 4})
eum (>@g0{>9})	illum[S++CMNEVL!t!c!b] (illud S+) {+ ? S++MNEV}
16:4	
inmissus (>@g0{>9})	missus[S+CMNVL!t] (= S++!c!b)(>E@g0{>10})
est (>@g0{>9})	=[SCMNVL!t!c!b] (>E{>10} @g0{>9}) (+ in !c)
vobis (>@g0{>9})	=[SCMNVL!t!c!b] (>E{>10} @g0{>9})
ignis	=[SCMNL!t!c!b](>E{>10}) (gladius ~V{s.a., v. 3})
et (>@g0{>10})	=[SCMNVL!t!c!b] (>E@g0{>10})
quis (>@g0{>10})	=[SMNVL!t!c!b] (>C,E@g0{>10})
est (>@g0{>10})	=[SMNV!t!c!b] (>CL,E@g0{>10})
qui (>@g0{>10})	=[SCMNV!t!c!b] (>L,E@g0{>10})
extinguat (>@g0{>10})	=[SMNL!t!b](exstinguat !c) (>E@g0{>10}) (extinguet C) (avertet ~V{s.a., v. 3})
eum (>@g0{>10})	illum[S++CMNVL!t!c!b] (>E@g0{>10})(illud S+) {+ ? S++MNV}
16:5	
inmissa {A++} (inmisa A+) (>@g0{>10})	missa[S+CMNEVL!t] (= S++!b)(immissa !c)
sunt (>@g0{>10})	=
vobis (>@g0{>10})	=
mala (>@g0{>10})	=

et	=
quis	=[SCMNEL!t!c!b](qui V)
est	=[SMNE!t!c!b](>CVL)
qui	=[SMNE!t!c!b](>CVL)
recutiet {@g1!w} (recuciet A+@g6) (recuciat A++)	repellet[CEVL] (repellat SMN!t!c!b)
ea	=[SCMNE!t!c!b](eam VL)
	{+ ? SMNE}
16:6	
numquid (nunquid @g3@g6)	=[SCMNVL!t!b] (nunquid @g3@g6E!c)
recutiet (recuciet @g6)	repellet[SCVL!t!c!b] (repellit MNE)
aliquis	=
leonem	=[SCNEVL!t!c!b](>M{>18})
esurientem	=[SCNEV!t!c!b](>~L,M{>18})
in	=[SCNEVL!t!c!b](>M{>18})
silva	=[SCNEL!t!c!b](>M{>18}) (silvam V)
	(+ esurientem ~L)
	{+ ? S}
aut	=[SCNEVL!t!c!b](>M{>18})
numquid (nunquid @g3@g6)	[>SCM{>18} NEVL!t!c!b]
extinguet {@g0} (extinguit A)	=[S++CEVL!t!b] (extinguat S+)(>M{>18})
	(exstinguet !c) (extinguit AN)
ignem	=[SCNEVL!t!c!b](>M{>18})
cum	in[SCNEV!t!c!b](= L) (>M{>18})
stramen	stipula[CEV!t!c!b] (stupa L)(>M{>18})
	(stipulam SN) (vel_messe W)
	(+ cum V{s.a., Fr})
	mox[~:SCNEVL!t!c!b] (>M{>18})
	(+ quae ~:!t!b)(que ~:S) (quando ~:!c)(ut ~:NE)
	coeperit[~:SNE!t!c!b] (>M{>18}) (ceperit ~:CVL) {s. Sp, 16:13}
incensum	ardere[SCNEVL!t!c!b] (>M{>18})
fuerit	[>~:SCM{>18} NEVL!t!c!b]
	{+ ? SNEV}
16:7	
aut (>@g0{>8})	[>SCM{>18} NEVL,@g0{>8} !t!c!b]
numquid (>@g0{>8})	=[SCNVL!t!b](nunquid E!c) (>M{>18})
	aliquis[SCNEVL!t!b] (>M{>18} ,~!c)
recutiet (>@g0{>8})	repellet[S++CNEVL!t!c!b] (repellit S+)(>M{>18})
	(+ aliquis ~!c)
sagittam {A++!w} (sagitam A+)(>@g0{>8})	=
inmissam {A++!w} (inmisam A+)(>@g0{>8})	[>~:SCMNEV,@g0{>8} !t!c!b] (missam L)
a (>@g0{>8})	=
sagittario {!w} (sagitario A)(>@g0{>8})	=
forte (>@g0{>8})	forti[SCME!t!c!b](= N) (fortissimam V)
	(fortissimo L)
	missam[~:SCMNE!t!c!b] (>~VL)
	{+ ? SMNEV}
16:8	
Dominus	=[SCMNEV!t!c!b](Domine L) (Domino L4)
Deus	=[SCMNEVL!t!b](fortis !c)
mittit (mittet @g0)	=[SCMNEL!t!b] (mittet V@g0) (immittit !c)
	(mittitur L4)

French Recension	Spanish Recension
mala	=
et	=
quis	=
(+ est @g0)	(+ est @g0!c)
(+ qui @g0)	(+ qui @g0!c)
(+ extinguat @g8{+10})	
(+ eum @g8{+10})	
(+ immissa @g8{+10})	
(+ sunt @g8{+10})	
(+ vobis @g8{+10})	
(+ mala @g8{+10})	
(+ et @g8{+10})	
(+ quis @g8{+10})	
(+ est @g8{+10})	
(+ qui @g8{+10})	
recutiet {@g1} (excutiet @g8) (recuciet A@g6)	repellet[S++CMNEV!t!b] (repellat S+!c) (repellete L) (repellere L4)
	=[SCMNEL!t!c!b](illa V)
ea	{+ ? SMNE}
16:9	
et	[>SCMNEVL!t!c!b]
exiet {@g1} (exiit A+) (exit A++) (exibit @g3@g4)	=[SCEVL!t!b] (exiit A+MN!c)
ignis	=
ex {@g0} (et A)	=[SCMNEL!t!c!b](et AVL4)
iracundia	=[SCMNEVL!t!c!b](iram L4)
eius	=
et	=
quis	=
est (>@g3@g4@g6)	=
qui (>@g3@g4)	=
	(+ eum ~V)
extinguat (extinguet @g0)	=[SCMNEL!t!c!b] (extinguet @g0V)
eum	=[SCMNEL!t!c!b](>~V)
	{+ ? SMNE}
16:10	
coruscabit (curuscabit A+)	=[S++C!t!c!b] (choruscabit MNE) (corruscabit S+V) (coruscavit L)
	(+ in L)
	(+ fulgoribus L)
et	=
quis	=
	(+ est M)
	(+ qui M)
non (nun A+)	=
timebit	=
	(+ eum CL)(Deum V)
	{+ ? SMNEL}
tonabit (thonabit @g6)	=[SCMNEL!t!c!b] (tonavit V)
	(+ cum L)
	(+ fortitudine L)
et	=
quis	=
non	=

French Recension	Spanish Recension
horrebit (terrebit @g8)	orrebit[CVL](= !b) (urguebit ME!t) (surgebit S) (pavebit !c)(urgebit N) {+ ? SMNEL}
16:11	
Dominus (Deus @g0)	=
comminatur {A!w} (comminabitur @g1) (cuncta_minabitur @g34) (cuncta_minabitur @g6)	conminatur[CL] (comminabitur @g1SMNE!t!c!b) (cominabitur V)
et {@g0} (>A!w)	=
quis	=
non	=
	funditus[SCMNE!t!c!b] (confunditur VL) {+ ? V}
conterretur {A+!w} (terretur A++) (terrebitur @g0) (+ . ~A@g3@g6){>@g1}	conteretur[CMNEVL!t!c!b] (conteritur S)
a	=
facie (faciae A)	=[SCMNEV!t!c!b] (faciae AL)
eius	ipsius[SCMNEVL!t!c!b]
. {@g1} (>~A@g3@g6)	={? SNE}
16:12	
	terra[~SCMNEVL!t!c!b]
tremet (tremit A++)	tremuit[SMNEVL!t!c!b] (tremit A++C)
terra	[>~SCMNEVL!t!c!b]
et {@g0} (a A!w)	=
fundamenta {@g0} (fundamento A!w)	=
eius (>@g0)	=
mare (maris @g0)	=
fluctuatur {A+} (fluctuantur @g1) (fluctuat A++)	fluctuat[A++CMNEV!c] (= S!t!b) (fluctuabuntur @g8) (fluctuavit L) (+ et V)
de	=[SCMNEV!t!c!b](ex L)
profundo (superbo @g6)	=
{@g ends here}	
et	=
fluctus	=
eius	=
turbabuntur	=[CV](turbabubuntur L) (disturbabuntur SMNE!t!c!b)
et	=
pisces	=
eius	=
	(+ conmiscebuntur L)
a	=[SCMNEL!t!c!b](>V{>8})
facie (faciae A)	=[SCMNE!t!c!b](faciae AL) (>V{>8})
Domini	=[SCMNEL!t!c!b](>V{>8})
et	=[SCMNEL!t!c!b](>V{>8})
a	[>S+MNEL,V{>8}] (= S++C!t!c!b)
gloria	=[SCMNEL!t!c!b](>V{>8})
virtutis	=[SCMNEL!t!c!b](>V{>8}) {M adds above line, 1st hand}
eius	=[SCMNEL!t!c!b](>V{>8})
16:13	
quoniam	=

French Recension	Spanish Recension
fortis	=
gloriae	dextera[SCMNEVL!t!c!b]
	eius[SCMNEVL!t!c!b]
qui	quae[SMNE!t!c!b](que C) (= V)(quia L)
	arcum[~:SCMNEVL!t!c!b]
tendit	=[SMNE!t!c!b](tendet CVL)
sagittam	[>~:SCMNEVL!t!c!b]
et	=[CVL](>SMNE!t!c!b)
acumen	sagittae[SMNE!t!c!b] (sagitte CVL) {s.a., Fr}
eius	=
acutum	acutae[MNE!t!c!b] (acute SC)(>V) (accute L)
quae	=[SMNEL!t!c!b](que CV)
	ab[~SCMNEVL!t!c!b]
	ipso[~:SCMNEVL!t!c!b]
dimissa {!w} (dimisa A)	mittuntur[SCMNEVL!t!c!b]
est	[>~:SCMNEVL!t!c!b]
ab	[>~SCMNEVL!t!c!b]
eo	[>~:SCMNEVL!t!c!b]
non	=
deficiet	deficient[SCMNEVL!t!c!b]
	cum[SCMNEVL!t!c!b]
	coeperint[SMNE!t!c!b] (ceperint CVL) {s. Sp, 16:6}
missa	mitti[SCMNEVL!t!c!b]
super	in[SCMNEVL!t!c!b]
fines	=
terrae	=[SMNEVL!t!c!b](terre C)
16:14	
ecce	=
mittuntur	=
mala	=
et	=
non	=
revertentur	=
donec	=
venient {A+} (veniant A++)	veniant[A++CMNVL!t!c!b] (= S)(veniat E)
super	=
terram	=
16:15	
et	[>SCMNEVL!t!c!b]
ignis	=
incendetur	succenditur[SCVL!t!c!b] (succendetur MNE)
et	=
non	=
extinguetur	=[SCMNEVL!t!b] (exstinguetur !c)
donec	=
excomedat	consumat[SCMNEVL!t!c!b]
fundamenta {!a} (frumenta A!f!w)	=
terrae	=[SMNEL!t!c!b](terre CV)
16:16	
quomodo	quemadmodum[SCMNEVL!t!c!b]
non	=
revertitur	redit[SCMNEVL!t!c!b]

French Recension	Spanish Recension
sagitta {A++!w} (sagita A+)	=
missa {A++!w} (misa A+)	=
a	=
	(+ valido ~!c)
sagittario {!w} (sagitario A)	=
valido	=[SCMNEVL!t!b](>~!c)
sic	=
non	=
revertentur	=
mala	=
quae	=[SMNEL!t!c!b](que CV)
fuerint	[>~SCMNEVL!t!c!b]
emissa {A++!w} (emisa A+)	missa[SCMNEVL!t!c!b]
	fuerint[~SCMNEVL!t!c!b]
	(+ a L)
	(+ Domino L)
in	=[SCMNVL!t!c!b](super E)
terram	=[SCMNE!t!c!b](terra VL)
16:17	
vae	=[SCML!t!c!b](ve NEV)
mihi	=[SNEV!t!c!b](mici C) (michi ML)
vae	=[SCML!t!c!b](ve NEV)
mihi	=[SNEVL!t!c!b](mici C) (michi M)
quis	=
me	=
liberabit {A++} (liberavit A+)	=[S++CMNEVL!t!c!b] (liberavit S+A+)
in	=
	illis[~SCMNEL!t!c!b](>~:V)
diebus	=
illis	[>~SCMNEL!t!c!b] (illius ~:V)
	{+ ? SMNE}
16:18	
initium	=[SCMEL!t!c!b] (inicium NV)
gemitus	dolorum[SCMNEVL!t!c!b]
et	=
copiosi	multi[SCMNEVL!t!c!b]
suspirantium	gemitus[SCL!t!c!b] (gement MNE) (gemitibus V) {s.a., Fr}
initium	=[SCME!t!c!b](inicium NVL)
famis	=
et	=
multi {A++!w} (multis A+)	=
disperient	interient[SCMNEVL!t!b] (interitus !c)
initium	=[SCMEV!t!c!b](inicium NL)
	(+ dolorum V)
belli	bellorum[SCMNEVL!t!c!b]
et	=[SCMNEV!t!c!b](>L)
timebunt	formidabunt[SCMNEVL!t!c!b]
	(+ potentes V)
potestates	=
initium	=[SCMEV!t!c!b] (inicium NL)
malorum	=[SCVL!t!c!b] (dolorum MNE)
et	=

French Recension	Spanish Recension
trepidabunt	=
	omnes[SCMNEVL!t!c!b]
{no punctuation -A}	(+ . C)
{Lat 16:19}	
ab	in[SCMNEVL!t!c!b]
eis	his{SCMNEVL!t!c!b]
.	[>~SCMNEL](= V)
quid	=[S+CVL!t!c!b](que S++) (qui MNE)
facient	=[CVL!t!b](faciam !c) (fecerint S) (defecerint
	MNE)
cum	=[SCNEVL](>M)
venerint	=[SCNEVL!t!c!b] (convenerint M)
mala	=
	{+ ? V}
16:19{Lat 20}	
ecce	=
famis	=[S+CVL] (fames S++MNE!t!c!b)
	et[SCMNE!t!c!b](>VL)
plaga	=
dimissa	[>~:SCMNEVL!t!c!b]
est	[>~:SCMNEVL!t!c!b]
et	=
tribulatio	=[SCMNEL!t!c!b] (tribulacio V)
eius	[>SCMNEVL!t!c!b]
	et[SCMNEVL!t!c!b]
	angustia[SCMNEVL!t!c!b]
	missa[~:SCMNEVL!t!c!b]
	sunt[~:SCMNEVL!t!c!b]
tamquam	[>SCMNEVL!t!c!b]
mastix	flagella[SCMNEVL!t!c!b]
castigatio	[>SCMNEVL!t!c!b]
in	=
disciplina	emendatione[SMN!t!c!b] (emendationem
	CEL) (emendaciunem V)
16:20{Lat 21}	
et	=
super	in[SCMNEVL!t!c!b]
his	=
omnibus	=
	(+ se ~SMNE!t!c!b)
non	=
se	=[CVL](>~SMNE!t!c!b)
avertent	convertent[SVL!t!c!b] (convertunt CMNE)
ab	=
iniquitatibus	=
suis	=
nec	neque[SCMNEVL!t!c!b]
super	[>SCMNEVL!t!c!b]
has	[>SCMNEVL!t!c!b]
plagas	flagellorum[SCMNEVL!t!c!b]
memorantur	memores[SCMNEVL!t!c!b]
	erunt[SCVL!t!c!b] (sunt MNE)
sempiterna	semper[SCMNEVL!t!c!b]

French Recension	Spanish Recension
16:21{Lat 22}	
ecce	=
erit	=
annonae	=[SMNE!t!c!b](annone CL) (annonebilitas V)
vilitas	=[SCMNEL!t!c!b](>~V)
	(+ vilitas L)
in	[>SCMNEVL!t!c!b]
brevi	[>SCMNEVL!t!c!b]
super	=
terram	=
	(+ non L)
ut	sicut[CMNEVL] (sic_ut S!t!c!b)
putent	=[SCL!t!c!b](putant V) (potest MNE)
sibi	=[SCVL!t!c!b](>MNE)
esse	=[SCMEVL!t!c!b](>N)
directam	=[SCVL!t!c!b](directa MNE)
pacem	=[SCVL!t!c!b](pace MNE)
	et[SCMNEVL!t!c!b]
tunc	=
superflorescent	germinabunt[SCVL!t!c!b] (germinabuntur E)
	(geminabuntur MN)
mala	=
super	=
terram	=
gladius	=[SCMNEVL!t!c!b] (gladio L4)
et	[>~:SCMNEVL!t!c!b](= L4)
famis {A+} (fames A++)	=[S+CL4] (fames S++A++MNEVL!t!c!b)
	et[~:SCMNEVL!t!c!b]
	magna[SCMNEVL!t!c!b]
	confusio[SCMNEVL!t!c!b]
16:22{Lat 23}	
	a[SCMNEVL!t!c!b]
	fame[SCMNEVL!t!c!b]
et	enim[SMNEVL!t!c!b] (aenim C)
aporiant {!w} (aperiant A+) (aporient A++)	[>SCMNEVL!t!c!b]
vitam	[>SCMNEVL!t!c!b]
	plurimi[SCMNEVL!t!c!b] (homines L4)
	qui[SCMNEVL!t!c!b]
	inhabitant[SCMNEVL!t!c!b]
super	[>SCMNEVL!t!c!b]
terram	=
	interient[~:SCMNEVL!t!c!b] (consumentur
	L4)
et	=
gladius	=
dispersit {A+} (disperdet A++)	disperdet[A++CVL] (perdet SMNE!t!c!b)
	ceteros[S++CNVL!t!c!b] (caeteros S+ME)
quae	qui[SCMNEVL!t!c!b]
superaverint	=[SMNEVL!t!c!b] (superaberint C)
a	=
fame	=[SCMNEV!t!c!b](famae L)
16:23{Lat 24}	
et	=

French Recension	Spanish Recension

mortui
quasi   =   tamquam[SCVL!t!b] (tanquam MNE)
           (sicut !c)

stercora   =
proicientur {A++} (proiecientur A+)   =[S++CMNEVL!t!c!b] (proiciuntur S+)
et   =
non   =
habent {A+} (habebunt A++)   erit[SCMNEVL!t!c!b]
qui   =
consolentur {A++} (consulentur A+)   consoletur[SCMNEVL!t!c!b]
                  (+ super L)

eos   =
et   [>~:SCMNEVL!t!c!b]
derelinquetur   =[S++CMNEVL!t!c!b] (derelinquitur S+)
                  enim[~:SMNEVL!t!c!b] (aenim C)(et L4)
                  terra[~SCMNELL4!t!c!b] (terram ~V)

deserta {A++!w} (desertas A+)   =[SCMNEVL!t!c!b] (desolabitur L4)
terra {A++!w} (terras A+)   [>~SCMNEVL!t!c!b]
et   =
civitates   =
eius   =
demolientur   deicientur[SCMNEVL!t!c!b]
16:24{Lat 25}
non   =
derelinquetur   =[SMNE!t!c!b] (relinquetur CVL)
agricola   =[CVL](>SMNE!t!c!b)
qui   =
colet {A+} (colat A++) (colit !w)   colat[SA++CMNEVL!t!c!b]
terram   =
et   =
qui   =
seminat {A+} (seminet A++)   seminet[S++A++CMNEV!t!c!b] (= S+L)
eam   =
16:25{Lat 26}
ligna   =
fructiferabunt   dabunt[SCMNEVL!t!c!b]
                  fructus[S++CMNEL!t!c!b] (fructos S+V)
                  (+ suos C)

et   =
quis   =
vindemiet {A+} (vindemiabit A++)   vindemiabit[S++A++CMNE!t!c!b]
                  (vindemiavit VL) (vindiamit S+)
illa   =[SMNE!t!c!b](illam CV) (eos L)
                  {+ ? SMNEV}

16:26{Lat 27}
et   [>SCMNEVL!t!c!b]
uva   =[SMNEVL!t!c!b](uba C)
                  matura[~:SCMNEVL!t!c!b]
tradet   fiet[SCMNEVL!t!c!b]
se   [>SCMNEVL!t!c!b]
ad   [>SCMNEVL!t!c!b]
vindemiam {A++!w} (vindimiam A+)   [>~:SCMNEVL!t!c!b]
et   =

French Recension	Spanish Recension
quis	=
	(+ illam ~V)
adligabit {A+!w} (alligabit A++)	calcabit[S++CMNE!t!c!b] (calcavit S+VL)
eam	illam[SCMNEL!t!c!b](>~V)
	{+ ? SMNEVL}
erit	=
enim	=[SMNEVL!t!c!b](aenim C)
et	[>SCMNEV!t!c!b,~L]
	(+ in S++MNE!b) {>S+CVL!t!c}
locis {A++!w} (locus A+)	=[SCMNEV!t!c!b] (locus A+L)
	(+ et ~L)
	magna[~:SCMNEVL!t!c!b]
desertio	=[SMNE!t!c!b] (desertatio CVL)
multa	[>~:SCMNEVL!t!c!b]
16:27{Lat 28}	
concupiscet	cupiet[SCMNEVL!t!c!b]
enim	=[SMNEV!t!c!b](aenim C) (>L)
homo	=
hominem	=
videre	=
vel	=
certe	[>SCMNEVL!t!c!b]
vocem	=
eius	=
audire	=
16:28{Lat 29}	
	(+ et VL)
	(+ nemo L)
	(+ inveniet L)
relinquentur	=
enim	=[SMNEVL!t!c!b](aenim C)
decem	[>~SCMNEVL!t!c!b]
de	=
civitate	=
	(+ homines L)
	decem[~SCMNEVL!t!c!b]
et	=[SCMNEL!t!c!b](>V)
duo	=
ex	=[CMNEL](de SV!t!c!b)
agro	=
qui	=
absconderint	=[SCMNEL!t!c!b] (absconderit{?} V)
se	=
in	=
	densis[SCMNEVL!t!c!b]
silva	nemoribus[SCMNEVL!t!c!b]
et	=
in	=[CVL](>SMNE!t!c!b)
fissuras {A++!w} (fisuras A+)	fissuris[SCMN!t!b] (scissuris !c) (sciscuris E)
	(fixuras V)(ficxuris L)
petrarum	=
16:29{Lat 30}	
quemadmodum	=[SMNEVL!t!c!b] (quemammodum C)

French Recension	Spanish Recension

relinquentur {A+!w} (relinquuntur A++) =[SCEV!t!b] (relinquetur L) (derelinquuntur
!c) (relinquuntur A++MN) {dot under 2nd
'-e-' -S}
(+ in L)
(+ singulis L)
(+ nemoribus L)

in =
oliveto =[SMNEVL!t!c!b] (olibeto C)
in[SCMNVL!t!b](et !c) (vel E)
singulis[SCMNEL!t!c!b] (>V)
arboribus[SCMNEVL!t!c!b]

tres =
vel =[CMNVL](aut SE!t!c!b)
quattuor =[SC!t!c!b] (quatuor MNEVL)
olivae =[SMNEL!t!c!b](olive V) (olibe C)
16:30{Lat 31}
aut =
sicut =
in =
vinea {A++!w} (vinia A+) =[SCMNVL!t!c!b](>E)
vindemiata {A++!w} (vindimiata A+) =[SCMNVL!t!c!b] (vindemia E)
et [>SCMNEVL!t!c!b]
racemi[~:S++CMNEVL!t!c!b] (racimi ~:S+)
subremanet relinquentur[SMNEVL!t!b] (relincuntur C)
(relinquuntur !c)
{dot under second '-e-' -S}
racemus [>~:SCMNEVL!t!c!b]
patens [>SCMNEVL!t!c!b]
ab =
his[SCMNEVL!t!c!b]
qui[SCMNEVL!t!c!b]
scrutantibus [>~:SCMNEVL!t!c!b]
(+ minus C)
diligenter[~SCMN!t!c!b,L{?}] (diligentur ~V)
(diligent~ {ambiguous} ~E)
vindemiam {A++!w} (vindimiam A+) vineam[SCMNEVL!t!c!b]
diligenter {A++!w} (diligentibus{?} A+) [>~SCMNEVL!t!c!b]
scrutantur[~:SCVL!t!c!b] (scrutabuntur
~:MNE)

16:31{Lat 32}
sic =
remanebunt relinquentur[SCMNEVL!c!b] (= L4)
{SA!w!c!b from here on} {now CMNEVL without S!c!b}
(+ terra V)
in =
illis{~}
diebus =
illis [>~]
(+ vel C)
tres =
vel {A} (aut S!c!b) =
quattuor quatuor[MNEVL](= C)
ab =

French Recension	Spanish Recension
	his
	qui
scrutantibus	[>~:]
	(+ in V)
domus {SA+!b} (domos A++!w!c)	domos[A++CMNEVL!w!c]
eorum	=[CVL](ipsorum MNE)
	scrutabunt[~:CVL] (scrutabuntur ~:MNE)
in	a[CVL](>MNE)
rompheam (rumphea A+) (rumpheam S!a!f!b)	gladio
(romphea A++!w) (rhomphaea !c)	
16:32{Lat 33}	
et	=
relinquetur (relinquentur S+)	=
deserta (>~!c)	[>~CMNEVL!c]
terra	=
(+ deserta ~!c)	deserta[~CMNEVL!c]
et	=
agri	=
eius	=
(+ in !b)	in[CMNEVL!b]
inveteraverunt {S+A+} (vepres !b)	vepre[CVL](vepres MNE!b)
(inveterabunt S++A++!c)	
(+ erunt !b)	erunt[CMNEVL!b]
	simul
et	=
viae	=[MNEL](vie CV)
eius	[>]
et	=
omnes	[>]
semitae	=[MNE](semite CVL)
(+ eius !c)	
	spinas[~CMNEL] (spinis ~:V)
germinabunt	=
spinas	[>~]
eo	=
quod	=
	oves[~CMNEV](>~L)
non	=
	sint
	(+ oves ~L)
transient (transeat A)	transiturae[MNE] (transiture CL)
	(transituri V)
oves (ovis A)(homines !c)	[>~]
per	=
eam	eas[MNE](illas CVL)
16:33{Lat 34}	
lugebunt	=
virgines	=
non	=
habentes	=
sponsos {SA+++} (sponsus A++)(>A+{>5})	=
lugebunt (>A+{>5})	=
mulieres (>A+{>5})	=

French Recension	Spanish Recension
non (>A+{>5})	=
habentes (>A+{>5})	=
viros	=
lugebunt	=[CMNEL](lugent V)
filiae	=[MNEL](filie CV)
earum	ipsarum
non	=[CMNEV](noti L)
habentes {erasure between 'e' and 'n' -A}	=
adiutorium	adiutoria
16:34{Lat 35}	
sponsi	=
earum	ipsarum[CMNEV](= L)
in	=
bello	=
consumentur	=
et	=
viri	=
earum	illarum[CMNEV](= L)
in	[>]
fame	=
exterentur (exterrentur A+)	interient
	{+ xxvi L}
16:35{Lat 36}	
audite	=[CMNEVL](audire L4)
vero	igitur
ista	haec[MNE](hec CVL)
et	=[CMNVLL4](>E)
cognoscite	intelligite[CMNL] (intellegite E) (intelligete V)
	(intelligere L4)
ea	[>]
servi	=[CMNEVL4](servvi L)
Domini	=[CMNEVLL4]
16:36{Lat 37}	
ecce	=
verbum	sermo[CMNEVLL4]
Domini	=[CMNEVLL4]
excipite	sumite
eum (illud A++!c)	illum
ne	=
	discedatis{s.b., Fr}
	a
	Domino
	et[CMNEVLL4]
	nolite[CMNEVL](non L4)
	(+ esse ~V,L4)
(+ diis S+!c)(dies A+) (dis S++A++)	
discredatis {!w!b} (credatis SA!f!c) {s.a., Sp}	increduli[CMNEVLL4]
	esse[CMNEL](>~V)
de	[>CMNEV](in L)
	his
quibus	quae[MNEL](que CV)
dicit	=[CMNEVL](dicta L4)
Dominus	=[CMNEVL](Deo L4)

French Recension	Spanish Recension

16:37{Lat 38}

ecce   =

                                                protinus{~:}
adpropinquant (appropinquant A++!c)   venient[CMNEVLL4]
mala   =
et   =
non   =
tardantur (tardant A++!c)   tardabunt
16:38{Lat 39}
quemadmodum   =

                                                mulier
praegnans   pregnans
(+ cum !c)
(+ parit !c)

                                                infantem{~:}
                                                suum[~CMNEL](>V)
                                                in
                                                utero
in   [>]
nono   [>~:]
mense   mensibus
                                                novem[~:VL](nobem ~:C) (octo ~:MNE)
                                                habens
filium   [>~:]
suum   [>~]
in (>S++!c!b)   ubi
                                                coeperit[MNE] (ceperit CVL)
adpropinquante {A+!w!b} (appropinquante A++!c) [>~:]
    (adpropinquantem S+) (apropinquante S++)
hora (ora S+)   =[C](>MNEV,~L)
partus (parti S+)   =
eius   =
                                                adpropinquare[~:CL] (appropinquare ~:MNE)
                                                    (appropinquans ~:V)
                                                (+ ora ~L)
ante   =
                                                duas{~}
horas   =[CMNEV](oras L)
duas   [>~]
vel   =
tres   =
gementes (>!c)   [>CMNEVL!c]
dolores   =[CVL](dolorem MNE)
circum (circumeunt !c)   circa
ventrem   =
eius   [>]
                                                patitur
et   =
prodiente (prodientem A) (prodeunte !c)   prodeunte[CMNEVL!c]
infante (infantem A)   =
de   =
ventre   =
non   =

French Recension	Spanish Recension
tardabit (tardabunt !c)	=
uno	=
puncto	=
	(+ exire L)
16:39{Lat 40}	
sic	=
non	=
morabuntur	=[MNE](tardabitur C) (morabitur VL)
mala	=[CMNEV](malum L)
ad	=
prodiendum (prodeundum !c)	prodeundum[CMNEL!c] (prodeundem V)
super	=[CMNEVLL4]
terram	=[CMNEVL](terra L4)
et	=
saeculum	=[MNEVL](seculum C)
gemet	parturit
et	=[CMNEV](>L)
dolores	=
circumtenent (circumtenebunt !c)	circumcingunt
illum (illud !c)	=[CVL](illud MNE!c)
16:40{Lat 41}	
audite	=
	(+ populus ~MNE)
	(+ meus ~MNE)
verbum	=
	Domini
plebs	populus[CVLL4](>~MNE)
mea	meus[CVL](>~MNE)(Dei L4)
parate	parati[CMNEVLL4]
	estote[CMNEVL](esse L4)
vos	[>]
ad {A!w} (in S!c!b)	=
pugnam	bellum
(+ et S!c!b)	
	aptate[MNE](abtate CVL)
	vos
in	ad
malis	mala
sic	=
estote	=
quasi	=
advenae (advene S)	incolae[MNEV] (incole CLL4)
terrae	=[MNEV](terre CL)
16:41{Lat 42}	
qui	=[CMNEL](quae V)
vendet {SA+} (vendit A++!w!c!b)	vendit[A++CMNE!w!c!b] (vendidit VL)
quasi {erasure between 'a' and 's' -A}	=
qui	=
fugiet {S} (fugit A) (fugiat !c)	fugiat[CMNE!c](fugient V) (fugiunt L)
et	=
qui	=
emit	=[CMNEL](emittit V)
quasi	=

qui (>A++)	=[MNE](>A++CVL)
perditurus {S} (periturus A)	=
	(+ est MNE)
16:42{Lat 43}	
qui (>A{>13})	=
mercatur (>A{>13})	=[CMNEL](merchatur V)
quasi (>A{>13})	=
qui (>A{>13})	=
fructum (>A{>13})	=
non (>A{>13})	=
capiat (>A{>13})	=[CMNE](capiet VL)
et (>A{>13})	=
qui (>A{>13})	=
aedificat (>A{>13})	=[MNEL](hedificat C) (edificat V)
quasi (>A{>13})	=
non (>A{>13})	=
habitaturus {S++} (>A{>13}) (habiturus S+)	=[CMNEV](habiturus S+L)
16:43{Lat 44}	
(+ et A)	
qui	=
seminat	=
quasi	=
(+ qui S!c!b)	qui[SCMNEVL!c!b]
non	=
messem {A!w} (metat S!b) (metet !c)	metat[SMNE!b](secet CL) (seccet V)
facturus {A!w} (>S!c!b)	[>SCMNEVL!c!b]
(+ sic S!c!b)	
et	[>CMEVL](= N)
qui	={+ 'non', crossed out -V}
(+ vineam !c)	
putat (portat A)	=[MNE](potat CV) (portat AL)
quasi	=
	(+ qui E)
non	=
vindemiaturus {S++A++} (vindimiaturus S+A+!f)	=[CMNVL](vindemiatur E)
16:44{Lat 45}	
qui	=
nubunt	nuptias[MNE](nubtias CL) (nupcias V)
	faciunt
sic	[>]
quasi	=
(+ si S)	(+ non ~E)
filios (filii S+)	=[CMNEV](>L)
non	=[CMNVL](>~E)
facturi	habituri
et	=
qui	=
non	[>~]
nubunt	nuptias[MNE](nubtias C) (nupcias V)
	(nubcias L)
	non[~CMNVL](>E)
	faciunt
sic	[>]

French Recension	Spanish Recension
quasi	=
vidui	viduitatem
	servaturi
16:45{Lat 46}	
propter	=
quod	=[CMNEL](>V)
qui	=
laborant	=
sine	=
causa	=
laborant	=[CMNEV](laborabunt L)
16:46{Lat 47}	
fructus	=[CMNEL](fructos V)
enim	=[VL](aenim C)(autem MNE)
illorum	=[CVL](eorum MNE)
alienigenae (alienigene S)	exteri
metent	manducabunt
et	=[CMNE](>VL)
substantiam	=[CMNE](substanciam V) (substancias L)
illorum	=[MNE](eorum CVL)
rapient (rapiant A+)	=
et	[>]
domos (domus A+!b)	=[CMNEL](domus A+V!b)
	ipsorum
evertent {S} (avertent A)	=
et	=
filios	=
eorum	ipsorum[CEV](illorum MN) (= L)
captivabunt	captivos
	ducent
	(+ ideo CV)(ideoque L)
	(+ sciant C)(sciunt V) (scient L)
quia	qui
	nubunt[CL](nubent MNEV)
	(+ quoniam CVL)
in	=
captivitate	=[CVL](captivitatem MNE)
et	=
fame	=[CV](famae L)(famem MNE)
	filios{~:}
	(+ filios L)
generant	generabunt
natos	[>~:]
suos	[>]
16:47{Lat 48}	
et	=
qui	=
negotiantur {!w!c} (negociantur SA!a!f!b)	mercantur
negotiantur {A} (>S!c) (negociantur !b)	[>~:CMNEVL,S!c]
in	ad
rapina	rapinam[MNEVL](= C)
	mercantur[~:CL] (mereantur ~:V)
	(mercabuntur ~:MNE)
	in

quamdiu (quantum !c)	quantum[CMNEVL!c]
(+ diu !c)	
	enim[MNEVL](aenim C)
exornant	ornant
civitates	=
et	[>]
domos (domus A+!b)	=
suas	[>~]
et	=
possessiones	=[CMNEV](possesiones L)
	suas{~}
et	=
personas	facies[MNE](faciem CVL)
suas	=[MNE](suam CVL)
16:48{Lat 49}	
	in
tanto	=[MN](tantum CEVL)
magis	=
adzelabor (zelabo S++)	zelabo[S++CMNEVL]
eos	illos
	(+ qui MNE)
	zelo
super	in[CMEVL](>N)
peccata	peccatis
(+ sua !c)	(+ suis L)(sua !c)
dicit	=
Dominus	=
16:49{Lat 50}	
quomodo	quemadmodum
zelatur (zelabor A+)	zelat
fornicaria (fornicariam S{S++} !b)	=[CMN] (fornicariam S{S++} EVL!b)
mulierem (mulier_rem !c)	=
idoneam (idonea S!b)	=[MNEVL](ydoneam C)
et	=
bonam (bona S!b)	=
valde	=[CMNEV](valdae L)
16:50{Lat 51}	
sic	=
zelabitur	zelavit[VL](zelabit C) (zelat MNE)
iustitia (iusticia S!a!f!b)	iusticia[SMNEV!a!f!b] (= C)(iusticiam L)
iniquitatem	=
cum	=
exornat	=[C](exornant VL) (exorta MNE)
se	=[CVL](sit MNE)
et	=
	(+ illam ~V)
accusat	=[CMNEV](acusat L)
eam	illam[CMNEL](>~V)
in	=
faciem (facie !c)	=[MNEL](facie CV!c)
cum	=
venerit	=
qui	=[CMNVL](>E)

French Recension	Spanish Recension
defendat	=[CMVL](descendat N)(>E)
(+ et A+){erased by A++}	
exquirentem	querens
omnem (omne S++!c)	omne[S++MNE,V{?} ,!c] (omnae L)(= C)
peccatum	=
super	in
terram	terra
16:51{Lat 52}	
propterea	ideo
nolite	=
	illius[~:CMNEV] (illis ~:L)
similari (similare A+)	similes{V?}
	esse[CMNEV](essae L)
eam (ei !c)	[>~:]
nec	neque
operibus	factis[CMNEV] (fructibus L)
eius	=
	neque
	malis[CMNEV](aliis L)
	(+ eius ~MNE]
	cogitationibus[CMNEL] (cogitacionibus V)
	eius[CVL](>~MNE)
16:52{Lat 53}	
quoniam	=
ecce (>!c)	[>CMNEVL!c]
{@r begins here}	
adhuc (crastina @r)	=
pusillum (die @r)	=
et (>@r)	=
tolletur (delebitur @r)	=
iniquitas [SA!w!c!b@r]	=
a (>@r)	=
terra (terrae @r)	=
et [SA!w!c!b@r]	=
iustitia (>~A~:@r) (iusticia S!a!f!b)	iusticia[SMNEVL!a!f!b] (= C)
regnabit [SA++!w!c!b@r] (regnavit A+)	=[CMNEL](regnavit A+V)
(+ iustia ~A)	
in (super @r)	=
nos [SA!w!b@r](vos !c)	nobis[CMNEV](vobis L)
(+ salvator ~:@r)	
(+ mundi ~:@r)	
{@r ends here}	
16:53{Lat 54}	
non	=[CMNEVLL4]
dicat	=
peccator	=[CMNELL4](pastor V)
(+ se ~!c)	se[~CMNEVLL4!c]
non (in A)	=
se (>~!c)	[>~CMNEVL!c]
peccasse	=[CMNEVL](iustificare L4)
	neque
	iniustus[CMNEV](iustus L)
	iniusticiam[MNEVL] (iniustitiam C)

French Recension	Spanish Recension
	(+ non MNEV)
	fecisse[C](feci MNEV) (fefecisse{?} L)
	(+ sed ~V)
quoniam	quia[MNEVL](= C)
carbones	=
ignis	=
conburet (comburet !c!b)	=[CL](comburet V!c!b) (comburit MNE)
super	=
caput	=
eius	suum
qui	=
dicit	=
non	=
peccavi	=[MNEVL](peccabi C)
coram	=
(+ Domino !c{s.b., Sp})	
Deo	Domino{E?}
et	=
gloria	=[CMNE](gloriam VL){E?}
ipsius	eius
16:54{Lat 55}	
ecce	=[CMNEV](eccae L) (quia L4)
Dominus	=[CMNEVLL4]
	Deus
cognoscit {A} (cognoscet S!c)	novit[MNEVLL4](nobit C)
omnia {A} (omnes S)	=[CMNEV](>L)
opera {A} (operas S)	facta[CMNEVLL4]
hominis (hominum !c)	hominum[CMNEVLL4!c]
et	=[CMNEVLL4]
	corda[~:CMNEVL] (cordis ~:L4)
	eorum{~:}
	(+ in E)
adinventiones	=[CMNV](adinvenciones L) (adinventionibus E)
illorum	[>]
et	=
cogitatum (cogitationes !c)	cogitationes[CMNELL4!c] (cogitaciones V)
illorum {words erased over line -A}	ipsorum[MEVL](= N) (eorum C)
et (>A+)	[>A+CMNEVL]
corda (>A+)	[>A+,~CMNEVL]
illorum (>A+)	[>A+,~:CMNEVL]
	malas
16:55{Lat 56}	
qui (>S!c)	=[CMNEVL](ipse L4)
dixit (>S)	=
(+ enim !c)	
fiat	=[CMNEVL](creavit L4)
terra	caelum[~CMNEV](celum ~L) (celos ~L4)
et	=[CMNEVLL4]
facta	factum
est	=
(+ et A)	
fiat	=

French Recension	Spanish Recension

caelum   terra[~:CMNEVL] (terram ~:L4)
et   =
factum   facta
est   =
16:56{Lat 57}
et   =
in   =[CVL](>MNE)
verbo (verba A+)   sermone[CMEV] (sermones NL)
illius   eius
stellae   =[MNEL](stelle CV)
fundatae (fundati A+)   =[MNE](facte CVL)
sunt   =
et   =
novit   [>~]
numerum   =
stellarum   ipsarum[CMNEL](ipsorum V)
                                                   novit[~MNEVL](nobit ~C)

16:57{Lat 58}
qui   =
scrutatur {A!c} (scrutat S!w!b)   =[CMNE](scrutor V) (inscrutantur L)
abyssum {S} (abysum A+) (abyssos A++)   =[MNE](abyssos A++CVL)
et   =
thesauros   =[MNEVL](tesauros C)
illorum (illarum !c)   eorum[CL](eius MNE)(>V)
qui {underlined -A}   =
metitus (meretus A+) (meritus A++)   mensus[CMNEL!c]
   (mensus !c){underlined -A}   (inmensus V)
est {underlined -A}   =
mare (manere A) {underlined -A}   =
et {underlined -A}   =
conceptum (concoeptum A) {underlined -A}   fundamenta
eius (>A)   =
16:58{Lat 59}
qui   =
conclusit (clusit A)   =
mare   saeculum[NEVL] (seculum CM)
in   [>~:]
medio   inter
aquarum   aquas
                                                   (+ . L)
                                                   et
                                                   aquas[CMNEL](aqui{?} V)
et   =[CMNEV](>L)
suspendit   =
terram   =[CMNEV](terra L)
super   =
aquam (aquas !c)   =[CMNL](aquas EV!c)
                                                   (+ in L)
verbo   =
suo   =
16:59{Lat 60}
qui   =
extendit   =[CMNEVL@z]

French Recension	Spanish Recension

caelum   =[CMNE@z](celum V)(>L)

quasi   ut[CMNEVL](sicut @z)

cameram   =[CMNE@z](camerum V) (camera L)
            (vel_ut_coreum W)
             {W could be 'cortum' or 'corcum'}
            (+ aer L)

et (>!c)   =

super   =

aquas   =

fundavit   =[MNEVL](fundabit C)

eum (illud A++)   illum[MNE](illud A++VL) (illut C)

16:60{Lat 61}

qui   =

posuit   =

in   =

deserto   =

fontes   =

aquarum   =

et   =

super   =

vertices (verticem !c)   =[CMNEV](verticem L!c)

montium   =[CMNEV](moncium L)

lacus   =

ad   =[CVL](>MNE)

emittendum (emittenda A++)   emittenda[A++CL] (emitenda V) (demittendo
            MNE)

flumina   =

ab {S++} (ad S+A!f) {underlined -A}   a[CMNEV](ad S+AL!f)

eminenti {underlined -A}   cacumine[CMNEV] (cacumen L)

(+ petra !c)   (+ collium L)(petra !c)

ut   =

potaret (portaret SA!f)   =[CNE](portaret SAMVL!f)

terra (terram !c)   =[MNE](terram CVL!c)

16:61{Lat 62}

qui   =

finxit (vinxit S)   =[CMNEL](fincxit{?} V)

hominem   =[CMNEVL](homine L4)

et   =

posuit (possuit A+)   [>~:]

cor   =

(+ suum !c)   illi[CMNEVL](suum !c)
            inposuit[~:CVL] (imposuit ~:MNE)

in   =

medio   =

corporis   corpore
            eius

et   =[CMNEVL4](>L)

misit (missit A+)   dedit[CMNEVL](posuit L4)

ei   illi

spiritum   =[CMNEVLL4]
            (+ vitae ~E)

et (>!c)   =
            intellectum{~}

French Recension	Spanish Recension
vitam	vitae[MNL](vite CV)(>~E)
et (>A+)	[>A+CMNEVL]
intellectum	[>~]
16:62{Lat 63}	
et (>A)	=[CMNEV](>AL)
	(+ ad V)
spiramentum (spiramen !c)	adspirationem[L] (a*spirationem C)
	(inspirationem MNEV)
	(+ . CMNE){>VL}
Dei	Dominus[CMNVL](Deus E)
omnipotentis	omnipotens
	hic[MNE](his VL)(scit C)
qui	=[CMNE](quoniam VL)
	(+ haec L)
	omnia[~CNEVL](>~M)
	(+ et V)
fecit	=
omnia	[>~CNEVL](= M)
et	=
scrutinat (scrutinatur A) {'-ur' erased,	scrutatur[CMNE]
'-r' added above line -A}	(scrutator VL)
	(+ est L)
(+ omnia !c)	
absconsa (>~A)	abscondita[CMNEV] (absconditorum L)
	et
in	=
absconsis	absconditis
(+ absconsa ~A)	
. {A!w!b} (>~S!f)	[>~SCMNEVL!f]
	(+ hic ~L)
certe {A!w!b} (certa S) (terrae !c)	certa[SCMNEVL]
(+ . ~S!f){>~A!w!b}	.[~SCMNEV!f](>~AL!w!b)
16:63{Lat 64}	
hic	=[CMNEV](>~L)
novit	=[MNEVL](nobit C)
	(+ . ~L)
	(+ quae L)
adinventionem	adinventiones
vestram	vestras
et	=
quae	=[MNE](que CV) (quaecumque L)
cogitatis	=
in	=
cordibus	=
vestris	=
vae (>!c)	=[CML](ve NEVL4)
	omnibus[CMNEL] (hominibus V)
	qui[CMNEVLL4]
peccantibus (peccantes !c)	peccant[CMNEVLL4]
et	=[MNE](ei CVL)
	(+ et L)
	qui
volentibus (volentes !c)	volunt[CVL] (voluerint MNE)

French Recension	Spanish Recension
occultare	[>~:]
peccata	=
sua (vestra !c)	=
	celare[~:CNEVL] (caelare ~:M)
16:64{Lat 65}	
propter	=
quod	=
Dominus (Deus A)	=
scrutinando	scrutans[MNE](>CVL)
scrutinavit {S+!c} (scrutinabit S++!w!b)	scrutavit[A+{?} VL]
(scrutatus A++) (scrutavit A+{?})	(scrutabitur MNE) (scrutabit C)
(+ est A++)	
omnia	=
opera	facta
eorum (vestra !c)	ipsorum
et	=
traducet	transducet
vos (nos A+)	=[CMNEL](>V)
omnes	=
	in
	illa
16:65{Lat 66}	
et	=
vos	[>CMNEL](non V)
confusi (confussi A+)	confundemini
eritis	[>]
cum	=
processerint	=[CMNEV](precesserint L)
peccata	=
vestra	=
coram	=
hominibus	=
et	=
iniquitates	iniquitas
erint {S} (erunt !c) (**** A+) (vestrae A++)	[>CMNEV](vestra L)
quae (quasi A++)	tanquam[CMNEV](tamquam L)
accusatores	accusator[CMNE] (accusatorum V) (acusator L)
stabunt	stabit[CMNEV](instavit L)
	(+ adversum L)
	(+ vos L)
	(+ . ~MNE)
in	=
	illa{~:}
die	=[CMNEV](diae L)
illo	[>~:]
.	=[CVL](>~MNE)
16:66{Lat 67}	
quid	=
	(+ ergo L)
facietis	=
aut	et
quomodo	=

French Recension	Spanish Recension
abscondetis (absconditis S+)	=[CMNE](absconditis S+VL)
peccata	=[CMNEL](>V)
vestra	=
coram	ante[CMNEV](antae L)
Domino {A} (Deo S!c!b)	Dominum
et	=
gloria {A} (angelis S!c!b) {final -'s' added above line in 1st hand -S}	gloriam[MNEVL](= C)
eius	=
	{+ ? SMNEL}
16:67{Lat 68}	
ecce	=
iudex	=[CMNEVLL4]
Deus	Dominus[CMNEVLL4]
	(+ est L4)
(+ et A)	
timete	=[CMNEVL](timere L4)
eum	illum[CMNEVLL4]
et (>S!c!b)	=
desinite (desinete A+)	=
a	=
peccatis	=
vestris	=
et	=
obliviscimini {S++A++} (obliviscamini !c) (obliviscemini S+A+!f)	=[MNEVL](oblibiscimini C)
iniquitates	=[CVL](peccata MNE)
vestras	=[CVL](vestra MNE)
iam	et[MNEVL](ut C)
	non
agere	faciatis
eas	haec[MNEL](hec CV)
(+ in !c)	
sempiterno {underlined -A}	semper
et	=
Deus	Dominus
	vos{~}
educabit {S++A++!w!b} (educavit S+!f) (**docavit A+) (educet !c)	deducet
vos (nos S+)	[>~]
	(+ ad L)
	(+ vitam L)
et	=
liberabit {S++A++} (liberavit S+A+!f)	=[CMNEL] (liberavit S+A+V!f)
de	ab
omni	=
tribulatione	pressura
16:68{Lat 69}	
ecce	=
enim	=[MNEVL](aenim C)
incendetur {A} (incenditur S!w!c!b)	succendetur[CMNEL] (succendentur V)
ardor	[>~]
super	=

French Recension	Spanish Recension
vos	=
	ardor{~}
	(+ angustiae L)
	et
turbae (turbe S)	turbabunt
	vos
	(+ populi ~N)
copiosae (copiose S)	multi
{'turbae' could go with 'populi'}	populi[CMEVL](>~N)
et	=
rapient	diripient
	res
	vestras
	et
	sument
quosdam	=
ex	=
vobis	=
et	=
cibabunt (cybabunt A++)	=[C](caecabunt ME) (cecabunt N) (suscitabunt VL)
	vos
	de
idolis	[>~:]
occisam {S} (occisum A) (occisos !c)	sacrificio
16:69{Lat 70}	
et	=
qui	=
consenserint	=[CMNEV](conseserint L)
eis	=
erunt (erint S+!b)	=
illis	=
in	=
derisum (dirisum A+)	=[MNE](derisu CVL)
et	=
in (>A)	=[CE](>AMNVL)
inproperium (improperium A++)	=[VL](improperium A++MNE) (inproperio C)
et	=
in	=
conculcationem	=[CMNEL](conculcacione V)
16:70{Lat 71}	
erit	=
enim	=[MNEVL](aenim C)
(+ in A++)	(+ in A++MNE)
lociis {A+} (*ocis S+) (locis S++A++!c!b) (+ lociis S)(locus !c!b)	locis[S++A++CMNE!c!b] (locus VL)
et	[>]
in	per
vicinas (vicinis A)	=
civitates (civitatis A+) (civitatibus A++)	=
exsurrectio (exresurrectio S+)	insurrectio
multa	=

French Recension	Spanish Recension

super

supra[CMNVL](= E)
hos
qui
timent

timentes
Dominum
16:71{Lat 72}

Deum[CMN](= EVL)

aporiati {!a} (>SA!f!w!c!b{>6})
enim {!a} (>SA!f!w!c!b{>6})
homines {!a} (>SA!f!w!c!b{>6})
a {!a} (>SA!f!w!c!b{>6})
malis {!a} (>SA!f!w!c!b{>6})
suis {!a} (>SA!f!w!c!b{>6})
erunt (erint S+!b)
quasi
insani
neminem {S} (nemine A+) (nemini A++!c)

=
=[MNEVL](aenim C)
=[CMNE](omnes VL)
=
=
=
=
tanquam[CMNE](tamquam VL)
=
nemini[A++CMNE!c] (nemine A+V)(= L)
    {later changed to 'nemini' -L}

parcentes
ad {A++} (a SA+!f)
diripiendum (deripiendum A+)
et
devastandum

=
=
=[CMNVL](deripiendum A+E)
=
exportandum[CMNE] (exportadum V)
    (expoliandum L)

adhuc

=
etiam[MNEVL](aetiam C)
horum
(+ qui CVL)

timentes
Dominum
16:72{Lat 73}
quia
devastabunt
et
diripient (eripient A+)
substantias
eorum (>!c)
et
de
domo (domos S+!b) (domibus !c)
sua (suas S+!b)(suo A+) (suis !c)
eos
eicient (iecient A+)

metuentes[MNE] (metuunt CVL)
Deum[CMNEV](= L)

[>]
=[CMNE](vastabunt VL)
[>]
[>]
res
[>CMNEVL!c]
=
=[CVL](>MNE)
domibus[CMNEVL!c]
suis[CMNEVL!c]
[>~:]
expellent
illos{~:} {illios with 'i' crossed out -V}

16:73{Lat 74}

et[CMNEL](e V)

tunc
parebit (apparebit A)
probatio
electorum
meorum

=
=
=[CMNEL](probacio V)
=
=
et
tolerantia[CMN] (tollerantia E) (tollerancia V)
    (tolerancia L)
ipsorum

French Recension	Spanish Recension
ut (prout A+)	quemadmodum[MNEVL] (quemammodum C)
aurum	=
	(+ per ~L)
quod	=
probatur	[>~]
ab	per[CMNEV](>~L)
igne	ignem[CMNEV](ignae L)
	probatur{~}
16:74{Lat 75}	
audite	=
electi (dilecti !c)	=
mei	=
dicit	=
Dominus	=
	(+ Deus V)
ecce	=
adsunt (assunt S++)	=[CMNVL](assunt S++E)
dies	=
tribulationis	=[CMNEL](tribulacionis V)
et	=
de	=
his	ipsis
liberabo	=
vos	=
16:75{Lat 76}	
ne	=
timeatis (tim*** A+)	=
neque {A} (nec S!w!c!b)	=
haesitemini {!w!b} (haessitemini A+) (esitemini S++) (sitemini S+) (haesitetis A++!c)	formidetis
quoniam	=
Deus	Dominus
dux	=
vester	=
est	=
16:76{Lat 77}	
et	[>]
qui	=[CMNEV](quia L)
servat {SA!c} (servatis !w!b)	servatis[CMNE!w!b] (servastis VL)
mandata	=
(+ mea A)	(+ mea AME,~V)
et	=
praecepta	precepta[CNEVL](= M)
mea	=[CMNEL](>~V)
dicit	=
Dominus	=
Deus	[>CMNEV](= L)
(+ liberabo A++)	
(+ eum A++)	
ne	non
praeponderent (praeponderint A)	preponderent[CNEVL](= M)

French Recension	Spanish Recension
vos	=
peccata	=
vestra	=
nec (ne !c)	=[CMNEV](neque L)
superelevent (superelebent S+)	extollant[CMNEL] (extollent V)
se (>S+!b)	=[MNE](>S+CVL!b)
iniquitates	=
vestrae	=[MNE](vestre CVL)
16:77{Lat 78}	
vae	=[CML](ve NEV)
qui	=
constringuntur	=[CMNE] (constringentur VL)
a	=
peccatis	=[CMNEL](peccato V)
suis	=
et	=[CVL](>MNE{>5})
	(+ qui V)
obteguntur	cooperiuntur[C](>MNE{>5}) (operiuntur V) (coobprimentur L)
ab	=[CL](a V)(>MNE{>5})
iniquitatibus	=[CL](peccatis V) (>MNE{>5})
suis	=[CV](>MNE{>5} L)
quemadmodum	=[MNEVL](quemammodum C)
ager	=[CMNEL](eger V)
constringitur	conclusus[CMNEL] (conclusa V)
a	=[CMNEL](>~:V)
silva	=
et	=
spinis	=
	(+ qui MNEL)
tegitur	cooperitur[MNE] (coperitur C) (cooperietur V) (operitur L)
semita {A} (semina S+!b) (semen S++)	=[CVL](semitis MNE)
eius	=
per	=
quam (quem S!b)	=[CVL](quem SMNE!b)
non	=
transiit {A+} (transiet A++!w) (transit S!c!b)	transivit[MNE] (transibit C) (transit SL!c!b) (transunt V)
homo	={no punctuation -L}
16:78{Latin: no verse division}	
et	[>]
excluditur (excludetur A)	=
et	=
mittitur (emittetur A)	fit
ad	in
devorationem	=[MNE](deforatione C) (devoracione V) (devoratione L)
ignis	=
{EXPLICIT OF THE BOOK}	
EXPLICIT (FINIUNT A+) (FINIT A++)	[>CMNEVL](FINIT A++L4)
(+ QUINQUE ~A+)	

French Recension	Spanish Recension
LIBER (LIBRI A+)	[>]
(+ QUINTUS ~A++)	
EZRAE	[>]
QUINTUS (>~A)	[>~A,CMNEVL]
(+ PROFAETE A)	
(+ COLIPHON A)	

6 Ezra: An Eclectic Latin Text

This text is identical to that printed, without parentheses, on the left side of the left column of Appendix 1.

15 : [1] Ecce loquere in aures plebi meae sermones prophetiae quos inmisero in os tuum, dicit Dominus, [2] et fac in carta scribi eos, quoniam fideles et veri sunt. [3] Ne timeas a cogitationibus adversum te nec conturbent te incredulitates dicentium, [4] quoniam omnis incredulus in incredulitate sua morietur.

[5] Ecce ego induco dicit Dominus super orbem terrarum, mala gladium et famem et mortem et interitum, [6] propter quod superposuit iniquitas omnem terram et adimpletae sunt operationes eorum. [7] Propterea dicit Dominus, [8] iam non silebo impietatibus eorum quae inreligiose agunt, nec sustinebo in his quae inique exercent. Ecce sanguis innoxius et iustus clamat ad me et animae iustorum clamant perseveranter. [9] Vindicans vindicabo illos dicit Dominus et accipiam omnem sanguinem innocuum ex illis ad me.

[10] Ecce populus meus quasi grex ad occisionem ducitur. Iam non patiar illum habitare in terra Aegypti, [11] sed educam eum in manu potenti et brachio excelso et percutiam Aegyptum plaga sicut prius et corrumpam terram omnem eius.

[12] Lugeat Aegyptus et fundamenta eius a plaga verberati et mastigati quam inducet Dominus.[13] Lugeant cultores operantes terram quoniam deficiet semina eorum et vastabuntur ligna eorum ab aurugine et grandine et a sidus terribile. [14] Vae saeculo et qui habitant in eum, [15] quia adpropinquavit gladius et extritio illorum et exsurget gens super gentem ad pugnam et romphea in manibus eorum.

[16] Erit enim inconstabilitio hominibus aliis; alii supervalescentes non curabunt regem suum et principem megestanorum suorum in potentia sua.[17] Concupiscet enim homo in civitatem ire et non poterit, [18] propter superbiam enim eorum civitates turbabuntur domus exterentur homines metuent.[19] Non miserebitur homo proximum suum ad irritum faciendum in domos eorum in gladium ad diripiendas substantias eorum propter famem panis et tribulationem multam.

[20] Ecce ego convoco dicit Deus omnes reges terrae ad movendum, qui sunt a borea et a noto et ab euro et a libano, ad convertendos in se et reddere quae dederunt illis. [21] Sicut faciunt usque hodie electis meis, sic faciam et reddam in sinum ipsorum. Haec dicit

Dominus Deus. [22] Non parcet dextera mea super peccantes nec cessabit romphea super effundentes sanguinem innocuum super terram. [23] Et exiit ignis ab ira eius et devoravit fundamenta terrae et peccatores quasi stramen incensum. [24] Vae eis qui peccant et non observant mandata mea dicit Dominus: [25] non parcam illis.

Discedite filii apostatae; nolite contaminare sanctificationem meam. [26] Novit Deus qui peccant in eum; propterea tradet eos in mortem et in occisionem. [27] Iam enim venerunt super orbem terrarum mala et manebitis in illis. Non enim liberabit vos Deus propter quod peccastis in eum.

[28] Ecce visio horribilis et facies illius ab oriente. [29] Et exient nationes draconum Arabum in curris multis et sibilatus eorum a die itineris fertur super terram, ut etiam timeant et trepidentur omnes qui illos audient. [30] Carmonii insanientes in ira et exient de silva et advenient in virtute magna et constabunt in pugnam cum illis et vastabunt portionem terrae Assyriorum in dentibus suis.

[31] Et post haec supervalescet draco nativitatis memores suae et si converterint se conspirantes in virtute magna ad persequendos eos, [32] et isti turbabuntur et silebunt in virtute illorum et convertent pedes suos in fugam. [33] Et a territorio Assyriorum subsessor subsedebit eos et consumet unum ex illis et erit timor et tremor in exercitum illorum et inconstabilitio in regno illorum.

[34] Ecce nubs ab oriente et a septentrione usque ad meridianum, et facies illorum horrida valde plena irae et procellae. [35] Et conlident se invicem et effundent sidus copiosum super terram et sidus illorum et erit sanguis a gladio usque ad ventrem equi [36] et femur hominis et suffraginem cameli. Et erit timor et tremor multus super terram. [37] Et horrebunt qui videbunt iram illam et tremor adprehendet illos.

[38] Et post haec movebuntur nimbi copiosi a meridiano et septentrione et portio alia ab occidente, [39] et superinvalescent venti ab oriente et recludent eum et nubem quam suscitavit in ira; et sidus ad faciendam exteritionem ab orientalem natum et occidentem violabitur.

[40] Et exaltabuntur nubes magnae et validae plenae irae et sidus ut exterant omnem terram et inhabitantes in eam, et fundent super omnem altum et eminentem sidus terribilem, [41] ignem et grandinem et rompheas volantes et aquas multas, ut etiam impleantur omnes campi et omnes rivi a plenitudine aquarum illarum. [42] Et demolient civitates et muros et montes et colles et ligna silvarum et faena pratorum et frumenta eorum [43] et transibunt constanter usque Babilonem et exterent eam. [44] Convenient ad ipsam et circuibunt eam et effundent sidus et omnem iram super eam, et subibit pulvis et fumus usque ad caelum et omnes in circuitu lugebunt eam. [45] Et qui subremanserint servientes his qui eam exteruerunt.

[46] Et tu Asia, consors in specie Babilonis et gloria personae eius: [47] vae tibi misera, propter quod adsimilasti ei. Ornasti filias tuas in fornicatione ad placendum et gloriandum in amatoribus tuis qui te cupierunt semper fornicari. [48] Odibilem imitata es in omnibus operibus eius et adinventionibus eius.

Propterea dicit Deus, [49] inmittam tibi mala, viduitatem paupertatem et famem et gladium et pestem, ad devastandas domos tuas ad violationem et mortem. [50] Et gloria virtutis tuae sicut flos siccabitur cum exsurget ardor qui emissus est super te. [51] Et infirmaberis et paupera a plaga et mastigata a vulneribus ut non possit vos suscipere potentes et amatores.

[52] Numquid ego sic zelabo te, dicit Dominus, [53] nisi occidisses electos meos, in omni tempore exultans percussionem manuum et dicens super mortem eorum cum inebriata es? [54] Exorna speciem vultus tui! [55] Merces fornicariae in sinus tuos; propterea redditionem percipies!

[56] Sicut facies electis meis, dicit Dominus, sic faciet tibi Deus et tradet te in malis. [57] Et nati tui fame interient et tu romphea cades et civitates tuae conterentur et omnes tui in campo gladio cadent, [58] et qui sunt in montibus fame peribunt et manducabunt carnes suas et sanguinem suum bibent a fame panis et siti aquae. [59] Propter priora misera venies et iterum excipies mala.

[60] Et in transitum allident civitatem oditam et exterent eam, portionem aliquam gloriae tuae et territorii tui, dum revertuntur a Babylonia. [61] Extrita illis eris in stramine et ipsi tibi erunt ignis. [62] Omnes hii comedunt te et civitates tuas et territoria tua et montes, et omnem silvam tuam et ligna pomifera igne consument. [63] Et natos tuos captivabunt et honestatem tuam spoliabunt et gloriam faciei tuae exterminabunt.

16 : [1] Vae tibi Babilon et Asia! Vae tibi Aegypte et Syria! [2] Praecingite vos saccos, plangite filios vestros et dolete de his, quia adpropinquavit contritio vestra. [3] Inmissus est gladius vobis et quis est qui avertat eum? [4] Inmissus est vobis ignis et quis est qui extinguat eum? [5] Inmissa sunt vobis mala et quis est qui recutiet ea? [6] Numquid recutiet aliquis leonem esurientem in silva aut numquid extinguet ignem cum stramen incensum fuerit [7] aut numquid recutiet sagittam inmissam a sagittario forte?

[8] Dominus Deus mittit mala et quis recutiet ea? [9] Et exiet ignis ex iracundia eius et quis est qui extinguat eum? [10] Coruscabit et quis non timebit? Tonabit et quis non horrebit? [11] Dominus comminatur et quis non conterretur a facie eius? [12] Tremet terra et fundamenta eius; mare fluctuatur de profundo et fluctus eius turbabuntur et pisces eius a facie Domini et a gloria virtutis eius. [13] Quoniam fortis gloriae qui tendit sagittam, et acumen eius acutum, quae dimissa est ab eo; non deficiet missa super fines terrae.

[14] Ecce mittuntur mala et non revertentur donec venient super terram. [15] Et ignis incendetur et non extinguetur donec excomedat fundamenta terrae. [16] Quomodo non revertitur sagitta missa a sagittario valido, sic non revertentur mala quae fuerint emissa in terram. [17] Vae mihi, vae mihi! Quis me liberabit in diebus illis?

[18] Initium gemitus et copiosi suspirantium; initium famis et multi disperient; initium belli et timebunt potestates; initium malorum et trepidabunt {Lat 19} ab eis. Quid facient cum venerint mala? [19] {Lat 20} Ecce famis plaga dimissa est et tribulatio eius tamquam mastix castigatio in disciplina. [20] {Lat 21} Et super his omnibus non se avertent ab iniquitatibus suis nec super has plagas memorantur sempiterna.

[21] {Lat 22} Ecce erit annonae vilitas in brevi super terram ut putent sibi esse directam pacem; tunc superflorescent mala super terram gladius et famis [22] {Lat 23} et aporiant vitam super terram et gladius dispersit quae superaverint a fame. [23] {Lat 24} Et mortui quasi stercora proicientur et non habent qui consolentur eos, et derelinquetur deserta terra et civitates eius demolientur. [24] {Lat 25} Non derelinquetur agricola qui colet terram et qui seminat eam.

[25] {Lat 26} Ligna fructiferabunt et quis vindemiet illa? [26] {Lat 27} Et uva tradet se ad vindemiam et quis adligabit eam? Erit enim et locis desertio multa. [27] {Lat 28} Concupiscet enim homo hominem videre vel certe vocem eius audire. [28] {Lat 29} Relinquentur enim decem de civitate et duo ex agro qui absconderint se in silva et in fissuras petrarum.

[29] {Lat 30} Quemadmodum relinquentur in oliveto tres vel quattuor olivae [30] {Lat 31} aut sicut in vinea vindemiata et subremanet racemus patens ab scrutantibus vindemiam diligenter,[31] {Lat 32} sic remanebunt in diebus illis tres vel quattuor ab scrutantibus domus eorum in rompheam. [32] {Lat 33} Et relinquetur deserta terra et agri eius inveteraverunt et viae eius et omnes semitae germinabunt spinas, eo quod non transient oves per eam.

[33] {Lat 34} Lugebunt virgines non habentes sponsos; lugebunt mulieres non habentes viros; lugebunt filiae earum non habentes adiutorium. [34] {Lat 35} Sponsi earum in bello consumentur et viri earum in fame exterentur.

[35] {Lat 36} Audite vero ista et cognoscite ea, servi Domini. [36] {Lat 37} Ecce verbum Domini: excipite eum! Ne discredatis de quibus dicit Dominus.

[37] {Lat 38} Ecce adpropinquant mala et non tardantur. [38] {Lat 39} Quemadmodum praegnans in nono mense filium suum in adpropinquante hora partus eius ante horas duas vel tres gementes dolores circum ventrem eius et prodiente infante de ventre non tardabit uno puncto, [39] {Lat 40} sic non morabuntur mala ad prodiendum super terram, et saeculum gemet et dolores circumtenent illum.

[40] {Lat 41} Audite verbum plebs mea; parate vos ad pugnam. In malis sic estote quasi advenae terrae:[41] {Lat 42} qui vendet quasi qui fugiet; et qui emit quasi qui periturus; [42] {Lat 43} qui mercatur quasi qui fructum non capiat; et qui aedificat quasi non habiturus; [43] {Lat 44} qui seminat quasi non messem facturus; et qui putat quasi non vindemiaturus; [44] {Lat 45} qui nubunt sic quasi filios non facturi; et qui non nubunt sic quasi vidui; [45] {Lat 46} propter quod qui laborant sine causa laborant.

[46] {Lat 47} Fructus enim illorum alienigenae metent et substantiam illorum rapient et domos evertent et filios eorum captivabunt, quia in captivitate et fame generant natos suos. [47] {Lat 48} Et qui negotiantur negotiantur in rapina.

Quamdiu exornant civitates et domos suas et possessiones et personas suas, [48] {Lat 49} tanto magis adzelabor eos super peccata, dicit Dominus. [49] {Lat 50} Quomodo zelatur fornicaria mulierem idoneam et bonam valde, [50] {Lat 51} sic zelabitur iustitia iniquitatem cum exornat se et accusat eam in faciem, cum venerit qui defendat exquirentem omnem peccatum super terram.

[51] {Lat 52} Propterea nolite similari eam nec operibus eius. [52] {Lat 53} Quoniam ecce adhuc pusillum et tolletur iniquitas a terra et iustitia regnabit in nos. [53] {Lat 54} Non dicat peccator non se peccasse, quoniam carbones ignis conburet super caput eius qui dicit, non peccavi coram Deo et gloria ipsius.

[54] {Lat 55} Ecce Dominus cognoscit omnia opera hominis et adinventiones illorum et cogitatum illorum et corda illorum. [55] {Lat 56} Qui dixit fiat terra et facta est; fiat caelum et factum est. [56] {Lat 57} Et in verbo illius stellae fundatae sunt et novit numerum stellarum.

[57] {Lat 58} Qui scrutatur abyssum et thesauros illorum, qui metitus est mare et conceptum eius, [58] {Lat 59} qui conclusit mare in medio aquarum et suspendit terram super aquam verbo suo, [59] {Lat 60} qui extendit caelum quasi cameram et super aquas fundavit eum, [60] {Lat 61} qui posuit in deserto fontes aquarum et super vertices montium lacus ad emittendum flumina ab eminenti ut potaret terra,[61] {Lat 62} qui finxit hominem et posuit cor in medio corporis et misit ei spiritum et vitam et intellectum [62] {Lat 63} et spiramentum Dei omnipotentis, qui fecit omnia et scrutinat absconsa in absconsis. Certe [63] {Lat 64} hic novit adinventionem vestram et quae cogitatis in cordibus vestris!

Vae peccantibus et volentibus occultare peccata sua. [64] {Lat 65} Propter quod Dominus scrutinando scrutinavit omnia opera eorum et traducet vos omnes. [65] {Lat 66} Et vos confusi eritis cum processerint peccata vestra coram hominibus et iniquitates erint quae accusatores stabunt in die illo. [66] {Lat 67} Quid facietis aut quomodo abscondetis peccata vestra coram Domino et gloria eius? [67] {Lat 68} Ecce iudex Deus! Timete eum et desinite a peccatis vestris et obliviscimini iniquitates vestras iam agere eas sempiterno, et Deus educabit vos et liberabit de omni tribulatione.

[68] {Lat 69} Ecce enim incendetur ardor super vos turbae copiosae et rapient quosdam ex vobis et cibabunt idolis occisam. [69] {Lat 70} Et qui consenserint eis erunt illis in derisum et in inproperium et in conculcationem.

[70] {Lat 71} Erit enim lociis et in vicinas civitates exsurrectio multa super timentes Dominum. [71] {Lat 72} Aporiati enim homines a malis suis erunt quasi insani neminem

parcentes ad diripiendum et devastandum adhuc timentes Dominum. [72] {Lat 73} Quia devastabunt et diripient substantias eorum et de domo sua eos eicient. [73] {Lat 74} Tunc parebit probatio electorum meorum, ut aurum quod probatur ab igne.

[74] {Lat 75} Audite electi mei, dicit Dominus. Ecce adsunt dies tribulationis et de his liberabo vos. [75] {Lat 76} Ne timeatis neque haesitemini, quoniam Deus dux vester est. [76] {Lat 77} Et qui servat mandata et praecepta mea, dicit Dominus Deus, ne praeponderent vos peccata vestra nec superelevent se iniquitates vestrae.

[77] {Lat 78} Vae qui constringuntur a peccatis suis et obteguntur ab iniquitatibus suis, quemadmodum ager constringitur a silva et spinis tegitur semita eius per quam non transiit homo; [78] et excluditur et mittitur ad devorationem ignis.

6 Ezra: Translation

15: [1] Behold, speak in the ears of my people the words of the prophecy that I will put into your mouth, says the Lord, [2] and cause them to be written (down) on paper, because they are reliable and true. [3] Do not fear the plots against you, and do not let the unbelief of those spreading rumors disturb you, [4] because every unbeliever will die in his unbelief.

[5] Behold, says the Lord, I am bringing evils upon the world—the sword, and famine, and death, and destruction—[6] because iniquity has overwhelmed the whole earth, and their evil deeds have reached the limit. [7] Therefore, says the Lord, [8] I will no longer be silent about their impieties which they sacrilegiously commit, nor will I tolerate the things that they do unjustly. Behold, innocent and just blood cries out to me, and the souls of the just cry out continuously. [9] Surely I will vindicate them, says the Lord, and I will take back all of the innocent blood from them to me.

[10] Behold, my people is led like a flock to the slaughter. I will no longer allow them to live in the land of Egypt, [11] but I will lead them out with a strong hand and an upraised arm, and I will strike Egypt with a blow [or: plague] as before, and I will destroy its whole land.

[12] Let Egypt and its foundations mourn because of the blow [or: plague] of beating and lashing that the Lord will bring about. [13] Let the farmers who work the earth mourn, because their seeds will fail and their trees will be destroyed by blight and hail and by a terrible storm. [14] Woe to the earth and those who live in it, [15] because the sword has drawn near, and their destruction, and nation will rise up against nation in battle, and the sword (will be) in their hands.

[16] For there will be turmoil among some people; others, growing very strong, will not respect their king and the chief of their [or: his] nobles in their power. [17] For a person will wish to go into a city and will not be able, [18] for because of their pride, cities will be thrown into confusion, houses will be destroyed, people will be afraid. [19] A person will not pity his neighbor enough to let their houses alone, but will pillage their property with a sword because of hunger for bread and great tribulation. [20] Behold, says God, I call together all the kings of the earth, to provoke them, who are from the north and from the south and from the east and from the west, to turn themselves and to return what they have given to them. [21] Just as they have done until this day to my elect, so I will do, and

I will repay into their bosom. Thus says the Lord God. ²² My right hand will not spare the sinners, nor will the sword desist from those who pour out innocent blood on the earth. ²³ And fire has gone forth from his wrath, and it has devoured the foundations of the earth and the sinners like straw that is burned up. ²⁴ Woe to those who sin and do not keep my commandments, says the Lord: ²⁵ I will not spare them.

Depart, faithless children; do not defile my holiness. ²⁶ God knows those who sin against him; therefore he will hand them over to death and slaughter. ²⁷ For now evils have come over the earth, and you will remain in them. For God will not deliver you, because you have sinned against him.

²⁸ Behold, a terrible vision and its appearance from the east, ²⁹ and the nations of the Arabian serpents will come out in many chariots, and their hissing is borne over the earth from the day of (their) march, so that all who hear them will also be afraid and tremble. ³⁰ The Carmonians, raging in wrath, will go out of the woods [MSS SMNE add: like wild boars] and (they) will arrive in great strength and will stand in battle with them, and (they) will destroy a portion of the land of the Assyrians with their teeth.

³¹ And after these things the serpent, remembering its origin, will become still stronger, and if they turn back [or: flee], agreeing in great strength to pursue them, ³² those [or: the former] also will be thrown into turmoil and will be silent because of their strength, and they will turn their feet in flight. ³³ And from the territory of the Assyrians, an ambusher will lie in ambush for them, and will destroy one of them, and there will be fear and trembling in their army and turmoil in their kingdom.

³⁴ Behold, clouds from the east and from the north across to the south, and their appearance (is) extremely frightful, full of wrath and tempest. ³⁵ And they will clash together, one against another, and pour out a huge storm over the earth, and their storm [*sic*], and there will be blood from the sword up to the belly of a horse, ³⁶ and the thigh of a human, and the hock of a camel. And there will be great fear and trembling upon the earth. ³⁷ And those who see that wrath will be terrified, and trembling will seize them.

³⁸ And after these things, huge clouds will be set in motion from the south and north, and another part from the west, ³⁹ and winds will swell up from the east; and they will drive away [or: lay open; uncover] it [antecedent unclear] and the cloud which it stirred up in wrath; and the storm that sprang up to cause destruction from the east [lit. add: and it] will be driven violently west [or: and a storm for causing destruction from the east will be driven violently north and west].

⁴⁰ And great and powerful clouds, full of wrath and storm, will be raised up, in order to destroy the whole earth and those living in it, and they will pour out over every high and lofty [place] a terrible storm, ⁴¹ fire and hail and flying swords and many waters, so that even all the plains and all the rivers are filled up with [lit.: from] the abundance of those waters. ⁴² And they will destroy cities and walls and mountains and hills and trees of the forests and grasses of the meadows and their grain, ⁴³ and they will go steadily across to Babylon and will destroy her. ⁴⁴ They will converge on her and surround her, and pour out a storm and every wrath upon her, and the dust [or: ashes] and smoke will rise up to the sky, and everyone around will mourn her. ⁴⁵ And those who remain behind will serve those who destroyed her.

⁴⁶ And you, Asia, consort in the beauty of Babylon and the glory of her person: ⁴⁷ woe to you, miserable one, because you have made yourself like her. You have adorned your daughters in fornication in order to please and glory in your lovers, who have always wanted you to fornicate. ⁴⁸ You have imitated that hateful one in all her deeds and designs.

Therefore, says God, ⁴⁹ I will unleash evils upon you—want, poverty, and famine, and the sword, and pestilence—in order to destroy your houses for injury and death. ⁵⁰ And the glory of your strength will be dried up like a flower, when the heat that has been sent upon you rises up.[51] And you will be weakened and (made) poor by a blow and beaten from (the) wounds [sic], so that it is impossible for you to receive powerful ones and lovers.

[52] Would I have acted so zealously against you, says the Lord, [53] if you had not killed my elect [pl.], always exulting with clapping of hands and talking about their death when you were drunk? [54] Make up the beauty of your face! [55] The wages of a whore (are) in your bosom; therefore, you'll get your recompense!

[56] Just as you will do to my elect, says the Lord, so God will do to you, and he will hand you over into evils. [57] And your children will perish with hunger, and you will fall by the sword, and your cities will be destroyed, and all of you who are in the plains will fall by the sword, [58] and those who are in the mountains and highlands will perish with hunger, and eat their own flesh and drink their own blood from hunger for bread and thirst for water. [59] At first you will come suffering, and again, a second time, you will receive evils.

[60] And in passing they will strike the hateful city and destroy her, some part of your glory and your land, while they are returning from Babylon. [61] You will be destroyed by them like straw, and they will be fire to you. [62] All of them will devour you and your cities and your land and mountains, and all of your forests and fruit-bearing trees they will consume with fire. [63] And they will take your children captive, and despoil your honor, and take away the glory of your face.

16: [1] Woe to you, Babylon and Asia! Woe to you, Egypt and Syria! [2] Gird yourselves with sackcloth, wail for your sons [or: children], and grieve for them, because your dismay has drawn near. [3] The sword has been sent against you, and who is there who can turn it away? [4] Fire has been sent upon you, and who is there who can put it out? [5] Evils have been sent upon you, and who is there who will repel them? [6] Will anyone (be able to) repel a hungry lion in the woods, or put out a fire when the straw has been kindled, [7] or repel an arrow shot by a strong archer?

[8] The Lord God sends evils, and who will repel them? [9] And fire will go forth from his wrath, and who is there who can put it out? [10] He will quake, and who will not be afraid? He will thunder, and who will not tremble? [11] The Lord threatens, and who is not terrified at his appearance? [12] The earth and its foundations will quake; the sea is shaken from the depth, and its waves and fish will be thrown into turmoil at the appearance of the Lord and the glory of his strength. [13] Because strong in [lit.: of] glory (is) the one who stretches the arrow—and its point (is) sharp—which has been shot by him; it will not fall short, having been shot over the ends of the earth.

[14] Behold, evils are sent out, and they will not return until they come over the earth. [15] And fire will be kindled, and it will not be put out until it consumes the foundations [Fr: grain] of the earth. [16] Just as an arrow shot by a strong archer does not return, so the evils that will be sent out over the earth will not return. [17] Woe to me, woe to me! Who will save me in those days?

[18] The beginning of groaning, and much sighing; the beginning of famine, and many will perish; the beginning of war, and those in power will be afraid; the beginning of evils, and they will tremble {Lat 19} at them. What will they do when the evils come? [19] {Lat 20} Behold, a plague [or: blow] of famine has been sent out, and its affliction (is) like a scourge, a punishment as discipline. [20] {Lat 21} And despite all of these things, they will not turn themselves from their sins, nor despite these plagues [or: blows] are they ever mindful.

[21] {Lat 22} Behold, in a short time produce will be cheap on the earth, so that they think that peace is assured for them [or: so that they think to themselves that peace is

assured]; then evils will break out over the earth, the sword and famine, [22] {Lat 23} and life will be under duress [lit.: and they are uncertain (about) life] on the earth, and the sword will scatter [lit.: has scattered] those who survive the famine. [23] {Lat 24} And the dead will be thrown out like dung, and they do not have anyone to comfort them, and the earth will be left deserted, and its cities will be demolished. [24] {Lat 25} There will be no farmer left to till the earth or sow it.

[25] {Lat 26} The trees will bear fruit, and who will gather from them? [26] {Lat 27} And the vine will be ready for [lit.: will present itself for] vintage, and who will bind it? For indeed, places will be completely deserted. [27] {Lat 28} For a person will long to see a(nother) person, or even to hear his voice. [28] {Lat 29} For ten will be left from a city, and two from a field, who have hidden themselves in the forest and in the clefts of rocks.

[29] {Lat 30} Just as three or four olives will be left behind in an olive grove, [30] {Lat 31} or as in a vineyard which is being harvested, a cluster of grapes (may) even remain behind, exposed by those who carefully search through the harvest,[31] {Lat 32} so three or four will be left behind in those days by those who search through their houses with the sword. [32] {Lat 33} And the land will be left deserted, and its fields have grown old [sc. with nonuse] [Sp: and its fields will be full of (lit.: in) briars], and its roads and all of (its) paths will grow thorn bushes, so that sheep will not wander through it.

[33] {Lat 34} Young women will mourn because they do not have grooms; women will mourn because they do not have husbands; their daughters will mourn because they do not have a helper. [34] {Lat 35} Their grooms will be killed in war, and their husbands will perish with hunger.

[35] {Lat 36} Indeed, listen to these things, and understand them, servants of the Lord. [36] {Lat 37} Behold, [or: This is] the word of the Lord: receive it! Do not disbelieve the things that the Lord says!

[37] {Lat 38} Behold, evils draw near, and they are not delayed. [38] {Lat 39} Just as a woman pregnant (with) her child in the ninth month, when the hour of her delivery draws near, groans for two or three hours beforehand (with) the pains around her womb [lit.: the pains around her womb groaning for two or three hours beforehand], and when the baby comes out of the womb, it will not delay for one moment, [39] {Lat 40} so the evils will not delay in coming forth over the earth, and the world will groan, and pains encompass it.

[40] {Lat 41} Hear the word, my people; prepare yourselves for battle. In the evils, be like strangers on [lit.: of] the earth: [41] {Lat 42} the one who sells, like one who will flee; and the one who buys, like one who is going to lose; [42] {Lat 43} the one who does business, like one who will not make a profit; and the one who builds, like one who is not going to inhabit; [43] {Lat 44} the one who sows, like one who is not going to reap; and the one who prunes, like one who is not going to harvest; [44] {Lat 45} those who marry, like ones who will not have children, and those who do not marry, like ones bereaved; [45] {Lat 46} because those who labor, labor in vain.

[46] {Lat 47} For strangers will gather their fruits and seize their property and destroy (their) houses and take their children captive, because they beget their children in captivity and famine. [47] {Lat 48} And those who do business, do business to be plundered [lit.: in plunder].

For as long as they adorn their cities and houses and possessions and their own persons, [48] {Lat 49} so much more will I strive zealously against them, because of (their) sins, says the Lord. [49] {Lat 50} Just as a whore strives very zealously against a dignified and good woman, [50] {Lat 51} so righteousness will strive zealously against iniquity, when she adorns herself, and accuses her to her face, when the one comes who will defend the one seeking out every sin on the earth.

[51] {Lat 52} Therefore, do not imitate her or her actions! [52] {Lat 53} Because behold, a little while longer and iniquity will be taken away from the earth, and righteousness will rule over [or: among] us. [53] {Lat 54} Let the sinner not say that he has not sinned, because coals of fire will burn on the head of the one who says, "I have not sinned before God and his glory."

[54] {Lat 55} Behold, the Lord knows all the actions of a person, and their designs and their intention and their hearts. [55] {Lat 56} He (is the one) who said, "Let there be earth," and it appeared; "Let there be sky," and it appeared.[56] {Lat 57} And by his word the stars were set up, and he knows the number of the stars.

[57] {Lat 58} He (is the one) who searches out the abyss and their [sic] storehouses, who has measured the sea and its capacity, [58] {Lat 59} who has enclosed the sea in the middle of the waters and suspended the earth over the water by his word, [59] {Lat 60} who stretched out the sky like a vault and established it over the waters, [60] {Lat 61} who put springs of water in the desert and, on the tops of the mountains, lakes, to send forth streams from the height so that the earth might drink; [61] {Lat 62} who formed a human being, and put a heart in the middle of (his) body, and sent to him spirit and life and understanding [62] {Lat 63} and the breath of almighty God, who made all things and searches out hidden things in hidden places. Surely [63] {Lat 64} he knows your intention and the things that you think in your hearts!

Woe to sinners and those who wish to hide their sins! [64] {Lat 65} Because the Lord has surely examined all of their deeds, and he will show up all of you. [65] {Lat 66} And you will be confounded when your sins come out in front of people, and it will be (your) iniquities that will stand as (your) accusers in that day! [66] {Lat 67} What will you do, or how will you hide your sins before the Lord and his glory? [67] {Lat 68} Behold, God is the judge! Fear him, and give up your sins and forget your iniquities, ever to do them again, and God will deliver you and free (you) from every tribulation.

[68] {Lat 69} For behold, the burning (wrath) of a great crowd will be kindled over you, and they will seize certain of you, and will feed (them) what was killed for [or: to] idols. [69] {Lat 70} And those who consent to them will be held by them in derision and disgrace and will be trampled under foot.

[70] {Lat 71} For there will be in (various) places [or: in Lociis/Locii/Lociae] and in neighboring cities a great [or: many an] insurrection against those who fear the Lord.[71] {Lat 72} For people pressed by their own evils will be like madmen, sparing no one, in order to pillage and destroy those who still fear the Lord. [72] {Lat 73} For they will destroy and pillage their property, and will drive them out of their house(s). [73] {Lat 74} Then the proving of my elect will become manifest, like gold that is proven by fire.

[74] {Lat 75} Listen, my elect, says the Lord. Behold, (the) days of tribulation are here, and I will deliver you from them. [75] {Lat 76} Do not be afraid or hesitate, because God is your leader. [76] {Lat 77} And the one who keeps my commandments and rules, says the Lord God: do not let your sins weigh you down or your iniquities mount up.

[77] {Lat 78} Woe to those who are choked by their sins and covered over by their iniquities, as a field is choked by the forest and its path covered over by thorn bushes, so that no one (can) traverse it; [78] and it is shut off and relegated to a devouring by [lit.: of] fire.

Textual Relationships between the Manuscripts of 4, 5, and 6 Ezra

These charts represent the exact percentages of verbal agreement between the manuscripts of 4, 5, and 6 Ezra. For example, in 6 Ezra, 72 percent of the readings in manuscript M are identical to the readings in manuscript L. When the text of one manuscript is longer or shorter than that of another (because of "additions" or "deletions"), each "added" or "deleted" word is counted as one verbal disagreement. Orthographic variations between manuscripts are also counted as disagreements.

"S" and "A" represent the original hands of these manuscripts, while "S++" and "A++" stand for the texts of the manuscripts after scribal changes. The chart for 6 Ezra excludes, for MS S, 15:59–16:30, where that manuscript switches affiliation from the French to the Spanish text.

Percentages of Verbal Agreement between the
Manuscripts of 6 Ezra (excluding, for S and S++,
15:59–16:30)

	S++	A	A++	M	N	E	C	V	L
S	I 96.3 I	81.7 I	82.0 I	56.7 I	57.4 I	57.3 I	57.4 I	53.9 I	52.9 I
S++	I ---- I	82.1 I	83.2 I	57.5 I	58.3 I	58.3 I	58.2 I	54.7 I	53.2 I
A	I	I ---- I	94.0 I	51.4 I	52.4 I	51.6 I	53.0 I	49.6 I	49.1 I
A++	I		I ---- I	53.4 I	54.6 I	53.6 I	54.8 I	50.8 I	50.3 I
M	I			I ---- I	93.7 I	90.6 I	82.4 I	74.0 I	72.0 I
N	I				I ---- I	93.8 I	80.3 I	74.4 I	72.0 I
E	I					I ---- I	78.7 I	73.4 I	70.5 I
C	I						I ---- I	80.1 I	77.7 I
V	I							I ---- I	75.4 I

Percentages of Verbal Agreement between the
Manuscripts of 4 Ezra 11–12 (Sample Unit)

	S++	A	A++	M	N	E	C	V	L
S	99.2	88.3	87.6	77.7	77.5	77.0	79.0	79.3	71.6
S++	----	87.9	88.0	78.1	77.9	77.4	79.2	79.6	71.8
A		----	95.4	76.7	76.1	75.8	78.7	78.3	71.1
A++			----	79.1	78.3	78.3	80.7	80.2	72.6
M				----	96.4	95.2	82.3	81.5	74.4
N					----	95.4	81.6	80.9	74.3
E						----	81.3	81.6	73.9
C							----	88.1	77.6
V								----	78.6

Percentages of Verbal Agreement between the
Manuscripts of 5 Ezra

	S++	A	A++	M	N	E	C	V	L
S	98.4	89.3	91.2	46.2	46.3	46.2	47.2	44.1	43.7
S++	----	89.2	91.9	46.5	46.6	46.3	47.5	44.4	43.8
A		----	94.3	44.5	44.5	44.3	45.8	42.5	42.5
A++			----	46.2	46.1	46.2	47.1	43.9	43.5
M				----	95.0	91.9	77.1	71.3	64.5
N					----	92.6	75.7	70.5	65.0
E						----	74.0	69.4	63.6
C							----	77.0	68.2
V								----	68.4

Index of Words in Latin Witnesses to the Text of 6 Ezra

The following index includes all the witnesses to the text of 6 Ezra that are listed in Appendix 1. The format of the index is based generally on the format for recording variant texts laid out by R. A. Kraft and E. Tov (eds.) in *Computer Assisted Tools for Septuagint Studies (CATSS)*. Volume 1: *Ruth* (SBLSCS 20; Atlanta: Scholars, 1986), pages 53–68. Some of the sigla used in this format are self-explanatory; others require explanation. Thus,

+	signifies	addition
>		deletion
:		variant reading
+:		addition with variants
:+		variant to an addition

The four-digit number in parentheses following the chapter and verse locator is made up of two parts: the first two digits represent the number of the lexical unit within the verse, while the second two indicate the type of reading (00 is a reading with no variants, 01 a reading in the main text that has variants, etc.). More precise details may be found in the volume by Kraft and Tov.

Also, many of the sigla used in the present index, including signs for manuscripts and other textual witnesses, are the same as those used in Appendix 1, and are explained in the introduction to that Appendix.

The following sigla are not explained in *CATSS* volume 1 or the introduction to Appendix 1:

Fr. All the French manuscript witnesses and the editions based on them (SA!w!c!b)
Sp. All the Spanish manuscript witnesses (CMNEVL)
edd The editions !w!c!b

The following common Latin words, in accordance with the practice followed in B. Fischer's *Novae concordantiae bibliorum sacrorum iuxta vulgatam versionem critice editam* (5 vols.; Stuttgart: Frommann-Holzboog, 1977), are omitted from the index in order to keep it within manageable space limits: *ad, de, ego, et, hic, ille, in, ipse, is, iste, meus, non, nos, noster, qui, sui, sum, suus, tu, tuus, vester,* and *vos*.

15:38(0700)   a
16:11(0900)   a
16:16(0600)   a
16:22(1800)   a
16:67(1000)   a
16:77(0400)   a
16:12(0402):   a A!w
15:20(1401)   a A!w]
15:20(1901)   a A!w]>Sp.
15:41(2101)   a ASp.!w]>S!c!b
15:60(2501)   a ASp.!w!b]
16:60(1502):   a CMNEV
16:36(0900)+   a Sp.
16:71(0401)   a Sp.]>Fr.!f{>6}
15:38(1000)+   a CVL
16:31(2002):   a CVL
15:19(1402):   a L
15:36(0200)+   a L
16:16(1800)+   a L
15:33(0201)   a Sedd]>~A
15:20(2501)   a Fr.]>Sp.
15:51(1201)   a Fr.]>Sp.
15:35(2001)   a Fr.CMNE]>VLL4
15:51(0601)   a SACMNEL!w!b]>~V,!c
16:77(1601)   a Fr.CMNEL]>{~} V
15:03(0301)   a Fr.CMNEL]>V
16:12(2001)   a Fr.CMNEL]>V{>8}
15:12(0601)   a SASp.!w!b]>!c
15:29(1501)   a SASp.!w!b]>!c
15:34(0901)   a SASp.!w!b]>!c
15:58(1901)   a Fr.Sp.]
16:52(0801)   a Fr.Sp.]>@r
16:07(0801)   a Fr.Sp.]>@g0{>8}
16:71(1202):   a SA+!f
15:13(1901)   a SA+CMNEVedd]>A++
              {>4},~L
16:22(0100)+   a SSp.!t!c!b
15:49(1602):   a S+!c
16:12(2401)   a S++ACedd]>S+MNEL,
              V{>8}
15:20(2202)   a V
16:77(1002):   a V
16:62(0304):   a*spirationem C
15:13(1400)   ab
15:23(0400)   ab
15:34(0300)   ab
15:38(1500)   ab
15:39(0400)   ab
16:20(0900)   ab
16:30(1100)   ab
16:31(1200)   ab
16:18(2401)   ab A!w]

16:13(1801)   ab A!w]>~SSp.!t!c!b
16:67(3202):   ab Sp.
15:34(0600)+   ab CVL
15:20(1902):   ab S!c!b
16:73(1501)   ab Fr.]>~L
16:77(1001)   ab Fr.CL]>MNE{>5}
15:39(2601)   ab SASp.!w!b]
15:20(2201)   ab Fr.CMNL]>E
15:28(0801)   ab Fr.MNE]
15:20(1402):   ab SSp.!c!b
16:60(1501)   ab S++edd]
16:13(1400)+   ab ~SSp.!t!c!b
16:28(1601)   absconderint Fr.CMNEL]
16:28(1602):   absconderit{?} V
16:66(0601)   abscondetis S++ACMNEedd]
16:62(1802):   abscondita CMNEV
16:62(2102):   absconditis Sp.
16:66(0602):   absconditis S+VL
16:62(1803):   absconditorum L
16:62(1801)   absconsa Sedd]>~A
16:62(2200)+   absconsa ~A
16:62(2101)   absconsis Fr.]
16:40(1402):+   abtate CVL
16:57(0303):   abyssos A++CVL
16:57(0301)   abyssum SMNEedd]
16:57(0302):   abysum A+
15:23(1704):   accendentur MNE
15:09(1401)   accipiam Fr.Sp.]
15:55(1502):   accipies !c
15:59(1202):   accipies SSp.!t!c!b
16:50(1001)   accusat Fr.CMNEV]
16:65(1502):   accusator CMNE
16:65(1501)   accusatores Fr.]
16:65(1503):   accusatorum V
16:13(1204):   accute L
16:13(1001)   acumen A!w]
16:50(1002):   acusat L
16:65(1504):   acusator L
16:13(1202):   acutae MNE!t!c!b
16:13(1203):   acute SC
16:13(1201)   acutum A!w]>V
16:71(1600)   adhuc
16:52(0301)   adhuc Fr.Sp.]
15:06(0902):   adimpleta SA+MNEV!f!c!b
15:06(0901)·   adimpletae A++!w]
15:06(0903):   adinpleta CL
16:54(1202):   adinvenciones L
16:63(0501):   adinventionem Fr.]
16:63(0502):   adinventiones Sp.
16:54(1201):   adinventiones Fr.CMNV]
16:54(1203):   adinventionibus E
15:48(1101)   adinventionibus Fr.MNE]

16:33(1602):	adiutoria Sp.
16:33(1601)	adiutorium Fr.]
15:60(0402):	adlident S+!t
16:26(1101)	adligabit A+!w]
15:37(1104):	adpreendet C
15:37(1101)	adprehendet S++L!w]
15:37(1102):	adprehendit S+A+!f!b
15:15(0203):	adpropinquabit C
16:02(1503):	adpropinquabit CL
16:37(0301)	adpropinquant SA+!w!b]
16:38(1901)	adpropinquante A+!w!b]
	>{~} Sp.
16:38(1903):	adpropinquantem S+
16:38(2300)+	adpropinquare {~} CL
15:15(0201)	adpropinquavit SA+L!w!b]
16:02(1501)	adpropinquavit S+A+!w!b]
15:47(0601)	adsimilasti SA+edd]
16:62(0303):	adspirationem L
16:74(0801)	adsunt S+ACMNVLedd]
16:40(2101)	advenae Aedd]
15:10(1700)+	advenam Sp.
16:40(2102):	advene S
15:30(1301)	advenient Fr.]
15:48(1103):	adventionem V
15:48(1102):	adventionibus CL
15:03(0700)	adversum
16:65(1700)+	adversum L
16:48(0401)	adzelabor S+Aedd]
15:53(1803):	aebria N
16:42(1001)	aedificat SMNELedd]>A{>13}
15:11(0202):	aeducam C
16:01(0804):	Aegipte N
15:10(1603):	Aegipti N
15:11(1203):	Aegiptum AN
15:12(0203):	Aegiptus AN
16:01(0802):	Aegyptae SA!f
16:01(0801)	Aegypte CEedd]
15:10(1601)	Aegypti Fr.E]
15:11(1201)	Aegyptum SCE!w!b]>!c
15:12(0201)	Aegyptus SEedd]
15:56(0303):	aelectis C
15:53(0303):	aelectos C
15:16(0202):	aenim C
15:17(0302):	aenim C
15:18(0302):	aenim C
15:27(0202):	aenim C
15:27(1602):	aenim C
15:29(2203):	aenim C
15:44(0202):+	aenim C
16:22(0303):	aenim C
16:23(1502):+	aenim C
16:26(1402):	aenim C
16:27(0202):	aenim C
16:28(0502):	aenim C
16:46(0202):	aenim C
16:47(1102):+	aenim C
16:68(0202):	aenim C

16:70(0202):	aenim C
16:71(0202):	aenim C
15:35(2702):	aequi S
16:59(0600)+	aer L
16:71(1702):+	aetiam C
15:51(0702):+	affligis ~:V
16:77(1401)	ager Fr.CMNEL]
16:67(1901)	agere Fr.]
16:32(0700)	agri
16:24(0301)	agricola ACVL!w]>SMN
	E!t!c!b
16:28(1400)	agro
15:03(0902):+	agunt L
15:08(0901)	agunt SSp.edd]>A{>10}
15:24(1002):	ait @g8
15:38(1401)	alia Fr.CVL]
16:46(0401)	alienigenae Aedd]
16:46(0402):	alienigene S
15:16(0901)	alii CMNEV]>~!w
15:16(0803):	alii S++A++!c!b
15:16(0801)	aliis A+CV]>MNE
16:51(1102):+	aliis L
15:16(0903):	aliis SA++L!c!b
15:16(0902):	alios A+
15:60(1201)	aliquam A!w]>~SSp.!t!c!b
15:60(1000)+	aliquam ~SSp.!t!c!b
16:06(0300)	aliquis
16:07(0300)+	aliquis SCNEVL!t!b
16:07(0500)+	aliquis ~!c
15:16(0802):	alisalios !w
15:16(0804):	alius S+L
15:60(0401)	allident S++ASp.edd]
16:26(1102):	alligabit A++
15:40(2700)	altum
15:51(2200)	amatores
15:47(2302):	amatores Sp.
15:47(2301):	amatoribus Fr.]
16:02(0103):	amicte L4
16:66(1202):	angelis S!c!b
16:19(1100)+	angustia SSp.!t!c!b
16:68(0800)+	angustiae L
15:08(2701)	animae Fr.MNEL]>V{>6}
15:08(2702):	anime C@y
16:21(0301):	annonae Fr.MNE]
16:21(0302):	annone CL
16:21(0303):	annonebilitas V
16:66(0903):	antae L
16:38(2500)	ante
16:66(0902):	ante CMNEV
16:22(0402):	aperiant A+
16:22(0401)	aporiant !w]>SSp.!t!c!b
16:71(0101):	aporiati Sp.]>Fr.!f{>6}
16:22(0403):	aporient A++
15:25(0601):	apostatae AEL!w!b]
15:25(0603):	apostate CMN!s
15:25(0602):	apostestate @g8
16:73(0302):	apparebit A

15:37(1103):	apprehendet A++MNEV!c
16:38(2302):+	appropinquans {~} V
16:37(0302):	appropinquant A++!c
16:38(1902):	appropinquante A++!c
16:38(2301):+	appropinquare {~} MNE
16:02(1504):	appropinquatur V
15:15(0202):	appropinquavit A++MNEV!c
16:02(1502):	appropinquavit
	S++A++MNE!c
15:30(0800)+	apri SMNE!c!b
16:38(1904):	apropinquante S++
16:40(1401)+:	aptate MNE
15:58(2401):	aquae AMNELedd]
15:41(0300)+	aquam E
16:58(1401):	aquam SACMNL!w!b]
15:41(2300)	aquarum
16:60(0600)	aquarum
16:58(0601):	aquarum Fr.]
15:41(1000)	aquas
16:59(0900)	aquas
16:58(0901)+:	aquas CMNEL
16:58(0602):	aquas Sp.
16:58(1402):	aquas EV!c
15:58(2403):	aque SCV
16:58(0902):+	aqui{?} V
15:28(0903):	aquilone L4
15:32(1900)+	aquilonem Sp.
15:29(0702):	Arabam{?} A+
15:29(0701)	Arabum SCVLedd]
15:29(0704):	arabunt MNE
15:29(0703):	Arabym A++
16:29(1000)+	arboribus SSp.!t!c!b
16:13(0600)+	arcum {~} SSp.!t!c!b
16:06(1902):	ardere SCNEVL!t!c!b
16:68(0401):	ardor Fr.]>~Sp.
15:50(1001)	ardor Fr.CMNEV]>L
16:68(0700)+	ardor{~} Sp.
15:44(2302):	ascendet Sp.
15:46(0301)	Asia SA++CMNEVedd]
16:01(0501)	Asia SA++CMNEVedd]
15:46(0302):	Assia A+
16:01(0502):	Assia A+
15:13(2005):	assidus L
15:47(0602):	assimilasti A++
15:30(2903):	Assirioru L
15:30(2904):	Assiriorum AL4
15:33(0402):	Assiriorum AV
16:74(0802):	assunt S++E
15:30(2902):	Assuriorum V
15:30(2901)	Assyriorum SCMNEedd]
15:33(0401):	Assyriorum SCMNELedd]
15:29(2901)	audient Fr.E]
16:27(1000)	audire
16:35(0102):	audire L4
16:40(0100)	audite
16:74(0100)	audite
16:35(0101)	audite Fr.Sp.]

15:29(2902):	audiunt CMNVL
15:01(1201):	aures Fr.]
15:01(1202):	auribus Sp.
15:20(2302):	auro S
15:13(1501):	aurugine MNE]
16:73(1100):	aurum
15:20(2003):	austro SSp.!c!b
16:30(0100):	aut
16:07(0101):	aut A!w]>SCM{>18}
	NEVL,@g0{>8} !t!c!b
16:31(1002):	aut S!c!b
16:66(0401):	aut Fr.]
16:06(0901):	aut Fr.CNEVL]>M{>18}
16:29(1202):	aut SE!t!c!b
15:16(0203):	autem E
16:46(0203):	autem MNE
16:03(1001):	avertat Fr.CMN]>@g0{>9}
16:46(1302):	avertent A
16:20(0801):	avertent A!w]
15:33(0302):	averterit_orio A
16:03(1002):	avertet E
16:04(1004):	avertet ~V
15:25(0604):	a_potestate SV!c
16:01(0301):	Babilon ACEVL]
15:43(0605):	Babilon L4
15:43(0601):	Babilonem S]
15:60(2602):	Babilonia CEVL
15:43(0603):	Babiloniam CNEVL
15:60(2603):	Babiloniam S
15:46(0701):	Babilonis SCEVL]
16:01(0302):	Babylon SMN!w!t!c!b
15:60(2604):	Babylonem !c
15:43(0602):	Babylonem Aedd
15:60(2601):	Babylonia AMN!w!b]
15:43(0604):	Babyloniam M
15:46(0702):	Babylonis AMNedd
16:18(1301):	belli A!w]
16:34(0400)	bello
16:18(1302):	bellorum SSp.!t!c!b
16:40(1202):	bellum Sp.
15:58(1802):	bibant S+
15:58(1801):	bibent S++ASp.edd]
16:49(0702):	bona S!b
16:49(0701):	bonam ASp.!w!c]
15:20(1501):	borea A!w]
15:11(0803):	bracchio !c
15:11(0801):	brachio SMNEVL!w!b]
15:11(0804):	bracio C
15:11(0802):	brahio A
16:21(0701):	brevi A!w]>SSp.!t!c!b
16:60(1603):	cacumen L
16:60(1602):	cacumine CMNEV
15:39(2200)+	cadavera L
15:57(2601):	cadent Fr.CVL]>~MNE
15:57(2200)+	cadent ~MNE
15:57(1101):	cades Fr.CMNEL]
15:57(1103):	cadet V

16:68(2503):	caecabunt ME
16:63(2402):+	caelare {{~} } M
16:55(1101)	caelum Fr.]
15:44(3001)	caelum Fr.CMNE]
16:59(0301)	caelum Fr.CMNE]>L
16:55(0502):	caelum ~CMNEV
15:45(0202):+	caeteri MNE
16:22(1502):+	caeteros S+ME
16:26(1103):	calcabit S++CMNE!t!c!b
16:26(1104):	calcavit S+VL
15:40(1204):	caliginis MNEV
15:36(0901):	cameli SA++CMNELedd]
15:36(0904):	camelis L4
15:36(0902):	camelli A+
16:59(0503):	camera L
16:59(0501):	cameram Fr.CMNE]
16:59(0502):	camerum V
15:36(0903):	camilli V
15:41(1700)	campi
15:57(2401):	campo Fr.MNEL]
15:42(1502):	camporum Sp.
15:57(2403):	campum CV
16:42(0701):	capiat SCMNEedd]>A{>13}
16:42(0702):	capiet VL
15:63(0401):	captivabunt A!w]
16:46(1701):	captivabunt Fr.]
15:63(0403):	captivas L4
16:46(2501):	captivitate Fr.CVL]
16:46(2502):	captivitatem MNE
16:46(1702):	captivos Sp.
15:63(0402):	captivos SSp.!t!c!b
16:53(1900)	caput
16:53(1500)	carbones
15:30(0105):	Carmine A++MNE
15:30(0102):	Carmini A+
15:30(0101):	Carmonii SCedd]
15:58(1201):	carnes Fr.Sp.]
15:30(0104):	Caronii L
15:02(0501):	carta S++A++CMNEV!w!b]
15:02(0504):	cartas A+L
15:02(0502):	cartha S+
15:51(1102):	castigata !c
16:19(1601):	castigatio A!w]>SSp.!t!c!b
15:12(1003):	castigatione !c
15:12(1002):	castigationes S
15:12(1004):	castigationis CMNEL!b
15:40(1202):	cataginis C
15:40(1203):	cathaginis L
16:45(0600):	causa
16:68(2504):	cecabunt N
16:63(2401)+:	celare {{~} } CNEVL
15:52(0405):	celassem L
16:55(0504):	celos ~L4
16:59(0302):	celum V
15:44(3002):	celum VL
16:55(0503):	celum ~L
15:63(0702):	censum SSp.!t!c!b

16:13(2302):+	ceperint CVL
16:06(1801):+	ceperit {~} CVL
16:38(1802):+	ceperit CVL
16:62(2503):	certa SSp.
16:27(0701):	certe A!w]>SSp.!t!c!b
16:62(2501):	certe A!w!b]
15:22(0801):	cessabit SA++CMNEedd]
15:22(0802):	cessavit A+VL
15:45(0201):+	ceteri CVL
16:22(1501):+	ceteros S++CNVL!t!c!b
15:02(0503):	charta !c
16:10(0103):	choruscabit MNE
16:68(2501)	cibabunt SA+Cedd]
16:02(0500)+	ciliciis SMNE!t!c!b
16:38(3303):	circa Sp.
15:44(0601):	circuibunt Sedd]
15:44(3400)	circuitu
16:38(3301):	circum SA!w!b]
15:44(0603):	circumcingent Sp.
16:39(1403):	circumcingunt Sp.
16:38(3302):	circumeunt !c
15:44(0602):	circumibunt A
16:39(1402):	circumtenebunt !c
16:39(1401):	circumtenent SA!w!b]
15:09(1000)+	cito @y
16:28(0800):	civitate
15:17(0800):	civitatem
15:60(0501):	civitatem Fr.CMNEL]
15:18(0600):	civitates
15:42(0300):	civitates
15:62(0700):	civitates
16:23(2000):	civitates
16:47(1300):	civitates
15:57(1301):	civitates Fr.Sp.]
16:70(0901):	civitates SSp.edd]
15:60(0502):	civitates V
16:70(0903):	civitatibus A++
16:70(0902):	civitatis A+
15:08(3001):	clamant Fr.]>V{>6}
15:08(2301):	clamat Fr.@y]
16:58(0202):	clusit A
16:13(2301)+:	coeperint SMNE!t!c!b
16:06(1800)+	coeperit {~} SNE!t!c!b
16:38(1801):+	coeperit MNE
16:54(1503):	cogitaciones V
16:51(1302):+	cogitacionibus V
16:54(1502):	cogitationes CMNELL4!c
16:51(1301)+:	cogitationibus CMNEL
15:03(0401):	cogitationibus SA++Sp.edd]
16:63(0900):	cogitatis
16:54(1501):	cogitatum SA!w!b]
16:54(0402):	cognoscet S!c
16:54(0401):	cognoscit A!w!b]
16:35(0501):	cognoscite Fr.]
16:24(0503):	colat SA++Sp.!t!c!b
16:24(0501):	colet A+]
ex 01(0800)+	COLIPHON A

237

16:24(0502):	colit !w
15:42(0900)	colles
15:35(0902):	collident !c
15:35(0202):	collident S++A++MNEV!c
16:60(1701)+:	collium L
15:62(2403):	comburent MNE!c
16:53(1702):	comburet V!c!b
16:53(1703):	comburit MNE
15:62(0402):	comedent A++
15:62(0401)	comedunt A+!w]
16:11(0204):	cominabitur V
16:11(0205):	comminabitur
	@g1SMNE!t!c!b
16:11(0201):	comminatur A!w]
15:62(2402):	conburent SCVL!t!b
16:53(1701):	conburet SACL!w]
16:57(1201):	conceptum Sedd]
16:77(1503):	conclusa V
16:58(0201)	conclusit SSp.edd]
16:77(1502):	conclusus CMNEL
16:57(1202):	concoeptum A
15:46(0402):	concors !c
16:69(1402):	conculcacione V
16:69(1401)	conculcationem Fr.CMNEL]
15:47(2802):	concupierunt EVL
16:27(0101)	concupiscet A!w]
15:17(0101)	concupiscet SCMNEVedd]
15:17(0102):	concupiscit AL
16:65(0303):	confundemini Sp.
16:11(0602):+	confunditur VL
16:65(0301)	confusi SA++edd]
16:21(2800)+	confusio SSp.!t!c!b
16:65(0302):	confussi A+
15:35(0201)	conlident S+A+CL!w!b]
16:11(0203):	conminatur CL
16:12(1900)+	conmiscebuntur L
15:11(1802):	conrumpam C
16:69(0301)	consenserint Fr.CMNEV]
16:69(0302):	conseserint L
16:23(1001)	consolentur A++!w]
16:23(1003):	consoletur SSp.!t!c!b
15:46(0401)	consors SASp.!w!b]
15:31(1703):	conspiranter MNE
15:31(1701)	conspirantes Fr.]
15:31(1702):	conspirantur CVL
15:16(0302):	constabilitio A!w
15:30(1800)	constabunt
15:43(0301)	constanter SACMN!w!b]>E
15:43(0302):	constantes !c
15:33(2302):	constantia S
15:43(0303):	constantur V,L{?}
16:77(0302):	constringentur VL
16:77(1501):	constringitur Fr.]
16:77(0301):	constringuntur Fr.CMNE]
16:23(1002):	consulentur A+
16:15(0802):	consumat SSp.!t!c!b
15:62(2401)	consument A!w]

16:34(0500)	consumentur
16:22(1101):+	consumentur L4
15:33(0901)	consumet Fr.CMNEV]
15:33(0902):	consummet L
15:25(0900)	contaminare
15:33(2303):	contentio !c
15:57(1501)	conterentur Fr.]
16:11(0704):	conteretur Sp.!t!c!b
16:11(0705):	conteritur S
16:11(0701):	conterretur A+!w]
15:15(1002):	contra A!w!c
15:03(1402):	contradicentium !b
15:15(0503):	contricio MVL
16:02(1602):	contricio MVL
16:02(1601)	contritio Fr.CNE]
15:15(0502):	contritio SA++CNE!c!b
15:03(1101)	conturbent AL!w]
15:31(0403):	convalescet CMNEV
16:18(3002):	convenerint M
15:44(0101)	convenient SSp.edd]
15:20(2801)	convertendos Fr.CVL]
15:20(2802):	convertendum MNE
15:32(1002):	convertens C
15:31(1503):	convertent !c
15:32(1001)	convertent Fr.MNEV]
16:20(0802):	convertent SVL!t!c!b
15:31(1502):	converterent A
15:32(1003):	converterent L
15:31(1501):	converterint SCVL!w!b]
15:31(1504):	converterit MNE
16:20(0803):	convertunt CMNE
15:20(0302):	convocabo V
15:20(0301)	convoco Fr.CL]
16:77(0904):	coobprimentur L
16:77(2104):	cooperietur V
16:77(2102):	cooperitur MNE
16:77(0902):	cooperiuntur C
16:77(2103):	coperitur C
16:68(1301):	copiosae Aedd]
15:38(0602):	copiosae MNE
16:68(1302):	copiose S
16:18(0401):	copiosi A!w]
15:38(0601):	copiosi Fr.CVL]
15:35(1100)	copiosum
16:61(0600)	cor
16:53(2500)	coram
16:65(0900)	coram
16:66(0901)	coram Fr.]
16:54(0901)+:	corda {~} Sp.
16:54(1801)	corda SA++edd]>A+,~Sp.
16:63(1100)	cordibus
16:54(0902):+	cordis {~} L4
15:30(0103):	coronii V
16:61(1102):	corpore Sp.
16:61(1101)	corporis Fr.]
15:34(1704):	corrigent MNE
15:11(1801)	corrumpam Fr.MNEVL]

16:10(0104):	corruscabit S+V	15:26(0606):	delincunt C
16:10(0101)	coruscabit S++A++Cedd]	15:26(0604):	delinqunt S++!s
16:10(0105):	coruscavit L	15:26(0607):	delinquoduunt V
16:52(0302):	crastina @r	15:26(0605):	delinquunt MNE!c
16:55(0402):	creavit L4	16:60(1304):	demittendo MNE
16:36(1402):	credatis SA!f!c	15:42(0201):	demolient SA+CL!w!b]
15:04(1100)+	credit Sp.	16:23(2201):	demolientur A!w]
15:13(0200)	cultores	15:42(0203):	demolientur A++MNE!c
16:50(0500)	cum	15:61(0202):	demolita SSp.!t!c!b
16:50(1400)	cum	15:42(0202):	demollient V
16:65(0500)	cum	16:28(1900)+	densis SSp.!t!c!b
16:38(0400)+	cum !c	15:30(3101)	dentibus SASp.!w!b]>!c{>3}
16:06(1301)	cum AL!w]>M{>18}	16:36(2002):	Deo L4
15:47(2700)+	cum A++	16:66(1002):	Deo S!c!b
16:10(1200)+	cum L	16:53(2701)	Deo Fr.]
in 01(0500)+	cum S	16:24(0201)	derelinquetur Fr.MNE]
15:53(1701)	cum Fr.]>{~} Sp.	16:23(1401)	derelinquetur S++ASp.edd]
16:18(2901)	cum Fr.CNEVL]>M	16:23(1402):	derelinquitur S+
15:30(2301)	cum Fr.CVL]>~MNE	15:26(0603):	derelinqunt S+
15:50(0801)	cum Fr.MNEVL]	16:29(0203):	derelinquuntur !c
16:13(2200)+	cum SSp.!t!c!b	15:53(1302):	deridens CMNEV
16:06(1500)+	cum V	16:71(1302):	deripiendum A+E
15:30(1900)+	cum ~MNE	16:69(0803):	derisu CVL
15:44(0102):	cum_venient A	16:69(0801)	derisum SA++MNEedd]
16:11(0202):	cuncta_minabitur	15:53(1303):	derridens L
	@g3@g4@g6	16:50(1702):	descendat N
15:47(2801)	cupierunt Fr.CMN]	16:32(0301):	deserta SA!w!b]>~Sp.!c
16:27(0102):	cupiet SSp.!t!c!b	16:23(1701):	deserta SA++Sp.edd]
15:16(1200)	curabunt	16:32(0500)+	deserta ~Sp.!c
15:29(0902):	curribus A++!c	16:23(1702):	desertas A+
15:29(0901):	curris SA+!w!b]	16:26(2002):	desertatio CVL
15:29(0903):	curros CVL	16:26(2001)	desertio Fr.MNE]
15:29(0904):	currus MNE	16:60(0400)	deserto
16:10(0102):	curuscabit A+	16:67(0902):	desinete A+
15:24(0702):	custodiunt Sp.	16:67(0901)	desinite SA++Sp.edd]
16:68(2502):	cybabunt A++	16:23(1703):	desolabitur L4
16:25(0202):	dabunt SSp.!t!c!b	16:70(1602):	Deum CMN
16:28(0601)	decem A!w]>~SSp.!t!c!b	16:71(2102):	Deum CMNEV
16:28(1000)+	decem ~SSp.!t!c!b	16:10(1002):+	Deum V
15:20(3400)	dederunt	15:56(1000)	Deus
16:61(1403):	dedit Sp.	16:64(0302):	Deus A
15:11(0203):	deducam MNE	15:26(0301)	Deus A!w]
16:67(2605):	deducet Sp.	16:54(0300)+	Deus Sp.
16:18(2804):	defecerint MNE	15:24(1200)+	Deus CMNVL
16:50(1701):	defendat Fr.CMVL]>E	16:62(0503):	Deus E
15:13(0702):	deficiat A+	16:11(0102):	Deus @g0
16:13(2102):	deficient SSp.!t!c!b	15:24(1102):	Deus @g5
15:13(0703):	deficient S++Sp.edd	15:26(1300)+	Deus S
16:13(2101):	deficiet A!w]	15:27(1901)	Deus Fr.]
15:13(0701):	deficiet S+A++]	15:48(3301)	Deus Fr.]
15:23(0802):	deforabit C	16:67(0301)	Deus Fr.]
15:62(0404):	deforabunt C	16:67(2401)	Deus Fr.]
16:78(0602):	deforatione C	16:75(0601)	Deus Fr.]
16:40(0703):	Dei L4	16:08(0201)	Deus SASp.!w!b]
16:62(0501)	Dei Fr.]	15:21(2201)	Deus Fr.Sp.]
16:23(2202):	deicientur SSp.!t!c!b	16:76(1101)	Deus Fr.L]>CMNEV
16:52(0602):	delebitur @r	15:20(0601)	Deus SSp.edd]

15:12(1502):	Deus SCMNVL!c	16:21(1502):	directa MNE
16:74(0600)+	Deus V	16:21(1501):	directam Fr.CVL]
16:72(0201)	devastabunt Fr.CMNE]	15:19(1502):	diripiendam CMNEL
15:49(1301)	devastandas Fr.Sp.]	15:19(1501):	diripiendas Fr.]
16:71(1501)	devastandum Fr.]	16:71(1301):	diripiendum
15:30(2602):	devastare L4		SA++CMNVLedd]
15:49(1302):	devastatas L4	15:19(1503):	diripiendum V
15:23(0803):	devorabit @g0MNE	16:68(1602):	diripient Sp.
15:62(0403):	devorabunt SMNEVL!t!c!b	16:72(0401):	diripient SA++edd]>Sp.
16:78(0603):	devoracione V	16:69(0802):	dirisum A+
16:78(0604):	devoratione L	16:36(0703):+	dis S++A++
16:78(0601):	devorationem Fr.MNE]	16:36(0800)+	discedatis Sp.
15:23(0801):	devoravit Fr.VL]	15:25(0400)	discedite
15:22(0300)	dextera	16:19(1801)	disciplina A!w]
16:13(0302):	dextera SSp.!t!c!b	16:36(1401)	discredatis !w!b]
15:29(1602):	diae L	16:22(1402):	disperdet A++CVL
16:65(2202):	diae L	16:18(1001)	disperient A!w]
16:53(0200)	dicat	15:58(0903):	disperient Sp.
15:03(1403):	dicencium L	16:22(1401)	dispersit A+!w]
15:53(1301)	dicens Fr.]	16:12(1503):	disturbabuntur SMNE!t!c!b
15:03(1401)	dicentium SACMNEV!w!c]	16:47(1000)+	diu !c
15:01(2300)	dicit	16:55(0201)	dixit ASp.edd]>S
15:07(0200)	dicit	15:01(0501)+:	dixit VL
15:20(0400)	dicit	16:02(1102):	doletae L
15:21(2000)	dicit	16:02(1101):	dolete Fr.CMNEV]
15:48(3200)	dicit	16:38(3202):	dolorem MNE
15:56(0500)	dicit	16:39(1300)	dolores
16:48(1100)	dicit	16:38(3201):	dolores Fr.CVL]
16:53(2200)	dicit	16:18(1902):	dolorum MNE
16:74(0400)	dicit	16:18(0202):	dolorum SSp.!t!c!b
16:76(0900)	dicit	16:18(1200)+	dolorum V
15:52(0701)	dicit Fr.CMNEL]>V	16:72(0903):	domibus Sp.!c
15:24(1001)	dicit Fr.Sp.]	16:08(0102):	Domine L
16:36(1901)	dicit Fr.Sp.]	16:35(0800)	Domini
15:09(1101)	dicit Fr.Sp.]>~@y	16:36(0300)	Domini
15:05(0601)	dicit Fr.MNE]>~CVL	16:40(0500)+	Domini Sp.
15:09(0400)+	dicit ~@y	15:34(2100)+	Domini L4
15:05(0200)+	dicit ~CVL	16:12(2201)	Domini Fr.CMNEL]>V{>8}
16:36(1902):	dicta L4	16:53(2600)+	Domino !c
16:52(0402):	die @r	16:66(1001)	Domino A!w]
15:29(1601)	die SACMNEV!w!b]>!c	16:36(1000)+	Domino Sp.
16:65(2201)	die Fr.CMNEV]	16:53(2702):	Domino Sp.
16:17(1000)	diebus	16:16(1900)+	Domino L
16:31(0600)	diebus	16:08(0103):	Domino L4
16:74(0900)	dies	16:66(1003):	Dominum Sp.
16:36(0702):+	dies A+	16:70(1601)	Dominum Fr.EVL]
16:36(0701)+:	diis S+!c	16:71(2101)	Dominum Fr.L]
16:74(0202):	dilecti !c	15:01(2400)	Dominus
16:30(1801)	diligenter A++!w]>~SSp.!t!c!b	15:07(0300)	Dominus
16:30(1600)+	diligenter ~SCMN!t!c!b,L{?}	15:21(2100)	Dominus
16:30(1802):	diligentibus{?} A+	15:56(0600)	Dominus
16:30(1601):+	diligentur ~V	16:48(1200)	Dominus
16:30(1602):+	diligent~ ~E	16:54(0200)	Dominus
15:26(0608):	diligunt L	16:74(0500)	Dominus
16:13(1602):	dimisa A	16:76(1000)	Dominus
16:13(1601)	dimissa !w]	15:20(0602):	Dominus A
16:19(0501)	dimissa A!w]>{~} SSp.!t!c!b	15:12(1501)	Dominus AE!w!b]

15:20(0500)+	Dominus Sp.	15:34(0100)	ecce
15:27(1902):	Dominus Sp.	16:14(0100)	ecce
15:48(3302):	Dominus Sp.	16:19(0100)	ecce
16:67(2402):	Dominus Sp.	16:21(0100)	ecce
16:75(0602):	Dominus Sp.	16:36(0100)	ecce
16:67(0302):	Dominus Sp.L4	16:37(0100)	ecce
16:62(0502):	Dominus CMNVL	16:67(0100)	ecce
15:01(0300)+	Dominus LL4	16:68(0100)	ecce
16:08(0101)	Dominus Fr.CMNEV]	16:74(0700)	ecce
15:52(0801)	Dominus Fr.CMNEV]>L	15:27(0102):	ecce CNEVL
15:24(1101)	Dominus Fr.Sp.]	15:05(0800)+	ecce L
16:11(0101)	Dominus Fr.Sp.]	16:52(0201)	ecce SA!w!b]>Sp.!c
16:36(2001)	Dominus Fr.Sp.]	15:01(0801)	ecce Fr.CMNEV]
15:09(1201)	Dominus Fr.Sp.]>~@y	15:05(0101)	ecce Fr.CMNEV]
15:05(0701)	Dominus Fr.MNE]>~CVL	16:54(0101)	ecce Fr.CMNEV]
16:64(0301)	Dominus SSp.edd]	16:42(1003):	edificat V
15:26(0302):	Dominus S@g8Sp.!c!b	16:67(2601)	educabit S++A++!w!b]
15:09(0500)+	Dominus ~@y	15:11(0201)	educam Fr.L]
15:05(0300)+	Dominus ~CVL,L4	16:67(2602):	educavit S+!f
16:72(0901)	domo S++A!w]	16:67(2603):	educet !c
15:49(1401)	domos ASp.!w!c]	15:51(0500)+	efficias L
16:31(1702):	domos A++Sp.!w!c	15:09(1402):	effuderunt @y
15:18(0802):	domos C	15:40(2304):	effundent A++CVL
16:46(1101)	domos SA++CMNEL!w!c]	15:35(0901)	effundent SACL!w!b]
16:47(1501)	domos SA++Sp.!w!c]	15:44(0901)	effundent Fr.CL]>V{>15}
15:19(1001)	domos SA++Sp.edd]	15:22(1201)	effundentes Fr.CVL]
16:72(0902):	domos S+!b	15:35(0903):	effundet V
15:19(1002):	domus A+	15:16(1706):	egentes_tenorum MNE
16:47(1502):	domus A+!b	16:77(1402):	eger V
16:46(1102):	domus A+V!b	15:16(1704):	egestanorum C
15:49(1402):	domus S!b	16:01(0807):	Egipte L4
15:18(0801):	domus Fr.MNEV]	15:10(1604):	Egipti L
16:31(1701):	domus SA+!b]	15:11(1205):	Egipto L4
15:18(0803):	domusque L	16:01(0806):	Egiptum L
16:14(0700)	donec	15:11(1204):	Egiptum VL
16:15(0700)	donec	15:12(0204):	Egiptus VL
15:44(1800)+	donec CMNEL	16:01(0803):	Egypte M
15:31(0501)	draco SASp.!w]	15:10(1602):	Egypti CMV
15:31(0502):	dracones !c!b	16:01(0805):	Egypti V
15:29(0501)	draconum Fr.]>Sp.	15:11(1202):	Egyptum M
16:38(2801)	duas Fr.]>~Sp.	15:12(0202):	Egyptus CM
16:38(2600)+	duas{~} Sp.	16:72(1201)	eicient SA++edd]
15:63(0500)+	ducent {~} SSp.!t!c!b	16:74(0201)	electi SASp.!w!b]
16:46(1800)+	ducent Sp.	15:21(0500)	electis
15:10(0801)	ducitur Fr.CMNEV]	15:56(0301)	electis AMNEVLedd]
15:10(0802):	duitur{?} L	16:73(0500)	electorum
15:60(2301)	dum A!w]	15:56(0302):	electos S
16:28(1200)	duo	15:53(0301)	electos SA++MNEVLedd]
16:75(0700)	dux	15:53(0302):	electus A+
16:73(0102):+	e V	16:19(1804):	emendaciunem V
16:03(0802):	e{?} L	16:19(1802):	emendatione SMN!t!c!b
15:53(1802):	ebria CMEVL	16:19(1803):	emendationem CEL
16:54(0102):	eccae L	15:40(2901)	eminentem Fr.]
15:08(1800)	ecce	16:60(1601)	eminenti Fr.]
15:10(0100)	ecce	16:16(1602)	emisa A+
15:20(0100)	ecce	16:16(1601)	emissa A++!w]
15:28(0100)	ecce	15:50(1201)	emissus Fr.]

16:41(0801)	emit Fr.CMNEL]	16:01(0503):	Esaye L
16:60(1303):	emitenda V	in 01(0402):	Esdre C
16:60(1302):	emittenda A++CL	16:75(0403):	esitemini S++
16:60(1301)	emittendum SA+edd]	16:51(0502):+	essae L
16:78(0402):	emittetur A	16:36(1500)+	esse CMNEL
16:41(0802):	emittit V	16:51(0501)+:	esse CMNEV
16:55(0300)+	enim !c	15:52(0500)+	esse E
16:23(1501)+:	enim {~} SMNEVL!t!c!b	16:40(0902):+	esse L4
15:54(0200)+	enim L	16:21(1401)	esse Fr.CMEVL]>N
15:44(0201)+:	enim MNEVL	16:36(1300)+	esse ~V,L4
16:47(1101)+:	enim MNEVL	15:53(2002):	esses !c
16:71(0201)	enim MNEVL]>Fr.!f{>6}	16:40(1900)	estote
15:18(0301)	enim Fr.MNE]>VL	16:40(0901)+:	estote Sp.
16:27(0201)	enim Fr.MNEV]>L	16:06(0501)	esurientem
15:17(0301)	enim Fr.MNEV]>~L		Fr.CNEV]>~L,M{>18}
15:27(0201)	enim Fr.MNEVL]	16:06(0800)+	esurientem ~L
15:27(1601)	enim Fr.MNEVL]	15:04(1800)+	eternum L
16:26(1401)	enim Fr.MNEVL]	16:71(1701)+:	etiam MNEVL
16:28(0501)	enim Fr.MNEVL]	15:41(1401)	etiam Fr.]>{~} Sp.
16:68(0201)	enim Fr.MNEVL]	15:29(2201)	etiam SAMNEVL!w!b]
16:70(0201)	enim Fr.MNEVL]	15:27(0103):	et_ce M
15:16(0201)	enim Fr.MNVL]	15:16(1707):	et_gestanorum V
16:46(0201)	enim Fr.VL]	15:20(2301)	euro ACMNLedd]>E
16:22(0302):	enim SMNEVL!t!c!b	15:57(0903):+	eversa V{?} ,L
15:17(0500)+	enim ~L	16:46(1301)	evertent SSp.edd]
15:35(2701)	equi ASp.!w!b]>!c	15:09(1800)	ex
15:44(2000)+	eradicent CMNEL	15:33(1100)	ex
15:42(1406):	erbas C	16:68(2200)	ex
15:42(1407):	erbasque L	16:28(1301)	ex ACMNEL!w]
15:52(0202):	ergo CVL	16:12(1002):	ex L
16:66(0200)+	ergo L	16:09(0401)	ex SCMNELedd]
16:65(1301)	erint S!w!b]>CMNEV	15:40(0200)	exaltabuntur
16:69(0502):	erint S+!b	15:53(0802):	exaltans S++!c
16:71(0702):	erint S+!b	15:40(1405):	examinent E
16:72(0402):	eripient A+	15:11(0900)	excelso
15:61(0501)	eris A!w]>~SSp.!t!c!b	15:40(2902):	excelsum Sp.
15:61(0300)+	eris ~SSp.!t!c!b	15:59(1201)	excipies A!w]
15:16(0100)	erit	16:36(0401)	excipite Fr.]
15:33(1400)	erit	16:78(0202):	excludetur A
15:36(1200)	erit	16:78(0201):	excluditur SSp.edd]
16:21(0200)	erit	16:15(0801)	excomedat A!w]
16:26(1300)	erit	16:08(1903):	excutiet @g8
16:70(0100)	erit	15:08(1601)	exercent SMNEVedd]>A{>10}
15:04(1600)+	erit CMNEL	15:08(1603):	exercerunt L
15:31(1200)+	erit MNE	15:08(1602):	exercescent C
16:23(0803):	erit SSp.!t!c!b	15:33(2003):	exercitu A{?} CMNEV!c
15:35(1801)	erit SSp.edd]>A	15:33(2001):	exercitum S++L!w!b]
16:65(0401)	eritis Fr.]>Sp.	15:33(2002):	exercituum S+
15:13(1505):	eruginae L	15:23(0202):	exibit @g1
16:65(1302):	erunt !c	16:09(0203):	exibit @g3@g4
15:61(1301)	erunt AVL!w]>~SCMNE!t!c!b	15:30(0600)	exient
16:32(1100)+	erunt Sp.!b	15:29(0201)	exient Fr.CMNEV]
16:20(1701)+:	erunt SCVL!t!c!b	15:29(0202):	exientque L
16:69(0501)	erunt S++ASp.!w!c]	15:23(0203):	exiet @g8CMEVL
16:71(0701)	erunt S++ASp.!w!c]	16:09(0201)	exiet SCEVL!w!b]
15:61(1100)+	erunt ~SCMNE!t!c!b	16:09(0204):	exiit A+MN!c
15:46(0303):	Esaye L	15:23(0201):	exiit Fr.N]

242

16:38(4600)+	exire L
15:29(0203):	exire L4
16:09(0202):	exit A++
15:54(0101):	exorna Fr.]
15:54(0102):	exornans Sp.
16:47(1201):	exornant Fr.]
16:50(0602):	exornant VL
16:50(0601)	exornat Fr.C]
16:50(0603):	exorta MNE
16:72(1203):	expellent Sp.
ex 01(0101)	EXPLICIT Sedd]>Sp.
16:71(1504):	expoliandum L
16:71(1503):	exportadum V
16:71(1502):	exportandum CMNE
16:50(1901):	exquirentem Fr.]
16:70(1002):	exresurrectio S+
16:04(1002):	exstinguat !c
16:06(1103):	exstinguet !c
16:15(0602):	exstinguetur !c
15:15(0801):	exsurget Fr.N]
15:50(0901)	exsurget Fr.NL]
16:70(1001)	exsurrectio S++Aedd]
16:59(0200)	extendit
15:40(1401)	exterant SA++!w!b]
15:45(1104):	exterent MNE
15:60(0801)	exterent SA++MNEedd]
15:43(0801)	exterent SA++Vedd]
15:18(0901)	exterentur Fr.MNEV]
16:34(1101)	exterentur SA++edd]
16:46(0403):	exteri Sp.
15:39(2501)	exteritionem S!w!b]
15:63(1600)	exterminabunt
15:60(2200)+	exterminabunt SSp.!t!c!b
15:31(2202):	exterminare L4
15:43(0804):	exterminari L4
15:40(1404):	exterminent CMNVL
15:40(1402):	exterrant A+
15:40(1403):	exterreant !c
15:43(0803):	exterrebit MNE
15:43(0802):	exterrent A+CL
15:60(0802):	exterrent A+CVL
15:45(1103):	exterrent CVL
16:34(1102):	exterrentur A+
15:18(0902):	exterrentur C
15:18(0903):	exterretur L
15:39(2504):	exterritationem !c
15:45(1102):	exterruerunt SA+!f!c
15:45(1101)	exteruerunt A++!w!b]
16:08(0700)+	extinguat @g8{+10}
16:09(1201)	extinguat Fr.CMNEL]
16:04(1001)	extinguat SAMNL!w!b]>E@g0{>10}
16:06(1102):	extinguat S+
16:04(1003):	extinguet C
16:09(1202):	extinguet @g0V
16:06(1101)	extinguet S++CEVL!w!b]>M{>18}

16:03(1004):	extinguet ~V
16:15(0601):	extinguetur SASp.!w!b]
16:06(1104):	extinguit AN
16:76(2003):	extollant CMNEL
16:76(2004):	extollent V
15:39(2503):	extricationem A++
15:61(0201):	extrita A!w]
15:15(0501):	extritio A+!w]
15:53(0801):	exultans S+ACVL!w!b]
15:53(0803):	exultasti MNE
15:15(0802):	exurget CMEV
15:50(0902):	exurget CMEV
in 01(0401):	Ezrae Sedd]>AMNEVL
ex 01(0501)	EZRAE Fr.]>Sp.
15:02(0200)	fac
16:11(1002):	faciae AL
16:12(2102):	faciae AL
15:21(0800)	faciam
16:18(2802):	faciam !c
15:09(0702):	faciam @y
15:10(1103):	faciam V
15:56(0802):	faciat S+
16:67(1902):	faciatis Sp.
16:50(1302):	facie CV!c
16:12(2101):	facie SCMNEedd]>V{>8}
16:11(1001):	facie SCMNEVedd]
15:63(1400)	faciei
15:32(1600)+	faciem Sp.
16:47(2103):	faciem CVL
15:34(1502):	faciem MNE
16:50(1301):	faciem SAMNEL!w!b]
15:39(2401):	faciendam Fr.]
15:39(2402):	faciendas Sp.
15:19(0800)	faciendum
16:18(2801):	facient ACVL!w!b]
15:28(0600)	facies
16:47(2102):	facies MNE
15:34(1501):	facies Fr.CVL]
15:56(0201):	facies Fr.VL]
15:56(0801):	faciet S++ASp.edd]
16:66(0300)	facietis
15:56(0202):	facis CMNE
15:21(0200)	faciunt
16:44(0300)+	faciunt Sp.
16:44(1600)+	faciunt Sp.
15:47(0800)+	facta Sp.
15:53(1900)+	facta Sp.
15:55(1200)+	facta Sp.
16:55(1302):	facta Sp.
16:64(0802):	facta Sp.
16:54(0603):	facta Sp.L4
16:55(0701):	facta Fr.]
16:56(0603):	facte CVL
16:51(0802):	factis CMNEV
16:55(0702):	factum Sp.
16:55(1301)	factum Fr.]
16:44(1001):	facturi Fr.]

16:43(0801)	facturus A!w]>SSp.!c!b
15:36(0304):	faemur A
15:42(1401)	faena !w]
15:58(0802):	famae A
15:58(2002):	famae A
15:57(0403):	famae AL
16:22(1902):	famae L
16:46(2702):	famae L
16:34(1000)	fame
16:22(1901)	fame Fr.CMNEV]
16:46(2701)	fame Fr.CV]
15:57(0401)	fame SCMNEVedd]
16:22(0200)+	fame SSp.!t!c!b
15:58(0801)	fame SSp.edd]
15:58(2001)	fame SSp.edd]
15:05(1500)	famem
16:46(2703):	famem MNE
15:19(1901)	famem Fr.CL]>MNE{>6}
15:49(0701)	famem Fr.CMNEL]
15:19(1902):	famen V
15:49(0702):	famen V
16:21(2502):	fames S++A++MNEVL!t!c!b
16:19(0202):	fames S++MNE!t!c!b
16:18(0700)	famis
16:19(0201):	famis S+ACVL!w]
16:21(2501)	famis S+A+C!w]
16:18(2803):	fecerint S
16:53(1202):+	feci MNEV
16:53(1201)+:	fecisse C
16:62(1200)	fecit
16:53(1203):+	fefecisse{?} L
15:36(0301)	femur CEL!w!b]
15:36(0302):	femus S+
15:36(0306):	femus{?} V
15:42(1402):	fena S!f!b
15:09(0300)+	feram @y
15:29(1800)	fertur
15:48(2500)+	fias Sp.
16:55(1000)	fiat
16:55(0401)	fiat Fr.Sp.]
16:28(2307):	ficxuris L
15:04(1301)+:	fide CMNEV
15:02(1300)	fideles
15:04(1302):+	fidem L
16:26(0402):	fiet SSp.!t!c!b
15:25(0502):	fili V
16:33(1201)	filiae Fr.MNEL]
15:47(1300)	filias
16:33(1202):	filie CV
15:57(0202):	filii CMNEL
15:25(0501)	filii Fr.CMNEL]
16:44(0802):	filii S+
16:02(0800)	filios
16:46(1500)	filios
16:46(2900)+	filios L
15:63(0202):	filios SSp.!t!c!b
16:44(0801)	filios S++ACMNEVedd]>L

16:46(2800)+	filios{{~} } Sp.
16:38(1501)	filium Fr.]>{~} Sp.
15:57(0203):	fillii V
15:36(0303):	fimus S++!c
16:61(0203):	fincxit{?} V
16:13(2600)	fines
ex 01(0103):	FINIT A++L4
ex 01(0102):	FINIUNT A+
16:61(0201):	finxit ACMNELedd]
15:51(0203):	firmaberis S+
16:28(2301):	fissuras A++!w]
16:28(2303):	fissuris SCMN!t!b
16:28(2302):	fisuras A+
16:78(0403):	fit Sp.
16:28(2306):	fixuras V
16:19(1502):	flagella SSp.!t!c!b
15:51(0701)+:	flagellis ~:CMNEL
16:20(1502):	flagellorum SSp.!t!c!b
15:29(1302):	flatus S!c
15:29(0301)+:	flatus V
15:50(0600)	flos
16:12(0803):	fluctuabuntur @g8
16:12(0802):	fluctuantur @g1
16:12(0804):	fluctuat A++CMNEV!c
16:12(0801):	fluctuatur SA+!w!b]
16:12(0805):	fluctuavit L
16:12(1300)	fluctus
15:29(0302):+	fluctus L
16:60(1400)	flumina
15:36(0305):	foemur MN
15:42(1403):	foena A
15:42(1404):	foenum !c
16:60(0500)	fontes
15:57(1800)+	fores L
16:18(1502):	formidabunt SSp.!t!c!b
15:29(2505):	formidant C
15:29(2504):	formident MNEL
15:29(2506):	formiderit V
16:75(0406):	formidetis Sp.
15:47(3402):	fornicare A+
15:47(3401):	fornicari SA++!w!c]
15:55(0302):	fornicaria A
16:49(0301):	fornicaria ACMN!w!c]
15:55(0301):	fornicariae SMNEVL!w!b]
15:47(3403):	fornicariam Sp.!b
16:49(0302):	fornicariam SEVL!b
15:55(0304):	fornicarie C
15:48(2902):+	fornicatione L4
15:47(1601)	fornicatione Fr.]
15:48(2900)+	fornicationibus CMNEV
15:55(0303):	fornicationis !c
15:48(2901):+	fornificationibus L
16:07(1001)	forte AN!w]>@g0{>8}
16:07(1002):	forti SCME!t!c!b
16:13(0200)	fortis
16:08(0202):	fortis !c
16:07(1003):	fortissimam V

16:07(1004):	fortissimo L
15:31(1902):	fortiter L4
16:10(1300)+	fortitudine L
15:62(2204):	fructaferum V
16:51(0803):	fructibus L
16:25(0201)	fructiferabunt A!w]
15:62(2202):	fructiferum SMNEL!t!c!b
16:25(0302):+	fructos S+V
16:46(0102):	fructos V
16:42(0501)	fructum SSp.edd]>A{>13}
16:46(0101)	fructus Fr.CMNEL]
16:25(0301)+:	fructus S++CMNEL!t!c!b
16:15(0902):	frumenta A!f!w
15:42(1701)	frumenta Fr.]
16:16(1501):	fuerint A!w]>~SSp.!t!c!b
16:16(1700)+	fuerint ~SSp.!t!c!b
16:06(2001)	fuerit A!w]>{~} SCM{>18}
	NEVL!t!c!b
15:32(1401)	fugam Fr.CVL]>MNE{>5}
16:41(0503):	fugiat CMNE!c
16:41(0504):	fugient V
16:41(0501):	fugiet S!w!b]
16:41(0502):	fugit A
16:41(0505):	fugiunt L
16:10(0300)+	fulgoribus L
15:44(2600)	fumus
16:59(1002):	fundabit C
15:12(0400)	fundamenta
15:23(0900)	fundamenta
16:57(1203):	fundamenta Sp.
16:12(0501)	fundamenta SSp.!c!b]
16:15(0901)	fundamenta SSp.!c!b]
16:12(0502):	fundamento A!w
16:56(0601)	fundatae SA++MNEedd]
16:56(0602):	fundati A+
16:59(1001)	fundavit Fr.MNEVL]
15:35(0904):	fundent MNE
15:44(0902):	fundent MNE
15:40(2301)	fundent S+A+MNE!w!b]
15:22(1202):	fundentes MNE
15:40(2302):	fundet S++
15:44(1900)+	funditus CMNEL
16:11(0601)+:	funditus SCMNE!t!c!b
16:18(0503):	gement MNE
16:38(3101):	gementes SA!w!b]>Sp.!c
16:39(1101):	gemet Fr.]
16:21(1904):	geminabuntur MN
16:18(0504):	gemitibus V
16:18(0201):	gemitus A!w]
16:18(0502):	gemitus SCL!t!c!b
16:46(3002):	generabunt Sp.
16:46(3001)	generant Fr.]
15:15(0900)	gens
15:15(1100)	gentem
15:63(0703):	genus W
16:32(2100)	germinabunt
16:21(1902):	germinabunt SCVL!t!c!b
16:21(1903):	germinabuntur E
15:16(1708):	gestanorum L
15:19(1302):	gladio A++
15:57(1005):	gladio Sp.
16:31(2106):	gladio Sp.
16:21(2302):	gladio L4
15:35(2101):	gladio Fr.Sp.]
15:57(2501):	gladio Fr.CVL]>~MNEX
15:57(2100)+	gladio ~MNE
16:03(0402):	gladioque L4
15:41(0704):	gladios CVLL4
15:05(1300):	gladium
15:49(0900):	gladium
15:19(1301):	gladium SA+Sp.edd]
15:15(0300):	gladius
16:22(1300):	gladius
16:03(0401):	gladius Fr.CMNEL]
16:21(2301):	gladius Fr.Sp.]
16:04(0502):	gladius ~V
16:66(1201):	gloria AC!w]
16:53(2901):	gloria Fr.CMNE]
16:12(2501):	gloria Fr.CMNEL]>V{>8}
15:46(0901):	gloria Fr.CMNEV]
15:50(0201):	gloria Fr.CMNEV]
15:63(1302):	gloria V
16:13(0301):	gloriae A!w]
15:60(1701):	gloriae AMNEedd]>C{>4}
	V{>4} L{>3}
15:46(0902):	gloriae L
15:50(0202):	gloriam L
16:66(1203):	gloriam MNEVL
15:63(1301):	gloriam Fr.CMNEL]
16:53(2902):	gloriam VL
15:47(2101):	gloriandum Fr.]
15:60(1702):	glorie S
15:48(2401)+:	gloriosa CMNEL
15:47(2102):	gloriosa Sp.
15:48(2402):+	gloriose V
15:03(0402):	gogitationibus A+
15:13(1702):	grandinae L
15:13(1701)	grandine Fr.CMNEV]
15:41(0500)	grandinem
15:10(0500)	grex
16:23(0802):	habebunt A++
15:63(1100)+	habebunt SCMNEV!t!c!b
16:38(1400)+	habens Sp.
16:23(0801):	habent A+!w]
16:33(0400)	habentes
16:33(1500)	habentes
16:33(0901)	habentes
	SA++Sp.edd]>A+{>5}
15:14(0501):	habitant ACNVL!w!c]
15:40(1904):	habitant MNV
15:31(0802):	habitantis V
15:10(1300):	habitare
16:42(1301)	habitaturus
	S++CMNEVedd]>A{>13}

16:44(1002):	habituri Sp.	15:62(2301)	igne A!w]
16:42(1302):	habiturus S+L	16:73(1601)	igne Fr.]
16:75(0401)	haesitemini !w!b]	15:41(0100)	ignem
16:75(0405):	haesitetis A++!c	16:73(1602):	ignem CMNEV
16:75(0402):	haessitemini A+	16:06(1201)	ignem
16:42(1002):	hedificat C		Fr.CNEVLedd]>M{>18}
15:42(1408):	herbam MN	15:62(2302):	igni SSp.!t!c!b
15:42(1409):	herbarum E	15:23(0300)	ignis
15:42(1405):	herbas V	15:61(1400)	ignis
15:21(0402):	hodiae L	16:09(0300)	ignis
15:48(0103):	hodibilem V	16:15(0200)	ignis
15:21(0401)	hodie Fr.MNEV]	16:53(1600)	ignis
15:60(0606):	hodiosam V	16:78(0700)	ignis
16:61(0302):	homine L4	16:04(0501)	ignis Fr.CMNL]>E{>10}
16:27(0400)	hominem	16:03(0403):	ignis ~V
16:61(0301)	hominem Fr.Sp.]	in 01(0700)+	II_CCXXX S
15:18(1000)	homines	15:48(0201):	imitata Fr.]>~Sp.
16:32(3003):	homines !c	15:47(3201)+:	imitata ~CMNE
16:71(0301)	homines CMNE]>Fr.!f{>6}	15:01(1902):	immisero MN!c
16:28(0900)+	homines L	16:05(0104):	immissa !c
16:22(0602):+	homines L4	16:08(0900)+	immissa @g8{+10}
16:65(1000)	hominibus	16:03(0104):	immissus @g3@g6!c
15:16(0501)	hominibus Fr.CMNE]	15:19(1202):	immittam M
16:63(1402):+	hominibus V	15:49(0102):	immittam MN!c
15:36(0400)	hominis	16:08(0302):	immittit !c
16:54(0701)	hominis SA!w!b]	15:19(0702):	impetum !b
16:54(0702):	hominum Sp.L4!c	15:08(0502):	impietates A!w
15:17(0400)	homo	15:08(0501)	impietatibus SMNE!c!b]
15:19(0300)	homo	15:41(1501)	impleantur Fr.MNEV]
16:27(0300)	homo	16:61(0802):+	imposuit {~} MNE
16:77(2800)	homo	16:69(1102):	improperium A++MNE
15:63(0701)	honestatem A!w]	15:23(1702):	incendentur CV
16:38(2001)	hora S++ACedd]>MNEV,~L	16:68(0301)	incendetur A]
16:38(2701)	horas Fr.CMNEV]	16:15(0301)	incendetur A!w]
16:10(1701)	horrebit A!w!b]	16:68(0302):	incenditur Sedd
15:37(0201)	horrebunt Fr.MNE]	15:23(1703):	incenduntur L
15:28(0401)	horribilis SAMNE!w!b]	16:06(1901)	incensum A!w]>M{>18}
15:34(1701)	horrida Fr.]	15:23(1701)	incensum Fr.]
15:35(2102):	humano L4	in 01(0101)	incipit Fr.]>Sp.
15:63(1900)+	humiliaberis L	16:40(2103):	incolae MNEV
15:08(0100)	iam	16:40(2104):	incole CLL4
15:10(0900)	iam	15:16(0303):	inconstabilicio NVL
15:29(2202):	iam !c	15:33(2301):	inconstabilitio A!w]
15:09(0100)+	iam @y	15:16(0301):	inconstabilitio SCME!c!b]
15:27(0101)	iam Fr.]	15:33(2305):	inconstancia VL
16:67(1701)	iam Fr.]	15:33(2304):	inconstantia CMNE!b
15:27(0300)+	iam VL	16:36(1403):	increduli Sp.L4
15:29(1201)+:	ibi CVL	15:04(0501)	incredulitate Fr.CVL]
16:51(0102):	ideo Sp.	15:04(0502):	incredulitatem MNE
16:46(1901)+:	ideo CV	15:03(1300)	incredulitates
16:46(1902):+	ideoque L	15:04(0300)	incredulus
16:68(2801)	idolis Fr.]>{~} Sp.	15:12(1303):	inducat A+
16:49(0502):	idonea S!b	15:12(1301):	inducet A++Sp.!w!c]
16:49(0501)	idoneam AMNEVL!w!c]	15:12(1302):	inducit S!f!b
16:72(1202):	iecient A+	15:05(0501)	induco Fr.CMNEV]>L
16:35(0202):	igitur Sp.	15:53(1801):	inebriata Fr.]
16:73(1603):	ignae L	16:38(3901)	infante SSp.edd]

16:38(3902):	infantem A
16:38(0600)+	infantem{{~} } Sp.
15:59(0100)+	infelix {~} SSp.!t!c!b
15:51(0201)	infirmaberis S++A++edd]
15:51(0202):	infirmaveris A+
15:51(0204):	infirmeris CMNE
15:51(0205):	infirmes V
15:40(2303):	infundent !c
15:31(0803):	inhabitans L
15:40(1902):	inhabitant CE
16:22(0800)+	inhabitant SSp.!t!c!b
15:14(0502):	inhabitant SME!b
15:40(1901)	inhabitantes Fr.]
15:40(1903):	inhabitent L
16:18(1102):	inicium NL
16:18(1802):	inicium NL
16:18(0102):	inicium NV
16:18(0602):	inicium NVL
15:08(1501)	inique SSp.edd]>A{>10}
15:06(0400)	iniquitas
16:65(1202):	iniquitas Sp.
16:52(0700)	iniquitas [Fr.Sp.@r]
16:50(0400)	iniquitatem
16:76(2200)	iniquitates
16:65(1201)	iniquitates Fr.]
16:67(1501)	iniquitates Fr.CVL]
16:20(1000)	iniquitatibus
16:77(1101)	iniquitatibus
	Fr.CL]>MNE{>5}
15:47(3203):+	inita {~} V
16:18(0601)	initium Fr.CME]
16:18(0101)	initium Fr.CMEL]
16:18(1101)	initium Fr.CMEV]
16:18(1801)	initium Fr.CMEV]
16:53(1001)+:	iniusticiam MNEVL
16:53(1002):+	iniustitiam C
16:53(0901)+:	iniustus CMNEV
16:57(0805):	inmensus V
16:05(0102):	inmisa A+
16:07(0702):	inmisam A+
15:01(1901)	inmisero SACEVL!w!b]
16:05(0101)	inmissa
	S++A++!w!b]>@g0{>10}
16:07(0701)	inmissam A++!w]>{~}
	SCMNEV,@g0{>8} !t!c!b
16:04(0101)	inmissus
	S++Aedd]>E@g0{>10}
16:03(0101)	inmissus S++A++!w!b]
16:03(0102):	inmisus A+
15:47(3202):+	inmitata ~L
15:19(1203):	inmittam E
15:49(0101)	inmittam SACEVL!w!b]
15:08(2004):	innocens L4@y
15:22(1403):	innocentem L
15:08(2802):	innocentum @y
15:22(1401):	innocuum SACMNEV!w!b]
15:09(1701)	innocuum S++ASp.!w]

15:08(2003):	innocuus A++CVL
15:22(1402):	innoxium !c
15:09(1702):	innoxium S+S+++!c!b
15:08(2001)	innoxius SMNEedd]
15:08(2002):	innoxus A+
15:08(0503):	inpietatibus CVL
15:41(1502):	inpleantur CL
16:61(0801)+:	inposuit {~} CVL
15:16(2003):	inpotencia L
15:16(2002):	inpotentia CMNEV
16:69(1103):	inproperio C
16:69(1101)	inproperium SA+VLedd]
15:08(0801)	inreligiose S+Sp.!w!b]>A{>10}
16:71(0900)	insani
15:30(0202):	insaniantes A+
15:30(0201)	insanientes SA++Sp.edd]
16:57(0204):	inscrutantur L
16:62(0305):	inspirationem MNEV
16:65(1603):	instavit L
16:70(1003):	insurrectio Sp.
16:61(2201)	intellectum Fr.]>~Sp.
16:61(1900)+	intellectum{~} Sp.
16:35(0503):	intellegite E
16:35(0505):	intelligere L4
16:35(0504):	intelligete V
16:35(0502):	intelligite CMNL
16:58(0502):	inter Sp.
16:22(1100)+	interient {~} SSp.!t!c!b
16:34(1103):	interient Sp.
15:57(0501):	interient Fr.Sp.]
16:18(1002):	interient SSp.!t!b
15:05(1900)	interitum
16:18(1003):	interitus !c
15:16(1002):	invalescentes SSp.!c!b
16:28(0300)+	inveniet L
16:32(1002):	inveterabunt S++A++!c
16:32(1001)	inveteraverunt S+A+!w]
15:35(0501):	invicem SSp.edd]>A
15:20(0303):	invoco MNE
15:23(0500)	ira
15:39(1501)	ira Fr.]
15:30(0401)	ira Fr.MNEVL]
15:34(2003):	ira V
16:09(0501):	iracundia Fr.Sp.]
15:17(0902):	irae L
15:34(2001)	irae Fr.MNE]
15:40(1001)	irae Fr.MNEL]>~V
15:30(0402):	iram C
15:39(1502):	iram Sp.
16:09(0502):	iram L4
15:37(0601):	iram Fr.CMNEL]>V
15:44(1301):	iram Fr.CMNL]>V{>15}
15:40(1002):	ire C
15:34(2002):	ire CL4
15:17(0901):	ire SCVedd]>~AMNE
15:17(1300)+	ire ~A
15:17(0600)+	ire ~MNE

15:40(0800)+	ire ~V
15:51(0206):	irfirmis L
15:08(0802):	irreligiose S++!c
15:19(0701)	irritum SACVL!w!c]
15:51(1400)+	ita CMNEV
15:41(1200)+	ita{~:} Sp.
15:59(0901)	iterum A!w]
15:29(1701)	itineris SASp.!w!b]
16:67(0200)	iudex
16:52(1300)+	iustia ~A
16:50(0302):	iusticia SMNEV!a!f!b
16:52(1102):	iusticia SMNEVL!a!f!b
16:50(0303):	iusticiam L
16:53(0702):	iustificare L4
16:50(0301)	iustitia AC!w!c]
16:52(1101)	iustitia C!w!c]>~A~:@r
15:08(2801)	iustorum Fr.CMNE]>V{>6}
16:53(0902):+	iustus L
15:08(2201)	iustus SSp.edd@y]>A
16:45(0702):	laborabunt L
16:45(0400)	laborant
16:45(0701)	laborant Fr.CMNEV]
16:60(1100)	lacus
16:06(0401)	leonem Fr.CNEVL]>M{>18}
15:20(2603):	liba V
15:20(2601)	libano Fr.MNEL]
ex 01(0301)	LIBER SA++edd]>Sp.
in 01(0201)	liber SA++Cedd]>A+MNEVL
15:27(1701)	liberabit A++CMNELedd]
16:67(3101)	liberabit S++A++CMNELedd]
16:17(0701)	liberabit S++A++Sp.edd]
16:74(1400)	liberabo
16:76(1200)+	liberabo A++
15:27(1702):	liberavit SA+V!f
16:17(0702):	liberavit S+A+
16:67(3102):	liberavit S+A+V!f
15:20(2602):	libia C
ex 01(0302):	LIBRI A+
15:02(1000)+	libro L
15:42(1100)	ligna
16:25(0100)	ligna
15:62(2101)	ligna A!w]
15:13(1201)	ligna SACVL!w!b]>MNE!c {>4}
15:23(1500)+	lignorum L
15:62(2102):	lignum SCMNEV!t!c!b
15:62(2103):	linum L
16:70(0401)	lociis A+!w]
16:70(0501)+:	lociis S
16:26(1701)	locis SA++CMNEVedd]
16:70(0403):	locis S++A++CMNE!c!b
15:40(2602):+	locum !c
16:70(0502):+	locus !c!b
16:26(1702):	locus A+L
16:70(0404):	locus VL
15:01(0900)	loquere
15:01(0502):+	loquitur L4
15:13(0101)	lugeant SASp.!w!b]
15:12(0101)	lugeat SASp.!w!b]
15:44(3502)	lugebant S+L
15:12(0102)	lugebit !c
16:33(0100)	lugebunt
15:13(0102)	lugebunt !c
16:33(1101)	lugebunt Fr.CMNEL]
16:33(0601)	lugebunt SA++Sp.edd]>A+ {>5}
15:44(3501)	lugebunt S++ACMNEVedd]
16:33(1102):	lugent V
16:48(0300)	magis
15:31(2000)	magna
16:26(1900)+	magna {~} SSp.!t!c!b
15:30(1601)	magna Fr.MNEL]
16:21(2700)+	magna SSp.!t!c!b
15:40(0401)	magnae AMNEedd]
15:30(1602):	magnam CV
15:40(0402):	magne SCVL!f!s
15:37(1000)+	magno L
15:33(1600)+	magnus L
15:27(0900)	mala
15:49(0300)	mala
15:59(1400)	mala
16:08(0400)	mala
16:14(0300)	mala
16:16(1300)	mala
16:18(3100)	mala
16:21(2000)	mala
16:37(0400)	mala
16:40(1702):	mala Sp.
15:56(1502):	mala CMNVL
16:08(1200)+	mala @g8{+10}
15:21(1300)+	mala L
15:48(0700)+	mala L4
15:05(1201)	mala Fr.CMNEL]
16:39(0401)	mala Fr.CMNEV]
16:05(0401)	mala Fr.Sp.]>@g0{>10}
16:54(2000)+	malas Sp.
15:05(1202):	male V
16:51(1101)+:	malis CMNEV
16:71(0501):	malis Sp.]>Fr.!f{>6}
15:56(1501):	malis SA!w!b]
16:40(1701):	malis Fr.]
16:18(1901)	malorum Fr.CVL]
15:56(1503):	malum E!c
16:39(0402):	malum L
15:24(0800)	mandata
16:76(0400)	mandata
16:46(0502):	manducabunt Sp.
15:58(1101)	manducabunt Fr.]>~Sp.
15:58(1400)+	manducabunt{~} Sp.
15:27(1202):	manebit CV
15:27(1201)	manebitis Fr.MNE]
15:27(1203):	manebunt L
16:57(1002):	manere A
15:15(1700)	manibus

15:16(0503): manibus L
15:11(0500): manu
15:53(1102): manum S+A++!f
15:53(1101): manuum S++Sp.edd]
16:58(0301): mare Fr.]
16:12(0701): mare Fr.Sp.]
16:57(1001): mare SSp.edd]
16:12(0702): maris @g0
15:51(1101): mastigata SA!w!b]>~:Sp.
15:12(1001): mastigati A!w]
15:12(1005): mastigationis V
16:19(1501): mastix A!w]
16:26(0300)+: matura {~} SSp.!t!c!b
16:61(1000): medio
16:58(0501): medio Fr.]
15:16(1701): megestanorum !w!b]>A{>4}
15:31(1003): memor CMNE
16:20(1601): memorantur A!w]
15:31(1001): memores S!c!b]>{~} A
16:20(1602): memores SSp.!t!c!b
15:31(1002): memoria !w
15:31(0600)+: memoriae {~} A
15:31(1004): memoriae V
15:31(1005): memoris L
16:38(1201): mense Fr.]
16:38(1202): mensibus Sp.
16:57(0804): mensus CMNEL!c
16:47(0703):+: mercabuntur {~} MNE
16:47(0701)+: mercantur {~} CL
16:47(0303): mercantur Sp.
16:42(0201): mercatur SCMNELedd]>A
                {>13}
15:55(0201): merces S++ASp.edd]
16:42(0202): merchatur V
15:55(0202): mercis S+
16:47(0702):+: mereantur {~} V
16:57(0802): meretus A+
15:38(0800): meridiano
15:34(1300): meridianum
16:57(0803): meritus A++
16:43(0701): messem A!w]
16:43(0703): metat SMNE!b
16:46(0501): metent Fr.]
16:43(0702): metet !c
16:57(0801): metitus S!w!b]
15:18(1101): metuent Fr.CMNE]
16:71(2002): metuentes MNE
16:71(2003): metuunt CVL
15:18(1102): metuunt VL
15:16(1702): me_gestanorum S
15:20(1102): me_vendum{?} S
15:20(1103): me_verendum !c!b
16:30(1500)+: minus C
16:16(0502): misa A+
15:59(0501): misera A++!w]>~>X>{~}
                SSp.!t!c!b
15:47(0301): misera Fr.CVL]

15:47(0302): miserae NE
15:47(0303): misere M
15:19(0200): miserebitur
16:61(1401): misit SA++edd]
16:19(1200)+: missa {~} SSp.!t!c!b
16:13(2401): missa A!w]
16:16(0501): missa SA++Sp.edd]
16:16(1603): missa SSp.!t!c!b
16:05(0103): missa S+Sp.!t
16:07(1100)+: missam {~} SCMNE!t!c!b
16:07(0703): missam L
15:59(0502): misserat{?} A+
16:61(1402): missit A+
15:05(0502): missurum_esset L4
15:50(1202): missus Sp.
16:03(0103): missus S+Sp.!t
16:04(0102): missus S+CMNVL!t
15:19(1204): mittam N
16:08(0303): mittet V@g0
16:13(2402): mitti SSp.!t!c!b
16:08(0301): mittit SACMNEL!w!b]
16:08(0304): mittitur L4
16:78(0401): mittitur Sedd]
16:14(0200): mittuntur
16:13(1603): mittuntur SSp.!t!c!b
15:38(0403): mobebuntur C
15:20(1104): mobendum C
15:39(3402): molabitur V
16:60(1002): moncium L
15:40(2601)+: montem MNE
15:53(1502): montem S++
15:42(0700): montes
15:62(1301): montes Fr.CMNEL]>V{>10}
15:58(0501): montibus Fr.Sp.]
16:60(1001): montium Fr.CMNEV]
16:39(0303): morabitur VL
16:39(0301): morabuntur Fr.MNE]
15:04(0700): morietur
15:49(1902): morte !c
15:53(1503): morte CMNEV
15:26(1503): morte L
15:05(1700): mortem
15:49(1901): mortem SA!w!b]>Sp.
15:26(1501): mortem Fr.CMNEV]
15:53(1501): mortem S+ALedd]
15:26(1802): mortem ~@g8
16:23(0200): mortui
15:38(0402): movebunt !c
15:38(0401): movebuntur SAMNEVL!w!b]
15:20(1101): movendum AMNEVL!w]
15:03(0901)+: moventur MNE
16:06(1600)+: mox {~} SCNEVL!t!c!b
16:38(0200)+: mulier Sp.
16:49(0401): mulierem SASp.!w!b]
16:33(0701): mulieres SA++Sp.edd]>A+
                {>5}
15:51(1302): mulieribus !c

16:49(0402):	mulier_rem !c
16:70(1100)	multa
16:26(2101)	multa A!w]>{~} SSp.!t!c!b
15:27(1000)+	multa @g1CMNEL
15:19(2302):	multa S
15:27(0800)+	multa ~@g8V
15:19(2301)	multam ACVLedd]>MNE{>6}
15:39(1900)+	multam L
15:41(2402):	multarum !c
15:41(1100)	multas
16:68(1303):	multi Sp.
16:18(0901)	multi SA++Sp.edd]
16:18(0402):	multi SSp.!t!c!b
15:38(0603):	multique L4
16:18(0902):	multis A+
15:29(1001)	multis Fr.N]
15:41(2203):	multitudine Sp.
15:36(1602):	multitudo E
15:29(1002):	multos CMEVL
15:36(1601)	multus Fr.CMNVL]
16:52(1700)+	mundi ~:@r
15:42(0501):	muros SA++CVLedd]
15:42(0502):	murus A+
15:39(2904):	natho A+
15:57(0201):	nati Fr.]
15:29(0400)	nationes
15:31(0801)	nativitatis Fr.CMNE]
15:63(0201)	natos A!w]
16:46(3101):	natos Fr.]>{~} Sp.
15:39(2901):	natum SCVL]>~MNE
15:39(3300)+	natum ~MNE
15:03(0100)	ne
16:36(0600)	ne
16:75(0100)	ne
16:76(1902):	ne !c
15:03(1002):	ne A+
16:76(1401)	ne Fr.]
15:22(0700)	nec
16:20(1201)	nec A!w]
16:75(0302):	nec Sedd
16:51(0701)	nec Fr.]
16:76(1901)	nec SACMNEV!w!b]
15:03(1001)	nec SA++Sp.edd]
15:08(1001)	nec SMNEVLedd]>A{>10}
16:47(0402):	negociantur !b
16:47(0302):	negociantur SA!a!f!b
16:47(0301):	negotiantur !w!c]
16:47(0401):	negotiantur A!w]>{~} Sp.,S!c
16:71(1003):	nemine A+V
16:71(1001):	neminem SL!w!b]
16:71(1002):	nemini A++CMNE!c
16:28(0200)+	nemo L
16:29(0500)+	nemoribus L
16:28(2002):	nemoribus SSp.!t!c!b
16:75(0301):	neque ASp.]
15:08(1002):	neque C
16:51(0702):	neque Sp.
16:51(1000)+	neque Sp.
16:53(0800)+	neque Sp.
16:76(1903):	neque L
16:20(1202):	neque SSp.!t!c!b
15:38(0501):	nimbi Fr.CVL]
15:38(0502):	nimphae MNE
15:53(0100)	nisi
16:38(1302):+	nobem {~} C
15:26(0202):	nobit C
16:54(0404):	nobit C
16:63(0202):	nobit C
16:56(1202):+	nobit ~C
15:06(1202):+	nociba C
15:06(1201)+:	nociva SMNEVL!c!b
15:25(0802):	nolitae L
16:51(0200)	nolite
16:36(1201)+:	nolite Sp.
15:25(0801):	nolite Fr.CMNEV]
16:38(1101)	nono Fr.]>{~} Sp.
15:20(2002):	notho A
15:39(2905):	notho A++
16:33(1402):	noti L
15:20(2001):	noto !w]
15:39(2902):	notum !w!b
16:38(1301)+:	novem {~} VL
16:54(0403):	novit MNEVLL4
16:56(0901):	novit Fr.]>~Sp.
15:26(0201):	novit Fr.MNEVL]
16:63(0201):	novit Fr.MNEVL]
16:56(1201)+:	novit ~MNEVL
16:44(1405):	nubcias L
15:39(1100)	nubem
16:46(2202):+	nubent MNEV
15:40(0300)	nubes
15:34(0202):	nubes A++Sp.L4!c
15:34(0201):	nubs SA+!w!b]
16:44(1403):	nubtias C
16:44(0203):	nubtias CL
16:46(2201)+:	nubunt CL
16:44(0201):	nubunt Fr.]
16:44(1401):	nubunt Fr.]
16:56(1000)	numerum
15:29(1702):	numerus !c
16:06(1001)	numquid A!w]>SCM{>18} NEVL!t!c!b
15:52(0101):	numquid SACMNVL!w!b]
16:06(0101):	numquid SACMNVL!w!b]
16:07(0201):	numquid SACNVL!w!b]> @g0{>8} >M{>18}
16:10(0802):	nun A+
15:52(0102):	nunquid E!c
16:07(0202):	nunquid E!c
16:06(1002):	nunquid @g3@g6
16:06(0102):	nunquid @g3@g6E!c
16:44(0204):	nupcias V
16:44(1404):	nupcias V
16:44(0202):	nuptias MNE

16:44(1402): nuptias MNE
16:67(1404): oblibiscimini C
16:67(1402): obliviscamini !c
16:67(1403): obliviscemini S+A+!f
16:67(1401): obliviscimini
S++A++MNEVL!w!b]
15:33(0603): obsedebit S+C
15:24(0701): observant Fr.]
15:33(0503): obsesor L
15:33(0502): obsessor S+CMNEV
15:33(0602): obsidebit S++MNEVL!c!b
16:77(0901): obteguntur Fr.]>MNE{>5}
15:38(1600): occidente
15:39(3202): occidente A++Sp.
15:34(0700)+: occidente Sp.
15:20(1700)+: occidente E
15:39(3201): occidentem SA+edd]
15:53(0202): occidisset A
15:60(0604): occisam !c
16:68(2901): occisam S!w!b]
15:26(1803): occisionae L
15:10(0700): occisionem
15:26(1801): occisionem Fr.CMNEV]
15:26(1502): occisionem @g8
16:68(2903): occisos !c
16:68(2902): occisum A
16:63(2101): occultare Fr.]>{~} Sp.
15:60(0605): ociosam N
16:38(1303):+ octo {~} MNE
15:48(0101): odibilem SA++CMNELedd]
15:21(0403): odie C
15:60(0602): odiosam CEL!t
15:60(0601): oditam A!w]
15:48(0102): odivilem A+
16:29(1403): olibe C
16:29(0702): olibeto C
16:29(1401): olivae Fr.MNEL]
16:29(1402): olive V
16:29(0701): oliveto Fr.MNEVL]
16:50(2003): omnae L
15:40(2502): omne C
16:50(2002): omne S++MNE,V{?} ,!c
15:40(1500): omnem
15:62(1601): omnem A!w]>E,V{>10}
15:06(0601): omnem Fr.CMNE]
15:44(1201): omnem Fr.CMNEL]>V{>15}
15:09(1501): omnem Fr.Sp.]>@y
15:40(2501): omnem Fr.MNEVL]
15:11(2101): omnem S+A!w]>~S++
CV!c!b,MNEL
16:50(2001): omnem S+AC!w!b]
15:41(1902): omnem V
15:11(1900)+: omnem ~S++CV!c!b
15:20(0700): omnes
15:29(2600): omnes
15:41(1600): omnes
15:44(3200): omnes

16:64(1300) omnes
15:62(0201) omnes A!w]>SSp.!t!c!b
15:37(0300)+ omnes Sp.
16:54(0502): omnes S
16:32(1701) omnes Fr.]>Sp.
16:41(1901) omnes Fr.CMNEL]
15:57(1701) omnes Fr.Sp.]
15:26(0400)+ omnes SSp.!c!b
16:18(2200)+ omnes SSp.!t!c!b
15:62(1602): omnes SCMNL!t!c!b
16:71(0302): omnes VL
16:67(3300) omni
15:53(0601) omni Fr.]>{~} Sp.
16:64(0700) omnia
16:62(1600)+ omnia !c
16:54(0501) omnia ACMNEVedd]>L
16:62(1301) omnia Fr.M]>~CNEVL
16:62(1000)+ omnia ~CNEVL
15:48(0500) omnibus
16:20(0400) omnibus
16:63(1401)+: omnibus CMNEL
15:16(0502): omnibus V
16:62(0602): omnipotens Sp.
16:62(0601) omnipotentis Fr.]
15:04(0200) omnis
15:04(0900)+ omnis Sp.
16:54(0601) opera Aedd]
15:48(0602): opera L4
16:64(0801) opera Fr.]
15:06(1102): opera SSp.!c!b
15:13(0301): operantes Fr.]>Sp.
16:54(0602): operas S
15:06(1101): operationes A!w]
16:51(0801): operibus Fr.]
15:48(0601): operibus Fr.Sp.]
16:77(2105): operitur L
16:77(0903): operiuntur V
16:38(2002): ora S+
16:38(2400)+ ora ~L
16:38(2702): oras L
15:27(0600) orbem
15:05(1001) orbem Fr.CMNEV]>L
15:06(0602): orbem VL
15:28(0403): oribilis V
15:39(2702): orientale A+
15:39(2701) orientalem Sedd]
15:39(2703): orientali A++
15:34(0400) oriente
15:39(0500) oriente
15:39(2704): oriente Sp.
15:28(0901): oriente Fr.MNE]
15:20(1502): oriente SCMNEL!c!b
15:28(0902): orientem CVL
15:20(1503): oriento V
15:13(1504): origine V
15:47(1202): ornando Sp.
16:47(1202): ornant Sp.

15:47(1201)	ornasti Fr.]
16:10(1703):	orrebit CVL
15:37(0202):	orrebunt CVL
15:28(0402):	orribilis CL!c
15:34(1702):	orrida CV
15:34(1703):	orridas L
15:01(2100)	os
15:60(0603):	otiosam SM!b
16:32(3001)	oves S!w!b]>~Sp.
16:32(2500)+	oves ~CMNEV
16:32(2800)+	oves ~L
16:32(3002):	ovis A
16:21(1602):	pace MNE
16:21(1601)	pacem Fr.CVL]
15:10(1102):	paciar L
15:58(2101)	panis Fr.Sp.]
15:19(2001)	panis Fr.CVL]>MNE{>6}
16:40(0801)	parate Fr.]
16:40(0802):	parati Sp.L4
15:25(0200)	parcam
16:71(1100)	parcentes
15:22(0201)	parcet Fr.Sp.]
16:73(0301)	parebit SSp.edd]
15:22(0202):	pareet @g7
16:38(0500)+	parit !c
15:30(2702):	partem Sp.
15:60(1600)+	partem SMNE!t!c!b
16:38(2102):	parti S+
16:39(1102):	parturit Sp.
16:38(2101)	partus S++ASp.edd]
16:53(0302):	pastor V
16:30(1001)	patens A!w]>SSp.!t!c!b
15:10(1101):	patiar Fr.CMNE]
16:38(3600)+	patitur Sp.
15:51(0403):	pauper CV
15:51(0401)	paupera SAL!w!b]
15:51(0402):	paupercula !c
15:51(0404):	pauperescas MNE
15:49(0500)	paupertatem
16:10(1706):	pavebit !c
16:53(2402):	peccabi C
15:24(0400)	peccant
15:26(0601):	peccant A!w!b]
16:63(1603):	peccant Sp.L4
16:63(1602):	peccantes !c
15:22(0601)	peccantes ASp.!w!b]
16:63(1601):	peccantibus SA!w!b]
16:53(0701):	peccasse Fr.Sp.]
15:27(2201)	peccastis Fr.MNEVL]
16:63(2200)	peccata
16:65(0700)	peccata
16:76(1700)	peccata
16:67(1502):	peccata MNE
16:48(0901)	peccata Fr.]
16:66(0701):	peccata Fr.CMNEL]>V
16:67(1100)	peccatis
15:27(2202):	peccatis C

16:48(0902):	peccatis Sp.
16:77(0501)	peccatis Fr.CMNEL]
16:77(1102):	peccatis V
16:77(0502):	peccato V
16:53(0301)	peccator Fr.CMNEL]
15:23(1200)	peccatores
15:22(0602):	peccatores S!c
16:50(2100)	peccatum
16:53(2401)	peccavi Fr.MNEVL]
15:26(0602):	peccavit @g6
15:32(1101)	pedes Fr.CVL]>MNE{>5}
15:47(2202):	penes Sp.
16:32(3100)	per
16:77(2400)	per
16:73(1502):	per CMNEV
16:70(0702):	per Sp.
15:04(1200)+	per L
16:73(1200)+	per ~L
15:55(1501)	percipies A!w]
15:11(1102):	percuciam VL
15:53(1002):	percussione Sp.!w!b
15:53(1001)	percussionem SA!c]
15:11(1103):	percutere L4
15:11(1101):	percutiam Fr.CMNE]
16:22(1403):	perdet SMNE!t!c!b
16:41(1101)	perditurus SSp.edd]
15:11(0204):	perducam{?} V
15:58(0901)	peribunt Fr.]
16:41(1102):	periturus A
15:31(2201)	persequendos Fr.Sp.]
15:08(3101)	perseveranter SMNLedd]
15:08(3103):	perseverantes ACV
15:08(3104):	perseverantur{?} E
15:46(1001)	personae Fr.MNEL]
16:47(2101)	personas Fr.]
15:46(1002):	persone CV
15:43(0202):	pertransient CVL
15:43(0203):	pertransiet MNE
15:59(0305):	per_maria !c
15:49(1101)	pestem Fr.]
15:49(1103):	pestilenciam VL
15:49(1102):	pestilentiam CMNE
16:60(1702):+	petra !c
16:28(2400)	petrarum
16:12(1700)	pisces
15:47(1802):	placeas Sp.
15:48(2700)+	placeas Sp.
15:47(1801)	placendum Fr.]
15:48(1601)+:	placitura CV
15:48(1602):+	placituram MNE
15:12(0700)	plaga
16:19(0400)	plaga
15:51(0901)	plaga SACMNEL!w!b]
15:11(1401)	plaga S++AVedd]
15:11(1402):	plagam S+
16:20(1501)	plagas A!w]
15:51(0902):	plagata !c

15:11(1403):	plagis CMNELL4	16:21(1203):	potest MNE
15:29(1303):	planctus CVL	16:18(1700)	potestates
15:51(0903):	planga V	16:76(0701):	praecepta Fr.M]
16:02(0702):	plangere L4	16:02(0101):	praecingite Fr.]
16:02(0701):	plangite Fr.Sp.]	15:63(1002):	praeda S!t!b
15:01(1301):	plebi S+A+!w!b]	15:63(1004):	praedam M!c
15:01(1302):	plebis S++A++!c	16:38(0301):	praegnans Fr.]
16:40(0601):	plebs Fr.]>~MNE	16:76(1501):	praeponderent SMedd]
15:40(0902):	plena S	16:76(1502):	praeponderint A
15:34(1901):	plena Fr.CV]	15:42(1501):	pratorum Fr.]
15:40(0901):	plenae AMNEedd]	15:01(0100)+	preceperat L
15:34(1902):	plenae MNEL	16:76(0702):	precepta CNEVL
15:34(1903):	plenas L4	16:65(0602):	precesserint L
15:40(0903):	plene CVL	16:02(0102):	precingite Sp.
15:41(2201):	plenitudine S++Aedd]	15:63(1003):	preda CV
15:41(2202):	plenitudinem S+	15:63(1006):	predabunt L
16:22(0601)+:	plurimi SSp.!t!c!b	15:63(1005):	predam NE
15:36(1001):+	poblites {~} CL	16:38(0302):	pregnans Sp.
15:62(2201)	pomifera A!w]	16:76(1503):	preponderent CNEVL
15:02(1100)+	ponantur L	16:67(3402):	pressura Sp.
15:36(1002):+	poplite L4	15:59(0304):	primaria SSp.!t!b
15:36(1000)+	poplites {~} MNE	15:48(1902):+	principalibus VL
16:68(1400)+	populi CMEVL	15:16(1601)	principem SSp.!w!b]>A{>4}
15:01(1303):	populi Sp.	15:16(1602):	principes !c
16:68(1200)+	populi ~N	15:48(1901)+:	principibus CMNE
15:10(0200)	populus	15:59(0301)	priora A+!w]
16:40(0602):	populus CVLL4	15:59(0302):	priorem A++
16:40(0200)+	populus ~MNE	15:11(1600)	prius
15:38(1302):	porcio NV	15:48(2802):+	pro L4
15:60(1102):	porcionem VL	15:61(0702):	pro SCVL!t!c!b
16:60(1902):	portaret SAMVL!f	16:73(0402):	probacio V
16:43(1303):	portat AL	16:73(0401)	probatio Fr.CMNEL]
15:38(1301):	portio Fr.CMEL]	16:73(1401):	probatur Fr.]>~Sp.
15:30(2701):	portionem Fr.]	16:73(1700)+	probatur{~} Sp.
15:60(1101):	portionem Fr.CMNE]	15:34(2303):	procella V
16:47(1802):	possesiones L	15:34(2301)	procellae AMNELedd]
16:47(1801):	possessiones Fr.CMNEV]	15:34(2302):	procelle SC
15:51(1703):	possint A++!c	16:65(0601)	processerint Fr.CMNEV]
15:51(1704):	possis A+++Sp.!w!b	15:08(3003):	proclamant CMNE
15:51(1701):	possit S]	15:08(2303):	proclamant V
15:51(1702):	possitis A+	15:08(3004):	proclamantes L
16:61(0502):	possuit A+	15:08(2302):	proclamat CMNEL
15:31(0200)	post	16:39(0603):	prodeundem V
15:38(0200)	post	16:39(0602):	prodeundum CMNEL!c
16:60(0200)	posuit	16:38(3803):	prodeunte Sp.!c
16:61(1404):	posuit L4	16:39(0601)	prodiendum SA!w!b]
16:61(0501):	posuit SA++edd]>{~} Sp.	16:38(3801)	prodiente SA!w!b]
16:60(1901)	potaret CNEedd]	16:38(3802):	prodientem A
16:43(1302):	potat CV	ex 01(0700)+	PROFAETE A
15:11(0602):	potentem S+	15:01(1702):	profetiae A
15:51(2001):	potentes Fr.CMNEL]	15:01(1703):	profetie C
16:18(1600)+	potentes V	16:12(1101):	profundo Fr.Sp.]
15:11(0601):	potenti S++ASp.edd]	16:23(0501)	proicientur S++A++Sp.edd]
15:16(2001):	potentia Fr.]	16:23(0503):	proiciuntur S+
15:48(1700)+	potentibus CMNEV	16:23(0502):	proiecientur A+
15:51(2002):	potentis V	15:01(1704):	propheciae L
15:17(1200):	poterit	15:01(1705):	prophecie L4

in 01(0800)+	prophete C	in 01(0900)+	quartus {~} C
15:01(1701)	prophetiae SMNEVedd]	15:12(1202)	quas S!c
15:06(0100)	propter	15:08(0702)	quas S++
15:18(0100)	propter	15:10(0400)	quasi
16:45(0100)	propter	15:23(1300)	quasi
16:64(0100)	propter	16:40(2000)	quasi
15:59(0201)	propter A!w]>SSp.!t!c!b	16:41(0300)	quasi
15:26(0902):	propter Sp.	16:41(0900)	quasi
15:47(0401)	propter Fr.]	16:43(0400)	quasi
15:19(1801)	propter Fr.CVL]>MNE{>6}	16:43(1400)	quasi
15:27(2001)	propter SSp.edd]	16:44(0500)	quasi
15:55(0902):	propter V!c	16:44(1800)	quasi
15:07(0100)	propterea	16:23(0301)	quasi A!w]
15:48(3100)	propterea	16:65(1402):	quasi A++
15:27(2002):	propterea A	16:59(0401)	quasi Fr.]
15:26(0901)	propterea Fr.]	16:71(0801)	quasi Fr.]
16:51(0101)	propterea Fr.]	16:42(0301)	quasi SSp.edd]>A{>13}
15:55(0901)	propterea SACMNEL!w!b]	16:42(1101)	quasi SSp.edd]>A{>13}
15:61(0803):	prostibulo MNE	16:29(1301)	quattuor Fr.C]
16:37(0200)+	protinus{{~} } Sp.	16:31(1101)	quattuor Fr.C]
16:73(1002):	prout A+	16:29(1302)	quatuor MNEVL
15:19(0402):	proximi A++MNEVL	16:31(1102)	quatuor MNEVL
15:19(0403):	proximo C!w	16:06(1702):+	que {~} S
15:19(0401)	proximum SA+!c!b]	15:08(0703):	que C
15:30(2202):	pugna CL	16:13(0503):	que C
15:15(1300)	pugnam	15:08(1402):	que CV
16:40(1201)	pugnam Fr.]	15:20(3302):	que CV
15:30(2201)	pugnam Fr.MNEV]	16:13(1302):	que CV
15:44(2400)	pulvis	16:16(1402):	que CV
16:38(4500)	puncto	16:36(1803):	que CV
16:52(0401)	pusillum Fr.Sp.]	16:63(0802):	que CV
16:21(1202):	putant V	16:18(2702):	que S++
16:43(1301)	putat SMNEedd]	15:03(0602):+	que V
16:21(1201)	putent Fr.CL]	15:20(1203):	que V
16:06(1701)+:	quae {~} !t!b	16:77(2502):	quem SMNE!b
16:22(1601)	quae A!w]	15:39(1202):	quem S+
15:01(1500)+	quae L	16:38(0100)	quemadmodum
15:20(1202):	quae L	16:49(0102):	quemadmodum Sp.
16:63(0400)+	quae L	16:73(1003):	quemadmodum MNEVL
15:03(0601):+	quae MNEL	16:29(0101)	quemadmodum Fr.MNEVL]
16:36(1802):	quae MNEL	16:77(1301):	quemadmodum Fr.MNEVL]
16:63(0801)	quae Fr.MNE]	16:16(0102):	quemadmodum SSp.!t!c!b
15:20(3301)	quae Fr.MNEL]	16:29(0102):	quemammodum C
16:13(1301)	quae Fr.MNEL]	16:73(1004):	quemammodum C
16:16(1401)	quae Fr.MNEL]	16:77(1302):	quemammodum C
16:65(1401)	quae SA+edd]	16:50(1902):	querens Sp.
16:13(0502):	quae SMNE!t!c!b	15:47(1602):	questum CMNE
15:08(1401)	quae SMNELedd]>A{>10}	16:02(1401)	quia A!w]
15:08(0701)	quae S+VLedd]>A{>10}	15:47(0402):	quia Sp.
16:41(0102):	quae V	15:03(1500)+	quia L
16:63(0803):	quaecumque L	16:13(0504):	quia L
15:12(1201)	quam ASp.!w!b]	16:76(0202):	quia L
16:77(2501)	quam ACVL!w!c]	16:54(0103):	quia L4
15:39(1201)	quam S++Aedd]>Sp.	16:53(1402):	quia MNEVL
16:47(0901)	quamdiu SA!w!b]	16:46(2101)	quia Fr.]
16:06(1703):+	quando {~} !c	16:72(0101):	quia Fr.]>Sp.
16:47(0902):	quantum Sp.!c	15:15(0101)	quia Fr.CMNEV]

15:47(1604):	quibus L
16:36(1801):	quibus Fr.]
16:66(0100):	quid
16:18(2701):	quid S+ACVLedd]
ex 01(0200)+	QUINQUE ~A+
ex 01(0601)	QUINTUS Sedd]>~A,Sp.
in 01(0301)	quintus Fr.]>{~} C,MNEVL
ex 01(0400)+	QUINTUS ~A++
16:08(0600)	quis
16:09(0800)	quis
16:10(0500)	quis
16:10(1500)	quis
16:11(0400)	quis
16:17(0500)	quis
16:25(0600)	quis
16:26(0900)	quis
16:08(1400)+	quis @g8{+10}
16:05(0601)	quis Fr.CMNEL]
16:03(0701)	quis Fr.Sp.]>@g0{>9}
16:04(0701)	quis Fr.MNVL]>C,E@g0{>10}
15:06(0200)	quod
15:27(2100)	quod
16:32(2400)	quod
16:64(0200)	quod
16:73(1300)	quod
15:47(0501)	quod Fr.]>Sp.
16:45(0201)	quod Fr.CMNEL]>V
16:66(0500)	quomodo
16:16(0101)	quomodo A!w]
16:49(0101)	quomodo Fr.]
15:02(1200)	quoniam
15:04(0100)	quoniam
15:13(0500)	quoniam
16:13(0100)	quoniam
16:52(0100)	quoniam
16:75(0500)	quoniam
16:46(2300)+	quoniam CVL
16:53(1401)	quoniam Fr.C]
15:26(0100)+	quoniam SSp.!c!b
16:02(1402):	quoniam SSp.!t!c!b
16:62(0802):	quoniam VL
15:01(1800)	quos
15:47(1603)	quos V
16:68(2100)	quosdam
15:50(0802)	quum C
16:30(0701)+:	racemi {~} S++Sp.!t!c!b
16:30(0901)	racemus A!w]>{~} SSp.!t!c!b
16:30(0702):+	racimi {~} S+
16:46(0902):	rapiant A+
16:68(1601)	rapient Fr.]
16:46(0901)	rapient SA++Sp.edd]
16:47(0601)	rapina Fr.C]
16:47(0602):	rapinam MNEVL
15:55(1504):	recipias V
15:55(1503):	recipies SCMNE!b
15:39(0701)	recludent Fr.]
16:05(0903):	recuciat A++
16:08(1902):	recuciet A@g6
16:05(0902):	recuciet A+@g6
16:06(0202):	recuciet @g6
16:05(0901)	recutiet !w]
16:08(1901)	recutiet !w]
16:06(0201)	recutiet A!w]
16:07(0401)	recutiet A!w]>@g0{>8} >M{>18}
15:21(1100)	reddam
15:20(3200)	reddere
15:55(1401)	redditionem Fr.]>~:Sp.
16:16(0302):	redit SSp.!t!c!b
15:16(1300)	regem
15:20(0800)	reges
15:33(2502):	reges SSp.!c!b
16:52(1201):	regnabit SA++CMNELedd@r]
16:52(1202):	regnavit A+V
15:33(2501):	regno A!w]
16:30(0803):	relincuntur C
16:28(0400)	relinquentur
16:29(0201)	relinquentur SA+CEV!w!b]
16:31(0202):	relinquentur SSp.!c!b
16:30(0802):	relinquentur SMNEVL!t!b
16:32(0202):	relinquentur S+
16:24(0202):	relinquetur CVL
16:29(0202):	relinquetur L
16:32(0201):	relinquetur S++ASp.edd]
16:30(0804):	relinquuntur !c
16:29(0204):	relinquuntur A++MN
16:31(0201):	remanebunt A!w]
15:45(0602):	remanserint MNV!c
15:45(0603):	remanserunt CL
16:05(0905):	repellat SMN!t!c!b
16:08(1905):	repellat S+!c
15:39(0702):	repellent Sp.
16:08(1907):	repellere L4
16:05(0904):	repellet CEVL
16:06(0203):	repellet SCVL!t!c!b
16:08(1904):	repellet S++CMNEV!t!b
16:07(0402):	repellet S++CNEVL!t!c!b
16:08(1906):	repellete L
16:06(0204):	repellit MNE
16:07(0403):	repellit S+
15:29(2503):	repetentur A
16:68(1700)+	res Sp.
16:72(0502):	res Sp.
15:55(1505):	respicies L
15:39(0900)+	retro MNE
15:60(2403):	revertentes SCMNEL!t!c!b
16:14(0600)	revertentur
16:16(1200)	revertentur
15:60(2402):	revertentur A++
16:16(0301)	revertitur A!w]
15:60(2401):	revertuntur A+!w]
15:15(1503):	rhomphaea !c
15:22(0904):	rhomphaea !c
15:57(1003):	rhomphaea !c

16:31(2105):	rhomphaea !c	15:09(1600)	sanguinem [Fr.Sp.@y]
15:41(0703):	rhomphaeas !c	15:35(1903):	sanguinis L4
15:19(0703):	ritum MNE	15:35(1901):	sanguis SA++Sp.edd]
15:41(2000)	rivi	15:08(1900)	sanguis [Fr.Sp.@y]
15:15(1505):	romfea C	16:46(2001)+:	sciant C
15:22(0902):	romphaea @g1	16:46(2003):+	scient L
15:57(1001)	romphea !w]	16:28(2305):	sciscuris E
16:31(2104):	romphea A++!w	16:28(2304):	scissuris !c
15:15(1501):	romphea A++!w]	16:62(0703):	scit C
15:22(0901)	romphea MEV!w]	16:46(2002):+	sciunt V
15:15(1504):	rompheae MNE	15:02(0602):	scribantur SSp.!c!b
15:15(1506):	rompheam V	15:02(0601):	scribi A!w]
16:31(2101)	rompheam]	16:64(0506):	scrutabit C
15:22(0908):	romphearumque L4	16:64(0505):	scrutabitur MNE
15:41(0701)	rompheas A++!w]>MNE	16:31(1901)+:	scrutabunt {~} CVL
15:22(0907):	ronfea L	16:30(1901):+	scrutabuntur {~} MNE
15:35(2200)+	ronphearum L	16:31(1902):+	scrutabuntur {~} MNE
15:15(1507):	rorifens L	16:64(0402):	scrutans MNE
15:39(2000)+	ruginem L	16:30(1401):	scrutantibus A!w]>{~}
15:22(0906):	rumfea C		SSp.!t!c!b
15:22(0903):	rumpfea @g8	16:31(1501):	scrutantibus Fr.]>{~} Sp.
16:31(2103):	rumphea A+	16:30(1900)+	scrutantur {~} SCVL!t!c!b
15:57(1002):	rumphea SA!a!f!b	16:57(0202):	scrutat S!w!b
15:22(0905):	rumphea SAN!a!f!b	16:62(1504):	scrutator VL
15:15(1502):	rumphea SA+!f!b	16:57(0201):	scrutatur ACMNE!c]
16:31(2102):	rumpheam S!a!f!b	16:62(1503):	scrutatur CMNE
15:41(0702):	rumpheas SA+!a!f!b	16:64(0503):	scrutatus A++
15:59(0903):	rursum SCMNEV!t!c!b	16:64(0504):	scrutavit A+{?} VL
15:60(2302):	rursum SSp.!t!c!b	16:64(0502):	scrutinabit S++!w!b
15:08(1700)+	rx{?} V	16:64(0401):	scrutinando Fr.]>CVL
16:02(0303):	saccis SSp.L4!t!c!b	16:62(1501):	scrutinat Sedd]
16:02(0302):	sacco A++	16:62(1502):	scrutinatur A
16:02(0301)	saccos A+!w]	16:64(0501):	scrutinavit S+!c]
16:68(2904):	sacrificio Sp.	16:57(0203):	scrutor V
15:14(0201)	saeculo Fr.MNEV]	16:43(0705):	seccet V
16:58(0302):	saeculum NEVL	16:43(0704):	secet CL
16:39(1001)	saeculum Fr.MNEVL]	15:14(0202):	seculo CL
16:16(0402):	sagita A+	16:39(1002):	seculum C
16:07(0602):	sagitam A+	16:58(0303):	seculum CM
16:07(0902):	sagitario A	15:55(1100)+	secundum Sp.
16:16(0802):	sagitario A	15:48(1300)+	secuta CMNEV
16:16(0401):	sagitta SA++Sp.edd]	15:11(0100)	sed
16:13(1002):	sagittae SMNE!t!c!b	15:09(0600)+	sed @y
16:13(0801):	sagittam A!w]>{~} SSp.!t!c!b	16:53(1300)+	sed ~V
16:07(0601):	sagittam SA++Sp.edd]>	15:53(0703):	sed_per L
	@g0{>8}	16:77(2203):	semen S++
16:16(0801):	sagittario SSp.edd]	15:58(1304):	semetipsorum L
16:07(0901):	sagittario SSp.edd]>@g0{>8}	15:13(0801):	semina SSp.edd]
16:13(1003):	sagitte CVL	16:77(2202):	semina S+!b
15:04(1502):+	salvabitur V	16:43(0300)	seminat
16:52(1600)+	salvator ~:@r	16:24(0901):	seminat S+A+L!w]
15:04(1501)+:	salvus CMNEL	16:24(0902):	seminet S++A++
15:25(1000)	sanctificationem		CMNEV!t!c!b
15:53(2200)+	sanguine L	15:13(0802):	semita A
15:22(1300)	sanguinem	16:77(2201):	semita ACVL!w!c]
15:35(1902):	sanguinem A+	16:32(1801):	semitae Fr.MNE]
15:58(1601)	sanguinem Fr.Sp.]	16:32(1802):	semite CVL

16:77(2204):	semitis MNE
15:47(3000)	semper
15:53(0702):	semper CMNEV
16:67(2202):	semper Sp.
16:20(1802):	semper SSp.!t!c!b
16:20(1801)	sempiterna A!w]
16:67(2201)	sempiterno Fr.]
15:34(1004):	septemtrionae L
15:34(1003):	septemtrione AM
15:38(1103):	septemtrione A++MV
15:38(1102):	septemtrionem A+
15:38(1101):	septentrione SCNELedd]
15:34(1001):	septentrione S++CNEVedd]
15:34(1002):	septentrionem S+
16:36(0202):	sermo Sp.L4
16:56(0303):	sermone CMEV
16:56(0304):	sermones NL
15:01(1601):	sermones Fr.CMNEV]
15:01(1602):	sermonibus L
16:76(0303):	servastis VL
16:76(0301):	servat SA!c]
16:76(0302):	servatis CMNE!w!b
16:44(2000)+	servaturi Sp.
16:35(0701):	servi Fr.CMNEV]
15:45(0702):	servient CMNEL!c!b
15:45(0701):	servientes SA!w]>V
16:35(0702):	servvi L
15:52(0302):	si L
16:44(0600)+	si S
15:31(1401):	si SASp.!w!b]>!c
15:29(1301):	sibilatus AMNE!w!b]
15:21(0700):	sic
15:56(0700):	sic
16:16(1000):	sic
16:31(0100):	sic
16:39(0100):	sic
16:40(1800)	sic
16:50(0100):	sic
15:29(2103):	sic CM
15:29(1202):+	sic S
16:43(0900)+	sic S!c!b
16:44(0401):	sic Fr.]>Sp.
16:44(1701):	sic Fr.]>Sp.
15:52(0301):	sic Fr.CMNEV]
15:50(0702):	sicabitur L
15:50(0701):	siccabitur Fr.CMNEV]
15:21(0100):	sicut
15:50(0500):	sicut
15:56(0100):	sicut
16:30(0200):	sicut
15:29(1203):+	sicut !c
16:23(0304):	sicut !c
16:21(1102):	sicut Sp.
15:29(2102):	sicut NEVL
15:11(1501):	sicut Fr.Sp.]
16:59(0403):	sicut @z
16:21(1103):	sic_ut S!t!c!b
15:13(2004):	sidere E!c
15:40(1201):	sidus Fr.]
15:35(1501):	sidus Fr.]>Sp.
15:44(1001):	sidus Fr.]>~CMNEL,V{>15}
15:40(3001):	sidus Fr.EVL]
15:39(1701):	sidus SA++EVLedd]
15:35(1001):	sidus SEVLedd]
15:13(2001):	sidus SV!w!b]>A++{>4}
15:44(1502):+	sidus ~EL
15:30(1102):	silba C
15:08(0300):	silebo
15:32(0501):	silebunt Fr.]
16:77(1700):	silva
16:28(2001):	silva A!w]
16:06(0701):	silva Fr.CNEL]>M{>18}
15:30(1101):	silva Fr.MNEVL]
15:62(1801):	silvam A!w]>V{>10}
16:06(0702):	silvam V
15:42(1200):	silvarum
15:62(1802):	silvas SCMNEL!t!c!b
16:51(0402):	similare A+
16:51(0401):	similari SA++edd]
16:51(0403):	similes Sp.
15:47(0603):	similis Sp.
16:32(1200)+	simul Sp.
16:45(0500):	sine
16:29(0400)+	singulis L
16:29(0900)+	singulis SCMNEL!t!c!b
15:55(0602):	sinos S+
15:55(1702):+	sinos ~:V
16:32(2700)+	sint Sp.
15:55(0603):	sinu Sp.!c
15:21(1502):	sinu SMNEVL!c!b
15:21(1501):	sinum AC!w]
15:55(0601):	sinus S++A!w!b]
15:55(1701)+:	sinus ~:CMNEL
16:01(1002):	Siria V
15:47(2000)+	sis Sp.
16:50(0702):	sit MNE
16:75(0404):	sitemini S+
15:58(2301):	siti SA++Sp.edd]
15:58(2302):	sitis A+
15:39(1702):	situs A+
15:46(0602):	speciae A
15:46(0601):	specie SSp.!w!b]
15:54(0300):	speciem
15:46(0603):	spem !c
16:32(2201):	spinas Fr.]>~Sp.
16:32(2001)+:	spinas ~CMNEL
16:77(1900)	spinis
16:32(2002):+	spinis {~} V
16:62(0302):	spiramen !c
16:62(0301):	spiramentum SA!w!b]
16:61(1600)	spiritum
15:63(1001):	spoliabunt A!w]
16:34(0100)	sponsi
16:33(0501):	sponsos SSp.edd]>A+{>5}

16:33(0502):	sponsus A++		16:68(0500)	super
16:65(1602):	stabit CMNEV		16:52(1402):	super @r
16:65(1601)	stabunt Fr.]		16:13(2501)	super A!w]
15:23(1402):	stamen MN		16:20(0201)	super A!w]
16:56(0501)	stellae Fr.MNEL]		16:20(1301)	super A!w]>SSp.!t!c!b
15:39(1800)+	stellam L		16:22(0901)	super A!w]>SSp.!t!c!b
16:56(1101)	stellarum Fr.]		16:16(2002):	super E
16:56(0502):	stelle CV		15:12(1600)+	super L
16:23(0400)	stercora		15:44(3600)+	super L
16:06(1402):	stipula CEV!t!c!b		16:23(1100)+	super L
15:61(0802):	stipula SCVL!t!c!b		15:27(0501)	super Fr.]
16:06(1404):	stipulam SN		15:53(1401)	super Fr.]
15:39(2505):	strages Sp.		16:50(2201)	super Fr.]
16:06(1401):	stramen A!w]>M{>18}		16:48(0801)	super Fr.]>N
15:23(1401)	stramen Fr.CEVL]		15:05(0901)	super Fr.Sp.]
15:61(0801)	stramine A!w]		16:70(1201)	super Fr.E]
16:06(1403):	stupa L		15:44(1601)	super SCMNELedd]>V{>15}
15:45(0400)+	sub ~!c		15:15(1001)	super SSp.!b]
15:44(2301)	subibit Fr.]		16:22(1702):	superaberint C
16:30(0801)	subremanet A!w]		16:22(1701)	superaverint Fr.MNEVL]
15:45(0601)	subremanserint SA!w!b]>E		15:18(0201)	superbiam Fr.MNEVL]
15:33(0601)	subsedebit A!w]		16:12(1102):	superbo @g6
15:33(0501)	subsessor S++Aedd]		16:76(2002):	superelebent S+
15:19(1603):	substanciam L		16:76(2001)	superelevent S++Aedd]
16:46(0702):	substanciam V		16:21(1901)	superflorescent A!w]
16:46(0703):	substancias L		15:39(0200)	superinvalescent
15:19(1602):	substantiam CMNEV		15:06(0302):	superpolluit !c
16:46(0701)	substantiam Fr.CMNE]		15:06(0301)	superposuit SASp.!w!b]
15:19(1601)	substantias Fr.]		15:31(0402):	supervalescent !c!b
16:72(0501)	substantias Fr.]		15:16(1001)	supervalescentes A!w]
15:36(0802):	substramen !c		15:31(0401)	supervalescet SA!w]
15:60(2801)+:	subversa Sp.!t!b		15:18(0202):	supervia C
15:60(2802):+	subversam S!c		16:70(1202):	supra CMNVL
15:57(1503):	subvertentur Sp.		16:10(1705):	surgebit S
16:68(0304):	succendentur V		15:15(0803):	surget L
16:68(0303):	succendetur CMNEL		15:59(0904):	sursum L
16:15(0303):	succendetur MNE		15:51(1900)	suscipere
16:15(0302):	succenditur SCVL!t!c!b		15:39(1302):	suscitabit A++CMNE
15:36(0801):	suffraginem SA!w!b]>{~} Sp.		16:68(2505):	suscitabunt VL
16:68(2000)+	sument Sp.		15:39(1301):	suscitavit SA+VLedd]
16:36(0402):	sumite Sp.		16:58(1100):	suspendit
15:22(0500)	super		15:08(3002):	suspirant @y
15:22(1100)	super		15:08(2900)+	suspirant L
15:22(1500)	super		16:18(0501):	suspirantium A!w]
15:29(1900)	super		15:08(1101)	sustinebo SSp.edd]>A{>10}
15:35(1200)	super		15:13(2003):	sydere MN
15:36(1700)	super		15:35(1002):	sydus ACMN!a!f
15:40(2400)	super		15:13(2002):	sydus A+C!a!f
15:50(1400)	super		15:39(1703):	sydus CMN
16:14(0900)	super		15:40(3002):	sydus CMN
16:21(0800)	super		15:44(1501)+:	sydus ~CMN
16:21(2100)	super		16:01(1001)	Syria Fr.CMNE]
16:39(0700)	super		16:01(1003):	Syrie L
16:53(1800)	super		16:19(1401):	tamquam A!w]>SSp.!t!c!b
16:58(1300)	super		16:65(1404):	tamquam L
16:59(0800)	super		16:23(0302):	tamquam SCVL!t!b
16:60(0800)	super		16:71(0803):	tamquam VL

16:71(0802):	tanquam CMNE	16:55(1103):	terram {~} L4
16:65(1403):	tanquam CMNEV	16:60(2002):	terram CVL!c
16:23(0303):	tanquam MNE	15:44(1302):	terram E
16:48(0201)	tanto Fr.MN]	15:13(0401):	terram Fr.]
16:48(0202):	tantum CEVL	16:50(2301):	terram Fr.]
16:38(4301)	tardabit SASp.!w!b]	15:06(0701):	terram Fr.CMNE]
16:39(0302):	tardabitur C	16:16(2101):	terram Fr.CMNE]
16:38(4302):	tardabunt !c	16:58(1201):	terram Fr.CMNEV]
16:37(0703):	tardabunt Sp.	15:35(1301):	terram Fr.Sp.]
16:37(0702):	tardant A++!c	15:39(0801):	terram Fr.Sp.]
16:37(0701):	tardantur SA+!w!b]	15:62(1003):	terram SCMNEL!t!c!b
15:47(2602):	tecum !c	16:23(1602):+	terram ~V
16:77(2101)	tegitur Fr.]	15:27(0700)	terrarum
15:53(0701)	tempore Fr.]	15:05(1101):	terrarum Fr.Sp.]
16:13(0702):	tendet CVL	16:23(1802):	terras A+
16:13(0701):	tendit Fr.MNE]	15:30(2803):	terras L4
15:36(1800)+	ter A	15:35(1302):	terras L4
15:10(1500)	terra	15:60(1302):+	terre {~} SC
16:32(0400)	terra	16:13(2702):	terre C
16:55(1102):	terra {~} Sp.	15:13(0403):	terre CL
16:12(0301):	terra A!w]>~SSp.!t!c!b	15:23(1002):	terre CL
16:23(1801):	terra A++!w]>~SSp.!t!c!b	15:30(2802):	terre CL
15:33(0303):	terra Sp.	16:40(2202):	terre CL
16:50(2302):	terra Sp.	16:15(1002):	terre CV
16:58(1202):	terra L	15:20(0902):	terre CVL
15:05(1102):	terra L4	15:06(0703):	terre L
16:39(0802):	terra L4	16:10(1702):	terrebit @g8
16:55(0501):	terra Fr.]	16:11(0703):	terrebitur @g0
16:52(0901):	terra Fr.Sp.]	16:11(0702):	terretur A++
16:60(2001):	terra SAMNE!w!b]	15:13(2103):	terribilae L
16:31(0300)+	terra V	15:40(3202):	terribile A++Sp.!w
16:16(2102):	terra VL	15:13(2101):	terribile SA+CV!w!b]>A++
16:23(1601):+:	terra ~SCMNELL4!t!c!b		{>4}
16:12(0100)+	terra ~SSp.!t!c!b	15:40(3201):	terribilem SA+!c!b]
16:62(2502):	terrae !c	15:13(2102):	terribili MNE!c
15:60(1301):+:	terrae {~} MNEVL!t!c!b	15:62(1001):	territoria A++!w]>V{>10}
16:52(0902):	terrae @r	15:60(2001)	territorii A++!w]>{~}
15:13(0402):	terrae MNEV		SSp.!t!c!b
15:20(0901)	terrae Fr.MNE]	15:33(0301):	territorio Sedd]
16:15(1001):	terrae Fr.MNEL]	16:57(0502):	tesauros C
15:23(1001):	terrae Fr.MNEV]	16:57(0501):	thesauros Fr.MNEVL]
15:30(2801):	terrae Fr.MNEV]	16:10(1102):	thonabit @g6
16:40(2201):	terrae Fr.MNEV]	16:75(0202):	tim*** A+
16:13(2701):	terrae Fr.MNEVL]	15:29(2301):	timeant Fr.MNEV]
15:06(0702):	terrae V	15:03(0200):	timeas
15:62(1002):	terraeturia A+	15:29(2303):	timeat L
15:60(2002):	terraeturiae A+	16:75(0201):	timeatis SA++Sp.edd]
15:11(2000)	terram	16:10(0900):	timebit
15:22(1600)	terram	16:18(1501):	timebunt A!w]
15:29(2000)	terram	15:32(0502):	timebunt Sp.
15:36(1900)	terram	15:29(2302):	timent C
15:40(1600)	terram	16:70(1502):	timent Sp.
16:14(1000)	terram	16:70(1501):	timentes Fr.]
16:21(0900)	terram	16:71(2001):	timentes Fr.]
16:21(2200)	terram	16:67(0602):	timere L4
16:22(1000)	terram	16:67(0601):	timete Fr.Sp.]
16:24(0600)	terram	15:33(1500)	timor

15:36(1300)	timor
16:73(0804):+	tolerancia L
16:73(0801)+:	tolerantia CMN
16:73(0803):+	tollerancia V
16:73(0802):+	tollerantia E
16:52(0601)	tolletur Fr.Sp.]
16:10(1101)	tonabit Fr.CMNEL]
16:10(1103):	tonavit V
15:56(1202):	tradent C
16:26(0401)	tradet A!w]
15:26(1101)	tradet ASp.!w]
15:56(1201)	tradet Fr.MNEVL]
15:26(1102):	tradidit S!c!b
16:64(1101)	traducet Fr.]
16:64(1102):	transducet Sp.
16:32(2902):	transeat A
16:77(2704):	transibit C
15:43(0201)	transibunt Fr.]
16:32(2901)	transient Sedd]
16:77(2702):	transiet A++!w
16:77(2701):	transiit A+]
16:77(2706):	transit SL!c!b
15:60(0302):	transitu S++CVL!t!c!b
15:60(0301):	transitum S+AMNE!w]
16:32(2903):	transiturae MNE
16:32(2904):	transiture CL
16:32(2905):	transituri V
16:77(2703):	transivit MNE
16:77(2705):	transunt V
16:12(0201):	tremet A+!w]
16:12(0203):	tremit A++C
15:33(1800)	tremor
15:36(1500)	tremor
15:37(0901)	tremor Fr.CMNEV]
15:37(0902):	tremore L
16:12(0202):	tremuit SMNEVL!t!c!b
16:18(2100)	trepidabunt
15:29(2502):	trepident !c
15:29(2501)	trepidentur S!w!b]
16:29(1100)	tres
16:31(0900)	tres
16:38(3000)	tres
16:19(0802):	tribulacio V
16:74(1002):	tribulacionis V
16:19(0801)	tribulatio Fr.CMNEL]
15:19(2202):	tribulatione S
16:67(3401)	tribulatione Fr.]
15:19(2201)	tribulationem ACVLedd]>
	MNE{>6}
16:74(1001)	tribulationis Fr.CMNEL]
15:42(1702):	triticum MNEVL
15:42(1703):	tritticum C
16:21(1800)	tunc
16:73(0200)	tunc
15:63(1800)+	tunc L
16:12(1502):	turbabubuntur L
16:68(1003):	turbabunt Sp.
15:18(0700)	turbabuntur
15:32(0300)	turbabuntur
16:12(1501)	turbabuntur ACV!w]
16:68(1001)	turbae Aedd]
16:68(1002):	turbe S
15:03(1102):	turbent SCMNEV!c!b
16:26(0202):	uba C
16:38(1702):	ubi Sp.
15:20(2303):	ueutro V
16:38(4400)	uno
15:44(0403):	unum CMNE
15:33(1001)	unum Fr.CMNEV]
15:13(1502):	uredine Fr.!f
16:10(1707):	urgebit N
16:10(1704):	urguebit ME!t
15:21(0300)	usque
15:34(1100)	usque
15:35(2300)	usque
15:44(2800)	usque
15:36(0502):	usque !c
15:36(0600)+	usque L
15:43(0401)	usque Fr.CMNEV]>L
15:40(1300)	ut
15:41(1300)	ut
15:51(1500)	ut
16:60(1800)	ut
15:51(0302):	ut !c
16:06(1704):+	ut {~} NE
16:21(1101)	ut A!w]
16:67(1703):	ut C
15:47(1702):	ut CMNE
15:48(2200)+	ut Sp.
16:59(0402):	ut Sp.
15:24(0103):	ut L
15:47(1902):	ut L
15:11(1502):	ut L4
15:51(0102):	ut MNE
15:61(0102):+	ut S
15:29(2101)	ut Fr.]
16:73(1001)	ut SA++edd]
15:02(0300)+	ut SSp.!c!b
15:30(0700)+	ut SMNE!c!b
16:38(0900)+	utero Sp.
16:26(0201)	uva Fr.MNEVL]
15:24(0101)	vae Fr.CM]
16:63(1301)	vae SACML!w!b]>!c
15:14(0101)	vae Fr.CML]
15:47(0101)	vae Fr.CML]
16:01(0101)	vae Fr.CML]
16:01(0601)	vae Fr.CML]
16:17(0101)	vae Fr.CML]
16:17(0301)	vae Fr.CML]
16:77(0101)	vae Fr.CML]
15:34(1802):	valdae L
16:49(0802):	valdae L
15:34(1801)	valde Fr.CMNEV]
16:49(0801)	valde Fr.CMNEV]

15:31(0404):	valescet L
15:40(0602):	valida S
15:40(0601)	validae A++MNEedd]
15:40(0603):	validas A+
15:40(0604):	valide CVL
16:16(0901):	valido SASp.!w!b]>~!c
16:16(0700)+	valido ~!c
15:03(1700)+	vanum L
15:11(1300)+	variis L4
15:30(2601)	vastabunt Fr.Sp.]
16:72(0202):	vastabunt VL
15:13(1101)	vastabuntur SACVL!w!b]>
	MNE!c{>4}
16:01(0602):	ve N{?} EV
15:14(0102):	ve NEV
15:24(0102):	ve NEV
15:47(0102):	ve NEV
16:17(0102):	ve NEV
16:17(0302):	ve NEV
16:77(0102):	ve NEV
16:01(0102):	ve NEVL4
16:63(1302):	ve NEVL4
15:08(3102):	vehementer @y
16:27(0600)	vel
16:38(2900)	vel
16:31(1001)	vel ASp.!w]
16:29(1201)	vel ACMNVL!w]
16:31(0800)+	vel C
16:29(0803):+	vel E
15:39(2100)+	vel L
15:30(0106):	vel_apri_carmeli W
15:16(1705):	vel_maiestanorum W
16:06(1405):	vel_messe W
15:23(1403):	vel_paleas W
16:59(0504):	vel_ut_coreum W
16:41(0201)	vendet SA+]
16:41(0203):	vendidit VL
16:41(0202):	vendit A++CMNEedd
16:18(3001)	venerint Fr.CNEVL]
16:50(1500)	venerit
15:27(0401)	venerunt Fr.CVL]
16:14(0802):	veniant A++CMNVL!t!c!b
16:14(0803):	veniat E
15:30(1302):	venient Sp.
16:37(0303):	venient Sp.L4
15:27(0402):	venient MNE
16:14(0801):	venient SA+!w]
15:59(0601):	venies SSp.!c!b]>A+
15:39(0300):	venti
16:38(4100)	ventre
15:35(2500)	ventrem
16:38(3400)	ventrem
15:39(2903):	ventum !c
16:32(1003):	vepre CVL
16:32(1004):	vepres MNE!b
16:56(0302):	verba A+
15:01(1000)+	verba L
15:12(0802):	verberata !c
15:12(0801):	verberati SA!w]
15:12(0803):	verberationis !b
15:12(0804):	verberum Sp.
16:58(1600)	verbo
16:56(0301):	verbo SA++edd]
16:40(0400)	verbum
16:36(0201):	verbum Fr.]
15:02(1500)	veri
15:39(2800)+	vero Sp.
16:35(0201)	vero Fr.]
in 01(0600)+	versis S
16:03(1003):	vertat{?} L
16:60(0902):	verticem L!c
16:60(0901)	vertices SACMNEV!w!b]
16:32(1401):	viae Fr.MNEL]
15:16(1703):	viae_gestorum !c
16:70(0801):	vicinas SSp.edd]
16:70(0802):	vicinis A
15:37(0500):	videbunt
16:27(0500):	videre
16:44(1901):	vidui Fr.]
15:49(0400):	viduitatem
16:44(1902):	viduitatem Sp.
16:32(1402):	vie CV
16:21(0500)+	vilitas L
16:21(0401):	vilitas Fr.CMNEL]>~V
15:32(0702):	vim CMNEL
15:33(1002):	vim L
16:30(0503):	vindemia E
16:25(0702):	vindemiabit S++A++
	CMNE!t!c!b
16:30(1701):	vindemiam A++!w]
16:26(0701):	vindemiam A++!w]>{~}
	SSp.!t!c!b
16:30(0501):	vindemiata SA++CMNVLedd]
16:43(1703):	vindemiatur E
16:43(1701):	vindemiaturus S++A++
	CMNVLedd]
16:25(0703):	vindemiavit VL
16:25(0701):	vindemiet A+!w]
16:25(0704):	vindiamit S+
15:09(0801):	vindicabo Fr.Sp.]
15:09(0701):	vindicans Fr.Sp.]
15:09(0803):	vindicetur L4
15:09(0802):	vindictam @y
16:26(0702):	vindimiam A+
16:30(1702):	vindimiam A+
16:30(0502):	vindimiata A+
16:43(1702):	vindimiaturus S+A+!f
16:30(0401):	vinea SA++CMNVLedd]>E
16:43(1200)+	vineam !c
16:30(1703):	vineam SSp.!t!c!b
16:30(0402):	vinia A+
16:61(0202):	vinxit S
15:39(3401)	violabitur Fr.CMNE]
15:49(1702):	violatione !c

15:49(1701)	violationem SA!w!b]>Sp.	16:63(2002):	volentes !c
16:33(0200)	virgines	16:63(2001)	volentibus SA!w!b]
16:34(0700)	viri	16:63(2004):	voluerint MNE
15:23(1600)+	viridis L	16:63(2003):	volunt CVL
15:32(0703):	virorum V	15:51(1301)	vulneribus SA!w!b]>Sp.
16:33(1000)	viros	15:54(0400)	vultus
15:32(0701)	virtute Fr.]	15:50(0302):	vultus Sp.
15:31(1901)	virtute Fr.Sp.]	16:49(0503):	ydoneam C
15:30(1501)	virtute Fr.MNEL]	16:50(0203):	zelabit C
15:30(1502):	virtutem CV	16:50(0201)	zelabitur Fr.]
15:50(0301)	virtutis Fr.]	15:52(0401)	zelabo SA!w!b]
16:12(2601)	virtutis Fr.CMNEL]>V{>8}	16:48(0402):	zelabo S++Sp.
15:28(0200)	visio	15:52(0402):	zelabor A+
16:61(2002):	vitae MNL	16:49(0202):	zelabor A+
16:61(1700)+	vitae ~E	15:52(0403):	zelassem CMNV
16:22(0501)	vitam A!w]>SSp.!t!c!b	16:49(0203):	zelat Sp.
16:67(2900)+	vitam L	16:50(0204):	zelat MNE
16:61(2001)	vitam Fr.]>~E	16:49(0201):	zelatur SA++edd]
16:61(2003):	vite CV	15:52(0404):	zelatus E
16:27(0800)	vocem	16:50(0202):	zelavit VL
15:39(3403):	volabitur L	16:48(0700)+	zelo Sp.
15:41(0801)	volantes Fr.CVL]>MNE		

APPENDIX 6

Index of Greek Words in Oxyrhynchus Fragment 1010

15:58(1602):	το αιμα X	15:58(2003):	λειμου X
15:58(1902):	απο X	15:57(0402):	{λει} μω X
15:58(2102):	αρτου X	15:58(0803):	εν λειμω X
15:58(1302):	αυτων X	15:57(2800)+	μαχαιρη ~X
15:58(1702):	αυτων X	15:59(0400)+	μεν X
15:59(1100)+	δευτερου X	15:58(0700)+	μετεωροις X
15:57(0502):	διαφθαρησεται X	15:57(2000)+	οι X
15:58(0902):	διαφθαρησονται X	15:58(0202):	οι X
15:58(2303):	διψης X	15:58(0502):	τοις ορεσι X
15:58(1102):	εδονται X	15:59(0902):	παλιν X
15:59(1000)+	εκ X	15:57(1702):	παντες X
15:57(0800)+	εν X	15:57(2402):	τοις πεδιοις X
15:57(2302):	εν X	15:57(1102):	πεση X
15:58(0402):	εν X	15:57(2602):	πεσουνται X
15:57(2700)+	εν ~X	15:58(1803):	πιονται X
15:59(0602):	ηκεις X	15:57(1302):	αι πολεις X
15:57(0602):	και X	15:59(0303):	{πρω} τα X
15:57(1202):	και X	15:57(1004):	ρομφαια X
15:57(1602):	και X	15:58(1202):	τας σαρκας X
15:58(0102):	και X	15:57(1402):	σου X
15:58(0600)+	και X	15:57(1903):	σου X
15:58(1002):	και X	15:57(0702):	συ X
15:58(1502):	και X	15:57(1502):	συντριβησονται X
15:58(2202):	και X	15:59(0700)+	ταλαινα ~X
15:59(0802):	και X	15:58(2402):	υδατος X

Bibliography

Material Relating to the 2 Esdras Corpus (4, 5, and 6 Ezra)

Basset, R. "Apocalypse d'Esdras." *Les apocryphes éthiopens.* Vol. 9. Paris, 1899; reprint ed., Milan: Archè, 1982. Pp. 18–21, 25–139.

Bensly, R. L. *The Missing Fragment of the Fourth Book of Ezra.* Cambridge: Cambridge University Press, 1875.

———, ed. *The Fourth Book of Ezra.* Introduction by M. R. James. Texts S 3,2. Cambridge: Cambridge University Press, 1895. [Cited as Bensly-James]

Berger, S. *Histoire de la Vulgate pendant les premiers siècles du Moyen Age.* Paris: Hachette, 1893; reprint ed., New York: B. Franklin, 1958.

———. "Un manuscrit complet du 4ᵉ livre d'Esdras." *RTP* 1885, 414–19.

Bergren, T. A. "Christian Influence on the Transmission History of 4, 5, and 6 Ezra." *The Jewish Apocalyptic Heritage in Early Christianity.* Ed. J. C. VanderKam and W. Adler. CRINT number 3, 4. Assen: Van Gorcum; Minneapolis, MN: Fortress, 1996. Pp. 102–27.

———. *Fifth Ezra: The Text, Origin and Early History.* SBLSCS 25. Atlanta: Scholars Press, 1990.

Biblisch-historisches Handwörterbuch. 4 vols. S.v. "Esrabücher, nichtkanonische," by L. H. Silberman. Ed. B. Reicke and L. Rost. Göttingen: Vandenhoeck & Ruprecht, 1962–66. Vol. 1, cols. 442–43.

Box, G. H. *The Ezra-Apocalypse.* London: Pitman, 1912.

Brou, L. "Le 4ᵉ Livre d'Esdras dans la Liturgie Hispanique et le Graduel Romain 'Locus iste' de la Messe de la Dédicace." *Sacris Erudiri* 9 (1957) 75–109.

Brou, L., and J. Vives, eds. *Antifonario visigotico mozarabe de la Catedral de León.* 2 vols. Monumenta Hispaniae Sacra, Serie Liturgica 5,1–2. Barcelona-Madrid: Viader, 1959.

Charlesworth, J. H. "Christian and Jewish Self-Definition in Light of the Christian Additions to the Apocryphal Writings." *Jewish and Christian Self-Definition 2: Apects of Judaism in the Greco-Roman Period.* Ed. E. P. Sanders. Philadelphia: Fortress, 1981. Pp. 27–55.

———, ed. "4 Ezra [and Ezra cycle]." *The Pseudepigrapha and Modern Research.* 2nd ed. SBLSCS 7S. Chico, CA: Scholars Press, 1981. Pp. 111–16, 284–86.

Collins, A. Y. "The Early Christian Apocalypses." *Apocalypse: The Morphology of a Genre. Semeia* 14 (1979) 61–121.

De Bruyne, D. "Un manuscrit complet du 4ᵉ livre d'Esdras." *RBén* 24 (1907) 254–57.

———. "Quelques nouveaux documents pour la critique textuelle de l'Apocalypse d'Esdras." *RBén* 32 (1920) 43–47.

Delling, G. *Bibliographie zur jüdisch-hellenistischen und intertestamentarischen Literatur 1900–1970.* 2nd ed. TU 106. Berlin: Academie, 1975. Pp. 160–62.

Dictionnaire de la Bible Supplément. S.v. "Esdras (Le cinquième livre d')," by L. Pirot. Ed. L. Pirot et al. Paris: Letouzey et Ané, 1926–. Vol. 2, cols. 1104–7.

Duensing, H. "The Fifth and Sixth Books of Ezra." English translation D. Hill. *New Testament Apocrypha.* 2 vols. Ed. E. Hennecke, W. Schneemelcher, and R. McL. Wilson. Philadelphia: Westminster, 1963–65. Vol. 2, pp. 689–703 (original: "Das fünfte und sechste Buch Esra." *Neutestamentliche Apokryphen.* 3rd ed. 2 vols. Ed. E. Hennecke and W. Schneemelcher. Tübingen: Mohr, 1959–64. Vol. 2, pp. 488–98).

Duensing, H., and A. de Santos Otero. "Das fünfte und sechste Buch Esra." *Neutestamentliche Apokryphen in deutscher Übersetzung.* 5th ed. 2 vols. Ed. W. Schneemelcher. Tübingen: J. C. B. Mohr [Paul Siebeck], 1987–89. Vol. 2, pp. 58–90.

Enciclopedia de la Biblia. 6 vols. S.v. "Esdras, Quinto y sexto libros de," by J. A. Gutiérrez-Larraya. Barcelona: Garriga, 1963. Vol. 3, col. 126.

Erbetta, M. "5–6 Esdras." *Gli Apocrifi del Nuovo Testamento.* 3 vols. Turin: Marietti, 1969. Vol. 3, pp. 317–31.

Fabricius, J. A. *Codex pseudepigraphus Veteris Testamenti.* 2nd ed. 2 vols. Hamburg: Felginer, 1722–41.

Fritzsche, O. F., ed. *Libri apocryphi Veteris Testamenti graece.* Leipzig: Brockhaus, 1871.

———. *Libri Veteris Testamenti pseudepigraphi selecti.* Leipzig: Brockhaus, 1871.

Gry, L., ed. *Les dires prophétiques d'Esdras.* 2 vols. Paris: Geuthner, 1938.

Gutschmid, A. von. "Die Apokalypse des Esra und ihre spätern Bearbeitungen." *ZWT* 3 (1860) 1–81.

Harnack, A. *Geschichte der altchristlichen Literatur bis Eusebius.* 2nd ed. Leipzig: Hinrichs, 1958.

Hilgenfeld, A. *Messias Judaeorum.* Leipzig: Reisland, 1869.

———. Review of *The Fourth Book of Ezra*, by R. L. Bensly. *ZWT* N.F. 4 (1896) 478–80.

Hunt, A. S., ed. *The Oxyrhynchus Papyri.* Vol. 7. London: Egyptian Exploration Fund, 1910. Pp. 11–15.

Klijn, A. F. J., ed. *Der lateinische Text der Apokalypse des Esra.* TU 131. Berlin: Akademie, 1983.

Knibb, M. A. "The Second Book of Esdras." *The First and Second Books of Esdras.* By R. J. Coggins and M. A. Knibb. Cambridge Bible Commentary. Cambridge: Cambridge University Press, 1979.

Kraft, R. A. "'Ezra' Materials in Judaism and Christianity." *ANRW* 2, Band 19.1. Ed. H. Temporini and W. Haase. Berlin: de Gruyter, 1979. Pp. 119–36.

Le Hir, A.-M. "Une livre apocryphe—du 4ᵉ Livre d'Esdras." *Etudes bibliques.* 2 vols. Paris: Albanel, 1869. Vol. 1, pp. 139–250.

Lexicon für Theologie und Kirche. 2nd ed. 5 vols. S.v. "Esdras," by H. Schneider. Ed. J. Höfer and K. Rahner. Freiburg: Herder, 1957–67. Vol. 3, cols. 1101–3.

Longenecker, B. W. *2 Esdras.* Sheffield: Sheffield Academic Press, 1995.

Lücke, F. *Versuch einer vollständingen Einleitung in die Offenbarung des Johannes oder allgemeine Untersuchung über die apokalyptische Literatur überhaupt.* 2nd ed. 2 vols. Bonn: Weber, 1852.

Marbach, C. *Carmina scripturarum (scilicet antiphonas et responsoria ex sacro scripturae fonte in libros liturgicos sanctae ecclesiae Romanae derivata).* Strasbourg: Le Roux, 1907; reprint ed., Hildesheim: Olms, 1963.

Metzger, B. M. "The Fourth Book of Ezra." *Old Testament Pseudepigrapha.* 2 vols. Ed. J. H. Charlesworth. Garden City, NY: Doubleday, 1983–85. Vol. 1, pp. 516–59.

———. *An Introduction to the Apocrypha*. New York: Oxford University Press, 1957.

———. "The 'Lost' Section of 2 Esdras (= 4 Ezra)." *Historical and Literary Studies: Pagan, Jewish and Christian*. NTTS 8. Grand Rapids, MI: Eerdmans, 1968. Pp. 48–51.

Myers, J. M. *1 and 2 Esdras*. AB 42. Garden City, NY: Doubleday, 1974.

New English Bible with the Apocrypha. Ed. W. D. McHardy et al. New York: Oxford University Press, 1971.

Noack, B. "Ezrabogerne." *Gads Danske Bibel Leksikon 1L*. Ed. E. Nielsen and B. Noack. Copenhagen: Gads, 1965–66. Cols. 482–83.

Oesterley, W. O. E. *An Introduction to the Books of the Apocrypha*. London: SPCK, 1953.

———. *2 Esdras (The Ezra Apocalypse)*. Westminster Commentaries. London: Methuen, 1933.

Oxford Annotated Bible with the Apocrypha. Ed. B. M. Metzger. New York: Oxford University Press, 1977.

Realencyklopädie für protestantische Theologie und Kirche. 3rd ed. 24 vols. S.v. "4 Esra," "5 and 6 Esra," "Pseudepigraphen des Alten Testaments," by G. Beer. Ed. A. Hauck. Leipzig: Hinrichs, 1905. Vol. 16, pp. 244–49.

Reallexikon für Antike und Christentum. 17 vols. S.v. "Esra," by W. Schneemelcher. Ed. T. Klausner. Stuttgart: Hiersemann, 1966. Vol. 6, cols. 595–612.

Die Religion in Geschichte und Gegenwart. 3rd ed. 7 vols. S.v. "Esrabücher. 4. Das 5. und 6. Esrabuch," by O. Plöger. Ed. K. Galling. Tübingen: Mohr, 1958. Vol. 2, cols. 699–700.

Riessler, P., ed. *Altjüdisches Schrifttum ausserhalb der Bibel*. Augsburg: Filser, 1928.

Sabatier, P. *Bibliorum sacrorum latinae versiones antiquae seu vetus Italica*. 3 vols. Rheims: Florentain, 1743; reprint ed., Munich: Ziffer, 1976.

Stone, M. E. *Fourth Ezra*. Hermeneia. Minneapolis: Fortress, 1990.

———. "Some Remarks on the Textual Criticism of 4 Ezra." *HTR* 60 (1967) 107–15.

Stone, M. E., with T. A. Bergren. "Second Esdras." *Harper's Bible Commentary*. Ed. J. L. Mays. San Francisco: Harper & Row, 1988. Pp. 776–90.

Thackeray, H. St. J. "Esdras, Second Book of." *A Dictionary of the Bible*. 5 vols. Ed. J. Hastings. New York: Scribner, 1903. Vol. 1, pp. 763–66.

Theologische Realenzyklopädie. 25 vols. S.v. "Esra/Esraschriften," by M. Saebo. Ed. G. Krause and G. Müller. Berlin, New York: de Gruyter, 1982. Vol. 10, pp. 374–86.

Turner, N. "Esdras, Books of." *Interpreter's Dictionary of the Bible*. 5 vols. New York: Abingdon, 1962. Vol. 2, p. 142.

Violet, B. *Die Esra-Apokalypse*. Teil 1: Die Überlieferung. GCS 18. Leipzig: Hinrichs, 1910.

Violet, B., and H. Gressmann. *Die Apokalypsen des Esra und des Baruch in deutscher Gestalt*. GCS 32. Leipzig: Hinrichs, 1924.

Volkmar, G. *Das vierte Buch Esrae ("Esdra Propheta")*. Handbuch der Einleitung in die Apokryphen 2. Tübingen: Fues, 1863.

Weber, R., ed. *Biblia Sacra Iuxta Vulgatam Versionem*. 3rd ed. 2 vols. Stuttgart: Deutsche Bibelgesellschaft, 1983.

Weinel, H. "Das sechste Buch Esra." *Handbuch zu den neutestamentlichen Apokryphen*. Ed. E. Hennecke. Tübingen: J. C. B. Mohr, 1904. Pp. 336–39.

———. "Das sechste Buch Esra." *Neutestamentliche Apokryphen*. 2nd ed. Ed. E. Hennecke. Tübingen: J. C. B. Mohr, 1924. Pp. 394–99.

Wood, J. S. "The Missing Fragment of the Fourth Book of Esdras." *Journal of Philology* 7 (1877) 264–78.

Other Material

Alföldi, A. *Studien zur Geschichte der Weltkrise des 3. Jahrhunderts nach Christus*. Darmstadt: Wissenschaftliche Buchgesellschaft, 1967.

Barnes, T. D. "The Lost *Kaisergeschichte* and the Latin Historical Tradition." *BHAC* 1968/69 (1970) 13ff.

Beasley-Murray, G. R. *Revelation.* NCBC. Grand Rapids, MI: Eerdmans, 1974.

Bergren, T. A. *A Latin-Greek Index of the Vulgate New Testament.* SBLRBS 26. Atlanta: Scholars Press, 1991.

Besnier, M. *L'Empire romain de l'avènement des Sévères au Concile de Nicée.* Histoire Ancienne, troisième partie. Histoire Romaine, Tome 4, première partie. Paris: Les Presses Universitaires de France, 1937.

Billen, A. V. *The Old Latin Texts of the Heptateuch.* Cambridge: Cambridge University Press, 1927.

Bird, H. W., ed. *The Breviarium ab urbe condita of Eutropius.* Liverpool: Liverpool University Press, 1993.

Blaise, A. *Dictionnaire latin-français des auteurs chrétiens.* Strasbourg: Le Latin Chrétien, 1954.

Bowersock, G. W. *Roman Arabia.* Cambridge, MA: Harvard University Press, 1983.

Breviarium Romano-Seraphicum. Vol. 1, *Pars hiemalis.* Patersonius: Societatis Sancti Antonii, 1943.

Bryan, D. *Cosmos, Chaos and the Kosher Mentality.* JSPSup 12. Sheffield: Sheffield Academic Press, 1996.

The Cambridge Ancient History. 12 vols. Cambridge: Cambridge University Press, 1923–.

Canfield, L. H. *The Early Persecutions of the Christians.* Columbia University Studies in History, Economics and Public Law 55.2. New York: Columbia University Press, 1913.

Charlesworth, J. H., ed. *The Old Testament Pseudepigrapha.* 2 vols. Garden City, NY: Doubleday, 1983–85.

Collins, A. Y. *Crisis and Catharsis: The Power of the Apocalypse.* Philadelphia: Fortress, 1984.

———. "Revelation, Book of." *Anchor Bible Dictionary.* 6 vols.Ed. D. N. Freedman. New York: Doubleday, 1992. Vol. 5, pp. 694–708.

Collins, J. J. *The Sibylline Oracles of Egyptian Judaism.* SBLDS 13. Missoula, MT: Scholars Press, 1974.

———, ed. *Apocalypse: The Morphology of a Genre. Semeia* 14 (1979).

Cooke, G. A. *A Text-Book of North-Semitic Inscriptions.* Oxford: Clarendon, 1903.

Coyecque, E. *Catalogue général des manuscrits des bibliothèques publiques de France. Départements.* Vol. 19: *Amiens.* Paris: Plon, 1893.

Dekkers, E., ed. *Clavis Patrum Latinorum.* 2nd ed. *Sacris Erudiri* 3 (1961). Steenbrugis: Abbatia Sancti Petri, 1961.

Delisle, L. *Inventaire des manuscrits de Saint-Germain-des-Prés conservés a la bibliothèque impériale, sous les numéros 11504–14231 du fonds latin.* Paris: Durand, 1868.

Denis, A.-M. *Fragmenta Pseudepigraphorum quae supersunt Graeca.* PVTG 3. Leiden: Brill, 1970.

Deshusses, J., ed. *Le sacramentaire grégorien.* 3 vols. Fribourg, Switzerland: Editions universitaires Fribourg, 1971.

Dumas, A., ed. *Liber sacramentorum Gellonensis.* 2 vols. CCL 159, 159a. Turnholt: Brepols, 1981.

Ensslin, W. *Zu den Kriegen des Sassaniden Schapur 1.* Sitzungsberichte der Bayerischen Akademie der Wissenschaften, Philosophisch-historische Klasse, Jahrgang 1947. Heft 5. Munich: Verlag der Bayerischen Akademie der Wissenschaften, 1949.

Feldman, L. H. *Jew and Gentile in the Ancient World: Attitudes and Interactions from Alexander to Justinian.* Princeton, NJ: Princeton University Press, 1993.

Fernández Marcos, N. *Scribes and Translators: Septuagint and Old Latin in the Books of Kings.* VTSup 54. Leiden: Brill, 1994.

Fischer, B. *Lateinische Bibelhandschriften im frühen Mittelalter.* AGLB 11. Freiburg: Herder, 1985.

————. "Limitations of Latin in Representing Greek." *The Early Versions of the New Testament*. By B. M. Metzger. Oxford: Clarendon, 1977. Pp. 362–74.

————. *Verzeichnis der Sigel für Handschriften und Kirchenschriftsteller*. Vetus Latina: Die Reste der altlateinische Bibel 1. Freiburg: Herder, 1949.

————, ed. *Novae concordantiae bibliorum sacrorum iuxta vulgatam versionem critice editam*. 5 vols. Stuttgart: Frommann-Holzboog, 1977.

Forcellini, A. *Lexicon totius latinitatis opera et studio*. Prati, 1858–75.

Frend, W. H. C. *Martyrdom and Persecution in the Early Church*. New York: University Press, 1967.

Gebhardt, O., and A. Harnack, eds. *Hermae Pastor graece addita versione latina recentiore e codice Palatino*. Patrum Apostolicorum Opera 3. Lipsiae: Hinrichs, 1877.

Gheyn, J. van den. *Catalogue des manuscrits de la Bibliothèque Royale de Belgique*. Vol. 1: *Ecriture sainte et Liturgie*. Brussels: Lamertin, 1901.

Glare, P. G. W., ed. *Oxford Latin Dictionary*. Oxford: Clarendon, 1982.

Grandgent, C. H. *An Introduction to Vulgar Latin*. Boston: Heath, 1907.

Gribomont, J. "L'Église et les versions bibliques." *Maison-Dieu* 62 (1960) 41–68.

————. "Latin Versions." *Interpreters Dictionary of the Bible*, supplementary volume. Nashville: Abingdon, 1976. P. 528.

Hayes, J. H. "The History of the Form-Critical Study of Prophecy." *Society of Biblical Literature 1973 Seminar Papers*. 2 vols. Ed. G. MacRae. Cambridge, MA: Society of Biblical Literature, 1973. Vol. 1, pp. 60–99.

Hennecke, E., W. Schneemelcher, and R. McL. Wilson, eds. *New Testament Apocrypha*. 2 vols. Philadelphia: Westminster, 1963–65.

Hesbert, R. J., ed. *Antiphonale missarum sextuplex*. Rome: Herder, 1935.

————, ed. *Corpus antiphonalium officii*. 6 vols. Rome: Herder, 1963–79.

Hilgenfeld, A., ed. *Hermae Pastor veterem latinam interpretationem e codicibus*. Lipsiae: Fues [Reisland], 1873.

Knipfing, J. R. "The Libelli of the Decian Persecution." *HTR* 16 (1923) 345–90.

Koch, K. *The Growth of the Biblical Tradition: The Form Critical Method*. Trans. S. M. Cupitt. New York: Scribner, 1969.

Kraft, R. A., and E. Tov, eds. *Computer Assisted Tools for Septuagint Studies (CATSS)*. Vol. 1: *Ruth*. SBLSCS 20. Atlanta: Scholars Press, 1986.

Kümmel, W. G. *Introduction to the New Testament*. Rev. ed. Trans. H. C. Kee. Nashville: Abingdon, 1975.

Lawlor, H. J., and J. E. L. Oulton. *Eusebius, The Ecclesiastical History and Martyrs of Palestine*. 2 vols. London: SPCK, 1928.

Lechner-Schmidt, W. *Wortindex der lateinisch erhaltenen Pseudepigraphen zum Alten Testament*. Tübingen: Franke, 1990.

Maas, P. *Textual Criticism*. Oxford: Oxford University Press, 1958.

Magie, D., ed. *The Scriptores Historiae Augustae*. 3 vols. LCL. Cambridge, MA: Harvard University Press, 1932.

March, W. E. "Prophecy." *Old Testament Form Criticism*. Ed. J. H. Hayes. San Antonio: Trinity University Press, 1974. Pp. 141–77.

Matzkow, W. *De vocabulis quibusdam italae et vulgatae christianis: Quaestiones lexicographae*. Berlin: Pilz & Noack, 1933.

Metzger, B. M. *The Early Versions of the New Testament*. Oxford: Clarendon, 1977.

Mitchell, S. *Anatolia: Land, Men, and Gods in Asia Minor*. 2 vols. Oxford: Clarendon, 1993.

Mohlberg, C., ed. *Liber sacramentorum Romanae Aeclesiae*. 2nd ed. Rome: Herder, 1968.

Mohrmann, C. *Etudes sur le latin des chr,tiens*. 4 vols. Storia e Letteratura 65, 87, 103, 143. Rome: Edizioni di Storia e Letteratura, 1958–77.

————. "Les origines de la latinité chrétienne à Rome." *VC* 3 (1949) 67–106, 163–83.

Molinier, A. *Catalogue des manuscrits de la Bibliothèque Mazarine.* Paris: Plon, 1885.

Mommsen, T., ed. *Gildae Sapientis de excidio et conquestu Britanniae. Monumenta Germaniae Historica* Auctores Antiquissimi 13 (Chronica minora 3). Berlin: Weidmannos, 1898; reprint ed., 1961.

Mounce, R. H. *The Book of Revelation.* NICNT. Grand Rapids, MI: Eerdmans, 1977.

Mussies, G. "When Do Graecisms Prove That a Latin Text Is a Translation?" *Vruchten van de Uithof* (H. A. Brongers Festschrift). Utrecht: Theologisch Instituut, 1974. Pp. 100–119.

Nestle, Eberhard, Erwin Nestle, K. Aland, L. M. Black, C. M. Martini, B. M. Metzger, and A. Wikgren, eds. *Novum Testamentum Graece.* 26th ed. Stuttgart: Deutsche Bibelgesellschaft, 1979.

Olmstead, A. T. "The Mid–Third Century of the Christian Era." *CP* 37 (1942) 241–62, 398–420.

Palmer, L. R. *The Latin Language.* London: Faber & Faber, 1954.

Paschoud, F., ed. *Zosime, Histoire Nouvelle.* Tome 1. Collection Budé. Paris: Les Belles Lettres, 1971.

Pichlmayr, F., and R. Gruendel, eds. *Sexti Aurelii Victoris Liber de Caesaribus.* 2nd ed. Leipzig: Teubner, 1970.

Plater, W. E., and H. J. White. *A Grammar of the Vulgate.* Oxford: Clarendon, 1926.

Potter, D. S. "Persecution of the Early Church." *Anchor Bible Dictionary.* 6 vols. Ed. D. N. Freedman. New York: Doubleday, 1992. Vol. 5, pp. 231–35.

————. *Prophecy and History in the Crisis of the Roman Empire: A Historical Commentary on the Thirteenth Sibylline Oracle.* Oxford Classical Monographs. Oxford: Clarendon, 1990.

Rahlfs, A., ed. *Septuaginta.* 2 vols. Stuttgart: Deutsche Bibelgesellschaft, 1935.

Rajak, T. "Was There a Roman Charter for the Jews?" *JRS* 74 (1984) 107–23.

Reynolds, J. M., and R. Tannenbaum. *Jews and Godfearers at Aphrodisias: Greek Inscriptions with Commentary.* Cambridge: Cambridge University Press, 1987.

Robert, L., ed. *Le Martyre de Pionios prêtre de Smyrne.* Washington, D.C.: Dumbarton Oaks, 1994.

Rönsch, H. *Itala und Vulgata: Das Sprachidiom der urchristlichen Itala und der katholischen Vulgata unter Berücksichtigung der römischen Volkssprache.* 2nd ed. Marburg: Elwert, 1875.

Sainio, M. A. *Semasiologische Untersuchungen über die Entstehung der christlichen Latinität.* Helsinki: Finnischen Literaturgesellschaft, 1940.

Schürer, E. *The History of the Jewish People in the Age of Jesus Christ.* New English version. 3 vols. Rev. and ed. G. Vermes, F. Millar, and M. Goodman. Edinburgh: T. & T. Clark, 1973–87.

Simon, M. *Verus Israel: A Study of the Relations between Christians and Jews in the Roman Empire (135–425).* Trans. H. McKeating. Oxford: Oxford University Press, 1986.

Smallwood, E. M. *The Jews under Roman Rule: From Pompey to Diocletian.* SJLA 20. Leiden: Brill, 1976.

Smith, M. "Ezra." *Ex Orbe Religionum* (G. Widengren Festschrift). 2 vols. Leiden: Brill, 1972. Vol. 1, pp. 141–43.

Souter, A. *A Glossary of Later Latin to 600 A.D.* Oxford: Clarendon, 1949.

Stevenson, J., ed. *Gildas, De excidio Britanniae.* London: Sumptibus Societatis, 1838.

Tcherikover, V. A. "Prolegomena." *Corpus Papyrorum Judaicarum.* 3 vols. Ed. V. A. Tcherikover, A. Fuks, and M. Stern. Cambridge, MA: Harvard University Press, 1957–64.

Thesaurus Linguae Latinae. Ed. Consilium ab academiis societatibusque diversarum nationum electi. Leipzig: Teubner, 1900–.

Thompson, L. L. *The Book of Revelation: Apocalypse and Empire.* New York: Oxford University Press, 1990.

Torre, M. de la, and P. Longás. *Catálogo de Códices Latinos de la Biblioteca Nacional.* Vol. 1: *Bíblicos.* Madrid: Biblioteca Nacional, 1935.

Trebilco, P. R. *Jewish Communities in Asia Minor.* SNTSMS 69. Cambridge: Cambridge University Press, 1991.

Tucker, G. M. *Form Criticism of the Old Testament.* Philadelphia: Fortress, 1971.

———. "Prophecy and the Prophetic Literature." *The Hebrew Bible and Its Modern Interpreters.* Ed. D. A. Knight and G. M. Tucker. Philadelphia: Fortress, 1985. Pp. 325–68.

———. "Prophetic Speech." *Int* 32 (1978) 31–45.

Valgiglio, E. *Le Antiche Versioni Latine del Nuovo Testamento.* Koinonia 11. Naples: D'Auria, 1985.

Van der Horst, P. W. "Jews and Christians in Aphrodisias in the Light of Their Relations in Other Cities of Asia Minor." *Nederlands Theologisch Tijdschrift* 43 (1989) 106–21.

Von Soden, H. F. *Das lateinische Neue Testament in Afrika zur Zeit Cyprians.* TU 3,3. Leipzig: Hinrichs, 1909.

West, M. L. *Textual Criticism and Editorial Technique.* Stuttgart: Teubner, 1973.

Westermann, C. *Basic Forms of Prophetic Speech.* Trans. H. C. White. Philadelphia: Westminster, 1967.

Williams, H., ed. *Gildae de excidio Britanniae.* Cymmrodorion Record Series 3. London: Society of Cymmrodorion, 1899–1901.

Williams, J. "A Contribution to the History of the Castilian Monastery of Valeranica and the Scribe Florentius." *Madrider Mitteilungen des Deutschen Archäologischen Instituts Madrid* 11 (1970) 231–48.

———. *Frühe spanische Buchmalerei.* Munich: Prestel, 1977.

———. "A Model for the León Bibles." *Madrider Mitteilungen des Deutschen Archäologischen Instituts Madrid* 8 (1967) 281–86.

Wilson, R. R. "Form-Critical Investigation of the Prophetic Literature: The Present Situation." *Society of Biblical Literature 1973 Seminar Papers.* 2 vols. Ed. G. MacRae. Cambridge, MA: Society of Biblical Literature, 1973. Vol. 1, pp. 100–127.

Winterbottom, M., ed. and trans. *Gildas: The Ruin of Britain and Other Works.* History from the Sources. London and Chichester: Phillimore, 1978.

Index of Passages

Index of Names and Terms